FORMS OF ENGLISH :   ACCENT, MORPHEME, ORDER

FORMS OF ENGLISH

ACCENT, MORPHEME, ORDER

Dwight L. Bolinger
Harvard University

Edited by

Isamu Abe	*and*	*Tetsuya Kanekiyo*
Tokyo Institute of Technology		*Yamagata University*

Harvard University Press
Cambridge, Massachusetts
1965

Copyright © *1965* by

Hokuou Publishing Company

Tokyo, Japan

First published 1965

EDITORS' NOTE

Readers of this volume might like to know how the editors first became acquainted with Professor Bolinger and why they decided to give a portion of his varied writings the form they take here.

In the spring of 1952, just before leaving for Japan after a year's study of English at the University of Texas, Abe wrote to Professor Bolinger, on an impulse, hoping to get some suggestions about English intonation. Some years later, in 1959, and on an entirely unrelated matter Kanekiyo also sent an inquiry.

This began a series of communications that have continued with hardly interrupted regularity ever since. It was a happy coincidence that the correspondence grew and that the correspondents, on the Japanese side, were later brought together. The Bolinger they came to know, as those familiar with his letters will be aware, is the embodiment of ready comment and good will, the kind of benevolent scholar and willing informant who has never discouraged anyone approaching him with an academic problem. His letters informed, but gave pleasure as well, for he was obviously enjoying himself in writing them; and their recipients came to feel close to a person for whom scholarship could evoke humor as quickly as careful explanation —over a range of everything linguistic, but especially sound and syntax. This feeling of intimacy was further enhanced when Abe visited him in the United States as a Fulbright Research Scholar a few years ago. His formal writing, we believe the reader will find, is disciplined but not heavy; and this points to a philosophical streak that is worth knowing too—the fighter, in his spare time, for educational causes—which it would be out of place here to do more than mention.

The value of Professor Bolinger's work is best appreciated by turning the pages. We will not extol the worth of each separate paper, and it is difficult to sum up in a few words where he stands in relation to other linguists, particularly the "phonemicists" of the American branch. Under the circumstances we can only recommend what he says about this himself, in the following Author's Preface.

The editors earnestly hope that readers will catch in this volume some of the flavor of controversy that enlivens contemporary linguistics. Of the papers gathered here, the longest is being published for the first time. The others have been reprinted in their original form except for minor alterations and the author's comments that precede each one.

For various reasons, especially those of typography, it has taken much longer than was originally planned for this volume to appear, and we must express our sincere apologies to Professor Bolinger.

EDITORS' NOTE

We take this opportunity to thank the several journals that kindly permitted the reprinting of the articles that appeared originally in their pages. Each source has been separately acknowledged under the title.

Not the least of our duties and pleasures is to thank the management and staff of Hokuou Publishing Company for their encouragement and assistance.

Finally we record the skilled assistance of Mr. Shigeji Ogawa of Keio University who helped read the proofs and prepare the Index.

Isamu Abe
Tokyo Institute of Technology

Tetsuya Kanekiyo
Yamagata University

June 1965

AUTHOR'S PREFACE

It is hard to find unity in essays written over a period of twenty years. Some can be achieved by selecting pieces on related themes; I have tried to do this from the three points of view that form the three parts of the book, and to fasten the pieces together with a paragraph or two of comment at the beginning of each.

Part I looks at those components of speech that come first for the child but last for the analyst: intonation, accent and stress, and rhythm. If the child could paint the picture, these would be the wave on which the other components ride up and down; but the linguist is older and stronger, and has his way—he calls them suprasegmentals, and makes the wave ride on top of the ship.

Part II looks at words and the smaller meaningful elements of words: how they are defined, what are their aids to survival, how their spoken forms and their written forms interact, and how they are sometimes shaped by meaning.

Part III looks at sequences and arrangements: how they are sometimes commandeered for a narrow but pressing need—that is, grammaticized—but how at other times the speaker is free to play on them to convey his sense of the important; and how they ally themselves with pitch and accent for clarity or emphasis.

Perhaps the real unity here is in the fact that the views expressed lie or have lain somewhat outside the mainstream of American linguistics. This is partly due to a defect of temperament. Most American linguists, like American Rotarians and American Baptists, are enthusiastic joiners. This is more visible at some times than at others, but hits the eye whenever a sizable number decide to change sides: as now, with the former soldiers of Phonology who have gone over to Transformations. I lack what it takes to warm me to collective action. I admire tagmemes, superfixes, and transforms, but I am too fickle to marry.

So the common thread—a virtue or a fault according to how you see it —is unorthodoxy. Some of the writing is unorthodox because it deals with questions that have been passed by, maybe through oversight or maybe because they were not worth attention; " Linear modification " and " Verbal evocation " are examples. Some of it is unorthodox because it attacks orthodoxy. American linguistics has had almost an official line on some questions: on meaning (it should be excluded); on writing (it is only an imperfect copy of speech); on intonation (there are four phonemic levels); on morpheme analysis (it should follow—in both senses—the analysis of phonemes) ; on stress (it is materialized by loudness) ; on purism (it is reprehensible). These positions have been defended with devotion, though recently a few with lessened zeal. Some I have criticized as manifestly wrong ; others as needing reform or reformulation.

I hope that some of my criticisms have been constructive. If not, I consider my efforts a failure, redeemed only by being occasionally entertaining. Linguistics is my business, though I came too late to get it in my blood. Perhaps being somewhat of an outsider has helped me to see one or two of the ten or a dozen questions treated here more clearly than if I had tangled with them hand to hand. I don't know. I hope so.

Most of the articles stand as they appeared in their original form. The only one with substantial changes is the last, and in both articles of Part III I have replaced most instances of the term *stress* with *accent* to accord with the definitions in Part I. The arrangement aims to be logical, and it is also almost chronological within each of the three parts, but not quite.

Dwight L. Bolinger

June 1962

TABLE OF CONTENTS

Part I

ACCENT AND RELATED MATTERS

I

INTONATION:
LEVELS VS. CONFIGURATIONS
Word 7. 199-210 (1951)

In the early Forties several linguists—Kenneth Pike, Zellig Harris, Rulon Wells—felt that they had discovered in English intonation an interplay of phonemic levels, out of which intonational morphemes were built just as linear morphemes are built of linear phonemes. The idea caught on, and has persisted, in spite of the lack of a respectable body of morphemes with which to test it. The popular phonemic concept was pushed into an untried field, and the standards of identification, in view of the severity of those held up to the identification of linear phonemes, seemed incredibly lax.

This article was a first attempt to show experimentally that English intonation does not lend itself to a layercake analysis.

The partisans of level-analysis of English intonation have made it plain that they consider the pitch levels (four is the favored number) to be relative. The most recent statement, that of G. L. Trager and Henry Lee Smith, Jr., includes this qualification explicitly: " it is relative, not absolute, pitch that is being discussed."[1] (In the remarks to follow I shall use Trager-Smith's analysis as a point of departure and return, since it represents the most concise and logical refinement of the phonemic technique transferred to intonation levels. The arguments apply, however, to all attempts to reduce intonation to the reciprocation of four levels of pitch.)

Unfortunately we are not enlightened on HOW relative these relative pitches are supposed to be. Adopting Trager's numbers[2] of 1 for lowest to 4 for highest, can we say that it is possible for [3] to be an allophone of /2/? Or, at an extreme, for [4] to be an allophone of /2/? Or are the zones of absolute pitch for each pitch phoneme mutually exclusive, for any given speaker on a given occasion? In other words, does the relativity of these " relative " tones allow of overlapping, or are they relative only within their proper limits?

Lacking this information, we shall have to make both assumptions, testing

---

1. *An outline of English structure* 41 (Norman, Oklahoma, 1951).
2. The reverse of Pike's.

them for internal consistency and to judge whether the conclusions that have been drawn will cohere in view of known pattern identities.

Assume, first, that the pitch phonemes are entirely relative. Each pitch phoneme would be free to range over the whole register of the speaker's voice, with no limitation save that /4/ would at a given moment always be higher than /3/, /3/ than /2/, and /2/ than /1/. Give the four pitches the benefit of the doubt and say that all intonation morphemes are expressible in terms of this number of variables.

On this assumption we gather that if there is a pitch morpheme that is keyed to four different pitches, the entire morpheme might be shifted to a higher or a lower set of frequencies without disturbing the internal relationships of the four pitches ; similarly the total range of pitch could be expanded or compressed without disturbing these relationships. It would follow that no pitch phoneme could be identified out of some context, and that a given absolute pitch could correspond to any of the four pitch phonemes.[3]

The consequences are embarrassing, for in any pitch morpheme keyed to fewer than four pitches, we could never tell which one or ones had been left out. There would be no way to distinguish 123 from 234, 121 from 232 or 242 or 343 or 131 or 141, and a morpheme consisting of but one pitch phoneme might be 1, 2, 3, or 4. If pitches were completely relative we could not, to take an example, fall back on a preceding morpheme such as 1342 to establish a kind of scale by which a 4 might be judged to be 4—1342 itself might be shifted up a fifth without having its identity destroyed.

The one heavy supporting argument for the assumption of unlimited relativity is that 231 and 241, for example, are actually synonymous. Trager-Smith's wording in likening the two is that " All the examples given so far can be said over again with a distinctly higher pitch replacing each instance of /3/."[4] This can only mean that the examples are the same examples, but to avoid too extreme an interpretation I have labeled them synonyms, which I agree that they are. Trager-Smith also identify a morpheme consisting solely of /3/ with another consisting solely of /4/, calling them an echo-question (*How do they study?*). I may add that in my dialect an echo-question may be uttered at a lower and a still lower pitch, so that if we are categorizing the synonymy as a case of " echo-questions," we get /1/ = /2/ = /3/ = /4/.

But—even though I would carry it farther in analyzing my own dialect —to say that /3/ = /4/ is enough to nullify my first assumption. Since

---

3. With the exception, of course, that the highest absolute pitch possible for /4/ would not, in a morpheme embodying all four pitches, be possible for /3/, and similarly down the line.

4. *Op. cit.* 43.

the two morphemes are synonymous, there would be no way of telling that a phoneme /3/ was involved in one and a phoneme /4/ in the other, if pitches were completely relative; the two morphemes could not be uttered simultaneously, and since our standard—on the assumption of absolute relativity—could shift in passing from one to the other, they would be indistinguishable. Yet they are distinguished with assurance in Trager-Smith's analysis. Despite the real and admitted synonymy of 231 and 241, or of 3 and 4, we must therefore conclude that those who adopt the four-level analysis are not talking about PURELY relative tones, but about tones that may rove each in its own bailiwick but no farther.[5]

So to the other assumption, that we are dealing with mutually exclusive ranges of pitch. I propose to test it with group reactions to a series of intonations. These have been set up to conform to the assumption, but comprise changes which, according to the assumption, would be regarded as allophonic. The object is to see whether the "allophonic" changes produce semantic contrasts.

Test I. Trager-Smith's analysis recognizes no contrast between a lower and a higher double-bar juncture (rising sentence-final intonation). So far as we are told, the end-pitch in their example [3]How [2]do they study ‖ can be anywhere from a semitone to an octave higher than the last preceding pitch; and since it is a fact that the end-pitch on such a question can vary within wide limits, we must take it that according to the system the differences in pitch are irrelevant. I may say in passing that in my own speech there is a difference in meaning between [3]Gee [2]I wish I hadn't forgotten to do it ‖ with a low end-rise and the same locution with a high end-rise—the latter is more self-accusing; this is something a group test could probably verify, though the tests that I shall report here do not bear upon it. For the moment I do not challenge the identification of [‖ (high)] and [‖ (low)] as allophones of /‖/.

My first test involves the same sequences as Trager-Smith's [3]How [2]do they study ‖, but I have substituted the locution cited above, [3]Gee [2]I wish I hadn't forgotten to do it ‖, to provide a little more bulk for the assumed allophones and also to imitate something well known to every radio-listener, the advertisement for Life Saver candy, *Gee, I wisht I had a nickel*, the intonation of which enters into the test.

---

5. Trager-Smith partly confirm this in the reference (p. 60) to "the scope of each of the pitch phonemes—that is, the extent of the material included under each pitch." This does not help us, of course, as far as possible overlappings, or of possible changes of scope from moment to moment, or as far as precisely WHAT is included at a given moment is concerned.

"Gee, I wish I hadn't forgotten to do it"

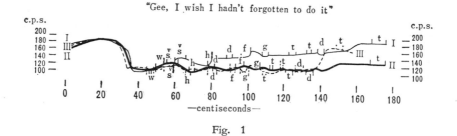

Fig. 1

A recording was made of the example, spoken in three different ways, which are traced in Figure 1.[6] In the first way my intent was to make as nearly as possible a steady rise in pitch beginning at the lowest pitch on the profile, imitating the intonation of the Life Saver advertisement. In the second way my intent was to hold a level tone after the drop and on to the end, with a slight rise on *it;* in the third way to do the same, but with a rise on *it* that would approximate the end-pitch of the first way (actually I came within one full tone of it). Since, after the initial fall and up to the rise in pitch on the final word *it* (which is by definition a double-bar juncture and consequently the same in all three), no one of the patterns exhibits a skip sufficient to justify invoking a transition from one of the four pitch levels to another,[7] all three are identical in terms of Trager-Smith's analysis as they have stated it. Configurationally, however, there is a marked difference: in the second way and the third way there is a fall succeeded by a level succeeded by an upskip; in the first way there is a fall succeeded by a steady rise which absorbs the end-rise as part of it.

The O's received the following instructions:

In this part you will hear the words *Gee, I wish I hadn't forgotten to do it!* spoken in three different ways. One of the three is somewhat of a misfit—the two others match pretty closely, but this one way, though similar to them, is a little more "foreign." Pick out the "foreign, misfit" one and check it, below (each way will be heard only once, but the recording will be played four times):

CHECK WHICH WAY IS THE "FOREIGN, MISFIT" WAY

The first way_____
The second way_____
The third way_____

---

6. Thanks go herewith to Professor Fred W. Householder, Jr., who kindly worked out the graphs on the sound-spectrograph machine at Indiana University.

7. The difference between the projected pitches on š in the first and second ways is only a little over a semitone, so that there is either a change of level on both or no change of level on either.

Responses were as follows.[8]

	I	II	III
Group A	12	0	2
Group B	13	1	1
Group C	9	0	0
Group D	7	2	1
Totals	41	3	4

The figures are conclusive. The O's identified the SIMILAR CON-FIGURATIONS and differentiated the DISSIMILAR CONFIGURATIONS without regard for any assumed identity of pitch-level sequences. If the example is a valid one, then, in terms of what Trager and Smith are attempting to measure, in order to accommodate it their scheme will have to be qualified in one or more of the following ways: (1) To allow for an ARBITRARY chopping up of a smooth rise; by thus "sacrificing the obvious to the ingenious" it would be possible to get a different sequence in the first of the three ways above. (2) To limit the rise permissible for double-bar juncture, which in turn would necessitate revising the treatment of juncture by introducing gradations or some other factor; this would differentiate the second and third ways above, making the test inconclusive since it is predicated on their identity. (3) To recognize an intonational continuum in this one instance[9]; this would save the day for the example in question, but not for others that might be devised. The first qualification would involve many contradictions, and the two others would be at best hard to digest.

In Test I no reference was made to a particular meaning; the O's were left to their own devices in choosing a criterion of similarity.

Test II approaches the same contrast—that between a steady rise and an upskip—on the basis of a more or less specific meaning. In the Trager-Smith example ³How ²do they study ‖ I am conscious of a different implication when the portion *do they stud-* rises gradually in pitch instead of remaining relatively level—the rise makes the question more wheedling, and the greater the rise, the more wheedling it is. Rather than this locution, however, I substituted ³He ²isn't going to hurt you ‖ as easier to define in terms of a concrete situation with specific attitudes.[10]

---

8. *A* was a class in remedial reading (mostly teachers) at Occidental College; *B*, two combined graduate-level classes at the University of New Mexico; *C*, an undergraduate class at the University of Southern California; *D*, a graduate-level class at the University of Michigan. I wish to thank Professor Charles N. Butt and Miss Helen J. Rogers of Occidental College, Professor R. M. Duncan of the University of New Mexico, and Professor L. B. Kiddle of the University of Michigan, for their assistance.

9. As Pike more or less does with the profile that consists of a series of downskips.

10. Several group tests with other phrases have convinced me that at this stage of

Figure 2 shows the two curves matched according to consonantal breaks.[11] The reader will note that in II the pitch again rises too steadily to afford any division other than an arbitrary one between levels in a four-level system—if there are levels at all, the number would have to be six plus terminal juncture or seven if the last rise is counted; but the levels are themselves slanted upward, which suggests that the breaks in the line are accidental—instead of counting the upslant as irrelevant and the breaks as significant, the breaks become irrelevant and the slant is significant. This is the more credible as the breaks correspond to the incidence of certain

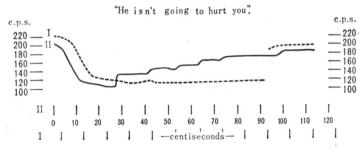

Fig. 2

consonants. Also worth noting is the fact that the terminal upskip in I actually attains a higher pitch than the end-pitch of II.

The O's received the following instructions:

In this part, imagine yourself as talking to someone, either a child or an adult, who is about to visit a dentist and dreads the visit. You want to be reassuring and so you say, *He isn't going to hurt you.* On the record you will hear this sentence spoken in two different ways. One of the two ways might be used with anyone, child or adult, on almost any occasion, and is more matter-of-fact. The other of the two ways is more likely to be used with a child, or with someone treated as a child, and is intended to comfort or coax. This latter way, the " child-comforting-coaxing " way, is the one you

---

unfamiliarity with intonation, self-judgment has to be based on the crudest materials that can be used consistently with the problem to be tested. It is not that discrimination is absent with more refined materials, but that to explicate it in an artificial setting requires distinctions that are relatively easy to grapple with. For the same reason I should point out that the meanings assigned to the intonations of the tests are not necessarily basic to the intonations, but may be partly colored by the verbal concomitants.

11. By slightly skewing the two time-scales it was—by coincidence—possible to match the consonantal breaks almost perfectly. The figure shows the second repetition of the first way and the first repetition of the second way.

are asked to mark. Check it, below (each way will be heard twice, and the recording will be played three times):

CHECK WHICH WAY IS THE "CHILD-COMFORTING-COAXING" WAY

The first way_____
The second way_____

Responses were as follows:

	I	II
Group A	2	12
Group B	3	12
Group C[12]	5	4
Group D	1	10
Totals	11	38

Again it seems to be demonstrated that the configuration-continuum is what counts, not a particular sequence of levels.

Test III is designed to meet an objection: that the difference between the two intonation morphemes of Test II is "esthetic," and that basically they are the same. By relegating Part II and its contrasts to a non-linguistic limbo, a four-level analysis that finds them to be "the same" is rescued.

But first a glance at the logic of the objection. Dismissing the "non-intellectual" follows the Prague definition of the phoneme, and has been applied (by Karcevskij, for example) to the analysis of intonation, and is in accord with the phonemic approach to intonation. Can intellectual and emotional meanings be distinguished in intonation? Obviously the distinction has been a good one in ordinary segmental phonemics, where its success testifies to its rightness.[13] But we must remember that in that area, contrasts of the sort just described are virtually absent (phonesthemes are the exception, not the rule), while in intonation they are ever-present. No one doubts that intonation does express emotion, part of the time at least; and if it is assumed that emotion is not always expressed, then those who make the assumption owe us an explanation. Where do emotional meanings stop and intellectual meanings begin? What is an intellectual meaning? What of the most extreme case: is "a question" an intellectual meaning? But the

---

12. The deviation in Group C is probably a reflection on the group, two members of which were natively bilingual. Its response to Part III is significant in this regard, differing in distribution and proportion from the three others.

13. The success, for example, achieved by disregarding affective length and so identifying all instances of the word *long* by reason of their having the "same" phonemic shape.

question *Will you help me?* subordinates the speaker to his interlocutor, while the command *Help me* superordinates him—these are two attitudes which, attenuate them as you please, are fundamentally emotional. All of the supposed intellectual meanings assigned to intonation carry some kind of emotional tone. The level-analysts have not equipped us with even a rough outline of what is essential in intonational meanings, much less a scale of importance for them. Until a tenable distinction is made, no analysis of intonation will be plausible that fails to account for any phonetic fact that reports an observed, objective, verifiable contrast.[14]

My test, however, assumes that the distinction is possible, and asks whether a four-level, three-juncture analysis takes care of all the differences commonly recognized as purely intellectual or grammatical. It takes the opposition question versus non-question to see whether the system deals with it satisfactorily.

Test III contrasts a simple end-rise with an end-rise preceded by a slight

---

14. The difficulty of getting an intonation with an unadulterated intellectual meaning is illustrated in the responses obtained by J. J. Dreher in his study of intonation-transfer in language-learning, *A comparison of native and acquired language intonation* (University of Michigan dissertation, 1950). Giving a group of O's a set of responses to be made to oral stimuli and instructing them to make their responses matter-of-fact, he obtained anything but uniform curves in a number of instances. The utterance *That's no good*, for example, had at least three contour-shapes. ⌐\, —\, and —/\. Clearly if one of these represents 'matter of factness,' the two others do not. The only reasonably satisfying solution is that no one intonation is purely matter-of-fact; there are merely feebler colorings of this or that emotion.

Trager-Smith use the terms *neutral, normal,* and *regular* (pp. 72, 73, 75, 76; the first two in quotes) to refer to patterns of stress, and presumably would apply the same adjectives to the intonation that they are describing. The same criticism fits as to *intellectual*, probably in regard to stress, positively in regard to intonation. There may be a "regular" intonation by the measure of statistical preponderance, but not in the sense of neutrality or absence of emotion. From the physicist's standpoint, cold is the absence of heat; from the physiological standpoint it is an entity in itself, for the body makes certain POSITIVE reactions to it—this is clear from the resistance that the physical fact had to meet before it was accepted, and from the everyday reference still to degrees of cold—*cold, colder, coldest.* From the standpoint of human reactions and attitudes there is no such thing as a mere absence of something —physical non-presence acquires a positive status of its own by reason of the polarities automatically set up where there are varying degrees of something. I would not emphasize this truism were it not for the fallacy in treatments like Trager-Smith's of apparently positing a hierarchy of intonations. In order to excuse themselves from the only valid treatment of a field—which is to treat the WHOLE of it before determinations of value are set—they must erect an entirely fictitious barrier between so-called neutral intonations and so-called non-neutral ones.

fall—so slight (it need not be more than a semitone) that it could not reach into a different level (where there are but four levels) from the one preceding it. In other words, the distinction is the one between the simple rising and the falling-rising sentence-final intonation.

Now the contrast—this explanation is necessary before detailing the test —is not automatically one between question and non-question, question being symbolized by simple rising and non-question by falling-rising, inasmuch as both intonation types figure in both sentence types. Falling-rising is common in questions of the "informed" type, e. g. *You're sure?*, where the speaker is pretty sure but asks in order to be absolutely sure. In my test, therefore, I am not imposing a non-question frame if I use falling-rising as a question.

Below are the instructions that were given:

In this part you will hear the following words (imagine them as all spoken continuously by one person): *You say that it's too late to ask them in? Why? They've already gone?* meaning, of course, 'Is it because they have already gone that you say it's too late?' The words will be spoken in three different ways, but the difference will be only in the last part (the *They've already gone?* part). One of the three ways will be nonsense—in fact, it will probably not even sound like a question to you. This last way, the "nonsense, no-question" way, is the one you are asked to mark. Check it, below (each way will be heard twice, and the recording will be played three times):

CHECK WHICH WAY IS THE "NONSENSE, NO-QUESTION" WAY

The first way_____

The second way_____

The third way_____

Figure 3 shows the falling pitch on the falling-rising close (the "second way") to be slightly under a full tone on the first repetition and slightly over a full tone on the second (the repetitions of the two other ways are also given, for comparison). In Figure 4 the second and third ways are matched, and found to parallel each other almost exactly in over-all pitch range—most significant of all, the difference between the two curves at the point where one turns perceptibly downward and the other does not is barely more than a semitone. From the standpoint of levels, II and III match more closely than I and III. If, then, the O's identify I and III rather than II and III, there must be something radically wrong with the four-level, three-juncture system.

Responses were as follows:

	I	II	III
Group A	0	13	1
Group B	0	14	1

Group C	3	6	0
Group D	0	8	3
Totals	3	41	5

The conclusion is inescapable that in this context the speaker is too curious to use as relatively incurious a question as would be the one employing a falling-rising end, whence the falling-rising end automatically becomes a non-question, and, as a non-question, is contradicted by the context. The two curves that were identified as questions were dissimilar in respect of levels but similar in respect of configuration (level followed by rise). The curve that was distinguished from both of them resembled one of the two in respect of levels but differed in respect of configuration (level followed by fall followed by rise). From the standpoint of level-analysis we have the unheard-of situation where identical phonemic shapes give homonyms (question and non-question) whenever a presumably non-phonemic differentia (drop in pitch of as little as a semitone) is present, and different phonemic shapes (high level and low level) give synonyms whenever the same presumably non-phonemic differentia is absent.

I think it has been sufficiently proved that the basic entity of intonation is a pattern, not a pattern in the relatively abstract sense of grammatical recurrences, but in the fundamental, down-to-earth sense of a continuous

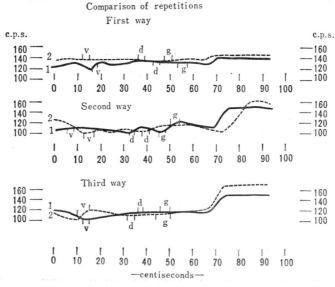

"They've already gone?"

Comparison of repetitions

First way

Second way

Third way

—centiseconds—

Fig. 3

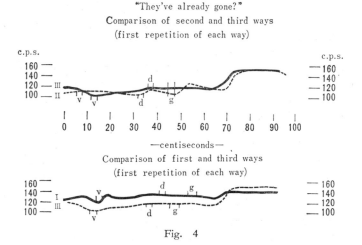

"They've already gone?"
Comparison of second and third ways
(first repetition of each way)

Comparison of first and third ways
(first repetition of each way)

Fig. 4

line that can be traced on a piece of paper. Two such patterns can be compared in the same way in which two freehand circles can be compared, and their existence as well as their comparability is completely objective. If we are to start in intonation with the evidence of our senses—any other beginning in science is reckless—we must start with units such as these, breaking them down later, if necessary, along lines congenial to them.

The analogy with the melodic line in music is inescapable. We have seen that the pattern can be shifted from one pitch range to another without becoming unrecognizable. It was this very fact about musical melody that laid the foundations of Gestalt psychology. If we must—as some linguists seem to think—affiliate ourselves with a particular brand of psychology in order to get along with our work, we had better turn gestaltists in analyzing intonation: the configuration may range within the limits of the voice register, or be expanded or diminished within that range, and still remain the same configuration; "size" and "position" do not materially affect it, and recognition is between pattern analogs as when a two-year-old recognizes a three-inch replica of a chair as "a chair" by attempting to sit on it—intonation could not be a more appropriate illustration of the Gestalt if it had been drawn from the book, and no unmodified behavioristic monadology can cope with it.

If we must analyze the configuration, what shall be the particles into which we break it down? Four levels are not enough, and with five or six levels there would still be left-over contrasts. Of course, as the size of our element approaches zero, we get a kind of infinitesimal calculus by which even a perfectly continuous figure can be accounted for. It is, however, accounted for in the same way in which the evenly spaced stippling on a half-tone accounts for the design of a photograph—it is an artificial atomizing imposed from outside that does not represent any of the segments or joints of the given. The syllabic phonemes have a counterpart in nature. Levels—four or six or sixty--have none.

I do not mean by this statement to dismiss absolute pitch entirely. A pattern that is discernibly higher than a previous pattern within a given context acquires a somewhat different value by reason of its change in pitch. The pattern may even be the same: when we ask *Is he coming?* with a rise on *-ing*, and have to repeat the question, we are apt to use the same configuration transferred to a higher pitch. Out of context, the difference would be insignificant; but related to the previous lower pitch it is meaningful. Aside from this contextual effect, however, and certain alterations of voice quality incident upon extreme pitches such as the falsetto, pitch range plays a role secondary to that of pitch pattern. The range is a sort of quantifier of the configuration; just as we find the "chair" configuration in all sizes, so we find different magnitudes of intonation patterns.

The necessary first step is to make a census of configurations. I question whether phonemic analysis would ever have been possible without a sizable corpus of words to begin with. To be sure, it is sometimes claimed that morphological and grammatical criteria should, or at least could, be kept out of phonemic analysis; perhaps so, but the argument would be more convincing if those who make it were not speaking through an enlightenment acquired by the application of the very mixed criteria that they would eschew. Whether, HISTORICALLY, phonemic analysis could have been possible without mixed principles is a different question; once having learned how through unrefined techniques, we may be in a position to refine our techniques. The given, which in that instance was mainly words and in this instance is mainly intonation morphemes or intonation configurations, must in the end determine the technique. And without enough of the given, refinements at this stage will simply misfire. My example of how they may misfire I again draw from Trager-Smith (p. 85): "Compare *What are we having for dinner, Mother?* with *What are we having for dinner— steak?* The pattern $\sqrt{2} \parallel$ on *Mother* might be called one of the forms of the 'vocative', while $\sqrt{3} \parallel$ on *steak* is part of the intonation of questions of certain kinds. The interchange of these two patterns gives ludicrous results because of incongruousness with possible cultural situations, pointing up clearly that the meaning analysis is not on the level of microlinguistic morphemics." Had the authors collected enough intonation morphemes minimally different from the two cited here, and confronted them with one another, they would have avoided comparing a phenomenon which is essentially a morpheme plus suffix (. . . *Mother*) with another which is essentially two independent morphemes. They would also have realized that the "patterns" are interchangeable without ludicrousness if the WHOLE CONFIGURATION is right (compare \What are we having for din/ner Mother? with \What are we having for din/ner. . . steak?, both of them identical ∨³ ‖ 's). The pause is more critical than the intonations in making the distinction that Trager-Smith have signalized; both intonations may be either vocative or interrogative.

Provided with a census of morphemes, we discover by direct observation what segments they have in common. A figure like ∩ is found to consist of a rise followed by a fall. The easiest sort of eye-analysis is sufficient at this stage to identify forms like this or like — and ‾ - _ . So long as the curves can be plotted, no two persons examining them can disagree overmuch as to their shape.

Of course, if these were merely chance similarities between unique configurations, they would have little more to commend them than would a calculus of levels. They do, to be sure, SEEM more plausible than do the large number of levels that would be necessary to account for all contrasts —we have to work with elements that lie well above the threshold of discrimination for the simple reason that too sharp a distinction would leave many speakers of the language unable to cope with it: rises, falls, and sustentions can be heard in or out of context, while levels grow progressively harder the more there are of them and can hardly be referred to any fixed standard—a narrow distinction of pitch must for most persons be referred to the immediate context, and judged not absolutely but only as higher or lower. Aside from this greater attractiveness, however, if both geometrical (pattern-segment) and mathematical (level) units were equally meaningless, the choice between them would be dictated by convenience.

Suppose, however, that configurations analyzed geometrically into rises, falls, and sustentions are responded to in a manner that tallies with the kind and number and relative position of the geometrical elements that each possesses. A rise terminated by a level, let us say, gets a response more similar to that of a continuous rise than to that of a continuous fall. *AB* is more similar to *A* than to *C*. This is the situation that I encounter in English intonation, and I believe that it enforces a different kind of analysis altogether from the one now in vogue. The specific deficiencies that I have pointed out in a treatment such as Trager-Smith's can be patched up by adding more levels and more junctures; but until the real units of intonation—and their phonesthetic character—are recognized, there will always be other deficiencies. A proper analysis of intonation must set the primary value on elements that make morphemes similar, not on elements that make them different: "231 and 241" (plus a note on synonymy) is less efficient than "rise-fall" (plus a note on pitch range), because the qualifying note in the latter can be generalized for all configurations and does not have to be repeated.

Oddly, a fact that would delight any other kind of scientist—that semantic value is correlated with formal shape, the surest guarantee that the forms singled out are no accident—seems to strike many linguists completely on the blind side.

2

A THEORY OF PITCH ACCENT IN ENGLISH*
Word 14. 109–149 (1958)

My first suspicions that stresses were not merely added to the ups and downs of pitch but were embodied by them, began to take shape in 1954, though without benefit of instrumental tests. I published "Intersections of stress and intonation" in 1955 (*Word* 11. 195–203), attempting to show that there are utterances in which the syllabic prominence that I now call *accent* can be signaled only by pitch. A year's experimenting at Haskins Laboratories forced me to credit pitch with a lot more than I had thought possible.

Unexpected confirmation came shortly from Wiktor Jassem, whose "Phonology of Polish stress" appeared in *Word* 15. 252–269 (1959), and proclaimed essentially the same findings for Polish. Other experimenters besides Cowan (p. 24 below) were finding that pitch was all that was required to specify "stress": Wang and Sivertsen in their work with synthesized speech made of reassembled "dyads" of natural speech observed that "except for weak syllables, stress is sufficiently closely correlated with vocal pitch level [so] that no additional conditions beyond those selected for intonation are required for stress" (*Journal of the Acoustical Society* 30. 741 [1958]). Most recently, Kerstin Hadding-Koch has found that in Southern Swedish "the syllable with a frequency pattern that deviated from that of the rest of the utterance was heard as stressed" (*Acoustico-phonetic studies in the intonation of Southern Swedish*, Lund, 1961, p. 161). Tests on Spanish have given the same results (Bolinger and Hodapp, "Acento Melódico, Acento de Intensidad," *Boletín de Filología*, XIII [1961], 33–48).

This study is the foundation of the remaining ones in Part I. The reader will find that the terms *stress* and *accent* are still confused to some extent—this was a concession to the reader's understanding of a conventional term. But I have tried to make clear that I regard *stress* as a potential only, a locus within a word where the sentence, for its own purposes, may or may not confer a prominence; the prominence itself is an *accent*, whose major cue is pitch and whose auxiliary and residual cue is length and—to a minor (and hardly more than "voice-qualifying" or emotional) degree—intensity.

On the subsidiary role of intensity I quote the conclusions of A. J. Vanvik (*On stress in present-day English*, Bergen and Oslo, 1961, p. 103): "In no way can the amplitude display unit serve as a meter for linguistic stress."

* Research at Haskins Laboratories, 1956–57, supported by a grant from the Carnegie Corporation of New York. The author gratefully acknowledges the cooperation of the Laboratory staff, particularly the hand-drawing of spectrograms by Prof. Pierre Delattre and the technical and editorial help of Dr. Louis J. Gerstman.

A THEORY OF PITCH ACCENT IN ENGLISH

1. THE FUNCTION OF PITCH

Like most other languages, English has contrasts of pitch. Unlike the pitch contrasts of certain languages, the English contrasts are not " phonemic " in the sense that raising or lowering the pitch of one syllable in a word such as *tower* will change its meaning in the way that replacing /t/ with /d/ will change it, causing it to point to something completely different in the world beyond language.

This much pitch in English does not do. No other phenomenon in language, however, has more firmly resisted efforts to find out what it does do. In the last two decades, linguists in the United States have attempted to take the garrison by main force. They have based their operations on a set of propositions which may be regarded either as assumptions or as conclusions from the evidence, depending on how far the evidence is credited. Among these propositions are the following:

1. That pitch functions in the same way as the segmental phonemes—the vowels and consonants—and that a sequence of different pitches will produce something potentially meaningful in the same way that a sequence of vowels and consonants may produce a word. In order to manage this, it is necessary to decide when one pitch is different from another. The segmental phonemes can be distinguished with relative ease because they are complex: each contains certain " distinctive features," whose presence or absence rather sharply separates one from another. Pitch has only one ingredient, the fundamental frequency of the voice. As a speaker moves up or down the normal range, there is no point at which the ear can detect that one thing ceases to occur and another begins—there is only up and down. So it is impossible to isolate a pitch as one can isolate a segmental phoneme: an untrained listener can identify a prolonged English /s/ without benefit of context; no amount of training will enable him to distinguish one linguistically significant pitch from another, however much prolonged, unless it occurs in context. Relying on contexts chosen for the purpose, analysts have discovered, or invented, " contrastive levels," each level representing a phoneme. Four is the usual number of levels.[1]

---

1. Zellig S. Harris, in *Language*, XX (1944), 189, marked seven. Rulon Wells, in *Language*, XXI (1945), 27–39, marked four, as did Kenneth L. Pike in his *Intonation of American English* (Ann Arbor, 1945). George L. Trager and Henry Lee Smith Jr., in their *Outline of English structure* (Norman, Okla., 1951), have followed Pike, and recent textbooks based on the *Outline* have propagated the number four. (For advanced classes: Charles F. Hockett, *A course in modern linguistics* [New York, 1958]; A. A. Hill, *Introduction to linguistic structures* [New York, 1958]; Henry A. Gleason, *An introduction to descriptive linguistics* [New York, 1955]; Velma Pickett, *An introduction to the study of grammatical structures* [Glendale, Calif., 1956]. For

2. That the meaningful something constituted by pitch phonemes is an intonation morph. The morph *231* (numbers refer to the "contrastive levels" of pitch) differs from the morph *221* as *tower* differs from *bower*. For those who follow Smith and Trager[2] the morphs are more complex, including, besides the pitch levels, "terminal junctures," which are ways of going from phrase to phrase or from phrase to silence, and which involve both pitch (direction, not level) and tempo. Such an intonation morph would be *231* #, which can be described phonetically as "mid-low level followed by mid-high level followed by low level followed by terminal fall and fade to silence, with a slowing down toward the end."[3]

3. That pitch and stress are phonemically independent. It is recognized that changes in stress may affect any level of intonation that happens to be running at the moment, but not, for example, in such a way as to raise a Level 2 pitch to a Level 3 pitch; the changes are phonetically slight and phonemically non-distinctive.

My purpose in this article is to deny the third assumption, and to reverse the roles of stress and pitch. I shall offer evidence that far from being a non-distinctive by-product or a completely independent variable, pitch is our main cue to stress.

2. Earlier Notions of Pitch as a Cue to Stress

The idea that stress may depend on pitch is not new. The experiment of John Muyskens in 1931, using kymographic records, purported to show that the familiar noun-verb pairs like *pérmit—permít* are distinguished by

---

beginning college classes: Donald J. Lloyd and Harry R. Warfel, *American English in its cultural setting* [New York, 1956]; W. Nelson Francis, *The structure of American English* [New York, 1958]; Paul Roberts, *Understanding English* [New York, 1958]. At least one for high school: Paul Roberts, *Patterns of English* [New York, 1956].) There has been no serious attempt to collect a real corpus of examples to test the theory, nor has it been proved experimentally. For intonational contrasts that the Trager-Smith *Outline* fails to account for, see my "Intonation: levels versus configurations" (pp. 3–16 in this volume).

2. *Outline*, especially p. 46.

3. The analysis of Spanish juncture and intonation made by Stockwell, Bowen, and Silva-Fuenzalida, *Language*, XXXII (1956), 641–665, which follows Smith and Trager, throws some doubt on the morphemic status of intonation patterns: "A sequence of pitches up to and including a terminal juncture will be referred to as an INTONATION PATTERN. Whether or not such a sequence of suprasegmental elements is a morph remains to be demonstrated on the morphological level of analysis" (p. 661). It is hard to see on what basis the levels and junctures are contrastive units, if sequences of them are not morphs.

higher pitches on their stressed syllables. Kenneth L. Pike[4] and Daniel Jones[5] demolish this argument by pointing out, in Jones' words, that "it often happens in a language that strong stresses are found on low-pitched syllables and weak stresses on high-pitched syllables." To demonstrate this, all we need to do is turn the *permit* example into a question: *pérmit?*

The refutation, however, is based on a persistent fallacy: that in order to serve as a cue to stress, pitch must RISE. Recent discussions and descriptions continue to look for this kind of relationship,[6] and, failing to find it, enter a verdict against pitch in general.

The experiments that I shall report suggest that it is not pitch RISE, but rather pitch PROMINENCE, that is essential to what we react to as stress. By prominence I mean a rapid and relatively wide departure from a smooth or undulating contour. A rise is only one kind of pitch prominence, though it is certainly the commonest kind. In the following

---

4. *Intonation*, pp. 16, 83.

5. *An outline of English phonetics* (New York, 1956), § 912 footnote.

6. Compare G. F. Arnold, "Stress in English words," *Lingua*, VI (1957), 226, and K. L. Pike and W. Kindberg, "A problem in multiple stresses," *Word*, XII (1956), 421. The latter deals with a complex relationship of stress and pitch in Campa; the wording on the page cited indicates that the investigators gave up associating pitch with stress when it became apparent that HIGH pitch was not systematically related to it. If applied to English—I cannot judge its application to Witoto—the following statement would illustrate the current fear of mixing levels: "There is a complex suprasegmental phoneme of stress accompanied by high pitch" (Eugene A. Minor, "Witoto vowel clusters," *International Journal of American Linguistics*, XXII [1956], 137)— rather like saying that the dawn breaks accompanied by sunshine. Uriel Weinreich draws my attention to the following from N. I. Žinkin, "The perception of stress in Russian words" (in Russian), *Izvestija Akademii pedagogičeskix nauk R. S. F. S. R.*, LIV (1954), 7–82, page 9: "The claim that under stress the fundamental pitch of the vowel is raised, is subject to doubt.... This raising should be attributed to sentence intonation, not to word stress. A pronunciation is possible without such raising. Furthermore, whispered pronunciation is possible, where the fundamental pitch ...is excluded altogether." Again pitch is dismissed as a cue to stress as a result of failure to find a pitch RISE. It is reasonable, of course, to assign to the role of sentence intonation, instead of to stress, a particular manifestation of pitch change, e. g., rise rather than fall. If, however, we find that either a rise or a fall, when certain conditions are met, is responded to as "stress," then we have pitch playing a dual role; I have preferred to keep the two functions intact, labeling them *accent*. (As for the absence of intonational contrasts in whispered speech, see my speculation on a change of vowel quality to substitute for it, *Studies in Linguistics* V [1947], 77, confirmed experimentally by Werner Meyer-Eppler, "Realization of prosodic features in whispered speech," *Journal of the Acoustical Society of America*, XXVIII [1956], 760.) These comments, of course, are beside the point if Russian stress and intonation are essentially different from English.

simplified diagrams, the "corners," or "sharp points," represented by dots, indicate some of the ways in which a syllable can be made to stand out by means of pitch:

3. STRESS AND INTENSITY

According to Bloomfield, "*stress*—that is, intensity or loudness—consists in greater amplitude of sound waves."[7] Jones gives more attention to gestural accompaniments, but he too insists on "the objective impression of *loudness*."[8] Nearly all linguists have followed this lead.[9] The unanimity of their opinion is a roadblock that must be got out of the way before an explanation based on pitch can gain acceptance. The removal will occupy a large part of this article.

I shall refer to *intensity*, the physical term for amplitude of sound waves, rather than *loudness*, the psychological impression that varies directly with amplitude, because the experiments are based partly on measurements of intensity. On the other hand, I shall refer to *pitch*, the psychological term, rather than *fundamental frequency*, the physical term, for the sake of brevity.

DEFINITION. By *stressed syllable* I mean one that occurs IN AN UT-TERANCE with the kind of prominence that listeners identify as "stress." The same distinction can be made for English that Charles A. Ferguson makes for Persian: "The syllable on which the stress falls when a given word is uttered in isolation is said to have 'inherent' or 'potential' stress, or simply the WORD STRESS. It must be noted that this concept of word stress is essentially morphological. A statement of the type 'The word X in Persian has (word) stress on the third syllable' means in effect that the word X has two alternants, one with stress on the third syllable, one with no stress at all."[10] *Stress* as I use it does not refer to potential, or word, stress, but to stress that is actually there, imposed within an utterance. And

---

7. Leonard Bloomfield, *Language* (New York, 1933), § 7.3.

8. *Outline*, § 909.

9. Pike (pp. 83, 96) gives first place to intensity, but allows that duration may be a factor. Trager-Smith (*Outline*, § 1.61) correlate stress with loudness, and Edith C. Trager (in *General Linguistics*, II [1956], 2) says unequivocally, "there is only one component that matters—loudness."

10. "Word stress in Persian," *Language*, XXXIII (1957), 124–125. See also Uriel Weinreich, "Stress and word structure in Yiddish," in *The field of Yiddish: studies in language, folklore, and literature* (New York, 1954), especially § 3.1.

for the most part the stress that I shall use as an example is the most prominent one in each of the utterances tested.

EXPERIMENTS BY OTHER INVESTIGATORS. Though a number of competent investigators have expressed doubts about intensity,[11] the only recent

---

11. Arnold says (pp. 440-441), "articulatory force is frequently a difficult and, sometimes, an impossible yardstick for the recognition of linguistic stress in English." He is not concerned with the syllable that carries the main stress, but, given that syllable, with predicting where other stresses will fall, which he does on rhythmic principles. His statement therefore is a denial of the importance of intensity not on the main stress, but on the stresses that Smith and Trager would mark with /ˊ/ and /ˆ/. They, of course, insist on loudness there also.

Using an approach similar to Arnold's, Wiktor Jassem, in "Stress in modern English," *Bulletin de la Société Polonaise de Linguistique*, Fascicule XI, pp. 23-49, is even more positive: "A definition of stress in terms of absolute force (or loudness) is an obvious impossibility. That the absolute breath-force (or loudness) of what are generally termed 'stressed' syllables may, under certain circumstances, be much less than the absolute force (or loudness) of 'unstressed' syllables hardly requires elucidation" (p. 29), and he cites Jespersen's *Lehrbuch*, p. 116, on this point. For him "the 'tonal accent' [is] wrongly called 'stress'" (p. 38).

Both Arnold and Jassem agree with the position that I adopt, which is that there is a special kind of syllabic prominence due to pitch, which should not be confused with other phases of stress.

H. E. Palmer "regards stressed syllables as those which take 'nucleus tones' in contrast to all other syllables which are pronounced with equal or nearly equal force" (quoted by Newman, p. 178; see below). Palmer's nuclei (see his *English intonation* [Cambridge, 1922]) are the nearest to the pitch accents that I describe in this article. The principal difference is that the nuclei are sentence stresses (p. 7), and while other syllabic prominences due to pitch are scored in his notation, he lumps them under "heads." For example,

What a re bly
mark a pretty little
house

contains, for him, a unclear tone on *house*, and what precedes is merely a "broken scandent head" (p. 46). As set forth in § 7 of this article, I would put pitch accents on *what*, *-mark-*, and *pret-*, those on *-mark-* and *pret-* being the same as the "nuclear" in Palmer's (p. 39)

Could you one?
spare me

on the word *spare*.

Stanley S. Newman, "On the stress system of English," *Word*, II (1946), 171-178, holds to the intensity theory but with reservations: "Altho force of articulation is the primary medium thru which the stress phonemes are externalized, this phonetic feature is not the exclusive medium of stress" (p. 171). He distinguishes between "expressive accents," in which articulatory force is secondary to or at least equaled by pitch and quantity (p. 173), and "stress accents," where intensity predominates.

published experimental study to my knowledge that calls it into question is "The linguistic relevance of intensity in stress," by H. Mol and E. M. Uhlenbeck.[12]   The authors adduce arguments from Franz Saran (1907), who pointed to the ear's well-known sensitivity to pitch and its relative unresponsiveness to intensity, but who failed to dissuade other phoneticians from their adherence to dynamic stress. Mol and Uhlenbeck experimented with the *pérmit—permít* pair, altering intensities in such a way that the stresses could not be signaled by them, and finding that nevertheless the stresses were clearly heard. They are perhaps too categorical about the absolute irrelevance of intensity, but their conclusions are probably true as regards its relative importance: "It is obvious that the decoding-system of the ear does not use any amplitude information. The system is concerned with the recognition of shapes or forms." The prominences to which I have referred are, of course, shapes—configurations of pitches.

At about the same time, Dennis Fry was conducting experiments at Haskins Laboratories using similar sets of minimal pairs, to determine whether pitch or duration was the better cue to stress. He had previously used the sets in pitting intensity against duration, and found that duration on the whole is a better cue.[13]   The later experiments showed pitch to be superior to

---

My view differs in that a large part of what Newman puts under the stress accents I would put under the expressive accents.

E. A. Glikina, in "An attempt at an experimental study of the elements of dynamic stress (with reference to English)" (in Russian), *Voprosy jazykoznanija*, 1958, no. 5, 18–85, showing no awareness of recent laboratory investigations in the United States, and employing no synthetic devices, found that in 250 pronunciations of compounds by native Englishmen, accentual prominence was generally achieved by a combination of intensity, duration and pitch, although any one factor could render the distinction when the others were equal.

12. *Lingua*, V (1956), 205–213. The same authors adduce other theoretical arguments against intensity in a later article, *Lingua*, VI (1957), 346.

13. "Duration and intensity as physical correlates of linguistic stress," *Journal of the Acoustical Society of America*, XXVII (1955), 765 ff.; "Experiments in the perception of stress," *Language and Speech* I (1958), 126–152.

In a sense the separation of duration and intensity may be a false dichotomy, if what we are seeking is determinations of "loudness." It is possible that increasing only the duration of a syllable, and not its intensity, may cause at least some hearers to report it as "louder," owing to the integration of intensities over a period of time: where two otherwise identical syllables have the same intensity level but one lasts twice as long as the other, the longer syllable could then be said to have twice as much acoustic energy. Another way of putting it is that there is a point below which the failure to discriminate between changes of intensity and changes of duration is determined biologically (sensory discrimination) rather than culturally (function of naming). Apparently duration does operate in some such way, at threshold

duration, from which it is reasonable to infer that pitch is superior to intensity.

A more direct attack was made by J M. Cowan, in an experiment whose results have not yet been published but which he has been kind enough to explain in a personal letter. It consists, essentially, in producing speech from which all intensity-control has been cut out. A harmonic-rich tone is fed from an artificial larynx through a tube to the back wall of the pharynx, where the operator, articulating in a whisper, re-emits it. The pitch of the tone is continuously variable; besides the tone-control there is an on-off switch to contrast voicing and non-voicing, but there is no control for intensity. Listeners report very good "stress" contrasts.

TESTS 1, 2, AND 3: INTENSITY AND PITCH IN NATURAL SPEECH.

Test 1. The sentence *Wouldn't it be easier to wait?* was recorded by the experimenter in two patterns of pitch, as seen in Fig. 1. In one (solid line), the syllable *wait* was "obtruded" from the pitch line by giving it a rapid fall. In the other (dotted line), the syllable *ea-* was obtruded by putting the rapid fall immediately after it, while the syllable *wait* was "embedded" in the following gradual curve. (This pitch contrast is the same one reported by James Sledd for the sentence *It's utterly ridiculous*, opposing the syllables *ut-* and *-dic-*.[14]) Intensities (peak value on vowel of syllable) were uniform in the four syllables: *ea-=wait=ea-=wait*.

—a sound with a given intensity which would be altogether inaudible becomes audible when prolonged (see W. R. Garner and G. A. Miller, "The masked threshold of pure tones as a function of duration," *Journal of Experimental Psychology*, XXXVII [1947], 293–303). More recent evidence indicates, however, that above threshold, and at durations significant for judgments of syllabic stress, this may no longer hold. The experiments of Irwin Pollack ("Loudness of periodically interrupted white noise," *Journal of the Acoustical Society of America*, XXX [1958], 181–185) suggest that for noises lasting longer than 1/10 second there is little change in loudness when duration is increased (provided the intervening "silences" are less than 1/3 second—a condition which is handily met in the normal stream of speech); and he refers to another study which sets the critical duration at around 1/20 second. A glance at Fig. 4 will show that durations of syllables normally regarded as stressable are well beyond the 1/20 to 1/10 second minimum, so that a further increase in duration would not create an impression of greater loudness, if these experiments have any bearing. I mention the point only because of the incidental observations in this article about duration and intensity, not because it affects the priority of pitch over intensity, or duration, or duration-intensity, however one may choose to look at the latter complex.

14. In *Litera*, III (1956), 38.

Eight listeners[15] were asked to say whether *easier* or *wait* contained the major stress. They had no difficulty, despite the lack of contrast in intensity: the vote in each instance was in favor of the similarly obtruded syllable.

Test 2. Smith and Trager[16] utilize an example that has been widely quoted: *The Pennsylvania Railroad is the main Pennsylvania railroad.* Without giving further details, it is enough to say (1) that *Pennsylvania Railroad* and *Pennsylvania railroad* are supposed to be distinguished by the arrangement of dynamic stresses (loudnesses), and (2) that in both instances in normal speech the principal stress on *railroad* is supposed to be louder than that on *Pennsylvania*.

As a less complicated example, since *Pennsylvania* contains what is usually marked as a secondary stress, I substituted the word *republican* in two contexts, which I infer to be analogous to those of *Pennsylvania*: (1) *He's a Methodist and belongs to the Republican Party* and (2) *It's too bad that Spain doesn't have a more republican government.* This test is reported more fully elsewhere,[17] but I reproduce the tracings in Fig. 2 to show a visual display of pitches in natural speech.

Six speakers recorded the two sentences. Only two could be judged by ear to have made a distinction between *Republican* and *republican*; the others apparently inferred a contrast with *Democratic*. Spectrograms were made of the phrases *Republican Party* and *republican government* as uttered by these two speakers. The pitch and intensity information appears in Fig. 2.

As the curves show, there are two kinds of pitch prominence. In *Republican Party* (solid line), the syllable *-pub-* stands out by reason of being skipped up to; after that the line remains fairly uniform until the syllable *Par-*, where there is a sharp drop. In *republican government* (dotted line), however, *-pub-* is obtruded both by an upskip and by following rapid downmotion, and *gov-* is obtruded in the same way.

The information from the intensity profile is irrelevant, and in one instance actually runs counter to the Smith-Trager markings: Speaker A gives slightly more intensity to *-pub-* than to *Par-*. His recording gave no impression of a contrastive stress.

Test 3. In a suggestive article comparing German and English intonation patterns,[18] Hugo Mueller observes that English numeral-plus-noun combinations tend to place the numeral on a higher pitch than the noun. He follows the Smith-Trager pitch-and-stress markings, giving an example such as ²*That*

---

15. Except as otherwise noted, listeners in all experiments were researchers and technicians at Haskins Laboratories.

16. § 4.3.

17. See pp. 57–66.

18. "Some German intonation patterns and their relation to stress," *Modern Language Journal*, XL (1956), 28–30.

Fig. 1

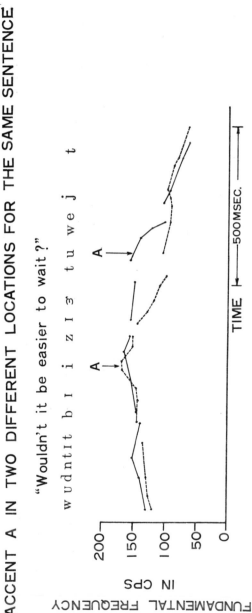

ACCENT A IN TWO DIFFERENT LOCATIONS FOR THE SAME SENTENCE

"Wouldn't it be easier to wait?"

Fig. 2

"Republican Party" <u>vs</u> "Republican government"

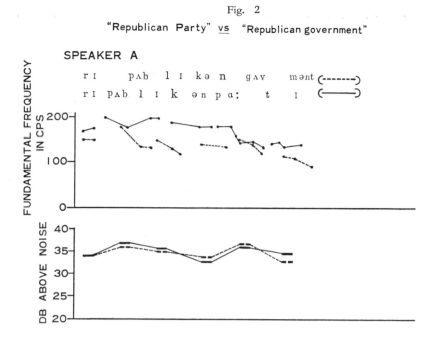

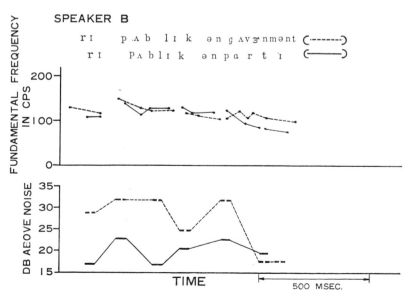

took [3]*twénty mínutes*[1]#, and interprets as follows: "In English, *the number* tends to have the highest pitch in the phrase, although it does not bear the strongest stress."

I judge this description to be correct as regards pitch. I would generalize it, however, to refer to all QUANTIFYING MODIFIERS, i.e., modifiers that show an amount or degree of something rather than a characteristic that distinguishes it from other things. I would expect the word *single* in *I couldn't contribute because I was flat broke; I didn't have a single dollar* to show the same trait as *twenty* in Mueller's example, and to contrast with the word *single* in a context where it is differentiating, e.g. *I'd have been glad to contribute if I'd had a single dollar, but all I had was some small change and a five-spot.*

This contrast with *single* was put to seven speakers, and the majority confirmed the predicted arrangements of pitch as judged by ear. An analogous contrast was made use of for more precise measurement: the word *solid* in the sentences *I waited a solid hour on that cold street corner* and [*How come it doesn't bend?*] *Because it has such a solid frame.* As this experiment is also reported in detail elsewhere,[19] I shall limit myself to the results that bear on the question of intensity:

Of six speakers, three produced both utterances as predicted (all six did *solid hour* as predicted). Pitch and intensity were measured for these three. Peak intensities for the three syllables of *solid hour* were as follows, in decibels above noise: 27-30-31; 34-32-35; 35-30-32. In only one of the three is *hour*, supposed to be the "strongest" stress, different by more than 1 db from both of the other syllables—this is the third example—and there it is 3 db LESS than *sol-*. It is obvious that the hearer is getting no information from intensity here.

TESTS 4, 5, 6, AND 7: INTENSITY AND PITCH IN SYNTHETIC SPEECH.

The Voback is a machine developed at Haskins Laboratories[20] enabling the experimenter to apply varying pitches or intensities to an artificial spectrogram by means of a hand-drawn pattern. For experimental purposes it has several advantages over natural speech; it is more flexible, for example, in that the pitch can be controlled within a fraction of a cycle per second, and in that a synthetic utterance can be stopped and held at any point to read off the precise pitch or to listen to any characteristic of the painted pattern. Spectrograms of natural speech will not yield precise information about pitch in jumps smaller than about 4 cps, and the effect of stopping a tape recorder is, of course, silence. The recordings used in the tests about

---

19. See p. 60.

20. See John M. Borst and Franklin S. Cooper, "Speech research devices based on a channel vocoder," *Journal of the Acoustical Society of America*, XXIX (1957), 777.

to be described were made by the Voback.

Test 4. The synthetic sentence *Break both apart* was given various treatments of intensity and pitch, designed to throw stress on one or another element. Seven listeners were asked simply to indicate the syllable or syllables that they heard as stressed. Here are some of the stimuli and their results:

1. Syllables *break* and *-part* given an inflected pitch of 120 cps dropping to 100 (about 3 semitones), other syllables held at 100. Syllable *both* 10.5 db more intense than *break* (at least "twice as loud"), and 7.5 db more intense than *-part*. Majority hear stress on *-part*.

2. Syllable *break* inflected, 120-100 cps, other syllables at 100 cps monotone. *Both* 11 db more intense than *break*, 9 db more intense than *-part*. Majority hear stress on *both*. A massive increase in intensity overcomes a comparatively small inflection of pitch, in this particular pitch pattern.

3. Syllable *break* at 120 cps, rest at 100 cps. *Both* 2 db more intense than *break* and 1 db more intense than *-part*. A large majority hear stress on *break*. The smaller difference of intensity is overwhelmed by the difference of pitch.

4. All syllables at 80 cps monotone. *Break* 10.5 db more intense than *both* and *-part*. A small majority hear stress on *break*. The massive increase of intensity here does not do as well as the comparatively small rise of pitch in (3), in putting the stress on *break*.

5. Syllable *both* given an inflected pitch of 90-80 cps, the rest at 80 cps monotone. Syllable *both* 6 db LESS intense than *break* and *-part*, but heard as stressed by the majority.

Other patterns and treatments could be listed, but these are typical, and indicate the ease with which changes in pitch register as stress and the difficulty that changes of intensity have in competing with them.

Test 5 is designed to show the relative power of certain changes of pitch and intensity. The synthetic sentence *Many are taught to breathe through the nose* was played at a monotone, and without manipulations of its intensities, to six listeners, to find how they considered it to be stressed. In 7 out of 12 judgments they favored *breathe* (3 *many*, and 1 each *nose* and *taught*). Knowing that the listeners already favored *breathe*, the experimenter now set about increasing the preference by adding intensity to this word, making it 3 to 7 db more intense than *taught* or *nose*.[21] The object was to see how it

---

21. The 3–7 fluctuation was not intended, but resulted from an inherent characteristic of the Voback.

would fare when changes of pitch were applied to these two other words.

The word *taught* was given 12 simple rises of pitch in 5 cps steps from 95 to 150 cps, the rest of the sentence being kept at a 90 cps monotone. The same treatment was given to *nose*, and in addition, the entire series was done again on *nose* with an inflected rise instead of a simple rise, the first half of the syllable being at the higher pitch and the second half at the reference pitch. Responses of the six listeners to the stimuli are shown in Fig. 3.[22]

A pitch rise of from 5 cps (less than a diatonic semitone) to 15 cps (less than a minor third) is sufficient to overcome both the initial bias in favor of *breathe* and its added intensity.

Test 6. The Smith-Trager system allows for rises in pitch associated with stress, but considers them " allophones of the pitch phonemes."[23] One to whom this point of view has become second nature is likely to say, " Of course if pitch rises when intensity rises, the hearer who is given a stimulus in which there is a change in pitch automatically interprets it as a change in intensity ; the pitch is only an indirect cue to the stress, but since it is the only cue present, it becomes effective." That is to say, a feedback is assumed from pitch, through intensity, to stress, While this argument hardly refutes the experiments where both pitch cues and intensity cues are present, it needs to be tested for whatever other plausibility it may have. This can be accomplished by asking the question in reverse : " When there are changes in intensity, can they be heard as changes in pitch?" If the answer is yes, this means that the gun shoots both ways.

The synthetic sentences *Break both apart* and *But would many return?* were given various treatments of pitch and intensity, including some in which the utterance was held at a monotone but one syllable was given an increase of intensity, and others in which the same utterance had both pitch and intensity changes. The listeners were asked to indicate the syllables that went higher or lower in pitch than the reference level.

Responses showed a tendency to hear a marked rise in intensity as a rise in pitch, when the stimulus was actually a monotone. This tells us that it is just as possible to mistake a change in intensity for a change in pitch as it is to mistake a change in pitch for a change in intensity. The feedback works both ways.

On the other hand, the responses showed no tendency to hear even a large

---

22. It should not be necessary to point out that normal precautions were taken in administering this and other tests. The stimuli were randomized and four other stimuli, two with pitch changes on *many*, were introduced to divert attention from the systematic changes lest the hearers assume that *breathe, taught,* and *nose* were the only words that could contain the major stress.

23. P. 43.

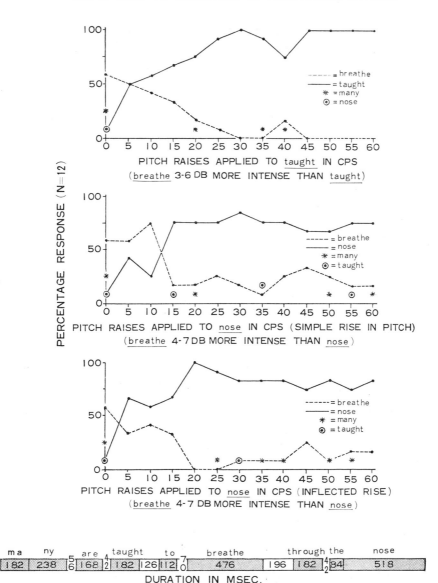

Fig. 3

VARIABLE PITCH VS CONSTANT INTENSITY-DURATION
AS A CUE TO LOCATION OF SENTENCE STRESS

DROP in intensity as a drop in pitch. Instead, the subjective impression was that of some external interference, as if the speaker had turned his face away or the wind had suddenly snatched part of a word. Intensity seems to be significant only when it rises—as we would expect if it were a voice qualifier rather than something linguistic in the narrower sense. Configurations of pitch work in either direction—up or down; in fact, some of the listeners responded to changes in pitch without knowing which way they went. Pitch is again the more reliable cue, in respect of this greater flexibility.

Test 7. Assuming now what seems to have been amply demonstrated—that intensity is at best UNNECESSARY as a cue to stress and that pitch alone will serve so long as an utterance is kept reasonably close to the normal range of intensity and duration—one may ask whether intensity perhaps at least contributes to the QUALITY of a stress, to making it " sound right." To inform ourselves on this point, we devised a test the results of which are published in another journal[24] and will merely be summarized here.

The synthetic sentence *Alexander's an intelligent conversationalist* was given pitch-marked stresses at points where the intensity was BELOW the maximum for the utterance. Boosts of intensity were then applied at those points, and the resulting stimuli, with and without added intensity, were judged for quality by 62 listeners.[25] Minimum intensities turned out to be slightly preferred to small additions of intensity; small additions were somewhat preferred over large additions of intensity; and the greatest preference was shown for no addition of intensity as against large additions.

TESTS 8 AND 9: INTENSITY OPPOSED TO OTHER CUES THAN PITCH.

Listeners might well feel that in sequences like *Pennsylvania Railroad, republican government*, etc., the stress at the end gives the subjective impression of greater prominence than the earlier stress or stresses. With this I would agree. As we have seen, however, measurements of intensity do not confirm it. Neither do the measurements of pitch in *republican government*, where the same kind of prominence (upskip followed by rapid downmotion) is present in both, but the second, instead of being more marked than the first, is less marked.

The only remaining measurable factor that is usually recognized to play a role in stress is duration. But a fourth possibility suggests itself: position. It is conceivable that stress is climactic, and that we attribute extra intensity to the position at the end, even when it lacks it phonetically. This is sug-

---

24. Bolinger, " On intensity as a qualitative improvement of pitch accent," *Lingua*, VII (1958), 175–182.

25. A pre-test by Laboratory personnel plus a large-scale test by naive listeners at the University of Connecticut.

Fig. 4

STRESS JUDGMENTS FOR SEVERAL VERSIONS OF THE WORD "UNDERTAKING"

FUNDAMENTAL FREQUENCY PATTERN IN CPS (UN-DER-TA-KING)

STRESS HEARD ON: (DURATION PATTERN IN MSEC.)	80-80-80-80 UN	80-80-80-80 TA	90-80-90-80 UN	90-80-90-80 TA	100-80-90-80 UN	100-80-90-80 TA
UN 170 / 65 / DER 170 / 65 / TA 155 / 70 / KING 320	7	1	2	5	3	5
210 / 40 / 95 / 60 / 180 / 30 / 310	4	4	2	5	2	6
230 / 30 / 80 / 55 / 200 / 50 / 260	4	4	0	7	1	7
145 / 15 / 80 / 85 / 215 / 50 / 250	1	7	1	6	4	4
180 / 30 / 70 / 45 / 25 / 170 / 250	6	2	1	6	6	2
RESPONSE TOTALS	22	18	6	29	16	24
NUMBER OF SUBJECTS	8		7		8	

33

gested by our tendency to shift the sentence stress toward the end at the price, sometimes, of distorting the word stress as a result.[26] If position overrides pitch, which in turn overrides intensity, we have one explanation of why the end stresses are so consistently marked as "louder."

Test 8 pits the cues of pitch and position against each other. Five patterns of the word *undertaking* were hand-drawn with varying syllable lengths, as shown in Fig. 4. Various combinations of pitch were superimposed, and the resulting stimuli were judged by several listeners, who were told to indicate whether they heard the word *úndertaking*, 'what a mortician does,' or *undertáking*, 'enterprise.' There were 16 pitch patterns comprising a total of 615 individual responses. In all but 3 patterns the majority of listeners reacted as the experimenter had predicted on the basis of pitch, and in only one of the 3 could the discrepancy be correlated with duration (i.e., the fault lay with a wrong interpretation of the pitches, not with the influence of duration). This confirms Fry's experiments where pitch overrides duration.

Fig. 4 tabulates the responses that bear on the problem of pitch and position. The first pitch pattern, a monotone, shows a bias in favor of *ún-*. When *un-* and *-ta-* are given equal pitch rises, however, the preference shifts radically to *-tá-*, and even when *un-* is made twice as prominent as *-ta-*, *-tá-* is still favored by the majority. This confirms the tendency to hear the latter of two pitch-marked stresses as "louder."

Test 9. In the Smith-Trager system, constructs such as *lighthouse-keeper* and *light housekeeper* ('housekeeper who is light rather than heavy') are supposed to be distinguished by different loudnesses at different points. As the naive speaker is likely to think that the difference depends more on degrees of separation than on loudness, an experiment was performed to oppose the two cues of disjuncture (separation of syllable centers) and intensity. Here again it developed that the information from intensity was irrelevant, and that the difference was in fact signaled by separation.[27]

With all the phonetic evidence pointing away from intensity as the thing that matters most in utterance stress, how can we account for its hold on the imagination? The answer lies, I think, in our folklore, and reflects not the acoustic signal but its linguistic function. The parts of our utterance that we stress most noticeably are the ones about which we want to be most forceful, and the kinetics of that force is felt and seen in a number of ways. A writer underlining the important parts of a message does it energetically.

---

26. For examples, see Bolinger, "Intersections of stress and intonation," *Word*, XI (1955), 199–201, and "English stress: the interpenetration of strata," § 6, in *Study of Sounds* (Tokyo, 1957), pp. 295–315.

27. See pp. 85–93.

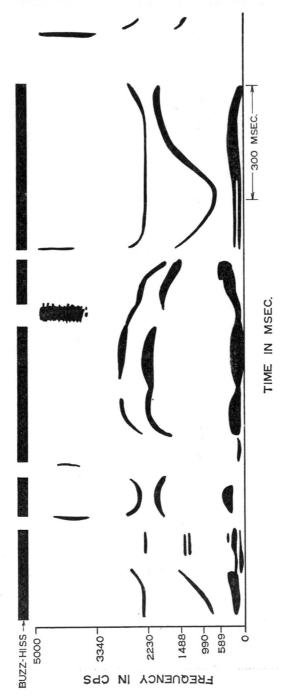

Fig. 5

TIME IN MSEC.

FREQUENCY IN CPS

BUZZ-HISS →
5000
3340
2230
1488
990
589
0

300 MSEC.

A speaker bobs his head and swings his arms in time with his stresses.[28] With this pugilistic obligato to the linguistic tune, it is hardly surprising that the tune became identified with the exercise that went with it; hence force, intensity, loudness. Finally, the pitch direction most fundamental to stress is up, and rising pitch bears a "pre-linguistic," physiological relation to physical tension.

Having given up the more usual definition of stress, I think it is wise, because of associations, to give up the term also. From this point on I shall therefore refer not to stress but to PITCH ACCENT, or simply ACCENT, meaning prominence due to the configuration of pitches.

4. PITCH PROMINENCE IN GENERAL

The experiments relegating intensity to a secondary position have shown that it is unnecessary to take great precautions about small random differences in intensity between one syllable and another in a synthetic utterance. Since the Voback does not deliver perfectly uniform intensities throughout the pitch range (nor does the human voice, though it is somewhat more stable in this regard), without these proofs it might have seemed necessary to specify intensities at every point. As it is, we may attend simply to pitch markings and let the minor fluctuations of intensity fall where they may.

Test 10 uses the same sentence, *Wouldn't it be easier to wait?*, as Test 1, but synthetic. The hand-drawn spectrogram is shown in Fig. 5. (This is done with white paint on transparent film. The pitch information, none of which appears here, is painted in a solid design at the top, with its upper edge tracing the rises and falls. The broken block lines directly beneath are for buzz (voice) and hiss (whisper). The rest of the painting controls the segmental phonemes—formants, transitions, bursts, releases, and frictions of the vowels and consonants.) Some 38 patterns of pitch were overlaid and judged by 9 listeners, who were told to indicate whether the principal accent ("stress" was the term used in the instructions) fell on *easier* or on *wait*. The responses indicated:

1. That when only one item is given pitch prominence, it is heard as accented. The pitch movement may be UP TO, DOWN TO, or DOWN FROM the accented syllable. Examples (the frequencies hold for all following syllables up to the next indicated frequency):

PATTERN	DIRECTION	VOTE FAVORING
100 *Wouldn't it be easier to* 120 *wait?*	up to	9-0, *wait*

---

28. A. J. Vanvik, observing the orators at Hyde Park, noted that how they stressed a word such as *salvation* could be determined by their gestures without actually hearing the syllabic contrasts. See *Maître Phonétique*, No. 103, Jan.-June 1955, p. 8.

100 *Wouldn't it be* 120 *easier to wait?*	— —	9-0, *easier*
100 *Wouldn't it be easier* 120 *to* 100 *wait?*	down to	9-0, *wait*
100 *Wouldn't it* 120 *be* 100 *easier to wait?*	— —	8-1, *easier*
100 *Wouldn't it* 120 *be ea*100*sier to wait?*	down from	9-0, *easier*
130 *Wouldn't it be ea*110-100*sier* 100 *to wait?*	— —	9-0, *easier*

Or the movement may be within the syllable:

100 *Wouldn't it be easier to* 100-130 *wait?*	up in	8-1, *wait*

2. That when one of the items is involved in some movement of pitch, but not enough to make it stand out from its environment, the other, if more clearly marked, is heard as accented. For example:

a) Movement down to the accented syllable, other syllable embedded in gradual upmotion:

80 *Would*85*n't* 90 *it* 95 *be* 100 *ea*105*si*110*er* 115 *to* 80 *wait?*	6-3, *wait*
80 *Would*85*n't* 90 *it* 95 *be* 80 *easier to wait?*	8-1, *easier*

b) Movement down from the accented syllable, other syllable embedded in more gradual downmotion:

130 *Wouldn't it be ea*110-100*sier* 98-92 *to* 90-70 *wait?*	7-2, *easier*
130 *Wouldn't it be ea*130-120*sier* 118-108 *to* 100-70 *wait?*	7-2, *wait*

These last two patterns reproduce the crux of Test 1—note the accent-forming 30 cps drop across *wait* in the second pattern as against the non-accent-forming 20 cps drop in the first.

c) Movement down from the accented syllable, with an undulation on the other syllable:

130 *Wouldn't it be ea*110-100*sier* 96-86 *to* 94-70 *wait?*	9-0, *easier*

3. That when two similar accents are obtruded with equal clarity, the second is more prominent (confirming the remark above about position). Example of two accents both skipped down to:

130 *Wouldn't it be* 115 *easier to* 100 *wait?*	8-1, *wait*

5. Predictable Ambiguity

If prominences of the kind that I have described are the true basis of the accents, it should be possible to predict when a given utterance may be taken in more than one way. For example, in a configuration of the shape ⌐ there are two "corners," either of which may be the significant one. If the top corner, we describe it as an accent that is "skipped down from." If the bottom corner, it is an accent that is "skipped down to." The fact that the linguistic signal is mixed does not refute it, but simply means that under the circumstances the hearer looks to another cue. Take the utterance

I
  broke it

in which both *I* and *broke* occupy corners. In the context where A says to B,

    ny!...   catch
John   you're going to   it for breaking this va se!

and C, a third party, confesses *I broke it*, it is *I* that is accented. But after

What happened to this va s_e?

the same *I broke it* is a disgusted reply accenting *broke*. The cue is contextual redundancy. In place of or along with the contextual cue, either *I* or *broke* may be phonetically degraded (though neither has to be), and when it is, the accent is thrown to the other word. In this sense, the allegro and lento forms of words perform an accentual function. Normally an accented syllable must not be phonetically degraded.

The commonest supporting cue is flanking by unaccentable syllables. The contrast between the following two utterances is clear:

It's the man who   It's   the man
            broke it   who broke it

The unaccentable syllable *who* helps to embed *man* in the first instance and *broke* in the second, giving *broke* the accent in the former and *man* in the latter. How we know that *who* is unaccentable will be discussed in the next section.

Test 11 embodies an ambiguity, contrived without phonetic degradation and with no flanking unaccentables, so as to force identification through context. It was decided to use a short command of the *Run along, Wait here, Come in* type, where American English readily puts the adverb at the low pitch when the speaker's intent is to coax, and to match it with the same phrase in a different context where the accent is clearly on the verb.

The experimenter made a tape recording of the following: *You say you want us to find your missing husband, but you certainly haven't given us much to go on, go on.* The two instances of *go on* were given the shape

Fig. 6

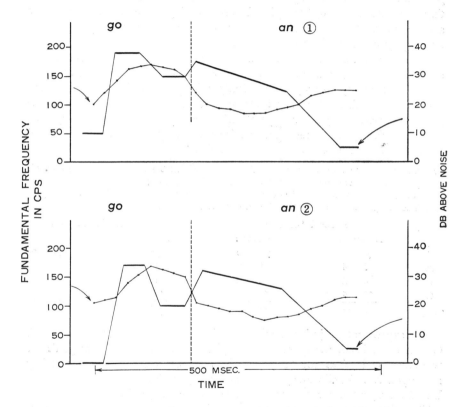

TWO PRODUCTIONS OF "Go on."

Go
  o^n

and made as nearly identical as possible. The pitch and intensity profiles appear in Fig. 6.

Copies were made of the recording. In one copy, the second *go on* was cut out, and the remainder constituted Stimulus II. In the other copy, everything was eliminated except *Go on, go on.* A second voice now recorded a long passage which was interrupted in the middle, at which point the *Go on, go on* was inserted, whereupon the second voice resumed. The effect was that of someone reading, stopping before reaching the end, being urged by another person to continue, and finally completing what was begun. This interchange constituted Stimulus I.

The listeners were asked to indicate which word carried the accent (instructions were explicit, using the terms *stress, accent,* and *emphasis,* to avoid a possible tendency to judge phonetically without regard to context), and also to say whether what they heard sounded like normal English. Three groups of varying degrees of sophistication participated: A, Laboratory staff and researchers; B, a class in Spanish phonology; C, a sophomore-level college class. Responses are shown in Table 1.

TABLE 1. JUDGMENTS OF ACCENT AND ACCEPTABILITY IN TWO CONTEXTS OF *go on.* (In Group B the same two marked "not normal" as marked *ón*; in Group C, however, none of those who marked "not normal" were among those who were judging 'continue' as *go ón.* There is therefore no correlation here.)

Group	Stimulus I 'continue'				Stimulus II 'rely on'			
	Accent on		Normal?		Accent on		Normal?	
	go	*on*	yes	no	*go*	*on*	yes	no
A	5	4	9	0	8	1	9	0
B	4	2	4	2	6	0	6	0
C	19	5	16	8	20	4	18	6
Totals	28	11	29	10	34	5	33	6

The experimenter's judgment that both instances are normal was confirmed. On the other hand, the greater tendency to locate the accent as *go ón* for 'continue' and *gó on* for 'rely on', while probably significant, is certainly not impressive. In all three groups the majority marked *gó* in both instances. Yet the analyst "knows" that 'continue' has to be *go ón.*

The reluctance of the listeners to hear the bottom pitch as an intentional prominence confirms the difficulty that we experienced in other tests, and suggests a reason why speakers—including phoneticians—instinctively look for correlations of HIGH pitch and stress. In the other tests, a downward obtrusion nearly always gave data which while reliable were not as clean as those obtained with an upward obtrusion.

Test 12 shows this graphically. From the hand-drawn patterns of *under-*

Fig. 7

VARIABLE PITCH VS CONSTANT INTENSITY—DURATION
AS A CUE TO LOCATION OF SYLLABLE STRESS

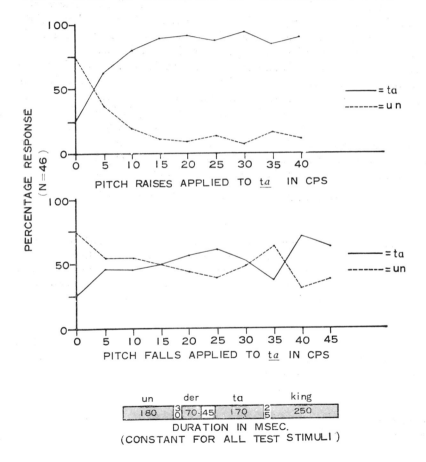

taking in Test 8, the one was chosen which had shown the clearest bias in favor of *un-* (the last pattern in Fig. 4). This pattern was then given pitch treatments similar to those in Test 5, with successive 5 cps rises on the syllable *-ta-*. In addition to the upward obtrusion, downward obtrusions also in 5 cps steps were put on the same syllable. The resulting stimuli, randomized and mixed with other stimuli, were played to 46 naive listeners at the University of Connecticut. The data are schematized in Fig. 7. The top diagram, representing the upward obtrusions, is similar to those of Fig. 3. The bottom diagram, representing the downward obtrusions, leaves little doubt that a prominence in that direction is effective, but also makes it clear that upward obtrusions are superior to downward ones.

The hypothesis that I advance to account for at least part of the difference in effectiveness between the two directions is that when we ask listeners to point to a " stress," and then give them a downward obtrusion, we miscue them. Downward obtrusions give perfectly normal syllabic prominences, as the judgments of Test 11 prove. But "stress" popularly means 'being emphatic about something.' The downward obtrusion seems to contradict this. Its use in situations where gentleness or restraint is called for is widely recognized.[29] Listeners are therefore willing to accept the downward syllabic

---

29. Pike (*Intonation*, § 4.3.1.) gives 'encouragement' as the meaning of

O
  ka^y

I have pointed out the frequency of the low pitch in questions addressed to a stranger, in " The intonation of ·ccosting questions," *English Studies*, XXIX (1948), 109–144. In Test 7 (text, above), listeners were apparently more reluctant to approve of added intensity on the bottom pitch than on higher pitches, suggesting a preference for " softness " there. Jones notes (§ 1069) that *All right* is usually

All
  rig^{ht}

and that if the directions are reversed one " may have the effect of a threat." Fred W. Householder, Jr., calls my attention to an example by Martin Joos involving a full answer to a yes-no question: in response to *Is this an ashtray?* it would probably be

                an
Ye^s it's   asht_ra^y

He suggests the meaning ' de-emphasis or restraint.' Palmer and Jassem, however, take their metaphors literally. Palmer considers

Be
  pa^{tie}n^t

to have " a protesting or exclamatory character " (*English intonation*, p. 80). Jassem regards

You've de
        ser_ted h^{im}?

prominence, but not always to interpret it as something " stressed."

What emerges from this is that while prominence as such gives the accent, accents are of more than one kind. It is best then to speak of PITCH ACCENTS, in the plural, and to look for kinships and differences. The search will also illumine that other part of the accentual complex, the un-accentable syllable.

6.   FAVORED ACCENTS AND THE LEARNING OF ACCENTUAL STRUCTURE

Of the two arrangements of *It's the man who broke it* (p. 38), one gives *who* the same kind of pitch prominence that *man* has in the other. If accent were a matter of pitch only, *who* would have the same kind of accent as *man*. But I have used *who* as a means of warding off an accent, not of it-self acquiring one, and referred to it as " unaccentable."[30]   There is an apparent contradiction.

The explanation probably lies in the manner in which the lexicon is learned. A child confronted with the two patterns

dai
      dʒɛstəbl̩   daɪdʒɛs təbl̩

would have no cue, from pitch, to tell whether the accent is on *dai-*, on

---

as " stupefaction, surprise combined with either incredulity or disapproval" (*Intonation of conversational English* [Wrocław, 1952], p. 29).   The verbal context does suggest this, of course, but the speakers are probably restraining themselves. The words and pitches pulling against each other are reminiscent of familiar paradoxes of literature, " an icy smile," " a cheerless laugh."   For Maria Schubiger, *English intonation: its form and function* (Tübingen, 1958), the lowered pitches are " regardful."

30.   Actually this is not quite true.   *Who* may be accented as a means of affirmation. Normally the configuration would differ slightly from the way it was set forth in § 5 above: specifically, the *who* would rise in pitch above what precedes:

                   who
It's the man   broke it

' He is the very person who did it,' analogous to the rise in pitch on other function words for the same purpose of affirmation, commonest in the auxiliary verbs, e. g.

              did
The man   break it

but also found on other words:

           to   for
There's no chance do it   There's no way doing it

Note the example *in Rumania*, text § 8.   But these instances are too infrequent to matter in the stigmatizing of most function words as unaccentables.

-*dʒɛs*-, or on -*tə*-, assuming that he has learned to respond to pitch prominence in a general way. This does not bother the adult, who KNOWS that only -*dʒɛs*- can receive the pitch accent, and is accordingly able to respond to and produce more than one KIND of pitch accent using the same phonetic data—high pitch, fall, and rise—differing only in the location of the accentable syllable on the configuration.

The question is, how does the adult know that only the one syllable is accentable, since pitch contrasts like those of the two examples did not give him this information as a learner? The answer is that it is a matter of frequency. About 70 percent of the time, the accented syllable is what might be called a cliff-hanger—it is obtruded by means of a subsequent fall in pitch.[31] Most of these—virtually all of them when they are citation forms and a large majority under other conditions of special emphasis (conditions under which learning is most likely to take place)—are skipped up to as well. With sufficient normal contexts of the type

$$\text{Cu} \qquad\qquad \text{ges}$$
$$\text{cumbers are indi} \qquad \text{tib}_{l_e}$$

it does not matter that the pitch relationships are occasionally reversed, for the syllables *cu-* and *-ges-* will have been learned quite early as the potentials for pitch accent in their respective words. Thereafter other obtrusions, with different meanings, become possible.

The reverse of the coin is the almost unbroken regularity with which certain segments are NOT obtruded. They are learned as "generally unaccented," and this expectation enables them to be used in locations of great pitch prominence without being understood as accented; for instance the stopgap subject *there* in

$$\text{There}$$
$$\text{wasn't any} \quad \text{troub}^{le.}$$

Similarly, certain syllable types are stigmatized as unaccentable. Typically these include the syllabic consonants and shwa, in words such as *dictum*, *turtle*, *warden*, *satchel*, and *forward*. A different syllable type flanked by these is in no danger of being misinterpreted, whatever the pitch direction.

Such is the built-in repertory of the language, on top of which the accents are laid. The English speaker's knowledge of the individual morphs and of morph and syllable types of his language gives permanent cues that

---

31. I derive this percentage from Pike, *Intonation*, whose examination of 804 contours (p. 159) in three sample texts (p. 150) yielded 559 in which the syllable marked with stress was dropped away from (pp. 157–158).

serve as a foil to the phonetic nonce cues of pitch.[32]

Looking a little farther, however, we find that pitch accent depends also on certain other phonetic cues, nonce like itself, of which one is especially important: duration. From the synchronic standpoint, duration is to a large extent a co-variable with accent. From the diachronic standpoint, duration accounts in part for how the unaccentables got that way.

A pitch obtrusion requires time for its execution. When the pitch accent is embraced completely by a single syllable, the syllable is lengthened to accommodate the necessary range of pitches; so *go* is probably longer in the first than in the second of the following two examples:

When did you   go \   o?   When did you   go   there?

And the second is in turn longer that the *go* of

When did you go   the re?

in which *go* is embedded in what precedes the accent.

The experiments have made it clear that in the duration-pitch complex it is pitch that primarily signals accent. I therefore assume that duration is ancillary. Figuratively speaking, it is there IN ORDER TO make room for the accent (though I would not say that duration has no other function). This is supported by the following considerations:

1. Accented syllables are normally longer than unaccented ones in comparable positions within the utterance (i.e., in reference to junctures). (Cf. Jones, *Outline*, § 870.)

2. A long syllable—and here I follow Jones in assigning to length and concomitant vowel quality rather than to intensity the prominence of the "medial stress" in words like *asphalt, teapot, hiccup* (*Outline* § 920, footnote) —other than the one carrying the potential for pitch accent tends to be unstable. This is demonstrated by the history of loanwords in which the potential for pitch accent shifts its position. The nouns *hurricane, program, crayon, address, rupee, caravan,* and *mascot* were imported with the potential on the final syllable. They accommodated themselves to the normal accentual

---

32. The fact that the speaker must know the morphs disposes of the suggestion, often made, that nonsense syllables be used to test these patterns. The suggestion is a plausible one, for the worst obstacle to agreement about pitch stimuli is that there are always syntactic, morphological, and other cues present, and untrained listeners are apt to go off on a tangent, while trained listeners are apt to interpret them in terms of their training. Tests in which everything is stripped off except pitch would seem to be an answer; but, as I have tried to show, they will not work with the pitch accents.

pattern of English nouns by shifting the potential forward. The syllable originally having the potential, however, did not lose its length immediately; for some speakers it is still long; for others it is short, with correspondingly centralized vowel (the *ACD* recognizes both stages for *máscot*, the earlier uncentralized [ɒ] and the later centralized shwa); for others it wavers. *Turquoise* has shifted without losing length, perhaps because of its syllable structure. *Intrigue* and *Portuguese* are shifting for some speakers, and have not had time to lose their length (which is furthermore supported rhythmically in *Portuguese*). This "medial stress" in many other words is uncertain: *cántŏn, cóncèrt, ínfidĕl, récŏrd, cónvĕnt, tăbóo, áncĕstor*.

3. A short syllable to which the potential is shifted becomes long. I do not have measurements of this, but the evidence of vowel-decentralization seems clear enough: *pecan,* from [pɪ-] in *pecán* to [piː-] in *pécàn*, in the dialects that have the latter; verb *survéy* [sɜʳˈveɪ] giving noun *súrvèy* [ˈsɜʳveɪ], etc. Verb-based nouns such as *cóme-òn, cómbìne, ímpòrt, pérvèrt, díscàrd*, and *tránsfèr* (or *tránsfer*) are typical. A favorite among linguists is the verb *to segmént* (or *ségmènt*), from the noun *ségment*, with shwa.

4. A long syllable other than the one carrying the potential is often the syllable that carries the potential in a cognate or popularly associated word —the pitch accent here is an indirect source of length. Newman lists[33] many examples of this "underlying theme" relationship: *nàturalizátion* ∽ *náturalize; matèrialístic* ∽ *matérial*. In citation forms, and sometimes elsewhere, the syllable in question actually develops a secondary pitch accent.

If my assumption is correct, the speaker has the gradient covariable of duration at his command in any case of ambiguity: by reducing the syllable (and also centralizing the vowel somewhat), he throws the balance toward another syllable as the receiver of the accent. So in

who's
I don't know   coming

either *know* or *who's* can be accented, depending on which is reduced in this fashion. Similarly

In
tri gue

can be distinguished as to whether we have a speaker of one dialect saying *íntrigue* with one kind of accent (Accent A; see next section) or a speaker of another dialect saying *intrígue* with another kind of accent (Accent C).

---

33. Pp. 184–185. I would add most if not all of his examples of "sonorous weak" (pp. 186–187): *légality*∽*légal, vibration*∽*víbrate, incúlcation*∽*incúlcate*.

7. Pitch Accents A, B, and C

It would be possible to view pitch accent as a matter of obtrusion per se, relegating manners of approach, sustention, and take-off to another level of analysis, i.e., to intonation.   This might seem the more advisable now that we know accent to be cued by the same kind of phonetic stimulus that we have always known operated in the sphere of intonation, namely, pitch change, and in view of the obvious difficulty of separating the different manners of achieving accent—apart from the fact of accent itself—from the domain of intonation.

That pitch can function in two equally complex ways at the same time, however, is well demonstrated by the tone-and-intonation languages.   Chinese and Japanese use pitch phonemically, and despite this fact have intonations in many ways similar to those of English.[34]   What happens in English with certain abrupt changes in a wider curve of pitch suggests that the same kind of line can be drawn between the pitch accents and intonation:

Two shapes like these are more alike, superficially, than they are different. Yet if we put an accentable syllable at the kink in the left-hand one and at the trough in the right-hand one, we get entirely different meanings:

(1) It wasn't John   (2) It wasn't John

For a contrastive context in which *John* comes as a potentially new datum, (1) is appropriate: " I wish I knew who did a thing like that."   —" It wasn't John (that much I'm sure of, though as to who else it might have been I'm not saying)."   But (2) is uncomplicated denial; *John* is not a new datum: " I think it was John."   —" It wasn't John—what are you talking about?" This contrast is pointed out by Maria Schubiger.[35]   On the other hand, if

---

34.   See Y. R. Chao, " A preliminary study of English intonation (with American variants) and its Chinese equivalents," reprinted from *The Ts'ai Yüan P'ei Anniversary Volume* (Supplementary Vol. 1 of the *Bulletin of the Institute of History and Philology of the Academia Sinica*) (Peiping, 1932). See also Isamu Abe, " Intonational patterns of English and Japanese," *Word*, XI (1955), 386–398. Weinreich, " Stress and word structure," treats stress in similar overlapping functions (phonemic, constructive, contrastive, expressive).

35.   " Again: fall-rise intonations in English," p. 2, reprinted from *English Studies*, XXXVII (1956).   Her example is *I hadn't expected to see him there*.   She credits " colleagues of University College, London," with having called the contrast to her attention.

we take a superficially disparate shape:

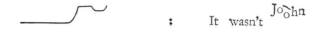

and put *John* at the peak, we again have implications of new-datum and contrast. The over-all similar curves carry something more dissimilar in meaning than the over-all dissimilar curves.

The phonetically similar fact in the two shapes with similar meanings is the way in which the accent is formed: it levels off from whatever kind of motion precedes it, and is followed by an abrupt drop. This differs from the other shape in that there the accent is formed by a drop TO the accentable syllable.

Now compare this all-or-none contrast (which is like the one on *intrigue* in the preceding section) with the gradient differences between

which can be laid on a smooth scale of 'degree of finality'. The pitch differences between the first and last in the series are great, but the accents are the same. There is no point along this scale, as there was in the utterance of Test 1 and Test 10 in which the listeners had to make up their minds whether they were or were not hearing a given kind of accent on the word *easier*, where it is necessary to say "yes" or "no" rather than "more" or "less." The all-or-none is the domain of the pitch accents; the gradient is the domain of intonation.

Because each distinctive accent is thus capable of maintaining its identity despite broader intonational changes, I believe that it is practical to recognize more than the mere fact of prominence, of obtrusion per se, i. e., to describe and identify the different ways of achieving prominence. These are the pitch accents.

Test 13 undertakes to show identifications among similar manifestations of accent in dissimilar intonational settings, and discriminations between dissimilar accents in similar intonational settings. The experimenter arranged the phrase *I did* in the following four ways:

These were presented in 12 separately recorded groups of 3 as an ABX test, i.e., the listeners were asked to match X with whichever of the two preceding stimuli it resembled more.[36]   Pattern (1) was present in each set of 3. Six listeners participated.   A majority in every instance treated (1) as the orphan.   This supports the theory that the four utterances have only two patterns of accent: in (1), the accent is formed by skipping down TO the accentable syllable.   In (2), (3), and (4) it is formed by moving rapidly down FROM it.

There seem to be sufficient resemblances and sharp enough differences among accents to group them about three kinds of obtrusion, which I describe and label as follows:

Accent A: A relative leveling off of the accentable syllable followed by a relatively abrupt drop, either within the accentable syllable (which is prolonged for the purpose) or in the immediately following syllable.   In very rapid speech the drop may be postponed to the second following syllable, but rarely beyond this.   There are affective (intonational) differences between a drop within the accentable syllable and a drop later.

The commonest type of approach (" head " in Palmer's terminology, " precontour " in Pike's) to the A accent in American English is from a lower pitch, with a skip up to the accentable syllable.   In British Received Pronunciation, if descriptions are accurate, an approach from a higher pitch would seem to be at least as common (the affective nuances need to be correlated as much with dominant social attitudes as with " dialect ").   One rather sharp deviation, which for semantic reasons I would class as a subtype of A, puts the accentable syllable at a lower pitch than the one immediately following, but requires that only that one weak syllable remain high—the syllable after it must come down rapidly.   An example from a radio dramatization,[37] with accent on *out:*

of
I am seldom out   my cas_{tle}

The least common denominator in all A's is the abrupt fall rarely more than two syllables after the accentable syllable.   In the following diagram the arrow represents a skip or skip-like motion, and solid lines denote essential movements while dotted lines indicate optional ones:

---

36.   For an example of ABX procedure, see Liberman, Harris, Hoffman, and Griffith, " The discrimination of speech sounds within and across phoneme boundaries," *Journal of Experimental Psychology*, LIV (1957), 358–368.

37.   Charles Dickens, *The Poor Relation*, broadcast from Station WABC, New York, 7 : 55 P. M., December 24, 1956.

Pike's 04–3–4 contour (pp. 56–57) is an example of this type of A accent compressed on a single syllable, *yes* and *no*, prolonged for the purpose.

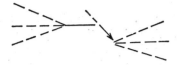

Accent C: This is a kind of anti-accent A, both in form and in meaning. The accentable syllable is approached from above, and skipped down to. What follows may level off or rise, but a further fall seems to be avoided:

Accent B: The characteristic of this accent is upmotion. It is neither skipped down to nor skipped down from. It may be approached from below and skipped up to, with the following motion continuing level, or rising (the usual thing), or falling slightly (an abrupt drop would create an A). Or it may be approached from a relative level and skipped up from, after which the movement usually continues upward slightly or levels off. This makes two diagrams necessary:

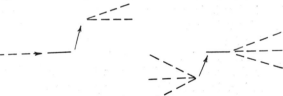

Examples of the accents:

<pre>
          B
Do you real ly hate your brother?
</pre>

<pre>
          B
        real ly hate your brother?
Do you
</pre>

<pre>
          B
Do you really hate your brother?
</pre>

<pre>
          B
        really hate your brother?
Do you
</pre>

<pre>
          A
        real ly hate your brother?
Do you
</pre>

<pre>
          A
Do you real ly hate your brother?
</pre>

Minimal contrast between A and B

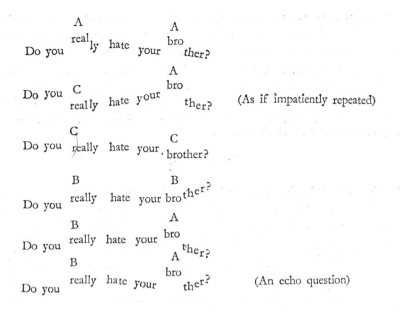

8. The Accents as Morphemes

The procedure that I have followed in grouping the accents about certain norms has been first to look for similarities and differences in meaning, and then to try to match them with similarities and differences in form. This reverses the approved order of business, but had to be adopted because pitch contours are if anything more fluid than meanings.

To take meaning as the starting point can be justified only if the accents are meaningful units. It assumes that they are morphemes, not phonemes. This assumption holds even in the most restricted sense of accent as mere fact-of-prominence. It opposes the current American theory, which is that stresses are meaningless sub-units that build themselves into morphemes ("superfixes") which give, in effect, a phonemic shape to syntax. I regard this view as untenable.[38] The older theory, that accent signals emphasis, has been re-stated by Weinreich for Yiddish: phonemic stress within the morpheme (i.e., word stress) is "the place at which relative loudness [sc. pitch change] occurs if the morpheme is emphasized."[39] This is to say that stress

---

38. See pp. 67–83 and 95–100.

39. Weinreich, "Stress and word structure," p. 2. The relevant part of this statement is that accent is not phonemic, whereas potential for pitch accent is. Whether Weinreich is right in not admitting any other kind of word stress than the potential is another matter. It has been disputed by Stockwell, *Language*, XXXII (1956), 374–383.

is phonemic only in the sense that a given syllable and not some other syllable within the morpheme carries the potential for pitch accent. When the accent occurs, it signals emphasis, i.e., is meaningful.

Accent A is assertive. It is used with items that are separately important, contrastive, and/or new to the discourse. It usually singles out the morph on which it falls, but this function of separation ("contour separation" in Pike's terminology) may be absent. I have heard a single syllable given as many as three successive A accents:[40]

$$\text{No}^{\nearrow\text{o}}\searrow {}_{\text{o}} {}^{\nearrow\text{o}}\searrow {}_{\text{o}} {}^{\nearrow\text{o}}\searrow {}_{\text{o}}\text{o}!$$

Also, instead of singling out one item, the A accent may put emphasis on the utterance as a whole. For this purpose, an item that is ordinarily incapable of receiving it is selected—an auxiliary verb, a preposition, or something of the sort. In the following example there is no contrast between 'in' and 'out of', nor is there any special attention of any other kind bestowed on the word *in*; it merely carries a sentence accent which, if it were to fall anywhere else, might be mistaken as contrastive: the speaker refers to someone who had been denied re-entry to the United States because of having worked for the Communist government of Rumania, and says

B   B   B   A

Well·· the De^fense maintained ·that everybody ^in Rumania worked for the government.

---

40. This freedom to " spread" syllables in order to accommodate more accents reflects a certain degree of freedom in the location of the potential for pitch accent in English. Not only is the normal locus of the potential free, i.e. unpredictable in terms of the total number of syllables and mechanical placement (in Arnold's terms, p. 440, " TONIC STRONG stress is undoubtedly free and not tied to any given position within the word "), but also other syllables may be raised to the status of potential-carrier when it is desired to lay on more than one accent. This is especially true when one word occupies the dimensions of a whole utterance. Note the successions of AAA and CCA in the following:

A   A   A   C   C   A

ab lute fu   so ly re fu

He so ly re ^used   He ab lute used

It also operates to shift the potential toward the end of a word when the word occupies the climactic position in the sentence, as when Thomas Mitchell said, in a TV program,

you   ti

What need is a little adver si_ng

The 'separateness' and 'newness' of A may be illustrated by what happens in a narrative. If one is telling a story in which a fog has been introduced, at a later point one may say

$$\text{The } \overset{\text{B}}{\text{fog}} \text{ had } \overset{\text{A}}{\text{deep}}_{\text{ene}_{\text{d}}}$$

But a B accent for something new and unexpected is unnatural. If we encountered

$$\overset{\text{A}}{\underset{\text{A}}{\text{bomb}}} \text{ had } \overset{\text{A}}{\text{wrecked}} \; \overset{\cdot}{\text{i}}_{\text{t}}$$

at all, it would probably be in a time of violence when bombs are commonplace. For something as inherently unlikely as a bombing,

$$\overset{\text{A}}{\underset{\text{A}}{\text{bomb}}} \quad \overset{\text{A}}{\text{wrecked}}_{\text{had}} \quad \overset{\cdot}{\text{i}}_{\text{t}}$$

with two A accents, or

$$\overset{\text{A}}{\underset{\text{A}}{\text{bomb}}} \quad \text{had } \text{wrecked} \; \text{it}$$

with one A accent, on *bomb* itself, is more probable.

Accent C is anti-assertive. It may be merely lackadaisical, as in a descending series like

$$\text{It's } \overset{\text{C}}{} \atop \text{never too } \overset{\text{C}}{} \atop \text{late to } \overset{\text{C}}{} \atop \text{mend}$$

or it may be clearly and even strenuously restrained, as in

$$\text{D'you think I'm } \overset{\text{C}}{\text{cra}_{\text{z}}\text{y}}?$$

Accent B means somthing like 'connectedness' and 'incompleteness.' In the question

$$\text{Were they } \overset{\text{B}}{\text{bet te}^{\text{r}}}?$$

it is terminal, and 'incomplete'. In the first clause of

$$\text{Were they } \overset{\text{B}}{\text{bette}^{\text{r}}} \text{ they'd be more } \overset{\text{A}}{\text{accep}_{\text{tab}_{\text{le}}}}$$

it is non-terminal and 'connected' to the following Accent A.

Test 14 relates this connectedness to compound words. A live-voice recording of *attorney-at-law* was made. The natural pitch pattern was removed, and the following artificial ones substituted:

(1) (90) *at*(110)*tor*(90)*ney-at-*(110-90)*law*

(2) (90) *at*(110)*torney-at-*(110-90)*law*

(3) (90) *at*(110)*torney-*(90)*at-*(110-90)*law*

The stimuli were mixed with others involving *mother-in-law*, and played to a group of seven listeners, who were asked to distinguish between those that seemed properly stressed and those that did not. Six approved (2) and (3), which have the B accent on *-tor-* that seems to characterize this kind of compound. Only three approved (1) with its A accent on *-tor-*.[41]

Much more testing needs to be done to make these definitions anything more than rough approximations. They are probably close enough to the truth, however, to credit separate semantic functions to separate kinds of pitch prominence.

9. ACCENT AND INTONATION

The pitch accents do not eliminate the problem of intonation. They merely narrow it by cutting out certain all-or-none contrasts. The residue is mostly gradient. Differences of meaning attach to:

1. Steep falls as opposed to gradual falls.

2. High approaches to a falling A accent as opposed to lower approaches.

3. In a succession of A accents that are skipped up to, the relative height of the peaks. Similarly for the relative depth of the troughs of successive C accents; note the difference between the "bright idea" of

$$\text{We could C}^{\text{them}}_{\text{buy}} \; _{a} \; ^{\text{C}}_{\text{coup}^{\text{le}}}$$

with an upward tangent to the troughs, and the more subdued implication where the tangent is down:

$$\text{We could } ^{\text{C}}_{\text{buy}} \text{ them } _{a} \; ^{\text{C}}_{\text{coup}^{\text{le}}}$$

4. A falling approach to a C accent as opposed to a high-pitched approach with steeper downskip:

---

41. Further contrasts of A and B have been described in "Certain functions of accents A and B." In addition, other tests have shown both B and C to be inappropriate to a contrastive context. See pp. 57–66.

He wouldn't believe you C   He wouldn't believe you C

Others could be added.

Furthermore, the problem of terminal junctures needs to be re-studied in the light of pitch accent. Something like the endings that Smith and Trager describe is probably correct, but with refinements. For example, it seems to make little difference after a B accent whether there is a slight fall, a level, or a rise; the differences here are gradient. But after an A accent there seems to be an all-or-none difference between a level and a rise, but a gradient difference between a level and a fall. In answer to *George asked for his shovel back* one might get

A
I thought he gave it to you

with *to you* at a fairly high tonal level, as if the speaker were wondering and half-questioning; but if there is a rise in pitch on *you*, the utterance either takes on an admonitory tone or, though these words scarcely lend themselves, becomes a perplexed iterative question. On the other hand, if *to you* remains level, it may stand at any height, with gradient differences of suspension and conclusiveness; or it may fall for still greater conclusiveness, but without the sharp difference created by the rise.

10. Conclusions

1. Tests with both natural and artificial speech have shown that the primary cue of what is usually termed STRESS in the utterance is pitch prominence.

2. Intensity is found to be negligible both as a determinative and as a qualitative factor in stress.

3. To avoid unwanted associations, it is better to speak of PITCH ACCENT and to leave the term STRESS to the domain of word stress. In the latter domain, one possible kind of phonemic stress is POTENTIAL FOR PITCH ACCENT.

4. While the upward obtrusion is basic, pitch prominence need not be merely upward, as commonly supposed, but may take other directions. The differences of form respond to differences of meaning, giving the accents a morphemic status. Differentiating them often calls for a repertorial cue (the user's knowledge of the morphs of his language, and what syllables have the potential for pitch accent) or a gradient phonetic cue (length of syllable and grade of vowel).

ON CERTAIN FUNCTIONS OF ACCENTS A AND B[1]

Litera 4.80-89 (1957)

A linguistic unit has a distinctive form and a distinctive function. If we imagine we have isolated a unit but it fails to qualify on either of these points, we have not proved that the unit exists. Traditional grammar often erred in setting up functions without forms. Structural grammar—particularly in the area of intonation—has sometimes erred in setting up forms without a convincing demonstration of functions.

What follows is an attempt to show distinctive meaning for two of the pitch accents whose distinctive forms were described in the preceding article.

The physical shapes of Accents A and B[2] suggest in a rough sort of way the difference in function between them; in fact, the function itself is probably of the same order of roughness as the analogy we draw from the physical shape. The drop in Accent A can be likened to a cut-off, by which what precedes it can be set out as a thing apart, as something separately told. The speaker is free to use this " separate telling " for something syntactically separate (it is the usual terminus for most non-questions and for many questions), for something logically separate (as when two things are individually contrasted with two other things):

```
            plea      morn              wret          no
It  was a        sant      ing  but  a      ched  after  on.
```

or, iteratively, in a kind of hectoring assertiveness on things that are not logically separate at all:

```
     ab  lute      fu    Ti        ga        go        go
I  so  ly   re  se.      me and    a  in.  It's    od,  but    od.
```

---

1. Research supported by a grant from the Carnegie Corporation of New York, 1956–57.

2. Accent A: a " stress " marked by a sharp drop in pitch after the accented syllable as against gradual movement or level pitch elsewhere. Accent B: a " stress " marked by a jump to a higher pitch on the accented syllable and with no sharp drop immediately afterward.

The sustained higher pitch at the end of Accent B is the opposite of the cut-off: it suggests connectedness, as in

$$\text{They were}\quad _{n}e^{c\,e\,s\,s}{}^{a\,r\,y}\quad ^{pre}_{cau}_{\text{tions,}}$$

where the B on *necessary* binds it to the A on *precautions;* and, when left suspended without an immediately following item to connect to, it suggests incompleteness:

$$\text{They were}\quad _{n}e^{c\,e\,s\,s}{}^{a\,r\,y^{?}}$$

The general distinction was confirmed in some exploratory tests at Haskins Laboratories. Precisely because the distinction is general, however, it needs to be followed in as many of its manifestations as possible. The present series of tests undertakes to add a few more, and particularly to supply what the exploratory tests lacked: pitch curves traced from spectrograms where Accents A and B were judged to occur.

I. Accent B with Enhancing Modifiers.

The connection of Accent B with numerals has been noted by Hugo Mueller[3]. Example:

$$\text{A}\quad \text{hundred}\quad m^{e}{}_{n}\qquad\text{rather than}\quad \text{A}\quad ^{hun}\text{dred}\quad ^{me}\text{n.}$$

We can probably generalize this and say that all *quantifying modifiers*—that show an amount or degree of something rather than a characteristic that distinguishes it from other things—tend to favor Accent B. A particular kind of quantifier is the one that is used not for precise degree but for enhancement. The purpose of the speaker, often carrying a shade of exaggeration, is likely to cause him to widen the intervals, which makes the B accent easy to detect.

The first experiment with enhancing modifiers involved the word *single* in contexts designed to elicit B and A accents in contrast, and merely auditory judgments of their occurrence. Seven persons read the following two passages aloud:

> 1. I'd have been glad to contribute if I'd had a *single dollar*, but all I had was some small change and a fivespot. (Double contrast intended to elicit A on *single* and A on *dollar*).

---

3. "Some German intonation patterns and their relation to stress," *MLJ* 40. 28 ff (1956). Mueller of course does not term the contrast one of accents.

"Solid hour" vs "Solid frame"

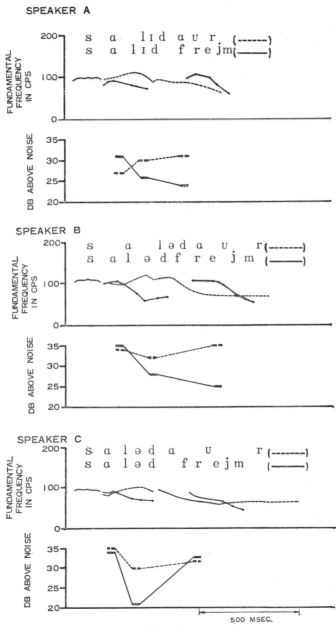

Fig. 1

2. I couldn't contribute because I was flat broke. I didn't have a *single dollar*. (Intended to elicit B on *single*, an enhancing modifier not in contrast with anything).

For the first passage, four speakers used AA with the second A higher in pitch than the first, one used BA, and two used just one A, on *single*. For the second passage, five speakers used BA with the B higher in pitch than the A, one used AA, and one used just one A.

The second experiment involved the word *solid*, in similarly differentiating contexts:

1. I waited a *solid hour* on that cold street corner.

2. [How come it doesn't bend?] Because it has such a *solid frame*. The first was intended to elicit BA, the second AA.

Six speakers recorded the utterances, and were judged, by ear, to have produced accents as follows: *solid hour*—AA, 0; BA, 6; *solid frame*—AA, 3; BA, 2; ambiguous, 1.

Spectrograms were made of the recordings of the three speakers who produced the expected distinction in *both* cases, and pitches were read off at all significant points. The curves appear in Fig. 1, with AA (*solid frame*) and BA (*solid hour*) superimposed one on the other to show the contrast. The three comparisons are alike in that *solid hour* has a gradual pitch descent, while in *solid frame* there is a sharp drop on the second syllable of *solid* plus an upward jump on *frame*.

(The irrelevance of intensity, both in magnitude and in direction, is apparent.)

The third experiment involved the words *evolutionary* and *revolutionary*, the first of which can hardly be other than differentiating, the second of which can readily be enhancing (compare the abnormal *What evolutionary ideas he has!* and the normal *What revolutionary ideas he has!*). The experimenter recorded them in the following two utterances, striving to make the two as nearly identical as possible, with B on *evolutionary* (which he regarded as abnormal) and on *revolutionary* (which he regarded as normal), and with A on *hypotheses*:

1. Darwin is best known for his *evolutionary hypotheses*.

2. Darwin is best known for his *revolutionary hypotheses*.

The two perceptually identical curves appear, superimposed, in Fig. 2.

The recording was played three times to nine listeners, who were told to assume that in one of the two sentences the modifier was not spoken normally, and to identify which sentence it was. Seven of the nine chose *evolutionary*.

(Irrelevance of intensity is again evident. The peak occurs on the syllable *-ry* while the " stressed " syllable *-lu-* of *evolutionary* is at the minimum).

II. *Accent B with Intermediate Compounds.*

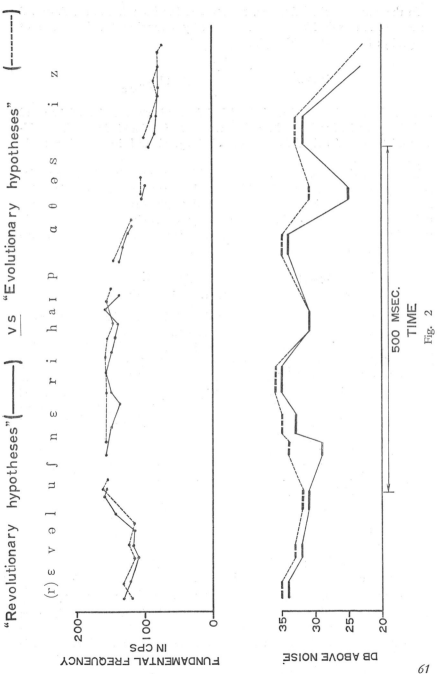

Fig. 2

In the examples cited thus far, the speaker has been free to use Accent B or Accent A to suit his purpose. The only limitation has been one of congruity: he would avoid saying

$$\text{his evo} \quad \overset{\text{lutionary} \quad \text{hy}}{\qquad} \quad \text{p o t h}_{\text{e s e s,}}$$

because the meaning ' differentiation' is inherent in the meaning of the word *evolutionary* as he has learned it; this avoidance is of a kind with the avoidance of *three-wheeled dogsled* or *soft-boiled junkyard*, and has nothing to do with grammar.

There is, however, a large class of partial stereotypes in which the choice is not quite free. Accent B is widely used as the first element in what might be termed " intermediate compounds ", phrases which have become unitary, whether because of unitary reference or as simple clichés, and in which the ' separateness' of two A accents is no longer appropriate. An example is the contrast between

$$\underset{\text{a}}{\text{flying}} \quad \overset{\text{fi}}{\underset{\text{sh}}{}} \quad \text{and} \quad \underset{\text{a}}{\text{fly}} \quad \underset{\text{ing}}{} \quad \overset{\text{fi}}{\underset{\text{sh}}{}}$$

where the first represents a variety of fish and the second a fish that flies or is flying, whether of that special variety or not. (Since the potential for pitch accent remains on the first element, however, the hectoring assertion described above can readily put an A accent where it would not normally come; in this respect the intermediate compound differs from the more usual forestressed compound, e.g., *shoestring*, *handy-man*, where the second potential is all but lost.) Similar contrasts exist in *performing monkeys* 'a special group trained to perform' vs. 'that perform or are performing', and in *galloping pneumonia* vs. *galloping horses*.

Other examples of intermediate compounds are *Canada goose, manifest destiny, helter-skelter* (and other reduplicative compounds), *living death, daily newspaper, fighting fool*. There is no sharp dividing line between intermediate compounds and phrases with enhancing modifiers. The more the phrase resembles the latter, the more likely the B accent is to have a pitch higher than the A:

$$\underset{\text{a}}{\text{fighting}} \quad \text{f}_{\text{o}\,\text{o}}{}_{\text{l}}\text{;} \quad \underset{\text{a}}{\text{daily}} \quad \overset{\text{news}}{\text{paper.}}$$

But in either case the B may be either higher or lower than the A.

The usual approach to intermediate compounds is to regard them as signaled by a pattern of loudnesses. The most-used examples are those originated by Trager and Smith: *Long Island* vs. *long island*, and *Pennsylvania*

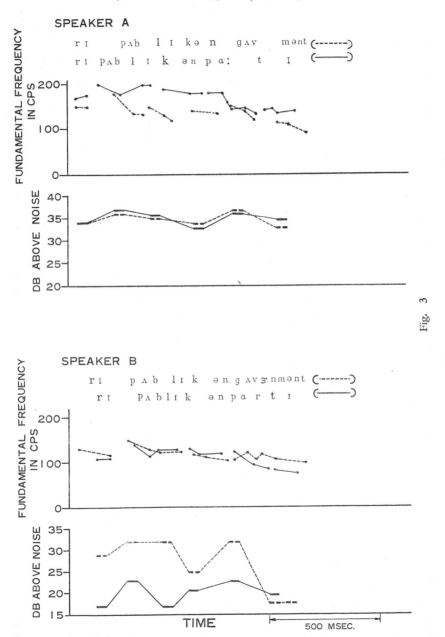

"Republican Party" vs "Republican government"

Fig. 3

Railroad vs. *Pennsylvania railroad*, with a (ˆ ´) superfix in the first member of the pair and a (ˆ ´) superfix in the second. *Our fourth experiment* is designed to show that the contrast is signaled by the pitch accents and not by loudness (intensity).

Since the word *long* consists of only one syllable and is accordingly insufficient for a full display of the pitches, while the word *Pennsylvania* contains what is usually marked as a secondary accent and is therefore needlessly complicated, we chose the word *Republican* as more suitable for testing. Six speakers recorded the following two sentences:

> 1. He's a Methodist and belongs to the Republican party. (Intended to elicit B on *Republican; Methodist* was introduced to avoid the suggestion of contrast with some other party.)

> 2. It's too bad that Spain doesn't have a more *republican government*. (Intended to elicit A on republican.)

The recordings, as judged by ear, gave the following combinations: *Republican Party*—BA, 2; AA, 4; *republican government*—BA, 0: AA, 6. It is characteristic of the instability of the intermediate compound that only two of the speakers made a perceptible distinction between *Republican* and *republican;* the others were evidently swayed by the latent contrast with *Democratic.*

The pitch and intensity curves of the two speakers who made the contrast are shown in Fig. 3, with one utterance superimposed on the other. The fairly regular downmotion of *Republican Party* is seen to contrast with the drop at the end of *republican* and rise at the beginning of *government.* Nothing, apparently, can be inferred from intensity.

III. Contrastive Function of A. Non-Contrastive Function of B.

A kind of subordinate role for Accent B can be inferred from the experiments already described. Its lack of the differentiating role in enhancing modifiers, and its dependence upon a larger whole in intermediate compounds, are opposed to the separateness and potential contrast of Accent A. It remains to demonstrate this explicitly. Two experiments do this. In the first, the sentence *The conference was postponed but the contest was held* was judged by listeners to be wrong with Accent B on *contest.* The second is reported in greater detail here, and shows the rejection of Accent A in a context where all newness and contrastiveness is excluded.

The experimenter recorded the sentences *Like hell I'll let you* and *I'm damned if I'll let you* each in two ways: with BA accents respectively on *hell* and *let*, and *damned* and *let;* and with A accents alone on *hell* and *damned.* The pitch curves are shown in Fig. 4.

These two sentences were chosen because, despite their near-synonymy, *like hell* is never used except to comment on something already introduced, while *I'm damned if* can comment either on something new or on something

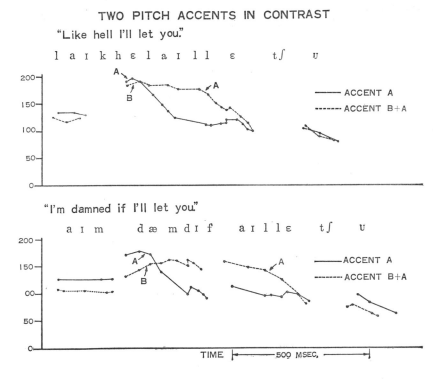

Fig. 4

old. *Like hell* therefore requires that whatever follows it be a resumptive or reprise, and should, if the assumptions about Accent A are correct, exclude Accent A from the word *let*.

Seven listeners were asked to assume that one of the four utterances was not normal English, and to mark it. All but one chose the utterance with the A accent on *let*. This confirms our prediction that Accent A is favored on items that are new and contrastive, but avoided on items that are merely resumptive.

4

STRESS AND INFORMATION

American Speech 33.5-20 (1958)

The editor of *American Speech* expressed the purpose of this article in his " Contributors' Column " : " a critique of certain rather over-simplified formulations." Phonological grammar, until it began to give way before the vogue of transformations, was endeavoring to define English phrase structures in terms of levels of stress interacting with transitions or " junctures." It seemed to me that whatever loose ends of syntax might be made a little more manageable by an appeal to stress, the real function of the top level of stress—i. e., pitch accent—lay elsewhere, and could best be accounted for by how much information was centered in the lexical items on which the accent was to fall. So I tried to give a sophisticated twist to a notion that has been around a long time—that speakers put the accent on what they regard as important.

Lee S. Hultzén's explanation of English stress through analogy with information theory[1] comes at a time when most American linguists are busy with a different kind of horticulture, cross-pollinating stresses, or stresses and junctures, in quest of hybrids that will give a phonemic shape to syntax.

It goes without saying that there are grammatical uses of stress. A simple example is the phrase *steel bár*, in which the arrangement of stress is like that of *green cóat*, and suggests an underlying kinship that the conventional classification of *steel* and *green* obscures. But are the uses systematic? If one stress acting independently marks the information-bearing part of an utterance, it is better regarded as a morpheme than as a phoneme. On the other hand, if stress is systematically grammatical there should be some obvious key to the system. A number of keys have been offered, fitting a variety of locks. Whether the doors that they open lead to blank walls, small closets, or all outdoors is the theme of what follows. And along the way we shall try Hultzén's passkey.

I

Hultzén criticizes Haugen's assumption ' that the stress pattern secondary-primary applies to most adjective-noun constructions,' a notion that is

---

1. *American Speech*, XXXI (1956), 195–201, especially 198–99. For my own almost identical formulation, see ' English stress : the interpenetration of strata,' in *Study of Sounds* (Tokyo, 1957).

'widely accepted and manifestly false.'[2] Hultzén's examples are pertinent, but the reader confirmed in the opposite point of view is apt to interpret them with the aid of the *deus ex machina* of the 'shift morpheme'—they are a bit too suggestive of contrastive stress. So I shall add a few where there is no suggestion of outright contrast, and where the stress on the adjective (optional, but highly probable) seems to be due to the relative pressures of information:

He has a lean and *húngry look.* (Reference to having looks is commonplace and redundant.)

We'll have our son to give us *légal advice* if we need it. (Advice is one of those things that come in packages with distinctive labels—legal, medical, etc.)

I like almost anything in the way of vegetables, except that I don't like a *bítter taste.* ('Bitterness'—the whole context suggests 'taste,' but nothing suggests 'bitter'; but the speaker may view it otherwise, and stress *taste.*)

In the four corners [of the stage] people were running through bits of their acts . . . the Italian Quartette . . . Rosie warming up, and the Arab Tumblers bouncing and rolling . . . wherever there was an *émpty space.*[3]

The bullet hit him in a *vítal spot* (*vítal organ*). ('In his vitals.')

'What do you notice most about him?' 'His *tíred expression.*'

'What don't you like about him?' 'It's that *sképtical attitude* of his.'

It has a *corréctive effect.*

What makes it difficult to understand is its *mathemátical emphasis* (*lógical nature*).

Naturally, if *emphasis* is introduced where its probability is lower, it is correspondingly more likely to receive the major stress, as it can even in the examples given. Furthermore, in the nature of things nouns are less predictable than attributes. It is noteworthy that precisely those adjectives (and other modifiers) which are most like nouns, i.e., lack the comparison, are the ones most readily stressed:

The *légal profession* (*more legal* impossible) vs. a *legal márriage* (*more legal* possible)

The *prínter's trade* vs. a *mother's lóve* (*mother* resembles the adjective *motherly*)

Military encampment vs. *military béaring*

---

2. The same assumption is implied in the Chomsky-Halle-Lukoff phonemicization of Newman's and Trager-Smith's data: forms such as *white house* and *White House* are transcribed differently both on the strength of phonology and on the strength of higher-order distinctions in syntax presumably converging with phonology. See their 'On accent and juncture in English' in *For Roman Jakobson* (The Hague, 1956).

3. *Atlantic Monthly*, CXCVIII (1956), 60. *Empty* and *space* are virtually names for the same thing, and one can be as easily stressed as the other. Compare Jones's examples in *An outline of English phonetics* (Cambridge, 1956), § 948: *óval-shaped* and *yéllowish-looking,* to which he might have added 'It has an *óval shape, yéllowish color, dún shade, órange tint.*'

A críminal investigation vs. *criminal négligence*

Relígious instruction vs. *religious wóman*

An eléctrical connection, eléctrical supplies, vs. *electric thríll*

A músical career vs. *a musical vóice*

An advísory committee, a theátrical agency, a téchnical school

I have said that in the nature of things nouns are less predictable than attributes. This is true of common nouns and common attributes. Given the noun *barn*, there is certain implication of its range of attributes; it will normally be referred to in terms of its size, color, shape, ownership, etc. Given the adjective *red*, the range of heads that can go with it is practically infinite, and any one head is highly unpredictable. These relative pressures do not exist when the adjective is one that lacks the comparison: *musical* goes with a much more restricted set of heads: *músical score, músical instrument*. But when it has the comparison, the possible heads run riot: *musical* in the sense 'having a musical quality' can modify anything from a voice to a telegraph wire or the wind in the trees.

Perhaps sheer frequency has led or is leading to a partial fossilization of the stresses in adjective-noun phrases; the grammatical binding of once-free combinations is nothing new in language. But it has not gone far enough to free us from taking stock of the pressure of information.

II

In his highly discerning article on English stress, Stanley S. Newman differentiates between two constructions:

The types of construction with middle stress are few, but they represent prolific types. One such construction is exemplified by such phrases as *bréad to èat, a fávor to àsk, instrúctions to gìve*. Here the middle stress [the weaker of the two marked ones, carrying the grave accent] indicates a syntactic relation in which the noun is the logical object of the verb: that is, *bréad to èat* has a relationship with 'to eat bread.' Other constructions composed of noun + *to* + verb occur without a middle stress, but in these constructions a different syntactic relation obtains between the noun and the verb: thus, in *a désire to éat* or *the wíll to líve*, the verb stands in the relation of complement to the noun, an appropriate paraphrase being 'a desire, namely to eat' and 'the will, namely to live'; there is no idea of 'to eat a desire' (as 'to eat bread') or 'to live the will.'[4]

Newman concludes with some minimal pairs, e.g., *I have instrúctions to lèave* ('I am to leave instructions') and *I have instrúctions to léave* ('I have been instructed to leave').

It is true that in the instances cited, the stress tells us something about the syntactic relationship. But is this identifying function essential to it, or is it like the green hat worn by a thief, which may help us to identify him but which he may change at any time? The answer depends on how many

4. *Word*, II (1946), 179.

contrary examples we can find. Unfortunately for the assumption of syntactic functions in stress, these are plentiful. Here are instances of (´´) rather than (´`) marking 'noun as logical object of verb':

1. With contrastive stress: 'A pocketbook is not a *bóok to réad*.' Of course no analyst would deny this, but there is no essential difference between it and the examples that follow.

2. Hackneyed expressions in which the verb is the logical center: 'There's no *tíme to wáste*'; 'There's not a *móment to lóse*'; 'He has *móney to búrn*.'

3. Expressions in which the infinitive is predicative: 'It's *nóthing to snéeze at*'; 'He's a *mán to remémber*'; 'He's a *pérson to respéct* (*admíre, trúst, be próud of*)'; 'That's the right *prínciple to maintáin*.'

4. Expressions in which the noun is generalized in meaning, almost like a pronoun; the semantic importance then passes to the verb by default: 'I have some *stúff to delíver*'; 'I have *things to atténd to*'; 'We have many *mátters to discúss*'; 'I can't stay now because I have too many *pláces to gó*'; 'Where are you going in such a hurry?'—'I have a *gúy to sée*'; 'The hotel is too small, and we have too many *péople to accómmodate*.'

5. Indefinite pronouns, same reason: 'She has a *lót to sáy*'; 'I have *too múch to dó*'; 'There's *nó one to belíeve*.'

6. Expressions in which the balance of informativeness is delicate, but inclines to the infinitive: 'He's no longer unhappy, because he has a *wóman to lóve*' (*wóman to lòve* would emphasize having the woman rather than having love); 'I can't leave yet—I still have a couple of *páges to próofread*, (editor speaking).

Now we look at Newman's examples, and see that it was not the construction, but the informativeness, that determined the stresses. In the narrow but frequent contexts typified by 'There's a...to...' and 'I've got a...to...' we usually find the *thing* pictured as constituting an *incentive* to perform the action that would normally be performed upon it anyway (bread has little other purpose than to be eaten, whence *eat* in such a context is relatively more redundant than *bread*) or that is foreknown to speaker and hearer as likely to be performed ('with my *pláns to wrìte*'—both already knew that having plans here signified having them to write).

III

Newman gives another example:

Special syntactic conditions demand the middle stress in a word; thus, a type of syntactic relation is indicated by the middle stress in *a móving vàn* ('a van for moving'), *a Frénch tèacher* ('a teacher of French'), *a desígning wòman* ('a woman engaged in designing'), as opposed to the heavy stress in *a móving ván* ('a van that is moving'), *a Frénch téacher* ('a teacher who is French'), *a desígning wóman* ('a woman who is artful').[5]

5. *Ibid.*, p. 175.

That the stresses here are not ' demanded ' by the syntactic relation is evident in the following: ' Architect Marcel Breuer characteristically designed such interiors in the home of fabric printer George Neumann and his *designing wife* Vera....'[6] Here, *wife* is essential, and is stressed, while in *She is a designing wòman* we are told only ' She is a designer '—*woman* is entirely redundant. But in another context *woman* may be stressed: *She is a wìcked wòman* refers to her personality, just as *She is a wìcked shòt* refers to her marksmanship.

It would be wrong to say that there is no syntactic function whatever in the stresses here, but it is one that has less to do with the syntactic interrelationships of the parts than with the suppression of such relationships. It would be more nearly accurate (though far from the whole story) to say that in *móving vàn* there are syntactic interrelationships, but in *mòving vàn* there are none. In *càt mèat* we are not told whether the meat is for cats or from cats. *A bódy blòw* is ' a blow TO the body '; *a hámmer blòw* is ' a blow LIKE a hammer's '; *a gúnstock blòw* is ' a blow WITH a gunstock.' In *bréakwàter* the stress is suppressed on the noun; in *wíndbrèak* it is suppressed on the verb.

The syntactic function, such as it is, is revealed in *There is no sùbstitute for mìlk*, which might appear as *There is no mìlk sùbstitute* but would not appear as *There is no mìlk sùbstitute*, except, of course, with contrastive stress. English words typically have but one potential for pitch accent, the one here marked (´) (I have put in the ' middle stresses ' to conform to the discussion but I question their relevance to syntax.) A syntactic marker for single words is therefore the loss of all but one such potential. Which element will lose the potential answers to intertwined mechanical and semantic forces. The forestress in *frée-for-àll* (' melee ') is mechanical. That in *Áddison's disèase* is partly semantic, for commonly it is used in contexts like *He was treated for* ..., *He died of* ..., *It was diagnosed as* ..., where *disease* is redundant. But a particular disease, say a fever, may keep the potential even when the sense is entirely unitary: *He has scárlet féver*. So far as the inner syntactic relations and unitary sense are concerned, *Hóbson's chóice* is the same as *Áddison's disèase*, yet it is afterstressed, probably answering to our lack of socially categorized choices of which Hobson's is one: *choice* is not redundant. In *coúntry Jàke*, *Jake* tells us less than *country*; in *cíty slícker* the balance is reversed. Possibly the most confirmed usage among noun compounds is that of object plus verb, applying to some recognized category, social or other: *man-eater*, *floorwalker*, *doorkeeper*, *jawbreaker*. But it is not the syntactic interrelationship that determines the stress; rather it is the otiosity of any separate meaning that determines the loss of all but one potential for pitch accent, plus the mechanical tendency to forestress nouns that puts the one potential where it is. But if the separate meanings are not otiose, afterstress may occur with the same syntactic inter-

---

6. *Interiors*, quoted in *New Yorker*, April 6, 1957, p. 75.

relationships (and with no need for contrastive stress to bring it about). Of seven persons who read the following passage aloud, all but one put the major stress on *bootleggers*: 'By 1949 the number had quintupled—yet the agencies were handling fewer than before. Baby-bootleggers did most of the business.'[7] *Bootlegger* is unexpected.

IV

Trager and Smith have this to say about combinations involving verb bases and adverb bases: 'In constructions involving a verb-adverb phrase, the superfix is basically $\sqrt{\ }\grave{\ }+\acute{\ }$; *gèt+úp, sìt+dówn, còme+ín*...; this contrasts with $\sqrt{\ }\acute{\ }+\grave{\ }$ in corresponding noun-like phrases *gét+ùp, sít+dòwn, cóme+òn*.'[8]

There is a question whether this contrast belongs at all in the syntax. The authors are obliged to follow their decision to treat all sequences containing more than one base as part of the syntax,[9] but for at least two reasons the decision is doubtful here: (1) We expect a degree of commutability in syntax, but the verb phrases and the nouns are completely at odds in this respect. The verbs, within the limits of sense, have something like unrestricted freedom: *come ín, come ón, come úp, come awáy, come dówn; scurry úp, scurry óff, scurry únder*, etc. The nouns have no freedom at all, beyond the diachronic one of being derivable more easily through this process than through any other. Neologisms are constantly appearing, but we immediately recognize a word like *gítalong* as a coinage and not as a freely formed phrase. We are not free, as we are with the verbs, to produce things like *a scúrry-off* or *a flý-through*. (2) The potentials for pitch accent are not the same. The verbs retain more than one, as true phrases should: a speaker may readily use two, for emphasis, in an utterance like *Shút úp!* The nouns behave like single words in that this is seldom possible.

The latter point is the important one, for it tells us that we have again, as with *móving ván* and *móving vàn*, a formal process of derivation in which a potential for pitch accent is lost. This differs fundamentally from the genuinely syntactic process in which, as in *Let's get a móving van for the job*, it is the whole element *moving van*, rather than *job*, that receives the pitch accent; i.e., it is not *moving* vs. *van* that counts, but the unit *moving van* vs. *job*. As before, two kinds of redundancy are involved: syntactic, in which the element least presupposed actually receives the pitch accent; and morphological, in which the otiosity of a separate meaning removes all but one *potential* for pitch accent in a single word. The first redundancy has to do with de-emphasizing what may be unnecessary because it is already known

---

7. *Harper's Magazine*, Jan. 1957, p. 58. The passage was read in context—thirty-seven words being included before the part quoted—so as to give no clue to the purpose of the reading.

8. *An outline of English structure* (Norman, Okla., 1951), p. 73.

9. *Ibid.*, p. 55.

or expected; the second has to do with de-emphasizing what may be un-necessary because it is no longer relevant.

But treat this reasoning as a cavil, and we are still left with the really crucial question: does the supposed contrast between the verb-adverb super-fix and the nounlike superfix exist, in a positive, predictable sense? Are there recognized nouns that have the wrong superfix? Here we appreciate the need of a real survey of the lexicon before such things as superfixes can claim to be more than artifacts.

First we must decide what is meant by 'nounlike.' Three definitions seem possible: (1) 'having the distribution of a noun (in other respects than in relation to the superfix)'; (2) 'having the / ´+` / superfix'; (3) 'having a referential meaning reminiscent of that of most nouns (e.g., "not referring to point-action").' The second of these is circular, and the third, though perhaps close to the heart of the matter, is too foreign to the philosophy of Trager and Smith to have been intended by them. We are left with the first, and in this sense there are nouns—many nonce ones and a few estab-lished ones—that do not fit the superfix. Unlike the nouns with forestress, the nonce nouns with afterstress have not been derived by a piecemeal his-torical process and firmly incorporated in the lexicon of nouns, but have been lifted from the status of verb and turned, by a syntactic process under the control of the speaker, into nouns for the purpose of his utterance: a true instance of syntactic conversion. As a test, I gave eight speakers, two male and six female, the following sentences to read aloud (hyphens were omitted, lest they cue 'permanency' and hence forestress):

1. If it hadn't been for that last-minute skin through of his, we'd never have made it.
2. That kind of cut in may do at a barn dance, but it won't do here.
3. With a spin around and a quick back away, he found himself suddenly, unexpectedly free.
4. Only a frantic wriggle loose saved the cub from the trap.
5. It was a premature sally forth.
6. With a dart up and a scurry off, the rabbit disappeared in the brush.

All these would be normal with afterstress in my speech, and the majority of the readers agreed.[10] A similar nonce use is possible without the adverb.

---

10. Specifically, all speakers stressed the adverb (or adjective) in 4, 5, and 6; all but one stressed the first adverb in 3, and three stressed the second adverb in 3; one, the same speaker, stressed the adverb in 1 and 2. All the female speakers regarded the pattern as normal; both male speakers objected to it. The semantic area seems to be that of 'quick action.' The style, as two speakers observed, is one that would be natural in telling a story to children.

I tried to avoid phrases where there would be an overlap with phrases where the

The following would probably cause no surprise, though *relent* n. is now re-corded as obsolete : ' With a quick *relent* and a quicker remorse.' Mono-syllables, of course, belong almost as much in one category as in the other, regardless of how the handbooks classify them : ' The slow *seep* of the water.'[11]

A few nouns have become established with stress on the adverb. In my speech there are at least two firm items of this kind (*set-tó*, recorded by *Oxford Universal* with plural *set-tós*, and *follow-thróugh*), and a few others limited to set phrases (*knock-dówn and drag-óut*, recorded by *DA* but stresses unmarked ; *turn-abóut's fair play;* as an adjunct, *a come-hither look*). The speakers I have consulted all agree on *follow-thróugh*, and some suggested *follow-úp* and *blast-óff* as possibilities.

Nouns, in the distributional sense, are not specified by stress. But this does not dismiss stress from the consideration of nouns and verbs, for half the story remains untold, the half that bears on referential meaning. If we pursue it, we find that a looser description than that of the superfix fits the mold of English more comfortably and inclusively.

There is a parallel, from start almost to finish, between nouns of the *cóme-on* type and nouns of the *pérvert* type, in their relation to their verbs. End-stressed verbs have been turned into nouns all along by back-shifting the stress : *to permít, a pérmit; to pervért, a pérvert; to rejéct, a réject.* What most effects this transformation is the sheer weight of numbers in the forestress of English nouns. But not all nouns from verbs have yielded to it, and there has been, I believe, a kind of crystallization of meaning among those that do and those that do not. It is as if with change of stress the noun were shrunk within the semantic area of the verb, or were detached from it, while without change of stress the semantic area remained more nearly the same. The test sentences above, with their end stresses, are instances of semantic closeness. So is *set-tó*, for the verb is already stereotyped and *They set tó* means substantially the same as *They had a set-tó*. (That others say *sét-to* is only evidence of the double pull to which all these forms are subjected.) Similarly with *follow-thróugh*, where the verb source already has a specific meaning in sports. On the other hand, *They came ón*, or even the command *Come ón*, is stringently narrowed in the noun *cóme-on*. A majority of noncompounds might well be found to show the same clustering : *to addréss* is narrowed in *an áddress*, but *to replý* is not narrowed in *a replý*. Other examples : narrowed or detached, *condúct-cónduct, invért-ínvert, discárd-díscard, digést-dígest;* same semantic area, *debáte-debáte, requést-requést, demánd-demánd, contról-contról, appéal-appéal.* The relevance

adverb qualifies an independent noun, e.g., *the ride back* paralleling *the trip home*. In ' Flag him down !'—' Huh, no *flág dówn* is going to stop hím. Look how fast he's going' the noun cannot be independent.

11. To someone on a buying spree : ' That was a big *spend* you had.' In a comment on a baseball game : ' That was the Dodgers' first *lose* of the season.' And especially in combination : ' With a *clamp* and a twist, we made it secure.'

of the semantic area can be seen in the stressing—often the altered stressing—of verbs like nouns when the nouns are the dominant member of the pair : *cómment-cómment, áccent-áccent, rébate-rébate, álly-álly.* These include numerous verbs stressed like the nouns that were in turn narrowed or detached from original verbs, a complete circuit, verb to noun to verb : *to contráct, a cóntract, to cóntract; to combíne, a cómbine, to cómbine;*[12] *to survéy, a súrvey, to súrvey.* A soldier released from service was heard to remark : 'After I was *díscharged* ['received my *dischárge*'] from the Army...' 'A notion like that has to be *discóunted* ['discrédited']' vs. 'His note was *discóunted.*' I sense a shadow of semantic influence, a sort of 'verbness,' even in nouns and adjectives that do not pair with verbs : *remórse, chagrín, concérn, sevére, contríte.*

The only important break in symmetry between compound and noncompound pairs is that on the noncompound side the circle is complete : verbs that gave nouns come back home again with their stresses altered. (See the schematic diagram.)

There is enough evidence of the assimilation of the *cóme-on* type to the ancestral pattern of verb-noun kinships to warn us against rules of stress for distribution classes that we cannot apply consistently everywhere. Stress tells us something about nouns and verbs, but it does not tell us when an item patterns grammatically as a noun or as a verb. Probably the only reason we have not yet seen the *to combíne-a cómbine-to cómbine* series extended to a *to come ón—a cóme-on—to cóme-on* series is the wholesale ambiguity that would result, itself a testimony to the instability of the stress in the verb phrase. But give it time.

V

Trager and Smith write further:

The primary stress of a phonemic phrase will come as near the end as possible; here 'as possible' means that some items, such as pronoun objects, certain adverbs, prepositions, and others, do not have primary stress even though they are normally the last thing in a phrase, and they get primary stress only with the shift morpheme.[13]

This statement seems to embody an attempt to identify the lack of stress with a set of forms rather than with a function of the stress irrespective of the forms with which it occurs. Let us see what common instances we can find of forms other than those cited which are destressed in total absence of the 'shift morpheme' (contrastive stress) :

'Why don't you like fluorescent lamps?' 'The *húm annoys me.*'

'Time flies.' 'I can't. They go *bý too fast.*'

'I can't see from here.' 'Why don't you change *pláces with me?*'

---

12. *American Speech*, XXV (1950), 87.
13. Trager and Smith, *op. cit.*, p. 75.

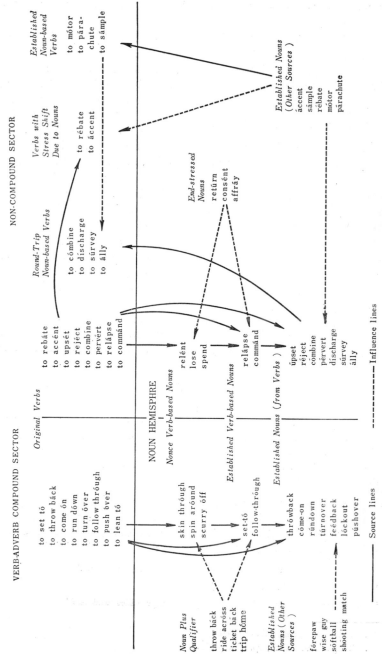

I have a *jób on my hands.*

The water in the lake is clear now because there are not so many *péople thrashing around in it as there were.*

I have some *búsiness to take care of.*

If you bypass that transformer somebody's *hóuse will get set on fire.*

There are more problems that I can *begín to deal with here.*

It's just about time for *Clárk to phone.* [Said of a bore whose habit was to telephone at mealtime.]

Somebody *chóked him to death.*

We'll go whichever way the *sígns point.*

In these the primary stress occurs well before the end, and in most instances rather obviously on the item that carries most information. In fact, it is often possible to omit the following destressed material with little loss of information: 'Why don't you like fluorescent lamps?' 'The hum.'

Apply this notion to the forms listed by Trager and Smith. Pronouns such as *it, him, them,* and *us* are not used unstressed unless the antecedents are clearly in mind. They are, then, more redundant than anything else. The same is true of the adverb *there* in the example they cite, *gét thêre,* where it too has an antecedent. But when the pronouns and *there* are less redundant, they are stressed: *I gave it to hím; I went thére* (speaker points).

It remains true that English tends to shift the major stress toward the end. But to what extent is this a structural tendency directly affecting the stress, and to what extent does it represent a tendency to prefer a climactic sentence order which puts the most informative item at the end, and accordingly drags the stress along with it? It is hard to improve upon the explanation offered by George O. Curme:

In Old English things were quite different. The chief stress was often upon the first word of a group: 'He *ín càme.*' 'He *úp stoòd,*' etc. In the course of the Old English period a great change took place. The heavily stressed word that stood at the beginning of a group took a position at the end of the group: . . . 'He *a létter wròte*' became 'He *wròte a létter.*' The old stress has been kept though the word-order has changed. The old word-order and stress are still preserved in group words . . . The object of the new development is evident. The heavily stressed word was withheld for a moment to create the feeling of suspense and thus render the word more prominent.[14]

VI

In her article ' Superfix and sememe: English verbal compounds,' Edith Crowell Trager concludes as follows:

Using Smith's term ' adjunctival '. . .to mean non-verb-noun-pronoun, it is possible to make this statement: In a sequence of a verb and an adjunctival, if one of the words has a *tertiary* stress, the adjunctival is a *preposition;* if one word has a primary

---

14. *Syntax* (New York, 1931), p. 572.

or secondary stress, and the other a *secondary*, then the adjunctival is an *adverb*.[15]

The familiar arguments for this are rather convincing. A number of neat minimal pairs can be quoted, such as Mrs. Trager's *Whât àre wè cóming tò?* vs. *Ìs hè côming tó?* and *Whât dìd yòu rîde òn?* vs. *Whŷ dìdn't yòu rîde ón?* (the marks are intended to register degrees of loudness: acute accent being 'primary,' circumflex 'secondary,' grave 'tertiary,' unmarked 'weak').

But if the definitions are not circular, that is, if calling an item an adverb is meant to predict its distribution and not merely to serve as a name for the stress pattern that it bears, then the consequences are uncomfortable. Not even these narrowly minimal pairs hold up. Consider a motorist who is not permitted to make a left turn, but has to go right and circle a block. He might then be asked, *Whîch blôck dìd yòu côme aróund?* This is the same as in *Hôw sôon dìd hè côme aróund?* (regain consciousness), yet in terms of distribution *around* is a preposition in the first and an adverb in the second. Worse still, we should be compelled to list as prepositions all the adjunctivals in commands such as *sìt dówn, còme ín, gò 'wáy* (whose first elements need have no more than tertiary stress, if even that much, as witness /kmin/), just as the author's *out* in *The chêcks gàve óut* is recorded, without comment, as a preposition. Similarly, *Whât dìd yòu híde behînd?* and '*Whât dìd yòu shóot fróm?*' 'A blind,' would have to contain adverbs, as does the author's *Whât àre yòu lóoking fôr?* ('Why are you looking?').

The business of what is meant by preposition and adverb in such unusual senses is one thing. The business of knowing which stresses are which, to begin with, is something else. Take the example *Is he coming to?* In order to make a case for a secondary on *com-* it is practically necessary to mark tertiaries on *is* and *he*; yet in most situations this utterance would be [zikʌmiŋtu], which hardly gives us the right to put more than a weak stress on *is* and *he*, and the basis for a real build-up to secondary on *com-* is lacking. But grant that it is a secondary, and consider how much influence there may be from the total situation on there being a secondary there. Compare *I doubt that he'll come to* and *He didn't come to for an hour*. I believe that there is a better chance for a heavier stress on *come* in the first of these than in the second (Trager seems to agree, for he marks *After an hour she came to* as *càme tó*, not *câme tó*[16]). In the second, the speaker refers to a past event, which may well be known to his hearer, the only point at issue being how long it took. In the first, he is deliberating about something that may or may not happen. If this is true, the degree of stress answers to the conditional probabilities of the word.

VII

In an aside in an article devoted to other matters, Noam Chomsky attempts

---

15. *General Linguistics*, II (1956), 13.
16. Trager and Smith, *op. cit.*, p. 75.

to relate syntax and stress. He gives as an example of identical syntax from which identical inferences cannot be drawn the sentences *The man is tall and thin* and *The flag is black and white*. The first is decomposable into *The man is tall and the man is thin*, but the second is not decomposable into *The flag is black and the flag is white*. As part of the syntax he evidently includes the pattern of stresses, for he adds in a footnote:

Though in the cited case the expressions are 'syntactically identical,' in other cases they will differ. Thus *tall* and *thin* are equally stressed in *a tall and thin man*, but *black* is more heavily stressed than *white* in *a black and white flag* (as if *black-and-white* were here a single word.[17]

The point of the observation seems to be that the one-wordness, as revealed in the stresses, reflects the different interrelationships; i.e., *táll and thín mán* construes the adjectives separately with the noun, *bláck and whíte flág* construes them jointly.

It would be satisfying, logically, if this were so. Unfortunately, none of the three steps entailed by the reasoning can be defended: (1) the stresses described are not a sure guide to one-wordness: (2) one-wordness is not a sure guide to the two kinds of modification; (3) the kinds of modification put no restrictions on the stresses.

1. We have structurally identical pairings with *and* in which the second member receives at least as much stress as the first, but which many considerations compel us to regard as just as unitary as *black-and-white*. Such are the inherently emphatic modifiers *black and blue*, *nice and hot* (*nice and soft*, etc.), and *spick and span*. In *That black and blue face of his told us definitely that he had been in a fight*, *blue* is strongly stressed.

2. It is the usualness and expectedness (hence redundancy) of the combination, not the kind of modification, that makes for rushing the syllables together and partially reducing the stresses toward the end. This can be demonstrated simply by turning the modifiers around: *a white and black flag*, *a hearty and hale fellow*. A really unusual combination holds the syllables up firmly: *an orange and purple flag*. There is some reduction in all the familiar pairings used attributively: *tried and true*, *free and easy*, *one and only*, *two or three*, *hale and hearty*. They do not have to be undecomposable: *a hale and hearty fellow* is a fellow who is hale and a fellow who is hearty.

3. Abundant undecomposables fail to reduce the second member: *a brick and steel building; her Indian and Scandinavian blood; a civil and military compact* (the sides arrayed opposite each other).

Before English stress can be treated successfully, we must avoid the classic confusion between *langue* and *parole*. The first step is to make a broad separation into two domains. The first domain is the *occurrence* of pitch

17. *Language*, XXXI (1955), 40.

accent in *utterances*. Where an assertive utterance contains more than one fraction, this will be found to answer pretty closely to the amount of information in the fractions. The second domain is the *potential* for pitch accent in *utterance fractions*. If a given syllable in a given utterance fails to receive the pitch accent, it may be because that syllable, within its utterance fraction, is incapable of receiving the pitch accent in any utterance;[18] or it may be because the semantic conditions of the utterance withhold the pitch accent from it. The syllable *-ing* of *coming* is incapable of receiving the pitch accent anywhere. The syllable *com-* may fail to receive it in the second part of ' He's coming'—' I know he's coming,' where, being redundant, it can be reduced practically to a whisper.

The separation between the two domains can be illustrated by an example in which the two come in conflict. Visiting New Haven in 1957 I was on the point of remarking how surprised I was that twelve years after the war the city still had *policewomen*, but corrected myself to *wómen polícemen*. The contradiction between *women* and *-men* was puzzling until I realized that something like *women policemen* had to be used if the separate information in *women* was to be shown. In *women policemen*, *women* has a potential for pitch accent; in *policewomen* the potential is virtually gone.

Mixing the two domains—especially attempting to find fixed correspondences in the first domain such as one might expect in the second—has been practiced extensively, but is not likely to be productive. In types like *Pennsylvania Railroad* and *Pennsylvania railroad* we can make a statistical guess; but there is no way to *predict* the stresses unless we know the dynamics of the utterance: both instances have two potentials for pitch accent, and the degree to which the potentials are realized depends not on P.R. and P.r. as classes but on the import of the message. In an experiment conducted in search of pitch contrasts in pairs of this type, I gave six speakers sentences to record, among which appeared *Republican party* and *republican government* with contexts carefully planned to elicit a difference; yet only two of the readers produced it; the others had in mind some latent contrast with *Democratic party*, and gave *Republican* and *republican* equal prominence. (See p. 64.)

Operations differ in the two domains. When American linguists speak of analyzing stress, they have in mind canons suitable to the second domain. Once a fraction that can occur by itself is found to contain only one potential for pitch accent, the relation between the syllable carrying the potential and the other syllables can be analyzed formally and correspondences can be sought between the resulting analysis and such things as nouns and verbs or derivatives and their sources. This is morphology, and involves the same difficulties in coping with patterns of stress as when we try to lay hold of

18. Except, of course, under contrastive stress in ' hypostasis,' which can occur anywhere.

regularities in affixes: *cóntent* and *contént*, both nouns; *combíne* and *cómbine*, both verbs; *fóretaste* and *foreknówledge*; *ínterplay* and *intercommunicátion*.

This is to say that English morphology is messy, in derivation by compounding as well as by affixing. The forces are various and the results are heterogeneous. The difference between *will-o-the wísp* and its synonym *jáck-o-lantern* is capricious. That between the two different senses of *misfit* n. and *misfit* n., recorded by the *ACD*, answers in part to meaning, for in the first the notion of 'fit' is more prominent. So with New York's *Long Ísland*, which is more of an island than California's *Lóng Beach* is a beach.

The important thing is that in the second domain we have left syntax and synchrony behind, and are involved with the historical development of words. A properly syntactic question can be framed out of the following contrast:

' Come dówn ! '
' I don't know how ! '
' Clímb down ! '

Come down and *climb down* have two potentials for pitch accent. If we regard the pitch accent as a morpheme, then the way it alights on one or the other half of *climb down* is a matter of syntax. A properly syntactic question cannot be framed out of:

' Come dówn ! '
' Here I come.'
' That was quite a cóme down.'

Such a remark is immediately tagged as a pun, for we recognize that there is no free relationship between *come dówn* as a verb and *cóme down* as a noun. The latter has only one potential for pitch accent. We can speak, diachronically, of its relation to its source. We cannot, as with the suffix *-ing*, speak syntactically of this relationship, because while *-ings* cannot be dated independently of their verbs, every noun of the *cóme down* type can theoretically be dated.

Confusion is understandable. Of all the frontiers between synchrony and diachrony, this is probably the one where it is easiest to lose one's way, for the domains overlap. If we overhear a snatch of conversation, *He lives in the* [*hwáit haus*], there is no way for us to know whether the speaker is referring to a *white house* by contrast with a red house, or to the *White House*. The phonetic result is the same, whether, as in the first instance, the loss of accent is syntactic, or, as in the second, bespeaks an utter loss of potential for the accent. With this phonetic sameness, the door is open to constant accretions to loss of potential by way of reinterpretations of loss of accent. A given phrase takes the accent on one of its elements by reason of greater informativeness there; in time the object to which the phrase is applied becomes standard equipment in our culture; the absence of the accent is reinterpreted as absence of potential for accent; result—a new compound. When *boy scout* first appeared it had two potentials, with the second usually realized as in other such attributive uses of nouns (*boy king, student prince*). Several forces came into play: boy scouts became institutionalized; scouts of other kinds figured less in the folklore; girl scouts were organized, called by contrast *gírl scouts*, and the analogy spread; the broader analogy of forestress in other noun compounds took hold. For many speakers this has meant the fossilization of *bóy scout*, with a loss of potential on the second element. Diachronic series of latent contrastives are commonplace. Pike notes one such in *Ro,yal Crówn Cola* coming on the heels of *Coca Cóla*.[19] Compare *atomic bómb, hýdrogen bomb, cóbalt bomb*.

Compared to other disputed frontiers of unhappy renown with their displaced persons, this one has a floating population of displaced words. Their relatively homeless status can be illustrated by describing, first, one or two more fortunate cousins securely lodged on the syntactic side of the frontier:

A subway wouldn't pay in Los Angeles; the *population density* isn't high enough.

Set the car bouncing by rhythmic pressure on bumpers, one corner at a time. Car should move up *or* down to *equilibrium position*.[20]

In these phrases, both nouns are about equally informative, and would receive the pitch accent in about equal measure. But if the situation rendered either redundant, it would be de-accented. (I use *accent* now on the syntactic side, and reserve *stress* for the morphological.)

If in place of *equilibrium position* we had *business position*, the second element would almost certainly lose the potential. This is an example of a displaced word. Like displaced persons, they exist in every degree between independence and indigence. Their tendency to lose the accent is both syntactic and morphological—syntactic because they name things that are relatively commonplace in our culture and the mention of them becomes to a certain degree redundant: the conditional probabilities of *game* after *baseball* are exceedingly high, whence *báseball game;* morphological because some have become virtual suffixes, as *man* in *the trásh man*, with vowels existing in every stage of fullness or degradation: full in *trash man*, less full in *milkman*, still less in *mailman*, less still in *postman*, completely degraded in *workman*. Some of them are floaters in every sense of the word, being found as verb affixes as well as noun affixes: ' Why is he in jail? ' ' Because he *shót a man*.'

At the frontier it becomes almost impossible to sort out allegiances. Close relatives belong on either side: *Wésleyan Cóllege* and *Wesleyan Univérsity; Wéldon Boulevard* and *Weldon Córt; lémon drops* and *lemon kísses; hotél room* and *hotel garáge; Cripple Creek* and *Kaw Ríver. Rap* in combination would

---

19. *The intonation of American English* (Ann Arbor, 1945), p. 81.
20. *Consumers Union Reports*, Feb. 1957, p. 60.

hardly receive the accent: *pérjury rap*. *Indíctment* might well receive it: *perjury indíctment*. The more independent floaters can readily recapture the accent: ' He's a member of the *enginéering proféssion* ' against ' Yes, that's one of the big drawbacks of the *engineering proféssion* ' (' of being what I am ').

Compounds of the *cóme-on* type are deceptively sharp, because the shift has been from one distribution class to another. The more typical noun compounds of the *toolbox* type are congenitally ambiguous, for they were nouns to begin with, and we can never tell when a syntactic loss of accent becomes a morphological loss of potential for accent. Under the circumstances about all the analyst can do is list the nouns that are likely to be de-accented and the circumstances under which the loss is likely to occur. He can say, for example, that in epithetical compounds referring to bodily traits, the distinctive mark carries the potential, while the part of the body loses it: *scárface, sóurpuss, múttonhead, bíg-nose, pégleg, éagle-eye*. He can add that common things of nature or commerce that exist under various aspects will have their common part de-accented and their distinctive part accented: *frúit can, súgar can; umbrélla handle, dóor handle; wíndstorm, sléet storm* (the point on the gradient is often shown by the way we space or hyphenate).

In short, the domains of synchrony and diachrony, of pitch accent and phonemic shape, syntax and morphology, are confused, and the analyst is tempted to become confused about them. This is an explanation, not an excuse.

5

DISJUNCTURE AS A CUE TO CONSTRUCTS

(with Louis J. Gerstman)

Word 13.246-255 (1957)

This is a companion piece to the preceding one. It is again concerned with the stress-and-juncture treatment of English phrase structure, but instead of concentrating on the top level of stress ("primary stress"), it looks to the interrelationships of the stress levels themselves, to try to discover, in one narrow experimental context, whether the supposed levels do discriminate phrases as they are supposed to do.

Recent research at Haskins Laboratories has demonstrated that in a number of test situations the stress of words is more efficiently marked by change of pitch than by change of either duration or intensity. The test items involved unit morphs (*súbject-subjéct*)[1] and derivatives (*úndertaking-underták-ing*) ;[2] the judgments were merely of stress vs. non-stress. Inasmuch as the structure of English words, particularly of compounds, has been identified with more than two levels of stress, it occurs to us that the relative importance of intensity should be tested in more complicated surroundings.

The test items chosen for the purpose are the presumably minimal pair *lighthouse-keeper* and *light* (with contrastive stress) *housekeeper*. The reasons for choosing them are two:

1. Spectrograms show, in addition to differences of pitch and intensity, a third factor which is conceivably significant: spacing. It is manifested in two ways: by wider or narrower gaps (intervals of relative silence) between the syllables, and by lengthening and shortening of the syllables themselves. This leads us to the hypothesis that one way in which connectedness between syllables may be signaled is by "disjuncture," which we define as ' separation of syllable centers.' It is not feasible to speak of mere ' separation of syllables,' because in an alternative pair such as *highline voltage* and *high* (contrastive stress) *line voltage* there are no interruptions, and yet the

---

1. Dennis Fry, see p. 23 footnote 13. It is assumed that the etymological prefix here is not to be regarded as a separate morph in the treatment of Modern English.
2. See p. 34.

spacing is still there in the form of lengthening.[3]   Such a pair, however, is not convenient for manipulation, because any attempt to vary the distance between syllable centers by cutting out or adding portions would mean altering not silences but sounds, and would degrade the sounds.   The gaps in *lighthouse-keeper* vs. *light housekeeper*, made possible by the voiceless consonants, provide something that can be cut or expanded with little or no distortion.   For the purpose of the experiment, disjuncture refers to separation by these gaps, although we attach no more importance to it than to separation by lengthening.

2.   The *lighthouse-keeper* vs. *light housekeeper* pair has been repeatedly used in the literature to illustrate certain assumptions.   According to Smith,[4] they are to be marked, respectively, *líght+hòuse+kêeper* and *líght+hôuse+kèeper*, with (′) signifying the loudest stress, (ˆ) the next loudest and (ˋ) the next, the weakest being left unmarked (these stresses are termed " primary," " secondary," " tertiary " and " weak ").   The plus sign refers to internal open juncture, a manner of transition between syllables that distinguishes, e. g., an intersyllabic cluster /s+k/ from an intrasyllabic cluster /sk/.   Smith's analysis is repeated by Stockwell[5] in a criticism of Weinreich,[6] and, in a modified form, by Chomsky, Halle, and Lukoff.[7]

In Smith's analysis, the systems of stress and of pitch (intonation) are regarded as independent,[8] interacting phonologically only to the extent of

---

3.   We acknowledge our recognition of this point to Professors Fred W. Householder, Jr., and J. D. O'Connor.

4.   Henry Lee Smith, Jr., *Linguistic science and the teaching of English*, Cambridge, 1956, 37–43.

5.   Robert P. Stockwell in *Language* 32.379 (1956).

6.   Uriel Weinreich, " Stress and word structure in Yiddish," in Weinreich, ed., *The field of Yiddish*, New York, 1954, 1–27.

7.   Noam Chomsky, Morris Halle, and Fred Lukoff, " On accent and juncture in English," in *For Roman Jakobson* The Hague, 1956, 65–80.   The Chomsky-Halle-Lukoff notation differs from the Smith notation in that it introduces an " external juncture " in *light housekeeper* (written *líght=hóuse-kéeper*).   This external juncture (equals sign) contrasting with internal juncture (hyphen) seems to suggest something like the varying disjunctures that are subject of our experiment, but actually are not, for the authors state : " The junctures . . . do not represent physical entities, but are introduced for the purpose of reducing the number of physical features that must be considered phonemic " (66).   The physical features are those noted by Trager-Smith and Newman (65 fn.), and accordingly do not involve disjuncture as we define it.   In the Smith analysis, neither *lighthouse-keeper* nor *light housekeeper* contains a " phonological juncture," which distinguishes " constructions " from " constructs," and accordingly both qualify as " constructs "—the latter are defined as segments characterized by predictable patterns of stresses and " plus " junctures only. See Smith, " Superfixes and syntactic markers," mimeographed brochure dated 13 April 1956, esp. p. 3.

8.   Pitch phenomena are described as significant in terms of levels (four) and junctures (three), the latter occurring at transition points.

allophonic changes in pitch, presumably slight, conditioned by changes in stress (loudness).[9] The minimal pair is therefore ideal for testing the reliability of intensity alone in making the distinction, since the pitch is defined as non-distinctive.

From the Smith analysis, and from our hypothesis, we derive two contrary sets of markings: one in which loudness (= intensity, under the conditions of the experiment) operates to distinguish the minimal pair by raising the intensity level of *house* above that of *keep*, or of *keep* above that of *house*; the other in which the disjuncture operates to distinguish the minimal pair by separating *light* and *house* more than *house* and *keeper*, or conversely, *house* and *keeper* more than *light* and *house*. The experiment attempts to determine whether the intensity differences are effective under two sets of conditions: (1) with disjuncture differences going counter to intensity differences, which may be called the extreme case; (2) with intensity differences carrying the burden alone and unopposed, which may be called the neutral case.

STIMULI. The original stimuli consisted of the words *light, house*, and *keeper*, recorded in three different contexts: M (Man) *He's a lighthouse-keeper;* W (Woman) *She's a light housekeeper*, with contrastive stress on *light;* and U (Unbiased) *light, house, keeper*, with wide pauses between the words. The M and W phrases were uttered according to the requirements of the Smith notation, and with the disjunctures as they occurred automatically, as detailed in Fig. 1.

The M version had an updash on *light* from 130 to 180 c(ycles) p(er) s(econd) and a downglide on *house* from 130 to 100; *keep* was at about 110 cps. *Keep* therefore rises somewhat above the lowest point reached in *house*, which satisfies the condition of an "allophonic" rise on the more heavily stressed syllable. The vowel in *keep* is about 3 d(eci)b(els) above that of *house*. The gap between *house* and *keeper* is three times as wide as that between *light* and *house*. The words *he's a* were cut out of the tape recording before any testing was performed.

The W version had an updash from 160 to 180 cps on *light*, a downglide from 140 to 120 on *house*, with *keep* at about 110 cps. The vowel in *house* is about 2 db above that of *keep*, so that *house* is both louder and "allophonically" higher in pitch than *keep*. The gap between *light* and *house* is seen to be twice as wide as that between *house* and *keeper*. The words *she's a* were removed from the stimulus.

The U version was a control stimulus in which relative disjuncture would

---

9. "English utterances containing more than one vowel exhibit marked differences in loudness, concentrated on the vowels." Trager and Smith, *Outline of English structure* § 1.61. Norman, Oklahoma, 1951. "There is only one component that matters—loudness." E. C. Trager, "Superfix and sememe," *General Linguistics* 2.2 (1956).

SCHEMATIC SPECIFICATIONS OF THE ORIGINAL STIMULI

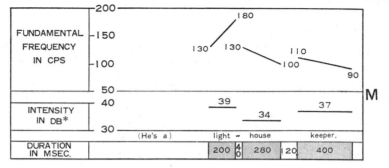

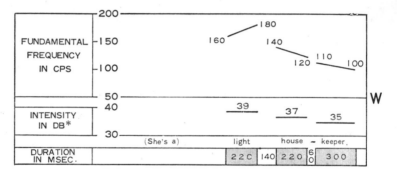

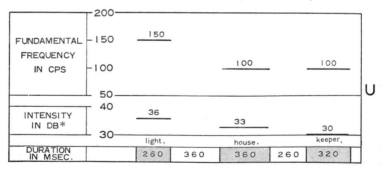

*Relative to background noise level.

Fig. 1. Measurements of the three original tape-recorded utterances. Durations, fundamental frequencies, and relative intensities (at the syllable peaks) were determined from Kay sonagrams and amplitude displays.

not be present to distinguish the two meanings.

Modified stimuli were derived from copies of the original stimuli through alterations of the disjunctures in the recordings. The gaps between the words were variously lengthened and shortened as schematized in the left-hand portion of Fig. 2. We see, for example, that the disjunctures of M were made to resemble the disjunctures of W (M→W) by increasing the gap between *light* and *house* while reducing the gap between *house* and *keeper*. M was made to resemble U (M→U) by enlarging both gaps. By means of similar alterations W was changed toward M and toward U (W→M, W→U), while U was made to resemble M and W (U→M, U→W).

There were in addition two other modified stimuli. One of these, shown at the bottom of the figure, was an attempt to see what would happen when the alterations U→M and U→W were combined. Since U→M had reduced only the gap between *light* and *house*, while U→W had reduced only the gap between *house* and *keeper*, it seemed reasonable to ask whether the reduction of both intervals would be equivalent to reducing neither interval.

The other modified stimulus was a second version of W→M, created because of the intrusion of the other feature of disjuncture, lengthening, in the production of the [s] of *house* in the original recordings. The friction portion of [s] occupied 140 m(illi)sec(onds) in M, 160 msec. in U, but only 100 msec. in W. The consequence of this was that *house* sounded too abrupt in the first version of W→M, which led us to attempt a second version wherein half the silence (100 msec.) consisted of additional [s] friction to ease the abruptness of [s]. This disparity in friction durations was also troublesome in the reverse direction, when we attempted to go from M to W and from U to W; here we simply removed some of the friction (60 msec. in M→W, 40 msec. in U→W), in each case without any degradation of the [s].

PROCEDURE. The three original and eight modified stimuli were arranged into several random orders to be judged by members of the laboratory staff on two separate occasions. With three exceptions,[10] each stimulus was heard five times by nine different subjects. Listeners were instructed to judge the stimuli as *lighthouse-keeper* or *light housekeeper* (contrastive context) or, if they had real difficulty deciding, as " either." In the results that follow we have tabulated these responses as M, W, and U, respectively.

RESULTS. The results are presented in the right-hand portion of Fig. 2, where, opposite each stimulus, is shown its percentage of M, W, and U re-

---

10. U→M was heard 6 times by 8 listeners, while M→U and W→U were heard 4 times by 7 listeners.

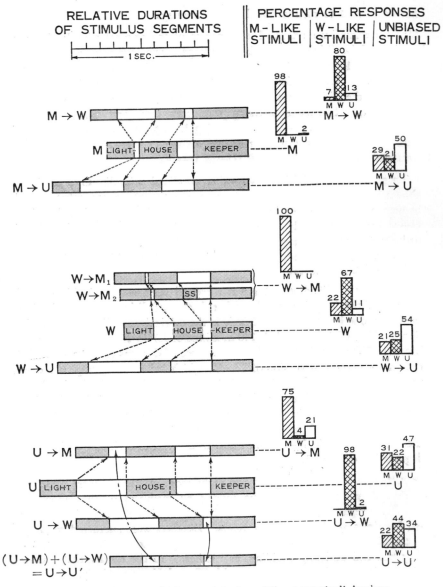

Fig. 2. Specifications and judgments of the eleven different test stimuli. As schematized at the left, the disjunctures in each of the three original utterances (M, W, and U) were modified by adding or subtracting pieces of magnetic tape to make eight new utterances. The arrows indicate these changes. The stimuli were judged to be M, W, or U utterances in proportion to the heights of the bars at the right.

sponses. The response blocks are placed in three columns corresponding to the three patterns of disjuncture. This arrangement enables us to see at once that the stimuli were judged overwhelmingly in accordance with their disjunctures rather than their sources. Intensity, even when unopposed by disjuncture (M→U, W→U), did not have an appreciable effect; there was simply an increase in the number of U responses.

Certain aspects of the experiment strengthen the case for disjuncture, and more particularly, for *relative disjuncture*, as the controlling feature. When the modified stimuli were prepared, we did not give the gaps exactly the same lengths as in the original stimuli, choosing instead to adjust them symmetrically. For example, in M→W, 233 msec. was added between *light* and *house* while 133 msec. was removed between *house* and *keeper*; in W→M₁, 133 mesc. was removed from the first interval while 233 msec. was added to the second. Often the effect of these operations was to make the modified disjunctures more extreme than the originals and, as seen in the results, such stimuli yielded more response agreement than did the original stimuli.

The three stimuli derived from U establish that neither of the disjunctures is, by itself, the controlling cue: U→M and U→U′ have the same first interval while U→W and U→U′ have the same second interval, yet the three stimuli are heard in radically different ways. Accordingly, we have sought some measure which would relate the two disjunctures and provide a simple description of the experiment. What seems to work best is the ratio of the interval between *light* and *house* to the interval between *house* and *keeper*.

In Fig. 3 we have arranged the stimuli in order of increasing relative disjuncture. (Values less than 1 mean that the first interval is shorter than the second; values greater than 1 mean that the first interval is longer.) Each bar represents all the responses made to a stimulus and is divided according to the distribution of judgments. We see that M responses predominate at the left, W responses at the right. In the light of this form of presentation, it is quite understandable why some of the modified stimuli should elicit a more positive response than the original stimuli.

It is apparent, from the way in which the data arrange themselves in Fig. 3, that if we attempted to apply a scale of relative intensity itstead of a scale of relative disjuncture, the results would be chaotic. Even in the most favorable case of all, that of U, in which the speaker was consciously striving to produce something that would be neither M nor W, a difference of 3 db crept in; but this difference had no effect on the responses: in fact, instead of favoring W as they theoretically should if the assumptions about intensity and stress are correct, the responses favored M.

Finally, we may ask why the original W stimulus, a presumably normal utterance, was not completely effective. The answer lies, perhaps, in the test format: the stimuli were presented in isolation whereas contrastive stress

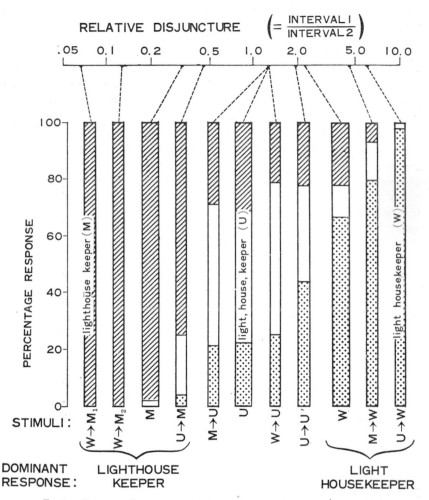

Fig. 3. The data of Fig. 2 replotted in terms of relative disjuncture. The stimuli are represented as bars, ordered according to the ratio of the interval between *light* and *house* (Interval 1) to the interval between *house* and *keeper* (Interval 2). The bars are divided in proportion to the percentage of M, W, and U judgments elicited by each stimulus.

usually relies on previous context to make the meaning clear. The absence of context may be thought of as an anti-W cue, requiring extreme disjuncture to be counteracted. The presence of this bias toward M should make us cautious in selecting a specific disjuncture as the dividing line between M and W responses.

CONCLUSIONS. All the modified patterns went in the direction of the modification, not only in an absolute sense but, in most instances, in proportion to the *degree* of modification. Neither in the extreme case of disjuncture opposing intensity, nor in the neutral case of disjuncture relatively balanced, did intensity appear to have the slightest influence in making the distinction.

If we insist that the type *lighthouse-keeper* is normally discriminated by stress from the type *light housekeeper*, the experiment compels us to:

1. Re-define phonemic stress to eliminate reliance upon loudness and to place it upon disjuncture (which would seem rather like a sophistication to save a term) ; or,

2. Re-define loudness to eliminate reliance upon intensity and place it upon disjuncture.

The common-sense conclusion, however, is that since in *lighthouse-keeper* the semantic bond between *light* and *house* is closer than that between *house* and *keeper* (immediate constituents are *lighthouse/keeper*), and since the disjunctures transparently supply a physical separation whose width corresponds inversely to the semantic bond, it follows that the disjunctures function directly to carry the information, and not indirectly as components of a hypothetical stress. Rather than attempt to salvage the stresses it would seem better to reconsider the juncture complex, for it is apparent that the uniform "plus" juncture with which Trager and Smith have marked the examples has overlooked the function of disjuncture.

6

INTONATION AND GRAMMAR
Language Learning 8 : 1,2.31-38 (1957-58)

Intonation has been invoked to define grammatical classes ever since the first discovery that most questions go up and most statements come down. Can we say that intonation is *part of* syntax, or are the two instead parallel systems, like Church and State, that sometimes contribute to one another's support but each of which claims a great deal more than lies outside the jurisdiction of the other? My vote is for the latter.

In this article I use the term *intonation* loosely, as the authors of the discussions that are criticized use it, to refer to vocal pitch in general.

The editors and contributors of *Language Learning* are doing good work in their encouragement of intonation and its uses in the teaching of language. I have in mind especially the editorial by Professor McCarus in *LL* 7 : 1, 2, and the articles by Louis C. Rus and B. J. Koekkoek in the same issue, cultivating a bit deeper the field that has engaged so many competent workers at Michigan for going on two decades. Among the virtues is a recognition of intonational forms, and a boldness in describing and defining them, a procedure that seems to frighten other researchers who are quick to set up intonation " phonemes " but unwilling to risk putting them into phonemic shapes whose existence can be verified or disproved, and along with them the existence of the phonemes themselves. There is also a virtue in the courage and good sense to call pitch pitch, instead of compressing pitches, intensities, and durations into a prosodic souse, cutting it into four sizes, and marketing it as large, extra-large, jumbo, and colossal " stress ".

Because I believe in this approach, I should like to venture a warning against claiming too much for it. Intonation signals meanings which in its own sphere are a steady and systematic illumination, but in a neighboring sphere may be only an occasional glimmer. The question is, can we infer from the intonation that covers a segment what the grammatical interrelationships of the segment are? And if we can, is it because the intonation carries the information directly or only, by a happy coincidence, gives us a clue? The difference is like the problem of a guest hunting on a dark night for the house of his host. If he has a flashlight, he may read the number and know, as well as systematic signs can tell him, when he is there. If not, he may have to blunder up to the first lighted porch that he sees. Lighted porches are good clues, but their relation to addresses is not systematic. What system they have is essentially self-contained.

In at least two places in his *Intonation of American English*, Kenneth L. Pike warns against taking the light on the porch for the number of the house: "Intonation contours cannot be defined in terms of the grammatical constructions with which they occur" (163), and, objecting to the British practice of using a notation of dots, "In addition it may lead to unnecessary—and inadvisable—complication of the definitions of the meanings of the contours by relating them to grammatical types instead of to speakers' attitudes" (41). I believe that Pike could have gone farther and said something like this: "Intonation applies to the whole of utterances, with little systematic relevance to their immediate constituents beyond its power to show connectedness or disconnectedness, completeness or incompleteness." For example, using what Pike terms "contour separation" we can discriminate between *Escaping, prisoner caught* and *Escaping prisoner caught*. But not even this tells us precisely and predictably that there is an IC cut between *escaping* and *prisoner*, for the same intonation might be used to emphasize the separate importance of 'escaping,' by a speaker who reiterates a statement after having been misunderstood by someone else.

Much too much has been claimed for the grammatical correlations of stress, as I have tried to show elsewhere.[1] Those who work with intonation have not exaggerated their claims to the same degree, but have still somewhat overextended them, as I shall illustrate.

1. The article by Rus discusses a relationship between intonation and IC's involving words of the class of *the*. With the intonation the girls bicycle the determiner is to be taken with *girl*, while with the intonation the girls bicycle it is to be taken with *bicycle*. Ambiguity "does not exist" if we take intonation into account, it is claimed.

Perhaps contrastive contexts were intended to be disregarded, for if they are included, the second intonation becomes ambiguous: "How did the boys get over there when both their bikes had flat tires?"—"They took the girls' bicycles."—"Their sisters'?"—"Yes." Here we understand 'The bicycles of *the* girls.' (Probably a double role should be assigned to the original *the*: '*The* bicycles of *the* girls'; but the critical question is the role with *girls*.)

But even without contrast the ambiguity persists. I give examples of "level 2 on the second Class 1 word" in which the determiner qualifies it rather than the first Class 1 word:

"How did she know?"—"Her woman's intuition" ('Her feminine intuition,' not 'Intuition of her woman').

---

1. See pp. 67–83.

96

"Why do you say that?"—"It's the God's⌐truth" ('The divine truth,' not 'Truth of the God').

"What happened?"—"There was a big fire over at the girls'⌐dormitory." ('The female dormitory,' not 'Dormitory of the girls').

I saw something flapping in the wind that gave me a start, and then realized that it was nothing but a woman's⌐handkerchief ('A feminine handkerchief').

The owner of a bike shop might say to his assistant, "Clear this part of the floor of those wagons and mount a couple of girls'⌐bicycles there."

The systematic relationship—the number on the house—is that between the high pitch (I would term it "pitch accent") and the semantically most-important item. The owner of the bike shop wants 'bicycles' on display. This is, as Pike would say, an attitude, and attitudes are the first business of intonation.

The light on the porch is the relatively high frequency of a special kind of no-importance: that of something which has just been mentioned. If we say the girl's⌐bicycle there is a better than even chance that the girl has just been mentioned or is too obvious to need mentioning, while the bicycle is only now being introduced and is the center of attention, the item with the most information. Guests about to leave, gathering up their belongings which include their youngster's paraphernalia, will say "You've forgotten the child's⌐coat." The low pitch on *child's* signals 'something known, something to which there is no need to draw special attention'; and this, in the context, means '*the* child' of the family.

By the same token, when we say the⌐child's⌐coat, accenting the possessor more often than not implies a generic sense if the name of the thing is at the same time de-accented. But such an intonation is less frequent because it implies that the identity of the thing is understood from the situation. When it is a new datum we tend to use an intonation different from either of the two presented: the⌐child's coat. And this more frequent intonation is quite ambiguous.

2. A differential role of intonation by which it is supposed to distinguish meanings such as those of *any*, 'any whatsoever' and 'just any,' has been discussed by W. R. Lee.[2] With the British preference for low-pitched accents, the examples would be hard for an American audience to interpret, but there are American equivalents that serve as well, or better. In They don't admit any students we understand that the students are picked carefully. In They don't admit any⌐students we understand that no students at all are admitted.

This is another light on a porch, illumining a passer-by and enabling us to

---

2. "English intonation: a new approach." *Lingua* 5.345–371 (1956).

identify him. In I won't play｜golf｜with｜you the intonation highlights 'golf' and at the same time is inconclusive. What is affirmed (or denied) about golf is not affirmed (or denied) unconditionally—I may be willing to play tennis with you. So we won't admit 'any (just any old)' students, but we may be willing to admit 'particular' students.

The differential role of intonation here is the chance result of there being two different lexical meanings for the word *any*, one of them common to affirmative contexts (*They'll take any student* 'They're not particular') and one limited to negative and interrogative contexts (*They won't take any students* 'They will take no students'). The latter meaning is all-excluding and only makes nonsense with an intonation, such as the contrastive-inconclusive one under consideration, that admits an alternative. The former meaning, though common to affirmative contexts, may also be used after a negative and, since it admits an alternative, it makes sense with this intonation. When we encounter the two together, we infer the sense and reject the nonsense, as we always do.

3. It is possible to overdo even one of the minimum roles of intonation, that of connectedness-disconnectedness, as may be seen in the next two examples taken from Pike.

In his *a man of the world* (p. 67), Pike creates what he calls a "double
$$3\text{-} \quad {}^{0}2\text{-} \quad \text{-}3\text{-} \qquad {}^{0}2\text{-}4//$$
function" to take care of the fact that the general impression conveyed by this utterance is about the same as in *a man of the world*. In other words, the fall
$$3\text{-} \quad {}^{0}2\text{-}3 \quad 3\text{-} \qquad {}^{0}2\text{-}4//$$
on *of* is equivalent to a fall within the syllable *man*, so that the syllable *of* serves both as the end-point of a preceding contour and the precontour of a following contour; it is "in double function."

But why not regard *of* as the end-point of the preceding contour and *the* as the precontour of the following contour? The reason for rejecting this seems to be that the IC cut is *a man / of the world*, and contours ought somehow to reflect the IC's. The truth is, however, that IC's need bear no relation to intonation contours. In *I will sir* the vocative is the end-point
$$3\text{-} \quad {}^{0}2\text{-} \quad \text{-}4//$$
of the contour on *will* and it makes no difference that the IC's *I will / sir* are straddled. For a better instance of double function we might cite *a man of God;* here, for reasons that are relevant to intonation, not to IC's, the syllable *of* has to provide both the low pitch following *man* and the low pitch preceding *God*, enabling us to have two high pitches distinctly marked.

4. In the examples *refugee?* and *effigy?* (p. 78) Pike finds, for *refugee*
$${}^{0}3\text{-} \text{-}2/ \qquad {}^{0}3\text{-} \text{-}2/$$
but not for *effigy*, the alternative *refugee?* (he has ${}^{0}2$ here, apparently a mis-.
$${}^{0}3\text{-} \text{-}(3)\text{-}2/$$

print), which he describes as the "option of a fairly slow rising glide from pitch three to pitch two on the last vowel (with resulting length of vowel) ; this variation is not permissible for *effigy*, although a much more fleeting glide is occasionally heard." "Since," he adds, "in the dialect cited, the vocalic quality is the same, the option of a second handling of the up glide on *refugee* is probably due to the fact that the relationship of a semantically full suffix like -*ee* to a full free underlying word like *refuge* is grammatically quite different from the relationship of a semantically weak ending like the -*y* of *effigy* to a semantically weak and dependent word part such as *effig-*." The point is evidently regarded as important, for it receives two more paragraphs and a long footnote.

The reason for the different treatment of *refugee* and *effigy* is incidentally, not essentially, grammatical and is indirectly, not directly, related to intonation.

On the grammatical side, it is true that the -*ee* suffix is pertinent. But it is pertinent only to the extent that it tells us that words assuming it are likely to have, at the outset, their primary stress (I prefer to call this the "potential for pitch accent") on the suffix. Coin a new word with it, and most speakers will give it the stress.

But English is averse to nouns with terminal stress, and pressure starts immediately to back-shift it. The result is that most -*ee* words waver. I am not sure myself how I should pronounce *employee, standee, returnee, deportee*. Recent dictionaries still mark *refugee* with primary stress on the suffix.

It is no wonder then that Pike finds something like a second contour possible on this syllable. It simply indicates our uncertainty as to where to put the potential for pitch accent, even to the extent of dividing it between two syllables of the word.

But if this, as far as intonation is concerned, is not something that can be tied directly to grammar, but is only a wavering in the locus of the potential for pitch accent, then we should be able to prove it by unit morphs which also waver. I have them in my speech. The word *obsolete* wavers between potential on the last and potential on the first syllable, and allows of the same "fairly slow rising glide" on the last syllable. A minimal pair is *chickaree* and *chicory; chickaree* has made the half-step from *chickarée* (*Oxford Universal*) to *chickaree* (*Webster, ACD*), and admits the glide. For speakers who forestress the word *shivaree*, it forms a minimal pair with *shivery*. *Obsolete, chickaree,* and *shivaree* are unit morphs, with no possibility of grammatical subdivision.

Intonation operates in its own sphere, and the uses that grammar makes of it are catch-as-catch-can. A brilliant contrast occurs to us, and we think we have discovered a systematic correspondence, only to find that it is valid with but few examples or only part of the time. I give two instances of such "discoveries." that have' occurred to me.

1. Pitch makes a useful distinction on the word *had,* in a sentence like *The general had conferred upon him a signal honor:*

   (1) had conferred upon him
   (2) had conferred upon him
   (3) had conferred upon him

The meaning of (1) is probably 'The general had conferred a signal honor on somebody else.' That of (2), 'The general received (got endowed with) a signal honor himself.' That of (3), 'The general possessed a signal honor, which had been previously conferred upon him.'

No. (3) we can dispose of in Pike's terms as "contour separation": *had* and *conferred* perform separate roles. This leaves (1) and (2) as competing auxiliary uses of the word *had.* Is there anything analogous in other auxiliaries? Take *was* and *got:*

   (4) was endowed with
   (5) was endowed with

No. (4) is natural, No. (5) would be used only in some special context, as in disputing the contrary or emphasizing the time; but there is no contrast similar to that in *had.*

   (6) got endowed with
   (7) got endowed with

Here both are perfectly natural, though (7) would be called for under circumstances of special emphasis.

The role of pitch change here is to focus on important words. Where the auxiliary has or approaches the meaning of 'possess,' it is more important than when it is merely a function word; but, as *got* with its dual possibilities proves, the intonational distinction is not at the level of grammar.

2. Another false promise was held out by a sign observed on a liquor store: *Liquors Reduced.* Here it seemed that Liquors Reduced and Pants Pressed should embody a contrast: that of 'act already performed' vs. 'service offered.' But a little reflection dispels it. An establishment offering a service may raise more than one pitch if the meanings are highlighted: Parcels Prepared for Export, Pants Cleaned and Pressed. And an establishment announcing an act already performed on one of many items in its inventory may, for contrast on that item, raise its pitch and lower the rest: Flash! Men's Suits Reduced! There is no correlation with grammar here.

Nor are we likely to find one elsewhere. The encounters between intonation and grammar are casual, not causal. Grammar uses intonation on those frequent encounters, but intonation is not grammatical.

7

CONTRASTIVE ACCENT AND CONTRASTIVE STRESS
Language 37.83-96 (1961)

One of the most durable concepts in American linguistics has been that of "contrastive stress." The term suggests not only a function but a form—it implies that stress (I substitute *accent*) is used for contrast, and that it is a special kind of stress. I examine this notion, find it faulty, and go on to describe a phonetic entity that is more nearly sui generis and more uniformly contrastive, but of a different order.

'This whiskey,' said O'Reilly, sampling spirits that claimed to be from his homeland, 'was not exported from Ireland; it was deported.'

This is the familiar phenomenon of contrast, by which two or more items are counterbalanced and a preference indicated for some member or members of the group. It is the most conspicuous of all the occurrences of phonetic highlighting by reason of its frequency and the extra oomph that we put into it, and because our attention is focused in a way that makes us aware of our speech and not just of our meaning.

The name we generally give is *contrastive stress*, but I propose *contrastive accent* because of the major contribution that the fundamental pitch of the voice makes to it.[1] I will keep the old term *contrastive stress* as well, but restrict its meaning in a way to be explained later.

The primary role of pitch in contrastive accent has been known for a long time. H. O. Coleman, in his oft-quoted article of 1914,[2] made it the basis of his distinction between 'prominence' and 'intensity.' As an example of prominence he gives

You   dark   bla

   may call it   I should say it was

        blu e,   ck.

and as an example of intensity,

---

1. For the distinction between accent and stress, see pp. 51–52.
2. "Intonation and emphasis," *Miscellanea Phonetica.*

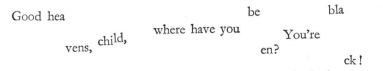

Good hea be bla

vens, child, where have you You're

en?

ck!

Daniel Jones follows Coleman, and says,[3] 'Contrast-emphasis is expressed mainly by intonation. The special intonation may be accompanied by extra stress or length, but these are secondary.' Most investigators nowadays agree on the pitch element of contrastive accent, however much they may disagree on the manner in which it works.[4]

But a question remains, which is whether contrastive accent is really a special kind of accent or only a particular way in which a more general kind of pitch contrast happens to be used at the moment. Kenneth Pike stated flatly in 1945 that 'there is no contrastive [accent]... as such.'[5] Einar Haugen asserted that the only thing special about a contrastive accent is its location.[6] Yet contemporary writers continue to refer to it as if it were a thing to itself.[7] It is worth citing some examples to see whether the presence or absence of logical contrast makes any audible difference, and also to ask a psychological question, which is why the notion of contrastive accent was and is so popular among linguists.

The popularity and the errors incurred by it are to be traced, I think, to a phonetic illusion created by the linguist's interference with his own data. Our main business is establishing contrasts at all levels. Ordinarily we can do this without distorting our material; the opposition between two vowels,

---

3. *An outline of English phonetics* § 1047 (New York, 1956).

4. Newman, writing earlier—*Word* 2.172 (1946)—said, 'Phonetically, the contrastively accented word is pronounced with an especially strong force of articulation.'

5. *The intonation of American English* 45.

6. *Language* 25.278 (1949). Haugen takes Newman to task for presumably making a categorical distinction between contrastive and noncontrastive accent. Newman, however, did not separate the two so sharply: 'The heavy stress which functions as the nucleus of an intonational unit or as the locus of an expressive accent will be termed the nuclear heavy stress' (*Word* 2.175)—nuclear heavy includes contrastive.

Trager and Smith, if their application by Stockwell represents their thinking, incorporate a contrastive accent within other primary accents (I substitute *accent* for *stress* to conform to my definitions here) so long as not more than one occurs in a given macrosegment, but ascribe additional contrastive accents to an overlaid voice-qualifier. See *Language* 32.376 (1956), and see Trager and Smith, *An outline of English structure* 73 (Norman, Oklahoma, 1951).

7. Cf. Chomsky, Halle, and Lukoff, who exclude from their analysis—*For Roman Jakobson 1956* 78—'all forms of expressive accent, including contrastive accent'. Also R. B. Lees, *Word* 16.123 (1960): '*any* under contrastive primary accent'. (Again I substitute *accent* for *stress.*)

for example, can be studied without warping any of the distinctive features of either vowel. But we no sooner begin to contrast accents than we are tripped by the fact that one of the functions of accent is to MEAN contrast, and in the act of performing the comparison we introduce one of the items to be compared. Suppose the utterance is *My mother is cóming*. The investigator wants to see what happens when the main accent occurs on prior words, so he tries it first on *is* (*My mother ís coming*), and concludes that this would imply a contrast with *is not*, then on *mother* (*My móther is coming*), and concludes that this would imply a contrast with *father* or *sister*, and then on *my* (*Mý mother is coming*), and concludes that this would imply a contrast with *your* or *his*. What is likely to escape him is that the contrastiveness of these accents is not only a function of the accents themselves but of the starting point. *My mother is cóming* already establishes a context in relation to which any other accent is contrastive. But if we fit the examples into a different context, for instance

> *Why are you in such a hurry to get home?*
> *My móther is coming.*

the accent on a prior word does not imply contrast. Similarly in

> *Why did you run?*
> *A policeman suddenly appeared around the corner.*

These are simply examples of the semantic peak occurring early in the utterance. The semantic peak includes contrastive accents along with other accents; and there is no predictable phonetic difference. In

> *How was the job?*
> *Oh, it was éasy.*
> *Was the job hard?*
> *No, it was éasy.*

the same pitch contour can be used in both answers.

But there are a few patterns of fundamental pitch where the first impression of contrast is harder to banish. In the type

where there are two peaks, the first higher than the second, Henry Lee Smith felt[8] that he had a pattern that could safely be labeled contrastive, and the examples that come quickest to mind, like

---

8. Personal letter, 10 April 1956.

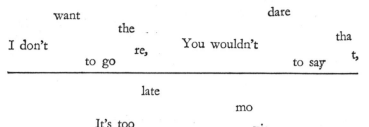

```
        want                              dare
              the  .                              tha
  I don't         re,        You wouldn't              t,
          to go                          to say
```

```
            late
                          mo
      It's too                     vie,
              to take in a
```

certainly imply a contrast. But it is a favorite trick of intonation to fool
us with the obvious, and we are as liable here as ever. The pattern in
question is simply one in which there are two semantic peaks, the first of
which makes a strong comment on the second, and in point of statistics
we have more use for this in assigning contrasts than in anything else.
But there are other uses. I can say, for example,

```
              ter
                                  live
      It's a                           with,
              rible thing to have to
```

using the same pattern, and not have in mind any contrast between living
and dying. It is easy to demonstrate the noncontrastiveness of this pattern
by making successive additions of dead weight to a sentence and noting how
the final accent slides right out to the end, regardless of any contrast. We
can start with something like

```
                              nick
                                      chan
      I wouldn't give a plugged              ces,
                              el for your
```

extend it to

```
                          nick
      I wouldn't give a plugged                      do
                                                  ing it,
                          el for your chances of
```

and further extend it to

```
                      nick
                                                      plan
  I wouldn't give a plugged                              to,
                      el for your chances of doing what you
```

and we find, in the same over-all pattern, the final accent first on *chances,* then on *doing it,* then on *plan to,* with no essential difference in meaning. The same is true of other patterns. In

mor

Why

don't you do it to

row?

there is clear contrast with *today* or some other day. But in

sup

Why

don't you have

Per with us?

there is no necessary contrast with *breakfast* or *dinner.* On a New York bus I heard a boy remark

Av

Here's nue.

e

Eighth

As there could be no idea of an Eighth *Street* in that neighborhood, this was not contrast but something affecting the utterance as a whole. Similarly in

What are you afraid bite

of? I'm not going to you,

there is contrast between treating ill, figuratively biting, and treating well. But in

him? ne that's

What'll I do to I'll

ck,

break his damn

all,
a

I'll break his damn neck has the same contour as *I'm not going to bite you,* but there is no contrast between *neck* and *arm* or *leg.*

The same is true of the pattern that consists of a low-pitched accent followed by a high-pitched one. It is often found with contrast, for example

$$\text{He}\ \text{did}_\text{n't}\ \text{buy}\ \text{a}\ \text{Fo}\ \text{rd,}\ \text{he bought a}\ \text{Ply}\ \text{mouth.}$$

But it is also used without contrast:

$$\text{Just}\ \text{leave}\ \text{him}\ \text{a}\ \text{lo}\ \text{ne,}\ \text{and}\ \text{he won't}\ \text{bo}\ \text{ther}\ \text{you.}$$

I would say then that as far as we can tell from the behavior of pitch, nothing is uniquely contrastive.

No less troublesome than our inability to find a uniquely contrastive pitch, however, is our failure to define what is meant by *contrastive.* Practically always the samples cited imply '*A* rather than *B.*' But when we try to pin this down we find that the 'ratherness' fades out gradually. In

> *I found a book.*
> *Whóse book?*
> *Jóhn's book.*
> *Not Jóe's?*

there is no difference between *whose, John's,* and *Joe's* as far as accent or reasons for accent are concerned, but we are likely to limit the term *contrastive* to the word *Joe's* in the last sentence of the series. In a broad sense every semantic peak is contrastive. Clearly in *Let's have a pícnic,* coming as a suggestion out of the blue, there is no specific contrast with *dinner party,* but there is a contrast between picnicking and anything else the group might do. As the alternatives are narrowed down, we get closer to what we think of as contrastive accent:

> *Where'll we have it?*
> *Let's have it in the párk.*
> *Can we all go?*
> *No, Jóhn can't.*
> *Bring some wíeners.*
> *I don't like wieners. I want hámburgers.*

Despite the difficulty, both phonetic and semantic, in finding a reality to correspond to contrastive accent in the traditional sense, there does remain one place where we can be fairly sure of our bearings. This brings us to the distinction between contrastive accent and contrastive stress.

I take as my definition of stress essentially that offered by Uriel Weinreich :[9] 'We can...consider phonemic stress within the morpheme as the place at which relative loudness occurs if the morpheme is emphasized.' I alter the phrasing somewhat: the stressed syllable of a word is the one where the accent falls if there is an accent, which is to say that it is the syllable with the potential for accent. This raises the question of syllabic length in English, for only long syllables have the potential for accent. Take the word *countersign*, in which the first and third syllables are both long. The first syllable is the one that normally gets the pitch accent when *countersign* is accented, and we can therefore say that in *countersign* the first syllable is stressed. In the sentence

He keeps insisting that we coun tersign it, but there's nothing to countersign,

the first accent falls on *countersign* and its stressed syllable, the first, is made to stand out sharply. But if we had to rely on the second part, where the accent is on *to*, we could not tell which syllable was stressed.

Contrastive accent usually occurs without contrastive stress. In the sentence

I said to re port the trouble, not broad cast it,

the words *report* and *broadcast* are contrastively accented, but normally stressed—that is, *report* appears with stress on the second syllable, where it regularly falls, and *broadcast* appears with stress on the first syllable, likewise the normal position.

This is possible because *report* and *broadcast* are about as unlike phonemically as any two words can be. There is already a built-in large-scale phonemic contrast, and none has to be added. But things change when we try to contrast words that are phonemically similar. We can tolerate some similarity, even a difference of only one linear phoneme if it is in the stressed syllable. This enables us to say *Not conféssion, concéssion,* or *Not deféction, defléction.* We can also tolerate identical stressed syllables if there is enough contrast elsewhere, and say *He's as insístent as any woman, but not really síssified.* But let the similarity of the contrasted words get any closer

---

9. *The field of Yiddish* 2 (New York, 1954).

and a change may be demanded. The typical case is the one that I used in my first illustration, where the verbs *expórt* and *depórt* were brought together with the result that the stress shifted:[10] *éxported, déported.* So frequently does this happen that a number of pairs of words whose members are more often encountered together than separately have undergone a permanent shift of stress: the verb *rétail* coupled with *wholesale,* the pairs *éxtroverted-íntroverted, éxhale-ínhale* (particularly *éxhale*), and the words of nationality ending in the syllable *-ese,* where one nowadays more often hears *Pórtuguese* than *Portuguése,* and where *Chinése* and *Japanése* are probably tending to shift to *Chínese* and *Jápanese* even when not joined in the same context. A similar phenomenon is the wavering in pairs like *outside-inside, outdoors-indoors, upgrade-downgrade.* Here, though the shift has not yet become permanent, we can observe it working covertly in situations where the speaker has the opposite member at the back of his mind, although he does not actually say it: I have caught myself producing sentences like *The only time it happens is when you íncrease the load.* Or the opposite member of the pair may have been mentioned, but some time previously. For example, a clerk at the Auto Club, after discussing motel accommodations in Mexico, said, *In Mexico City I recommend a hótel.*

One reason perhaps why this temporary shift takes place is that English permits unstressed syllables to become progressively degraded phonetically, with the result that the stressed syllable is forced to carry almost the whole burden of contrast between words of equal length. Then when the stressed syllables themselves are identical, something may have to be done to make another part of the word conspicuous enough to mark the distinction. When *pre-ténd* becomes *p'ténd* and *in-ténd* becomes *n'ténd,* it is not surprising that contrast brings about a shift of stress to the first syllable: *It isn't what you prétend, it's what you íntend.*

But there are restrictions on where the stress may shift. Ordinarily it may shift to a long syllable regardless of position: *The book refers to cýtology, not to hístology,* where *cytólogy* shifts the stress from the second to the first syllable, both of which are long; or similarly in *I would call that legal action pérsecution, not prósecution.* Likewise when the long syllable follows the stress: *Which kind of compound is it, sulfáte or sulfíte?* Where the shift is to a weak syllable, however, it cannot go freely in both directions. It may shift to the left, as we have already seen: *You may détain them but don't rétain them.* The leftward shift is especially notable when a negative is contrasted with its morphological affirmative. Here is a sentence in which the shift may be to either of two left-hand syllables: *The phenomenon we are*

---

10. The 'shift' noted by Trager-Smith 73 refers to a change in the position of the accent within the utterance. It is not the same as the shift noted here, which affects the position of the potential for accent, i.e. the stress, within words.

noting may be called the relationship between length and únfamiliarity, or between condensation and fámiliarity (or, as it was actually used in this context, *between condensation and familiarity*). It is obvious that in pairs where everything is identical except a prefix, a shift to the left is necessary if anything like a balanced contrast is to be achieved. The interesting thing is that the shift may not only be to the prefix itself, as in *dísintegrate* contrasted with *íntegrate*, or to a syllable in the same position as in the negative word, for example *cónsent* or *ássent* matched with *díssent*, but to a makeshift position in the other member of the pair, for example *On the one hand you have the densest únintelligibility, and on the other the clearest íntelligibility* (or *intélligibility*).

The leftward shift is of course at least as feasible when long syllables are involved. In answer to the question *Was it yésterday?* one may get either *No, dáy before yesterday* or *No, day befóre yesterday*. The first of these, *dáy before yesterday*, seems less logical, but is probably helped along by the traditional English tendency to forestress noun compounds as soon as they are completely fused.

Two additional causes contribute to the ease of the leftward shift. One is the relatively high frequency of functionally active prefixes in English. In pairs like *denounce-pronounce, command-demand, interrupt-disrupt*, though the independent meaning of the prefixes has been dimmed, being coupled to morphs that are related in meaning they are able to serve as differentiating elements. This is assisted of course by prefixes that are truly productive in the language, like *anti-, un-, pre-*, and *non-*, with meanings that lend themselves to contrast in a way that is seldom to be found among suffixes.[11] The second cause is the large number of cognates, especially nouns and verbs, which are distinguished by stress—*ímpound* and *impóund, cómbine* and *combíne, pérvert* and *pervért*, etc.—which has produced a good deal of wavering within categories (e.g. noun *áddress* or *addréss*, verb *áccent* or *accént, bísect* or *biséct*), and has also made us somewhat deaf to vowel quality in this position.

A shift to the right onto a weak syllable is much less usual, and we tolerate more similarity between contrasted words before we resort to it. An extreme case is the contracted negative, where we are satisfied to say *Yes he ís!, No he ísn't!* In order to stress the negative we have to pull it loose: *Yes he ís!, No he's nót!*

---

11. The obvious exception is the suffixes *-less* and *-ful*. But most pairs carrying them have ceased to be—if they ever were—true contraries: we speak of a *cheerful* person, but a *cheerless* room; the person himself may be *soulless*, but only his eyes are generally *soulful; mindful* means 'remembering', *mindless* 'idiotic'. Many, perhaps most, morphs carrying one of the suffixes do not carry the other: *beautiful, hapless, penniless, spiteful, gainful*. Finally, *-less* is productive, *-ful* is not: *footless, eyeless*, coined *penless*, etc.; this may reflect the homonymic competition of *-full: eye-full, drawer-full, cupful*, etc.

In words where matching weak syllables after the normal position of the stress are the only phonemically contrasting parts, we again do not as a rule shift the stress; for example, *Did you say advénturesome or advénturous?*, *Would you rather be réverend or réverent?*, *The word I used was not régiment but régimen.* It would surprise us a bit, I think, if we heard *The word I used was not regimént but regimén.*[12]

Our recourse with these weak syllables then is to be overprecise in their pronunciation if it seems necessary in order to establish the contrast. We may not shift the stress in the word *regiment*, but we can exaggerate the release of the final /t/: [rédʒəmn̩tʰ]. One who misunderstands the full name of a girl nicknamed *Kathy* will ask *Did you say Cath-er-ine or Kathryn?*—exaggerating the length of the weak syllable without necessarily shifting the stress. One result of this is the frequent appearance of what J. H. D. Allen Jr. calls a 'reconstituted vowel'[13]—in other words, a spelling pronunciation. Normally the two words *forward* and *foreword* are homonyms in my speech, but if I contrast them I am apt to produce an /a/ in *forward* that I never normally produce between a /w/ and an /r/, and at the same time to exaggerate the length of the weak syllable in *foreword*. One notes something similar under conditions other than contrast, in both a leftwise and a rightwise direction. Allen points out our tendency to distinguish in this manner the words *affect* meaning 'work a change in' and *effect* meaning 'accomplish.' If the two words were in contrast, we would use both the spelling pronuncia-

---

12. We would be less surprised by *regimént* than by *regimén*, because of the support that *regimént* would have (even though in a different category, as verb rather than noun) from the numerous pairs in which a verb is distinguished from an adjective or a noun by reason of having its final syllable either lengthened or stressed. This is to say that a stress shift can occur more readily if the result is some morphemic shape already familiar than if it is relatively unfamiliar. Examples of distinctive length are *affiliate* [-ejt] verb versus *affiliate* [-ət] noun, *separate* [-ejt] verb versus *separate* [-ət] adjective, *compliment* [-ment] verb versus *compliment* [-mənt] noun. Of stress, a number of examples have already been cited. A. A. Hill, in his note on Stress in recent English as a distinguishing mark between dissyllables used as noun or verb, *American Speech* 6.443-8 (1931), was of the opinion that new nouns could be derived from old verbs by the process, but not new verbs from old nouns. While it is true that examples of nouns from verbs are overwhelmingly more numerous, there are a few recent creations of verbs from nouns exhibiting both the length and stress features already illustrated. *Certificate* [-ejt] comes from *certificate* [-ət], and a favorite among linguists is the verb *to segment* [-ment] from *segment* [-mənt], where I waver between [ségment] and [segmént] in my own speech and have heard both pronunciations from others. I would also readily use the verb *to fragment*. The area of *-ment* is perhaps the most active one, with new pairs supported by old ones like *augmént-áugment* (only stress distinguishes these, as both have two long syllables), *régiment* [-ment]—*régiment* [-mənt] (length only), etc. See p. 160 footnote 59.

13. *Word* 12.252 (1956).

tion and the shift in stress : *I said áffect* [æf-] *the results, not éffect* [ef-] *them.*
It usually happens that a leftwise shift onto a weak syllable forces a spelling
pronunciation, for the vowel is generally shwa, difficult to stress even under
these unusual circumstances. So in place of *I didn't say* [kə́nvəᵗt], *I said*
[də́vəᵗt], we hear *I didn't say* [kánvəᵗt], *I said* [dájvəᵗt]. I have already
referred to our partial deafness to vowel quality in this position.

But we cannot say that absolutely no shift of stress to a weak syllable ever
occurs to the right of the normal stress. If it appears that we can make our
point only by going almost the limit, we may shift. For example, if someone misunderstands our word *latter* for *ladder*, we can interpose *I said lat-tér,
not lad-dér;* or if *albumin* meaning ' water-soluble protein in general' is misunderstood for *albumen* meaning ' egg white,' we may explain *I meant albumín,
not albumén.* The limit, the final step, would be to spell the words out.

Where we generally find the greatest freedom is with contrasting pairs in
which one or both members have as the contrasting element a long syllable.
First, the contrast may be satisfactory as it stands, and then there will be no
alteration at all save perhaps a slight lengthening : *I said whítefish, not whíting;
I said cát nap, not cátnip ; I said cátbird, not cátfish.* In the pair *cát nap* vs.
cátnip there is the contrast both in the vowels and in the length of the syllable,
and usually that is sufficient; but we also have the option of changing it to
I said cat náp, not cátnip, or even to *I said cat náp, not catníp* if more contrast
is needed, automatically lengthening as well as stressing the weak syllable in
catnip. Where both unstressed syllables are already long, as in *cátbird* and
cátfish, we are more likely to shift the stress than not : *I said catbírd, not cat-
físh.* An interesting sidelight is our ability nevertheless to use the unshifted
form, which then can serve as a test for the fusion of compounds. The
fact that we can use *cátbird* and not necessarily *catbírd* in contrast with *cátfish*
indicates that these compounds are fused, whereas the unlikelihood of our
saying *I want a piece of ápple pie, not a piece of ápple cobbler*, indicates that
ápple pie is less fused, despite the compounding forestress that one hears
from many speakers.

In the example *cát nap* and *cátnip* I pointed out that there is enough contrast already to make a shift unnecessary, since there is a difference both in
vowel and length of syllable. But if the vowel contrast is reduced, it may
be necessary to shift the stress even though there is a difference in length
of syllable. Take the word *chíckaree* meaning ' red squirrel' and the word
chícory meaning something you mix with coffee. I doubt that one would
hear *I said chíckaree, not chícory.* It would probably come out *I said chickarée,
not chícory.* On the other hand the related contrast between *bóotee* meaning
' small boot' and *booty* meaning ' swag' is sufficiently carried by an exaggeration of the plosive versus the flapped /t/, in addition to the length, so that
no shift of stress is necessary, though of course it is possible : *I said* [bútʰij],
not [búɾi]. It seems apparent that each separate contrast is judged to some

extent on its own merits, and while there are certain general tendencies, the speaker himself has wide latitude in deciding how much contrast is needed and how to work it out. The phonemicist would be interested here in the fact that it is not merely the presence of contrast but the quantity of it that has to be decided on. It has often been noted that minimal pairs are the exception in a language; the relatively bulky, multiphonemic distinctions that surround contrastive stress are the best illustration of this, as well as of the fact that not all contrasts are of equal rank. I offer a few more examples.

Where two words are paired—especially an affirmative and negative of the same concept—and the first undergoes shift, it may not be necessary for the second to undergo it also; there may already be enough difference between them. In the nature of the case this is most likely to happen when a word with a distinctive prefix onto which the stress has been shifted is the one that precedes. So we get utterances like *Avoid índigestible foods in your diet and favor digéstible ones;* it would be quite unsatisfactory to say *Avoid indigéstible foods in your diet and favor digéstible ones*—without some stress shift there is not enough contrast. It is possible but not ordinarily necessary to add a shift on the second word and say *Avoid índigestible foods in your diet and favor dígestible ones.* But if the words are longer, a shift of stress on just one member of the pair may not be enough. To paraphrase an example already quoted, we would not find an utterance like *The densest únintelligibility and the clearest intelligibílity* very satisfying, even though there is a shift of stress in the first word, the negative member of the pair. Without a second shift of stress the contrasting items are identical in seven syllables and different in only one,[14] so we prefer to say *The densest únintelligibility and the clearest íntelligibility* (or *intélligibility*). The matter of amount of contrast becomes even more critical where only one member of the pair is actually mentioned, or where some distance separates the two. Ordinarily a pair such as *stalactite* and *stalagmite* are sufficiently different, and we can easily have a sentence like *Is it a staláctite or a stalágmite?* But if one member stands alone but in implied contrast to the other, the normal difference is not enough. In a *New Yorker* cartoon[15] a man stands upside down, with feet on the ceiling, in a psychiatrist's office. The psychiatrist says to the man's wife, ' In a case of this kind, Mrs. Hall, our first concern is to persuade the patient that he is a stalag*mite*' (last syllable underlined in original). If the normal stress had been left on the word, ' persuade the patient that he is a *stalágmite*', the hearer would infer something like ' a stalagmite rather than an icicle '. The shifted stress implies ' What is in contrast here is not just another concept, but one

---

14. This is partly the result of the close match between the stressed *-bil-* of *intelligibílity* and the subdued but nevertheless prominent *-bil-* of *unintelligibility*, which reduces the contrast.

15. 14 April 1956, p. 36.

that is similarly named '.[16] In a radio ad for Carter's Little Liver Pills that ran for a long time,[17] the announcer emphasized the wisdom of *natural régularity*, in a context that implied an opposition to *irregularity*. A somewhat similar situation occurs when on saying the first member of the contrasting pair the speaker has not yet established a contrast, which may then come as something of an afterthought. By definition there would have been no shift on the first member, and in pairs identical except for a prefix it then becomes necessary to make a shift on the second. So one hears *Avoid foods that are indigéstible—favor those that are dígestible*. Had there been a shift on the first word, there might or might not have been one on the second. This works out most satisfactorily, of course, when the otherwise marked member of the pair—the one that has the distinctive syllable—comes last: *Favor foods that are digéstible—avoid those that are índigestible*.

A minor point concerns the order of the items when a long syllable is contrasted with a similar short syllable. In the pairs *sequins-sequence, raider-radar, confident-confidant*, and *surplice-surplus*, there is more satisfactory contrast when the word with the long syllable comes first, e.g. *I said séquence, not séquins*, rather than *I didn't say séquins, I said séquence*. In the other order, the intonational fall wipes out much of the differentiating quality of the long syllable.

We complete the consideration of stress-shift within words by looking at the two main situations in which it occurs. The first is that of contrast within a context of homonymic or near-homonymic conflict. It is well known that when homonyms occur a large part of the time in similar environments, an accommodation of some sort has to be worked out. One solution is the liquidation of one of the members of the conflicting pair. One never hears *succor* nowadays in the sense of ' help ', nor *quean* in the sense of ' hussy '. Another solution is to restrict the distribution of one of the members. The words *light* and *green* as antonyms of *dark* applied to fruit are both troublesome. If we wish to refer to *dark grapes* we may do so ; but it is inconvenient to refer to *light grapes* because we seem to mean grapes that are not heavy, and equally inconvenient to say *green grapes*—which is the true color of varieties like the Thompson and muscat—because it may be taken to mean ' unripe '. So we call them *white grapes*. This is of course the conflict of homonyms in general. It becomes specific to our problem when the speaker must counterbalance two concepts whose names are similar. Unlike the general situation, we have here a conflict of words that do not ordinarily occur in the same context ; it is a momentary collision, not a constant friction, and can hardly be solved by liquidating one of the members. The speaker can of course reject one of the members in favor of a synonym, which is a

16. I have since heard the identical shift on the *stalactite-stalagmite* pair, under circumstances similar to those of the cartoon. (Conversation recorded May 1957.)

17. E.g. Station WRCA, New York, 8 : 28 P.M., 18 December 1956.

kind of temporary liquidation; but the more usual recourse is to liquidate whatever excess of homonymy there may be by creating an artificial phonemic contrast.

The second situation is that of contrast within what Pike terms hypostasis, wherein language becomes an instrument to probe itself rather than some other part of reality. The linguist works in a constant frame of hypostasis, using bits of language as specimens rather than in their normal functions. In everyday conversation a remark such as *The word I used was x* or *What I said was x* is hypostatic. The relationship of this to quotative contexts is apparent: it is only a step from the quotative sentence *The name on the door was John Jones* to the contrastive sentence *The name on the door was John Jones, not Alfred Hayes.* The same pitch prominence highlights both instances of *John Jones.*

These two situations do not affect the shift of stress in the same way. The conflict-of-homonyms situation, where the speaker is only trying to keep his meaning clear, does not press so hard for abolishing similarity. An utterance such as *No, the plant they were studying was dógwood, not dógbane,* is normal. There is already enough contrast, in the two long but unstressd syllables, to make the distinction. But if the speaker is misunderstood and has to focus on the word itself, that is, to hypostasize, he will probably say *No, the plant they were studying was dogwóod, not dogbáne,* in which he sets his interlocutor right not only about the meaning but about the words.

A measure of the stability of stress position is how readily it yields to pressures to move it somewhere else. Though English words withstand the pressures pretty sturdily, the postion of the stress is not an absolute. A certain degree of instability shows up not only in situations of contrast like the ones we have examined, but also in another situation, which I shall only touch upon so as not to leave the impression that contrastive stress is unique. I refer to the still fluid tendency of the accent to formalize its position in the utterance. Most English declaratives of any considerable length have two marked peaks of pitch, one toward the beginning and one toward the end. There is a tendency to push them as far to these extremes as possible.[18] Usually this does not affect word stress, but sometimes it does, especially when two conditions are met—one is rapid or emphatic speech, the other is the presence at the accent point of some word with more than one long syllable. Take the word *ordinary*, with normal stress on the first syllable. A neighbor, inviting us to dinner, gave the following friendly warning:

---

18. It might be said that the accent here is emphasis on the meaning of the utterance as a whole rather than any of its parts. Cf. Bolinger, " English stress : The interpenetration of strata " 301-2, *Study of Sounds* (Tokyo, 1957).

Won't be e^{lab}ate, just be ordi^{na}ry,
or   ry,

with the accent shifted to the third syllable. Here are two more examples, the second of which was recognized as a lapse and corrected on the spot:

They ^{pushed} to get the Demo^{crat} that they want^{ed} and then endorsed Knight.

You were on the out^{skirts} of it.

The stress was shifted in *Democrat* and *outskirts*. The forestressing of adjectives, in phrases like *a cómplex problem* as against *The problem is compléx*, is of course well known.[19]

Up to this point we have been treating stress as if all words contained it, i.e. contained a potential for pitch accent, on equal terms. This is not quite true. Some words rarely receive the accent, and may properly be said to lack the phoneme of stress.[20] At the opposite extreme are words that are rarely used unless they do receive the accent. When a normally stressless word is accented, we may say that the phoneme of stress has been added, and the chances are that it is a contrastive stress. The articles are at this extreme. An utterance like *It's thé picture to see* or *He may be á doctor but he's not thé doctor I'd hoped to find* is pretty sure to be identified as containing a contrastive stress. Similarly with the prepositions in their usual position before the noun, e.g. *He came áfter the meeting*, if there is no following accent; but not when at the end of the utterance, e.g. *I didn't know what the meeting was abóut*. Even when before the noun with no following accent, however, an accent on a preposition does not necessarily mean an added contrastive stress, for one often hears emotionally motivated accents as in this sentence: *Thróugh the house, úp the stairs, ínto the bathroom, óver the rugs—those kids tramp*

---

19. An instance of how these two pressures can meet head-on occurred to me when I was about to voice the following complaint: *The other day those peanuts were only nineteen cents a pound; today they're thirty-nine;* I fumbled the accent on the last word. The aim was a contrastive accent on *thírty-níne*, such as might easily have worked in contrasting it with *twénty-níne*, but this would not work against the background of the already stress-shifted *níneteen* (shifted by reason of the phrase *nineteen cénts*, as against an unshifted *They cost ninetéen*), carrying an accent on the element that was not in contrast.

20. Unless stress is defined as prerequisite to "word" status.

mud in everywhere. Similarly with the personal pronouns, but always with the likelihood of contrastive stress, never the certainty. The utterance *Why don't you give it to mé?* is contrastive in response to *I don't know who to give it to,* but not contrastive, at least in the narrow sense, in response to *I don't know what to do with it.*[21] If at a lodge meeting someone inquires *Where's Joe?* and receives the reply *Oh, he's over at mý place,* there is a kind of residual contrastive stress on the possessive *my,* although in this setting there is no overt contrast with any other possessor.

The contrary case, where a word that normally gets an accent fails to get one, is significant for contrastive stress because then it usually happens that some other word has become contrastive.[22] We noted this interplay above in *He came áfter the meeting,* with de-accented *meeting.* The best examples are unmodified personal names. If instead of *He plays with Jóhn,* which might come in answer to *What does he do all afternoon?* and not imply any contrast, we hear *He pláys with John,* the inference of contrastive stress is almost inescapable. But again we can't be sure, for the accent may be emotionally motivated:

I like

John;   I don't know   w h y,   I   just o.

While we can with some justification speak of contrastive stress on words which normally carry no stress, the clues to it are less clear-cut than with words which do carry a stress and reveal their contrastiveness by shifting its position.

I sum up: (1) Contrastive accent is not phonetically definable. It is the same as other highlighting by means of pitch accent, though it leans to the extreme of the scale. (2) Contrastive stress is phonetically definable as a shift

---

21. In the latter case it is virtually interchangeable with *Why don't you make me a présent of it?*—no contrast on *me* in the other sentence, and no contrast on *present* here.

22. Cf. Newman 178: "the degree of emphasis is actualized not only by the intensity of the nuclear heavy accent itself but also by the contrasting weak intensity of the subordinate heavy accents occurring in the same prosodic context." (*Accent* substituted for *stress.*) In an utterance like [*Hey, Joe!*] *I want you to hélp me tomorrow* with no accent on *tomorrow,* there is no reason, in the absence of more context, to infer a contrast; but if generally unaccented *tomorrow* receives the accent, we almost necessarily do infer contrast. (Not with absolute certainty, however. In

Would you like me to help you?

Yes, I want you to help me tomórrow.

the accent merely covers something previously unspecified. Its function is the general one—which includes that of contrast—of marking the point of least redundancy.)

in stress, although one cannot predict with precision when, where, and how the shift will occur.   (3) Contrastive stress normally implies the presence of contrastive accent,[23] but the converse is not necessarily true.

---

23. A contrary example: in the following, the main accentual prominence falls elsewhere than on the contrasted words : *It would be a terrible blow to American unions if the conspiracy device again comes into common usage in the prosecution and persecution of unions* (*Frontier*, Sep. 1960, p. 12).

8

AMBIGUITIES IN PITCH ACCENT
Word 17.309-317 (1961)

One confirmation of a theory about a linguistic contrast is being able to predict where the contrast will break down. In § 5 of the " Theory of pitch accent " article I had found—under artificial conditions—a kind of situation where the contrast of pitch would fail to come through. The following describes an instance of this failure under conditions that were not contrived to reveal it.

The data on which this report is based came to light accidentally, in the course of looking for something else. The experience is a familiar one, where new insights are often gained by identifying the nuisances that disturb our predictions.

The source was a more or less routine assignment to a group of four graduate students, who were to discover for themselves, by canvassing native speakers, one way in which American English handles the stress of noun compounds made up of a verb plus an adverb. Each was to interview five speakers, who were to read aloud the following list of fifteen sentences:

1. What usually wins the game for him is that terrific follow through of his.
2. It's that eternal shrivel up that annoys me about thin bacon.
3. He got the quail in the sights of his gun; this time they didn't manage their usual scatter off and it was fatal.
4. What I'm afraid of is a sudden topple over, so let's watch our footing.
5. You'll note that after the first rotation the spindle does a kind of swivel around and then comes to rest.
6. If it hadn't been for that last-minute skin through of his, we'd never have made it.
7. That kind of cut in may do at a barn dance, but it won't do here.
8. With a spin around and a quick back away, he found himself suddenly, unexpectedly free.
9. Only a frantic wriggle loose saved the cub from the trap.
10. It was a premature sally forth.
11. With a dart up and a scurry off, the rabbit disappeared in the brush.
12. They had a regular set to.
13. It was a regular knock down and drag out at that party.
14. With a slow and bumbling lumber off, he made his way down the road.
15. With a streak off that was like greased lightning, the jet vanished.

The student was to keep a record of the stress pattern of each compound, that is, whether the adverb was heard as accented or as de-accented; an accent was expected on the verb in any case. There had been no previous discussion of pitch accent, nor was there any thought that the inquiry would provoke one.

As will be observed, the compounds used in the sentences are a rather special group, with a strong likelihood of having an accent on the adverb; this was shown in an earlier test.[1] So it came as a surprise that the twenty persons consulted were reported as de-accenting the adverb almost three-fourths of the time. Here are the figures:

		Accent only on verb	Accent also on adverb
1.	follow through	15	5
2.	shrivel up	15	5
3.	scatter off	16	4
4.	topple over	12	8
5.	swivel around	11	9
6.	skin through	18	2
7.	cut in	19	1
8.	spin around	19	1
9.	back away	16	4
10.	wriggle loose	14	6
11.	sally forth	9	11
12.	dart up	14	6
13.	scurry off	9	11
14.	set to	16	4
15.	knock down	18	2
16.	drag out	16	4
17.	lumber off	8	12
18.	streak off	15	5
	TOTALS	260	100

---

1. See p. 73. My feeling about these now is that they represent the same kind of nominalization that is almost universally applicable to one-syllable verbs: *dash, run, shake, spill, drive, turn*—even verbs like *sow, pray, send, pry,* and *dine* have been used in the sense of 'act of —ing.' Their tendency to equalize the semantic range of the verb and noun —in contrast to the semantic narrowing of forms like *leanto, turnout, brushoff, shoo-in, pérvert, cómbine*—suggests that they are the English counterpart of the infinitive used as a verbal noun (one, that is, which can have adnominal modifiers, as the infinitive with *to* cannot), though it does not have quite the dual status that it enjoys in some other languages since many polysyllabic infinitives cannot be used as nouns. It is not difficult to imagine it being said of a gossip that *He specializes in the quick tell,* or of somebody showing annoyance that *He has an irk on*; but *indispose* and *communicate* can scarcely be used as nouns.

An obvious guess was that the interviewers differed from their subjects, and perhaps among themselves, in their stress habits, and were reporting in some instances not what they heard but what they thought they heard. To check this, each one was tested on his own reading of the sentences. It turned out that 38 of the 100 votes for accent on the adverb were obtained by the person who herself accented the adverb about twice as often as she de-accented it; the others de-accented the adverb 50%, 59%, and 100% of the time.

There is nothing momentous about the fact that we listen with a pre-judiced ear. Were the percentages more evenly distributed among the eigh-teen compounds, they could be dismissed as nothing more than the margin of error to be expected from interpretations made by untrained listeners. But there are inconsistencies that appear to make no sense. Why should *knock down* and *drag out*, in the same sentence, give different results? Or *back away* and *wriggle loose*, and most of all *dart up* and *scurry off*, the second being one of only three instances where an accent was favored on the adverb?

This latter pair offers two clues. The first is that syllable structure may have something to do with the discrepancies. If we add separately those compounds (numbers 1–5, 8–11, 13, 17) which have one or more unstressed syllables between the two stressable ones, the figures are 144 for accent just on the verb, 76 for accent on both verb and adverb, a ratio of about two to one. Adding together the remaining compounds that have no unstressed syllable between, we get 116 to 24, or roughly five times as many favoring an accent on the verb only. With three exceptions (*spin around, dart up*, and *streak off*), this division also sets 16–4 as the dividing line—on one side are all items in which de-accenting the adverb is more favored, on the other are all items in which accenting it is more favored. The presence of the un-stressed syllable seems to make for hearing an accent on the adverb.

The second clue offered by the *dart up, scurry off* pair is that position in the utterance may count for something: *dart up* is medial, *scurry off* is directly before pause. If we check the compounds that occur before an unmistakable pause (4, 9, 11, 13, 14, 17) we find that with one exception they include all those in which the vote for accenting the adverb was eight or more; the totals are: verb only, 70, verb plus adverb, 50. Looking at the matter of position in a slightly different way, in terms of the relationship with the main accent in the sentence, we find that the compound coincides with this accent in items 1, 2, 4, 10, 11, 13, 14, 16, and 17, and that this set comprises all but three of the items in which the vote for accenting the adverb was five or more. In addition, the six compounds that occurred paired in one sentence point to the relevance of position with respect either to pause or to accent: in each such pair (8, 9; 12, 13; 15, 16) the compound occupying that position was biased in favor of accenting the adverb.

To verify the effect of position, a new set of sentences was devised and submitted to fifteen speakers, interviewed by three of the original four. The items to be tested were before pause, mostly at the end of the sentence, and received the main accent. I give the examples and the tallies; the first figure is for accenting only the verb, the second for accenting both verb and adverb:

1. What annoys me about thin bacon is that eternal shrivel up (5, 9).
2. We managed to make it to the goal post, thanks to that last-minute skin through (9, 6).
3. Quail are pretty sly. They'll wait until you're just ready to squeeze the trigger and then pull their favorite trick, a quick scatter off (8, 7).
4. She refused to dance with him after that rude sort of cut in (12, 3).
5. Then a back away (8, 7) and a quick spin around (4, 11). He was free!
6. The cub was saved from the trap only by a frantic wriggle loose (2, 13).
7. With a prick of the ears and a dart up (3, 12), the rabbit scurried off into the brush.
8. That party was a regular knock down (9, 6) and drag out (7, 8).
9. I watched him hobble down the stairs, and then his slow and bumbling lumber off (3, 12).
10. A straining upward as if against a thousand Lilliput leashes, then a dizzy gathering of momentum, and a final streak off (8, 7). The rocket was out of sight.

The shift in the preferences is striking. Disregarding *back away* and *knock down*, which are medial and lack the main accent, the adverb is now favored to receive an accent: to de-accent 61, to accent 88. Considering *back away* and *knock down*, we find that again when the compounds are paired, the one with the main sentence accent, before pause, has the adverb favored. And once more a separate accounting of those having one or more unstressed syllables shows those having it favoring an accent on the adverb 22 to 52, and those not having it favoring no accent on the adverb 39 to 36. The one interviewer who herself uniformly accented only the verb changed proportions radically from the first set to the second. Totaling just those items common to both sets (and again disregarding *back away* and *knock down*) her figures were 32 to 8 versus 16 to 24.

Part of the shift is undoubtedly due to the increased sensitization of the interviewers, but there is more than that. We have encountered two situations, one in which the thing the interviewers were directed to listen for is easy to hear, and one in which it is not. This assumes, of course, that with perhaps three exceptions (*follow through*, *cut in* and *set to* are evidently forestressed stereotypes for many speakers, like *comeon* and *fallout*), the majority of the compounds would, for most, call for an accent on the adverb. The interviewers, having been cued to listen for compounds and associating these with the multifarious forestressed type, expected the adverb to be de-accented, and wrote it that way whenever it was indistinct.

Our problem now is to examine why the speaker's intentions are " easier to hear" when there are intervening unstressed syllables and when the item in question carries the main accent and occurs directly before pause. Or, putting it the other way around, why without these advantages there tends to be ambiguity.

At this point I should interpose one or two definitions. I use the term *stress* to refer not to anything phonetically manifest but to a POTENTIAL. I would say that the word *compost* is stressed on the first syllable; but this would not mean that in any given instance the syllable *com-* was more prominent than the syllable *-post*. Indeed, in an utterance having the pitch profile of the following,

               do

What did you

                  with that compost?

com- and *-post* would be about equal in prominence, or lack of it. The pitch prominences, or accents, belong not to individual lexical items but to the utterance, which in this example happens to have conferred one on *do* and none on *compost*. Saying that *compost* is stressed on the first syllable is then to say only that if *compost* receives an accent, the syllable *com-* is the one that will be made prominent by it, as in the following:

                        com

What   do with that

      did you   post?

—where pitch accents are conferred on *what*, *do*, and *compost*. As this implies, a pitch accent is a relatively wide separation of a given syllable from the contour as a whole.[2]

To return to the two sets of conditions described—presence of intervening unstressed syllables and position relative to accent and pause—we find that both depend on the movement of pitch, and confirm predictions made in an earlier study. There it was noted that "the commonest supporting cue" for an accent "is flanking by unaccentable syllables."[3] In the first set, the

---

2. For the different kinds of pitch movement by which a syllable may be obtruded, see pp. 47–51.

3. See pp. 37–43. The flanking unaccentable provides a foil for the accent even when a competing syllable is undegraded, as happens with the *-post* of *compost*, the *can-* of *canteen*, etc. It is not a phonetic but a repertorial cue, one that comes from lexical storage. Our experience with citation forms and other instances where the word is in a favorable position with respect to accent (e.g., *This is called a canteen*) tells us that the syllable *can-* is unaccentable; and this helps to mark *-teen* as accented in an ambiguous situation like

Can

        te$^{e^{n?}}$

only examples in which an accent on the adverb was favored were *sally forth*, *scurry off*, and *lumber off*, all having a flanking unaccentable. When the speakers said, for example,

```
        scur    o
    a      ry  ff
```

the pitch-marking of *off* was unmistakable. Similarly with

```
        scurry
    a          o
                ff
```

where the holding of the unaccentable at the high pitch, away from *off*, left *off* free to be marked both as " skipped down to " and as " skipped down from." The only way to de-accent *off* is either to hold it at the pitch of *-ry* (with or without a slight rise) :

```
        scurry off        scurry o^ff
    a                  a
```

which is an unlikely intonation in this context, or to embed it at the lower pitch by dropping to *-ry* and not rising again :

```
        scur
    a
            ry off
```

which is the intonation that was probably used by those who actually did de-accent *off*.

But the monosyllables give trouble. The contour used for the thirteenth sentence of the first set was probably like this:

There are of course phonetic cues as well, in the shape of degraded syllables. Since accented syllables are always undegraded, any suggestion of degradation immediately marks the syllable affected as unaccented. Mostly degradation has to do with length— the degraded syllable is shortened and this in turn leads to a centralizing of the vowel. But there is no precise rule for this. In the object pronouns *him* and *her*, for example, at times there is neither loss of length nor centralization of vowel; here, the consistent mark of degradation is loss of the [h]. So in

```
          i              hi
    Kill  m   vs.   Kill  m
```

with no difference except [h] versus zero, the first is accented on *kill* (an " anticipated A " accent—see p. 49), the second on *him* (a normal A accent).

knock do^{wn} drag

reg

It was a   ular   and ^{o}ut at that party.

With no flanking unaccentable, it is diffiuclt to hear an accent on *out* even
when one is intended.   An accented *out* will have a significant drop in pitch
within the syllable, but an unaccented *out*, one that is merely a trailer for
drag, will have a certain amount of non-significant drop, and the difference
between the two may be too slight to notice.   There would be no ambiguity
if the contour were

drag o

and   ut at that party

with a marked drop in *out*, but the speaker would have to be more aroused
than the mood of the sentence seems to call for.   The pitch accent is lost
because the intonation interferes with it and there is no extra syllable to save
it.   The effect is even more serious in the last sentence of the second set,

final streak

a ^{o}ff

where the four interviewers agreed that they themselves could not tell the
difference between an accented and an unaccented *off*.   The difficulty is com-
pounded by the shortness of the checked syllable *streak*.   Even if the speaker
intends to de-accent *off* by making *streak* carry the drop in pitch, he can
hardly manage it because the syllable does not last long enough, unlike what
he could easily do if the words were

final zo
          o

a   m off.

These examples have enjoyed either position before pause, or the main accent,
or both, conditions which make for the possibility of a falling pitch on the
adverb.   Other conditions, which make the drop unlikely, introduce a new
kind of ambiguity.   This occurs between an utterance having a single B accent[4] with rising trailer and one having two B accents.   Pike's example of
the " extension of a long question "[5] illustrates the kind of situation where
this occurs, though he does not note the ambiguity :

re yes^{ter} day?

Was he ^{he}

Unless the pitch intervals are exaggerated, e.g.

---

4.   An accent marked by an upward skip in pitch. See pp. 50–51.

5.   *The intonation of American English*. Ann Arbor, 1945, pp. 59–60.

Was he here yes ter day?

it is difficult to tell whether *yesterday* is accented as a new, contrastive item, or unaccented and serving merely as the trailer of the accented *here*.   With the drop in pitch of the A accent[6] we can readily distinguish *wild flowers* from *wildflowers*,[7] and we are confident of the distinction because we base it on citation forms or definitions which use this accent:

They wi flow were ld ers.   They were wild flowers.

But without the drop, it is harder:

They were wild flow ers?

Similarly in a question like *Shall we send him to the electric chair?* it may be difficult to tell whether the speaker is one who treats *electric chair* as a fore-stressed compound or keeps a stress on *chair*.   Ambiguities like these are pervasive among all linguistic contrasts, and only prove once again how much we depend on redundancy.

Applying these observations to the third sentence of the first set, we see how even with the unaccentable flanking syllable the accent remained ambiguous:

their usual scatter of f

is the likeliest contour, and it is difficult to tell whether *off* is being accented or not.   The same is true of

with a spin aro u nd

which in spite of its flanking syllable was one of the two that favored the adverb least in the first set.   So also for

a reg ular knock do w n

6.   An accent marked by being jumped down from (and often up to or down to as well).   See pp. 49–50.

7.   Unless, of course, *wild flowers* has a contrastive accent on *wild* with *flowers* deaccented.

in both sets, for *streak off* in the first, and for *back away* in the second. As for *dart up* in the first set, I suspect that the slightly greater-than-average favoring of the adverb was due to a widening of the interval as a kind of sound-symbolic treatment of the word *up*,

```
                up
          dart
   with a
```

which made the possible accent on *up* more audible.

The class of words exhibiting the ambiguity that we have been studying is a small one, with only some of its members—those without flanking syllables—seriously affected, and others affected only in certain positions. Ambiguity of no wider scope than this can be tolerated. But its existence anywhere is a reminder that the language may have found a way to prevent it from occurring on a larger scale. Does English have devices that enable pitch accent on the whole to play its role more effectively? Do word classes, or sentence positions, tend to arrange syllables so as not to interfere with the hearing of accents? Is the lengthening of monosyllables in English to some extent compensatory, to allow for the lack of flanking syllables? In particular—having to do with the two-stress compounds investigated here— is it significant that such compounds more readily persist as verbs with a tendency to end position in the sentence, where the double accent stands out, than as nouns with a tendency to pre-position where the second accent is often lost? Evidence for the presence and survival value of some adjustments that English makes to surmount these difficulties will be offered in a sequel to this article.[8]

---

8. The sequel is " Pitch accent and sentence rhythm," pp. 139–180.

9

BINOMIALS AND PITCH ACCENT[1]
Lingua 11. 34-44 (1962)

We can conceive of prominence as due to a static scheme of values, or to a dynamic scheme.

A static scheme is some set of more or less fixed points or quantities. In terms of length, it might mean that a prominent syllable is twice as long as a subdued one; of loudness, that it is twice as loud; of pitch, that it is twice as high. There can be two, three, or more points along the scale, but a scale is essential.

A dynamic scheme achieves prominence through patterning. To be prominent, a syllable must be different from its neighbors, not just different from syllables that are more subdued. For example, on the static side, two or more syllables which are made prominent by length can stand next to each other. We know that they are prominent because they are substantially longer than other syllables in the environment, and it does not matter whether the contrasting environment is immediate or only proximate. Similarly, two or more syllables that are prominent by reason of high pitch can stand side by side. We know that they are prominent because they are substantially higher than other syllables that are near but not necessarily next door. But in a dynamic scheme, say one in which a syllable in order to stand out must be raised or lowered from adjoining syllables, it is not so easy for two or more to stand side by side. If the first syllable has already been raised in order to make it stand out, and the second also has to be raised, and the third also, the pitch can conceivably mount until it is out of hand. " Higher than " rather than simply " high " calls for more freedom to maneuver.

To avoid this trouble in a dynamic scheme of pitches, the directions of pitch can be alternated so that for each centrifugal movement there is a centripetal one. The centrifugal movement thrusts the syllable out; the centripetal one pulls the line back in readiness for another thrust. The most convenient arrangement of syllables, then, is one in which those to be made prominent alternate with those to be kept subdued.

" Binomials and pitch accent " offers some evidence that English words do tend to fall into position so that prominent and subdued syllables alternate with each other.

1. I gratefully acknowledge the help of Seymour Chatman, Pauline Marshall, Robert S. Pease, and Harold Tarver in administering the tests for this paper to their classes.

" Why do you always saý *Joan and Margery*, yet never *Margery and Joan?*" – .. " It just sounds smoother ".[2]

In his article on " irreversible binomials ",[3] those expressions on the order of *odds and ends, back and forth, fine and dandy*, Yakov Malkiel poses two questions. After noting (149) that " Modern English displays a very marked partiality to short plus long : either monosyllable plus (normally paroxytonic) disyllable, or two monosyllables of unequal size ", he goes on to ask, apropos of *bright and shiny* (note 43) with five phonemes each, " Does the fact that the latter spreads them over two syllables recommend it for the position of B [second member] ?" And in reference to cases like *pots and pans* he says (note 43), " Where the number of phonemes is equal, does the phonetic duration of contrastable sounds merit separate consideration?" I offer evidence that the answer to both questions is yes, and that the reason for it is a practical one.

Binomials are affected by what I believe is a general tendency in English to have prominent syllables flanked by subdued ones. This seems to be a requirement of prominence itself. The verbal population is as undemocratic as most societies ; it needs peons to give status to the aristocrats. I have shown elsewhere,[4] and will merely summarize here, that if an accented syllable is not flanked by unaccentable ones, it is liable to be misinterpreted. How the unaccentables work may be seen in the following examples :

Gregory   Greg
     Peck   ory Peck

Depending on whether *Peck* is detached in pitch from *-ory* or on relatively the same pitch level as *-ory*, it will be heard as accented or as unaccented. The first is appropriate to answer the question *What's his name?*, the second to answer *Which Peck do you mean?* If no flanking unaccentable is present, as happens in

John
    Peck

there is a problem. It can be partially solved in favor of making *John* the only accented syllable by giving *John* a turn of pitch :

---

2. Roman Jakobson, " Linguistics and poetics ", *Style in language* (Cambridge, Mass.; 1960), pp. 356–357.

3. *Lingua* VIII (1959), pp. 113–160.

4. " Ambiguities in pitch accent ", pp. 119–127.

John
Peck

But when we try to do the same for *Peck,*

John
Peck

we can only barely manage it because a syllable like *Peck* is too short. *John Jones* would give less trouble.

So we have two conditions that are met by the answers to Malkiel's questions. First, if a syllable is to be accented it is convenient to have it flanked by unaccentable ones. Second, in the absence of flanking unaccentables, it is convenient to have the accented syllable as open and sonorous as possible. A third condition is corollary to the second: since lengthening is easier directly before a pause, terminal position frees us to a certain extent from the other conditions. We will not be stopped from communicating if these conditions are not fulfilled, but we will have more trouble, and the forms that avoid the trouble will in the long run have more resistance. They will " sound better " to us. So, in our binomials, we look for the following three things: the accented syllable flanked by unaccentable ones; the accented syllable open and sonorous; the accented syllable in terminal position.

The binomials pertinent to our study are the ones that lend themselves to comparing each of the three conditions with its absence. Potentially interior position is a requirement, and the most suitable group for this purpose is that of the modifiers which may but need not be adnominal, that is, the adjective pairs like *fine and dandy, tried and tested,* and the potentially adnominal noun pairs like *peaches and cream (complexion), drum-and-bugle (corps).* We shall narrow our attention to this set.

Also we narrow the question of accent to the second member of the pair. The first member has a built-in unaccentable, practically always *and,* which automatically meets the first condition.

What of Malkiel's examples? He gives ten that are explicitly adnominal:

cold and obvious fact
long and beautiful friendship
strong and bitter (political factor)
a bows-and-arrows project
fresh and frisky pups

a red and yellow river
drum-and-bugle corps
furred and feathered creatures
up-and-coming writer
floor-to-ceiling window

In all of these the binomial ends in one or more unaccentable syllables.

Malkiel's text contains, *passim,* 45 additional examples that could be adnominal but are not expressly shown to be. All but four have terminal un-accentables, and of these, three end in voiced continuants: *tattered and torn, peaches and cream, merry and wise*. The fourth, *open and shut*, is clearly, like *early and late, down and out*, one of those exceptions to the rule that " can almost invariably be accounted for by powerful constellations of special circum-stances " (Malkiel, 150).[5]

Since the auditory effect of the binomials is what we are interested in, not the listener's recollection of tightly memorized forms, the best items for a test will be binomials that are original or at least not highly stereotyped. With this in mind I prepared the following set of stimulus sentences, which was administered as a test to a class of 17 undergraduate students. Their votes are given after each sentence:

TEST 1

Say the expressions over to yourself and then put a check mark beside one out of each pair, the one that seems to sound better to you.

1. a. He made a frank and candid statement. 16.
   b. He made a candid and frank statement. 1.
2. a. We looked out across the placid and calm water. 1.
   b. We looked out across the calm and placid water. 16.
3. a. I'd say that all we have are pretty slim and slender chances. 16.
   b. I'd say that all we have are pretty slender and slim chances. 1.
4. a. It was a lengthy and dull speech. 0.
   b. It was a dull and lengthy speech. 17.
5. a. She wrote me a curt and hurried note. 15.
   b. She wrote me a hurried and curt note. 2.
6. a. They were carried off, as captive and bound slaves. 1.
   b. They were carried off, as bound and captive slaves. 15.
7. a. What a loud and noisy company ! 16.
   b. What a noisy and loud company ! 1.
8. a. The signal was to raise a purple and red flag. 5.
   b. The signal was to raise a red and purple flag. 12.
9. a. Did you hear that wild and crazy uproar? 12.
   b. Did you hear that crazy and wild uproar? 5.

5. I list the remaining 41 : *black and sooty, blue and silver, bright and rosy, bright and shiny, bruised and battered, cheap and nasty, cloak and dagger, drawn and quartered, fast and furious, fat and fulsome, fat and sassy, fine and dandy, fine and fancy, free and easy, full and equal, gay and laughing, grim and weary, hale and hearty, high and handsome, high and mighty, hot and bothered, hot and healthy, hot and heavy, hot and spicy, lean and lanky, long and lazy, low and lonely, married or widowed, plain and fancy, poor but honest, pure and simple, rough and ready, rough and tumble, slick and slimy, slow and steady, straight and narrow, strong and stormy, tried and tested, true and trusty, warm and winning, wild and woolly.*

10. a. What senseless and mad slaughter ! 0.
    b. What mad and senseless slaughter ! 17.
11. a. It was a long and tedious speech. 16.
    b. It was a tedious and long speech. 1.
12. a. I listened to her quiet and soft voice. 1.
    b. I listened to her soft and quiet voice. 16.
13. a. Everyone remembers those sweet and joyous days. 17.
    b. Everyone remembers those joyous and sweet days. 0.
14. a. The chairman made a simple and short statement. 1.
    b. The chairman made a short and simple statement. 16.
15. a. It was depressing, that bleak and lonely countryside. 16.
    b. It was depressing, that lonely and bleak countryside. 1.
16. a. She's such a thoughtful and shy person. 2.
    b. She's such a shy and thoughtful person. 15.
17. a. From the summit you could see the broad, expansive plains. 17.
    b. From the summit you could see the expansive, broad plains. 0.
18. a. They all knew that sound. It was a dreadful and dire warning. 5.
    b. They all knew that sound. It was a dire and dreadful warning. 12.

The totals are 277 to 28, or 91% favoring the terminal unaccentable. One person was responsible for seven of the " wrong " votes and seven persons voted unanimously for the predicted choices.

Now we need to know whether listeners will react more favorably to having the binomial end in an oxytone if the following noun provides the flanking unaccentable, i.e., does not itself begin with an accented syllable. No dramatic reversal of the preferences is to be expected ; from the standpoint of pitch accent, more than one unaccented syllable between accented ones at best gives an extra margin of safety and at worst does no more than create a slight redundancy. Furthermore, to the extent that adnominals as a class are required to do service before all nouns, they will tend to adjust themselves to the prevailing pattern of noun stress, which is on the initial syllable, and this means supplying an unaccentable syllable before that stress ; a habit formed to meet a stringent requirement will be retained to some extent when the requirement is relaxed. Nevertheless, with some of the pressure off, the proportions should change. To get a rough measure of this I rewrote the first test altering only the nouns : *statement* became *appraisal*, *water* became *Atlantic*, *uproar* became *commotion*, etc. This was tried on a different undergraduate class of thirteen students, whose responses follow (I list the noun only ; the first figure indicates the preference for having the paroxytone the second member of the pair, the second, the oxytone) :

Test 2

1.	appraisal, 11–2	10.	destruction, 9–4
2.	Atlantic, 13–0	11.	oration, 13–0
3.	expectations, 13–0	12.	endearments, 9–4
4.	oration, 12–1	13.	adventures, 11–1
5.	invitation, 12–1	14.	explanation, 12–1
6.	defendants, 9–4	15.	ravine, 11–2
7.	assembly, 11–2	16.	young lady, 11–2
8.	device, 9–4	17·	Sahara, 13–0
9.	commotion, 11–2	18.	forewarning, 5–8

It will be noted that in No. 18 the preferences have been reversed, and that several others have been substantially altered. Totals show 195 to 38, or 84% and 16%. Almost twice as many preferred the oxytone last as did in the first test. (Our confidence in the reactions of the two groups is increased by the fact that in No. 18, and probably also in No. 8, both seem to have responded to some additional, unidentified force).

On the basis of the last of our three conditions, it would be expected that if the binomial were in terminal position, having or not having the unaccentable syllable at the end would be less important. Again, there should be a certain amount of carry-over of the preference for a non-oxytonic ending, but the different circumstances should produce results significantly different from those of the first test. Accordingly a third test was devised, using the same binomials as those of the first and second but now placed at the end of the sentence. Here is the test, and the reactions of a third class of 32 college undergraduates:

Test 3

(The instructions were the same. To save space, I give only the form with the non-oxytonic ending. The first figure represents the vote for that form, the second the vote for the same sentence but with the members of the binomial reversed.)

1. His statement was frank and candid, 19–13.
2. The water was calm and placid, 27–5.
3. Our chances look pretty slim and slender. 24–8.
4. The speech he made was dull and lengthy, 15–17.
5. The note she wrote me was curt and hurried, 14–18.
6. They were carried off as slaves, bound and captive, 22–10.
7. That company of yours is much too loud and noisy, 23–9.
8. It was a handsome flag, all red and purple, 18–14.
9. Why act so wild and crazy?, 19–13.
10. All war is mad and senseless, 16–16.

11. The speech he made was long and tedious, 31-1.
12. Her voice was like music, soft and quiet, 27-5.
13. I look back on those days, so sweet and joyous, 17-15.
14. The chairman's statement was short and simple, 30-2.
15. It was a depressing countryside, bleak and lonely, 18-14.
16. She's more expressive and outgoing than shy and thoughtful, 12-20.
17. Out to the distance spread the plains, broad, expansive, 26-6.
18. They all knew that sound—a warning, dire and dreadful, 22-10.

The totals are 380 to 196, the votes for the oxytonic ending making a sharp increase to 34%. In four items (4, 5, 10, 16) they equal or exceed the vote for the non-oxytonic ending. Terminal position clearly makes a difference.

Testing the condition of "openness and sonorousness" is a bit more difficult. Following would seem to be the syllable endings that ought to be considered, from "most open-sonorous" to "least open-sonorous": (1) a vowel, (2) a voiced continuant, (3) a voiced stop or affricate, (4) an unvoiced continuant, (5) an unvoiced stop or affricate.[6] These should be paired against one another,

We can take our hint from existing binomials like *drum-and-bugle corps* vs. *fife-and-drum corps* (Malkiel, note 35), but the requirement of minimal pairs makes nonsense words a virtual necessity. I accordingly devised the following test with imaginary pre-adjunct modifiers. It was administered to three classes of three different age levels: a class of 28 junior high school students (seventh grade), a class of 27 college undergraduates, and a class of five graduate students. I give the tallies with the examples, which have been de-randomized to get the predicted choice first.

TEST 4

	7th grade	Col. under-grad.	Grad.	Total
1. He lives in a plap and plam house.	11	14	4	29
plam and plap	17	13	1	31
2. They let out a crit and crin yell.	18	16	4	38
crin and crit	10	11	1	22
3. They say he has a shrick and shring way of talking.	17	17	3	37
shring and shrick	11	10	2	23
4. It's his flope and flobe anger that gets me.	15	15	5	35
flobe and flope	13	12	0	25

---

6. There are of course intermediate steps. Among the vowels, for example, an [a] is more open than an [i]; this would be relevant to a study of reduplicative forms such as *flimflam, tick-tock, rick-rack, shilly-shally, mishmash, fiddle-faddle, riffraff, seesaw, knickknack,* but I pass over it here.

	7th grade	Col. under-grad.	Grad.	Total
5. That kind of prook and proog dance never interests me.	16	18	1	35
proog and prook	12	9	4	25
6. It isn't safe to keep up that blit and bliz speed all the time.	14	12	0	26
bliz and blit	14	15	5	34
7. I don't like to have to decide these jode and jore matters so fast.	13	16	3	32
jore and jode	15	11	2	28
8. Let's have less of this drid and drin nonsense.	17	14	4	35
drin and drid	11	13	1	25
9. He said good-bye with a blite and blide wave of his hand.	16	13	3	32
blide and blite	11	14	2	27
10. Don't give me any of that trabe and trame nonsense of yours.	14	12	4	30
trame and trabe	12	14	1	27
11. They came at us emitting glog and glong yells.	12	21	3	36
glong and glog	16	6	2	24
12. Get rid of that flope and flome grin on your face.	16	18	5	39
flome and flope	12	9	0	21
13. Wasn't that a plap and plab meeting!	10	13	3	26
plab and plap	18	14	2	34
14. Suddenly a brip and briff gust of air hit us.	12	14	2	28
briff and brip	16	13	3	32
15. Our little dog greeted us with a sprit and spriss bark.	15	14	2	31
spriss and sprit	13	13	3	29
16. If only he didn't have such a prid and prill temper!	20	16	4	40
prill and prid	8	11	1	20
17. She gave him a skrit and skrill look and turned away.	20	22	3	45
skrill and skrit	8	5	2	15
18. His sarp and sarve accent gave him away.	15	13	1	29
sarve and sarp	13	14	4	31
19. It was a blyme and blye day.	19	15	4	38
blye and blyme	9	12	1	22

	7th grade	Col. under-grad.	Grad.	Total
20. We could hear the ploot and ploo cries of the bird.	16	15	2	33
ploo and ploot	11	12	3	26
21. He unsheathed that speen and spee blade and took after me.	11	13	1	25
spee and speen	16	14	4	34
22. For one steet and stee moment, nobody knew what was going to happen.	18	16	3	37
stee and steet	10	11	2	23
23. One more plab and plam answer like that and I'll let you have it.	15	14	3	32
plam and plab	13	13	2	28
24. It was a blyde and blye sorrow that overtook us.	10	14	4	28
blye and blyde	17	13	1	31
25. With a broat and broe moan, the stricken animal collapsed.	19	15	4	38
broe and broat	9	12	1	22
26. It was a sproam and sproe effort, but it failed.	11	12	3	26
sproe and sproam	17	15	2	34
27. They smeared it all over with swite and swy colors.	18	18	4	40
swy and swite	10	9	1	20
28. It was a snafe and snay insult, that's what it was.	13	16	4	33
snay and snafe	15	11	1	27
29. They celebrated a glawb and glaw Christmas.	10	13	3	26
glaw and glawb	18	14	2	34
30. The water penetrated every spreak and sprea crack.	13	16	4	33
sprea and spreak	15	11	1	27

Voting as
predicted:
1st group 444=53%; 2nd, 455=56%; 3rd, 93=62%; all, 992=55%
Contrariwise:
      390=47%;   354=44%;   57=38%;   801=45%

The majority favoring the predicted choices is small but consistent. Also it is normally distributed in terms of individuals, as may be seen by the following chart (note also in the chart that only two persons came within nine points of a " zero " score, but nine persons came within nine points of a " perfect " score): [7]

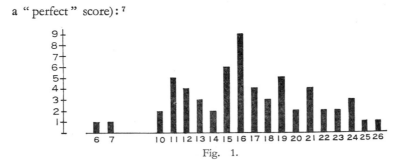

Fig. 1.

It is probably significant that the more mature the group is, the more pre-dictable are the reactions. Some of the contrary figures invite speculation. In No. 21, the suggestion of *keen* undoubtedly influenced the preference for *speen*—not even nonsense words exist in a vacuum. Possibly *flophouse* influenced No. 1, *sharp* No. 18, and *supreme* No. 26. Nos. 6 and 13 may reflect an ob-jection to the abutting homorganic consonants [z]-[s] and [b]-[m] with a difference of only one distinctive feature. I have no theory to account for Nos. 24 and 29.

If on the five-point scale mentioned above we compare the extremes, vowel or voiced continuant versus unvoiced stop (Nos. 1, 2, 3, 6, 12, 17, 18, 20, 22, 25, 27, 30), the figures are 424 in favor of the predictions and 295 against, or 59% and 41%—not impressively different from the over-all figures but different enough in the direction that would be expected to make the theory more plausible.

To sum up: Adnominal binomials unquestionably favor a non-oxytonic end-ing. This is particularly acute in adnominal constructions; a terminal oxytone is not particularly objected to (in fact, investigation will probably show that when emphasis is desired the terminal oxytone is preferred, where it does not have to fight some other pattern such as that of binomials). Binomials also seem to favor—at least in adnominal constructions—an ending that is relatively open and sonorous. I am inclined to think that there is more than coincidence in the fact that these characteristics are the same ones which, in the view of pitch accent, make speech more intelligible.

---

7. The figures 1–9 on the *y* axis indicate "number of persons"; those on the *x* axis indicate "number of cases in which predicted choices were favored." Thus e.g. nine persons favored the predicted choices in sixteen of the thirty pairs.

PITCH ACCENT AND SENTENCE RHYTHM

This study is published for the first time here. In it I bring together the material of the two preceding articles, along with other observations about rhythm, to show the struggle waged by pitch accent to arrange the phonetic bulk of utterances in a way that will serve its needs.

I. INTRODUCTION

Although Jespersen credits James Elphinston with having noted in 1765 the rhythmic shift of stress in words like *almost, forthwith, therein*,[1] for example, *the laws written therein* versus *the laws thérein written*, it remained for P. Fijn van Draat to conceive of the principle as one affecting not just pre-adjunct modifiers but the language as a whole, shifting stresses within words, causing one of two alternative constructions to be preferred over the other, contributing to the preservation of a form that might otherwise have been lost, leading to phonetic compensations where the beat would otherwise be disturbed, and making itself felt in other ways.[2] Unfortunately, having struck gold,

---

1. Otto Jespersen, *A modern English grammar on historical principles*, Vol. I, Heidelberg, 1909, § 5.42. Subsequent references to J. will be by volume and section, e.g. J I §5.42.

2. His views appear in three items, which I shall refer to as V1, V2 and V3: V1, *Rhythm in English prose, Anglistische Forschungen*, Heidelberg, 1910; V2, " Rhythm in English prose : the adjective," *Anglia* 36.1–58 (1912) ; V3, " Rhythm in English prose," *Anglia* 36.492–538 (1912). Unless indicated by section (§), the references will be to pages, e.g. V1 65.

Like most discoverers, Van Draat lays claim to too much territory. Where this is most obvious is in his treatment of the split infinitive, V1 103 ff, which he credits primarily to rhythm, overlooking the greater importance of immediate constituents. In *It was my intention to then ask her to marry me* (121) the position of *to* and *then* is not a mere unrythmical " mannerism " but an attempt to make *then* unambiguously temporal and unambiguously immediate to *ask*.

He is also—with his eyes fixed on poetic meters—too exacting. While he admits the anapest and the dactyl, he feels (V1 16–17) that the iamb and the trochee are what rhythmic prose is consciously or unconsciously striving for, and in a number of passages he treats the three-syllable meters as if they were somehow defective. For example, he praises Carlyle's " Amelia's love *makes* the burning sand *grow green* beneath him and the stunted shrubs *to blossom*," but depreciates Swift's " I fell on my knees and

Van Draat has no eyes for other metals in his diggings and when he comes across a pocket of pitchblende he tramps over it indifferently : observing with Sievers that a turn of pitch is often found as a phonetic compensation, he remarks, " For our investigation this . . . mode of avoiding the clash of two stresses is of no importance." (V1 12.)

While I am not prepared to claim that the vein thus overlooked is what transmutes the gold, I do believe that the two lie in intimate relationship to each other and must be studied together. Whether pitch causes rhythm or only takes advantage of its presence is hard to say. The best I can hope to do is to show how some of the oversights and overstatements about rhythm in prose can be corrected if we take into account the utility of the rhythmic pulse to pitch accent.

Most explanations of rhythm attempt to be either biological or esthetic or both. It answers to a poetic streak in human nature, or is simply the linguistic copy of the heartbeat, the length of one's stride, the skip of the eye movements in reading, or the limit of air that can be put out with a single exhalation. As for the esthetic argument, it is as hard to settle as whether a potter's wheel was invented to make things more symmetrical or to make them faster ; probably it was both, with a value to survival inherent in the enjoyment of what is workmanlike. Jespersen gives a practical reason (I 5.41) : " It is easier to alternate between strong and weak syllables than to pronounce several equally strong or equally weak syllables consecutively." But do we do it because it is easier, or is it easier because we do it, the habitual becoming easy in the process of acquiring the habit?

In an earlier article I attempted to show that unless there is a due proportion of accentable and unaccentable syllables, a pitch accent is liable to be miscued.[3] This I believe is one reason, if not the main reason, why accented and unaccented syllables tend to alternate with each other. I shall now try to demonstrate how rhythm serves pitch accent as an aid to practical communication.

---

made my master *to* understand as well as I could "—the *to* in the latter " interferes with the rhythm " (V1 8). He criticizes Sheridan's *Hére are thrée or fóur of ús páss our tíme agréeablý enóugh* (V3 502), which I have marked with the accents that he reads in to show the basis of his objection—two strongs, on *us* and *pass*, occur together, and he feels that it would be better not to omit the *who*. He reads his poetic prejudice into *John took ten, but I took thirteen* (V1 56), where he thinks that *thirteen*, with its variable stress, will appear as *thírteen* to preserve the trochee. In my speech it is regularly *thirtéen* when terminal and non-contrastive (*1913* could be either). All that is called for, as I shall try to demonstrate, is that pitch accent be aided by flanking unaccentable syllables ; one is usually enough, but a little redundancy does no harm—recognizing this would have saved him a struggle to account for the alternation of *in* and *into*, V1 36–43.

3. " Ambiguities in pitch accent." See this volume pp. 119–127.

II. PATTERNS OF ALTERNATING STRESS

In general, the tendency to separate accented syllables by unaccented ones manifests itself in three ways : (1) By backshifting the stress.[4] This affects pre-posed items (particularly adjectives) of more than one syllable which in other positions may be oxytonic. (2) By causing a form to yield to a companion form—often a cognate one—which is non-oxytonic. Again it is adjective pairs that are most often affected. (3) By replacing one construction with another. Satellite-plus-head combinations are the most typical examples here too, but not the only ones. Since the same principle affects all of them, there is no need to list them strictly by syntactic type.

1. Backshifted stress. This is found most readily among modifiers whose stress may be characterized as " unstable " to begin with. I use this term only as a suggestive label for words containing more than one long, undegraded syllable.[5] The typical case is the compound :[6]

---

4. Less frequently by moving the stress the other way. For example, there are two ways of handling the following sentence tonally : *A lot of it is not just plain ordinary correspondence.* We can bend the syllable *plain* so as to make it cover the pitch inflexion :

		pla		or		pon	
just	in			dinary	corres		dence

or we can shift the stress on *ordinary*—this is more apt to happen in rapid speech :

		plain		nary		pon	
just		ordi			corres		
						dence	

Another example, overheard from a questioner at a lecture : *a rélatively smáll inflúence.* The same speaker a moment later said *ínfluence.* The stress on this word is unstable ; I have recorded the following, all from different speakers : *his unbiased, unprejudiced, uninflúenced opinion* (bank president) ; *has inflúenced other countries* (newscast) ; *They've gót to have been inflúenced by that course* (linguist). The last speaker, about an hour later, again said *inflúenced* and immediately corrected it to *ínfluence.* Instability makes for rhythmic shift.

5. The type distinguished by G. F. Arnold, " Stress in English words," *Lingua* 6.221–267, 397–441 (1957), as the basis for his definition of stress. Arnold's work is of interest here for two reasons : he assigns the difference between " loud " and " medial " to pitch (p. 226 and passim), which implies a recognition of pitch accent ; and he appeals to the principle of rhythm in describing the sequence of stressed (i.e., long and undegraded) syllables within words. See e.g. p. 437 for types a, b, and c, words in which the stress may shift when preceding an accented syllable.

6. The instability is reflected in the status of the first element of the compound, which is sometimes accented, sometimes not, when the second carries an accent. Accented :

The problem was clear-cút; a cléar-cut próblem
This variety is long-éared; a lóng-eared jáckass
See how red-nósed he is; the réd-nosed réindeer
such hard-bóiled (hárd-boiled) aggressiveness; a hárd-boiled égg
a firm-búilt (fírm-built) reactor; a fírm-built hóuse
The sky was overcást; an óvercast ský
The places are far awáy; fár-away pláces
He's good-nátured; a góod-natured féllow (J II 14.11)
That father of yours is no góod; that nó-good fáther of yours
The sizes were cut-dówn ones; those cút-down sízes
This cereal is whole-gráin; a whóle-grain céreal
He lives in New Yórk; He takes the Néw-York Céntral[7]
He's all ríght; an áll-right féllow
I say I cannót (cánnot); I cánnot sáy[8]

Compound adverbs behave similarly when used prenominally or in some other construction directly before an accent:

He went upstáirs; an úpstairs báth
There's a lot of room overhéad; a lot of óverhead róom
" Are you ready? "—" Almóst (álmost)"; I'm álmost réady[9]

Daniel Jones lists *red-hot*, *second-hand*, *inside*, *greengage*, *inland*, and *uphill* as

Unaccented:

See p. 172, discussion of the " sacrifice " of an accent.

7. And so with *Colorado*, *Alabama*, *Mississippi*, and other names having an undegraded syllable before the stress. In *Pénnsylvania Ráilroad* we note a tendency to overshoot the mark. *Pennsylvánia Ráilroad* would provide a buffer between the accents, but there is a backshifting nevertheless, imposed by the larger sentence pattern; see pp. 161–164, and cf. Daniel Jones, *An outline of English phonetics*, New York, 1956, § 922, and Wiktor Jassem, " Stress in Modern English," *Bulletin de la Société Polonaise de Linguistique*, Fascicule XI (1952), p. 28 note 44. But observe how the accent is jockeyed when it receives a push from the other direction: *the máin Pennsylvánia ráilroad* vs. *the príncipal Pénnsylvania ráilroad* (the latter could vary).

8. V1 28 lists *onto*, *into*, *until*, and *always*, which for most speakers are now fixed and would not shift.

9. But possibly *I'm almóst ready*, when *ready*, being repeated, is de-accented.

examples of the phenomenon, which he calls "rhythmical variation."[10] J I 5.42 adds *overland, oversea, overnight, afternoon,* and *farewell.*[11] His examples *sound-asleep steamboats, fast-asleep baby, half-alive people,* cited (II 14.17) to prove that forms like *asleep* can occur prenominally, really only prove that a compound pre-adjunct will shift its stress, for these are normally *sóund-asleep, fást-asleep,* and *hálf-alive* in this position. Compound numerals are affected similarly:

> The books number twenty-fíve; I have twénty-five bóoks
> There were sixtéen; I said it síxteen tímes[12]

Where we make a distinction between compound with preposition (*His clothes look slépt in*) and compound with adverb (*His ears look lopped óff*), that distinction disappears prenominally:

> Those slépt-in clóthes of his
> Those lópped-off éars of his

It is as hard here as anywhere else to draw the line between compounds on the one hand and derivative with isolable prefix on the other. The latter, when the prefix is a long syllable (normally a mark of isolability), may readily backshift:

> The word is misspélt; a místspelt wórd
> Those traits are inbórn; ínborn tráits
> The package was untíed; an úntied páckage

V2 §§ 15–17 points out *unchánged caréer* vs. *únborn spírits,* and notes that when a preposition serves as buffer, the stress does not shift: *unhéard-of wonders.*

A few words are unstable by virtue of frequent contrastive use: *his soon considerably íncreased stáff,*[13] *dísplaced pérsons.*[14]

Other words with a prior long syllable likewise shift:

> He's so robúst; a róbust féllow
> The colonel was iráte; an írate cólonel
> The problem is too abstráct; an ábstract whát?
> Ábsolute pówer corrupts absolútely
> The model is obsoléte; an óbsolete módel[15]

---

10. *Op. cit.* § 954.

11. His example *halfway house* does not necessarily shift, since *house* in this combination is normally de-accented; at least, in my speech I would say *halfwáy house.*

12. This should not be confused with shifts due to contrast: *Did it happen in 1910? —No, in nineteen sixtéen* vs. *Did it happen in 1915?—No, in nineteen séventeen.*

13. *Language* 37.192 (1961).

14. Cf. Jassem pp. 44–45.

15. So in my dialect, though the dictionaries give *óbsolete* for both positions.

This river is the Oságe; the Ósage Ríver
He lives in Kankakée; a Kánkakee résident
The curtain is bambóo; the Bámboo Cúrtain[16]
That lawyer's a millionáire (míllionaire) ; a míllionaire láwyer
The chair is rattán; a ráttan cháir
She cooks at the cantéen; the cánteen cóok
The surface is convéx; a cónvex súrface
How augúst he is!; an áugust pérsonage
Too much routíne; a róutine tásk
The figures are too ornáte; órnate fígures
He's Chinése; a Chínese lámp

Similarly words which may or may not have a prior long syllable according to dialect, but shift apparently with little regard to dialect:

Sell the excéss (éxcess) ; éxcess gárbage [əksés, éksɛs]
He has a mustáche (místache) ; místache wax[17] [məstǽš, mʌ́stæš]
The reasons are too compléx (cómplex) ; a cómplex réason[18]
    [kəmpléks, kámplɛks]

The echo of an earlier long syllable, degraded since, is perhaps to be
detected in similar backshiftings noted by J I 5.53: *obscene, occult, contrite,
inverse, serene, extreme, impure.* Some of these, and others like them, are still
normal in my own speech: *impure wáter, for díverse réasons, a cóntrite héart*

---

16. Cf. Jones §§ 928–932. So for *Waterloo, inbred, etc.* While the *Ámen Córner* ex-
emplifies the shift I am illustrating here, *amen* differs from Jones's other examples in that
—for my speech at least—the stress is otherwise only on the second syllable, no matter
how much I may lengthen the first. So while for me

puts the accent on either syllable,

puts it only on the second, as the inflexion on *-men*, both times, shows.

17. Here the pattern is so unstable—I have heard the same speaker use *místache* and
mustáche only a sentence or two apart—that even de-accented *wax* is sufficient to re-
pulse the accent.

18. Consider the embattled adjective *expert*, which for most American speakers has
shifted from [ɪkspə́t] to [ékspət], regardless of position. Was Fowler responsible for
propagating the puristic insistence on *expért*? See *Modern English usage* s.v. " Noun and
adjective accent."

(the latter only in verse).[19] But while it is not so hard for a stress to shift to the left onto a degraded syllable as for it to shift to the right,[20] for the most part we do not get a backshift onto a degraded syllable. We must then either put up with juxtaposed accents or find some other way out of the difficulty. Shakespeare's *lick ábsúrd pómp* would now be *absúrd* in prose utterance for speakers of my acquaintance. I would say *extréme únction*,[21] *insáne áctions, He gave me an expréss nó*. A low-frequency word I might avoid, whether or not it had a long first syllable: *The essay was too prolíx*, but not *a prólix éssay and probably not *a prolíx éssay.

Similar to combinations of modifier and head are proper names consisting of two elements, of which the most typical are given name plus surname. So, with intervening weak syllable, we get *Iréne McDermott*, but without it *Írene Cárstairs*; *He lives in Tennessée* (or *Ténnessee*), but *Ténnessee Williams*. While English nouns are notorious for their tendency to backshift the stress, nowhere is this tendency so marked as with given names. Of the 385 polysyllabic masculine names listed in the Webster *Collegiate*, Fifth Edition, only six (*De Witt, Eugene, Gerard, Ibrahim, Jerome, Leroy*) are stressed on the last syllable.[22] This is eloquent testimony to the effect of combination with generally forestressed or monosyllabic surnames. Compare also the *Árchduke Férdinand* and *Férdinand the Archdúke* (or *Árchduke*).

2. *Companion forms.* The type of adjective most frequently cited in discussions of what can and what cannot precede the noun is the one containing the prefix *a-*. Jespersen lists (II 14.15) *asleep, awake, afloat, aswim, aglow, ablaze, aslant, agape, aquiver*, etc., pointing out that the limitation to predicative use is due to their origin as prepositional phrases; but others (14.16), such as *afraid, aghast*, and *averse*, have been influenced analogically.[23]

There is another reason too—also related to their origin—why these forms resist pre-position: their semantic range. We do not normally say *I saw a biting dog* (there are no problems of accent here) unless we mean one that

---

19. For other examples from Shakespeare, see Helge Kökeritz, *Shakespeare's pronunciation*, Yale, 1953, pp. 332–339.

20. See p. 109.

21. Pronounced *éxtreme únction* in a production of G. B. Shaw's *Don Juan in Hell*, TV Play of the Week, 3 Sep. 1961.

22. And *Ibrahim* is obviously an unassimilated loan, while *Jerome* for British speakers is stressed on the first syllable as is *Leroy* for many Americans. *Eugene* has a sufficiently undegraded first syllable to shift the stress: *Éugene Ádams*. As a curiosity I list *for Ývonne's sake, I'd*... "Meet McGraw" TV program, 11 July 1961.

23. Jespersen's *averse* also belongs among his examples in 14.14, which avoid prenominal position because of calling for a complement: *averse* is normally specified by what one is averse *to*. So with *replete with, instinct with*.

habitually bites.[24]   The range of the *a-* words parallels that of the *-ing* words of the progressive construction: *He was asleep, He was a-sleeping*; both refer to something momentary. Pre-adjunct modifiers, however, are used to CHARAC-TERIZE.   If we say *a sleeping figure* or *a dying man* we have in mind not just the act of sleeping or dying, but the way one looks under those circumstances. Where a word such as *aloof* comes to be used prenominally, we note a shift in the semantic range: *an aloof person* is one who is characteristically this way.[25] *Two thoroughly alive bears came at us* categorizes the bears—they are not the "kind" of bears we expected.   *A half-asleep child* is one who is sleepy-eyed (and *half-asleep* can overcome its accentual problem by suppressing the accent on *asleep*).   *Awry* has shifted its stress as well as its semantic range: *orey-eyed.*[26]

So when we examine the related forms which are used instead of the *a-* ones prenominally, we must bear in mind that the meaning is not usually the same, and replacing the *a-* form with the other one is due only partly, if at all, to accent.   Here are some examples:

ablaze—blazing	alive—living
aslant—slanting	alike—similar
akin—kindred[27]	alert—watchful

But no semantic snag lies in the way of past participles, which are freely used prenominally and offer the best examples of companion forms selected for stress:

The case is proved; a proven case
The sailor is drunk; a drunken sailor
They had hid(den) the treasures; hidden treasures
He had broke(n) the stick; a broken stick
They've bought the goods; boughten goods
They've fought the field; foughten field
His skin had shrunk; shrunken skin

---

24.   "Particles...are construed before nouns to denote quality...when they reject the idea of time and denote something customary or habitual, rather than a transient act or state." Goold Brown, *The grammar of English grammars*, New York, 1884, p. 415. A striking example is the stereotyping of *mad: The mad king* 'insane'; *He was mad* 'angry.'

25.   So it is with *a bunch of aware men and women*, in *Frontier*, April 1962, p. 10.   V2 § 19 overlooks the semantic restrictions and cites *an imperial, aloof politeness* as an example of a suitable prenominal use, supposing that *the aloof people* is unacceptable.   It is true that the latter is more displeasing, but it is not excluded.   As elsewhere, Van Draat depends too much on examples from verse, despite the title of his work.

26.   H. L. Mencken, *The American language, Supplement One*, New York, 1945, p. 266.

27.   "They have an akin grammatical structure," Felix M. Keesing, *The Philippines*, Shanghai, Kelley and Walsh, 1937, p. 61.

He was bound to do it; bounden duty
The head was misshaped; a misshapen head
The garden was sunk ten feet below the surrounding area; a sunken
garden

The *-en* suffix maintains various degrees of attachment to its companion term. In some cases it has gone its own way to the point of becoming an independent adjective, displacing the other form even in predicative position for certain senses: *These biscuits are beaten* (probably even for the person who would say *had beat*); *He looks stricken*; *Their hoofs are cloven*; *a tree that was writhen and bare*. Also, dialects differ: *boughten bread*[28] for some may be *stóre-bought bréad*, with another solution of the accentual problem, for others; and *drunk* as a prenominal has made its way in, partly through the abbreviation common to newspaper headlines.

The *-ed* suffix exhibits similar redundant forms selected at least partly by accent. V2 § 22 offers *lighted window* vs. *moonlit scene*. Other examples:

His knee is bent; on bended knee
The main had burst; a bursted main
These drawers have never fit(ted) very well; fitted drawers
She had knit(ted) the sweater; a knitted sweater
They were wont to ride; their wonted ride

But the *-ed* suffix is historically more complex. This is not so much because of its two separate origins (*-ed* etc. participle, e.g. *strung*, and *-ed* adjective, *stringed*[29]), which have now virtually merged, but because of an uneven phonological development that seems in part to underlie the participle-adjective contrast. We can distinguish three sets of endings to verbal stems: (1) /t/ and /d/; (2) other stops and affricates, and clusters not ending in /t/ or /d/; (3) continuants and vowels. The treatment of (1) is completely uniform; it retains the *-ed* as a separate syllable regardless of its function: *excited, fleet-footed, breaded, one-handed, double-breasted*. As there is no accentual problem in this class, we are not concerned with it.

The status of (2) and (3) is also settled as far as verb uses are concerned; the *-ed* is not a separate syllable: *hatched, budged, financed, barged, scorched, lisped, scathed*. But there are a number of vestiges of *-ed* adjective as a separate syllable in (2), and a few, mostly archaisms, in (3). It appears that the two forces, phonological (avoidance of terminal clusters) and accentual (avoidance of juxtaposed accents in pre-position) have combined to preserve them: *dogged, ragged, crabbed, wicked, wretched, crooked, rugged, jagged, aged, learned,*

---

28. H. L. Mencken, *The American language*, New York, 1955, p. 429.
29. See H. Poutsma, *A grammar of late Modern English*, Groningen, 1926, Chapter 57, §§ 42–43; also J II 15.34,35.

naked. Others, however, are wavering and tending more and more to reduce the syllable: *hooked, peaked, striped, streaked, (bow-)legged.* Even *aged* does not for all speakers maintain the distinction between *an aged man* and *aged wine.*[30]

Comparing the types where the separate syllable is vigorously maintained (e.g. *wicked*) and the ones where it is being lost (e.g. *striped*), it appears that we must reckon with a third force, separate from the phonological and accentual ones but ultimately with accentual ties. This is the abundance of adjectives in graphic *-id*, phonologically identical to those with graphic *-ed*: *solid, squalid, timid, rigid, putrid, pallid, stupid, fluid, acid, vivid, morbid, turgid,* The *-ed* adjectives that bear least resemblance to anything derivable from a verb or a noun used as a verb have assimilated themselves to this set, and thereby clung to their extra syllable.[31] Thus *wicked* does not relate to any verb *wick* nor, semantically, to the noun *wick*. *Crooked* does not relate to the verb *crook* for most speakers, who have stopped using the verb, and the noun *crook* is not normally converted to a verb. *A learned person* relates better to *teach* than to *learn*, if viewed as a participle: *a taught person*. On the other hand, *striped* can as readily be 'having been striped,' from a verb *to stripe*, as 'having stripes': so with *streaked*. *One-armed* suggests a verb 'to provide with arms.' It is these *-ed* words that are assimilating themselves to the verbs and losing their extra syllable.[32]

The support given by the *-id* adjectives raises the question of why these adjectives have not undergone the same phonetic erosion as the forms in *-ed*. It would seem that *rigid* and *ridged, squalid* and *squalled, horrid* and *whored* must have had about equal chances of losing the syllable. This brings us

---

30. Gen. Douglas MacArthur in his Republican keynote address, 7 July 1952, referred to the *aged* [ejdžd], 'old people.' The reduction of *-ed* has been perhaps the most striking phonological change in English in the past century and a half. Poutsma (Part II, § 2, p. 569) quotes Bradley to the effect that "Within the memory of living persons it was still usual in the reading of the Bible or the Liturgy to make two syllables of such words as *loved* or *changed*, which are now pronounced in one syllable." As a child I gave *striped* and *streaked* two syllables each. The disintegration continues; I have heard *jagged* pronounced as one syllable by a twelve-year-old.

31. It is likely that the same family of adjectives is at least in part responsible for the pattern that we observe in certain *-ed* words—those with stem ending in a stressed syllable—when they receive the *-ly* adverbial suffix: regardless of the consonant at the end of the stem, these keep *-ed* as a separate syllable. Examples: *advisedly, assuredly, markedly, aggrievedly, designedly, reportedly, avowedly, confessedly, unconcernedly, restrainedly.* Cf. Poutsma pp. 569–570 and Jones p. 145 note 10. With the complete freedom of *-id* adjectives to take the *-ly* suffix, the less readily adverbialized *-ed* forms were probably assimilated to them.

32. As for *peaked*, in its one-syllable pronunciation there is probably the influence of spelling, the same thing that for some speakers coverts short-[lajvd] to short-[lɪvd]. Cf. Poutsma p. 561.

back, I think, to accent. The forms with a high frequency of prenominal use needed the extra syllable and kept it.[33]

As for -*ed* forms of the third class—those with stem ending in a vowel or continuant—the few that have kept the extra syllable are mostly archaisms, kept half alive by ties with the ritual: *blessed, beloved,* and the minced oaths *cursed, dashed,* and *deuced,. Hallowed* barely retains its third syllable in the Lord's Prayer; elsewhere it has two: *hallowed ground.* Others have lost the extra syllable: *creased, two-faced, wreathed.*

Outside the verb system and the old *a-* phrases, we find sporadic examples of synonyms whose selection is influenced by accent:

áutumn flówers; the fáll seméster (cf. V2 § 32)
He was contént(ed) ; conténted cows
a more incénsed young lády; an ángry mán[34]
a glád occásion; a háppy dáy
He went and did it quick(ly) ; He quickly went and did it
They blessed war outright; Few clergymen outrightly blessed war[35]
It is fast becoming a nuisance; It is rapidly getting to be a nuisance
the jóurney óut; the óutward (óutgoing) jóurney[36]
a múch-repéated (óft-repéated) phrase; a fréquently úttered phrase
an intént regárd; a wátchful gáze
This number is less; the lésser númber
sóund asléep; He was sóundly thráshed (cf. V1 98)

These differ in the kind and degree of restrictions imposed on them. The non-oxytonic forms can for the most part be freely used in all positions; the extra syllables do no harm accentually. In some, there is a restricted distribution with a slight difference in meaning: *The waters fast receded (fast ebbed* is unlikely) combines an evaluation (pleasure, approval, surprise) with a fact; *The waters rapidly receded* is neutral. In others, the avoidance of juxtaposed accents may be stronger or weaker: *It was a glad day* is more likely to be

---

33. Was there also possibly a resistance to homonymy in pairs like these?

34. Conflict of homonyms (*íncensed* 'having incense') bars a backshift here.

35. *Progressive*, June 1950, p. 21.

36. Probably other uses of -*ward* likewise. As for *out*, we find other resistances to pre-position besides that of accent. First, its frequent use as a prefix creates a homonymic conflict. Second, it shares with *in* (*on, back,* etc.) and the *a-* words a tendency to retain an adverbial, non-characterizing meaning, so that while *the trip out*, reflecting the verbal *to travel out*, is normal despite its accent, *the out trip* is not; this excludes *the out retreat*, even though there is a buffer syllable. The word *off*, on the other hand, has developed a characterizing meaning: *an off day* 'a bad day'; *an off brand* 'a non-standard brand.' As to how much of the failure of this class of words to acquire a characterizing meaning may have been due to accentual resistance to pre-position in the first place, we can only guess.

avoided, in my speech, than is *It was a glad day for all of us*—in the latter, *day* does not occupy one of the two principal accent positions, being displaced from it by *all*.[37] *Content* and *contented* differ much as do *alive* and *living*. A speaker may deliberately aim at a spondee effect ; *twice-told tales*. But accent functions even among the exceptions. If *fast becoming* is a stereotype, perhaps stereotyping itself is a result of accentual compatibility; V2 § 10 points out that of the set phrases with noun plus adjective, all early borrowings—*time immemorial, heir presumptive*—are rhythmic, and only the later, unassimilated loans—*prince regent, court martial*—are likely to deviate. If *content* assumes a shade of meaning not associated with prenominal position, it is likely that failure to be used in that position—as a result of accent—is partly the cause of the meaning.

Related to the choice of synonyms for the sake of accent, especially to the selection of one or the other of two cognate forms, is the power of accent to arrest the phonetic erosion of a word. V1 68 points out the two competing forms of *heaven*, [hɜbm] and [hɛvən], the first of which would be encountered in *Our Father Which art in Heaven* and the second in *Across high heaven streaming*. Terminal position requires no intervening syllable. We note the same difference in the de-accented

```
                        do
    What    are    you
                            ing     there    for    Heaven's    sake?
and the accented
```

```
                                sa
                        Hea
        Well    for         ven's
                                    ke!
```

Jespersen (I 5.41) gives *through* and *thorough* as a pair whose differentiation, once rhythmic (*through thick and thin*—*through* de-accented ; *a thorough beating*—*thorough* prenominal and accented), has now been formalized.

V2 § 38 promised a study on "Rhythm and synonyms," e. g. *ancient* vs. *old*. I have been unable to find it.

3. Alternate constructions. Satellite elements are so regularly placed before their heads in English that variations due to accent are difficult to find.[38] One form of accommodation is to insert a more or less otiose element:

37. But see p. 177 for B accent plus A accent with such a phrase as *glad day*.

38. As a curiosity I undertook to find what would happen in Spanish, where the pattern of pre-posing adnominals is almost as weak as that of post-posing them in English. For the purpose I used names of colors, as this set comprises both oxytones and paroxytones. It turned out that a combination like *la verde (morada, roja, negra) casa* was judged quite acceptable, as was also a plural like *las azules casas*, but the singular *la azul (gris) casa* was rejected. In this case, the requirements of accent were strong enough to obliterate the conflicting pattern.

an aloof (alert, adept, remiss) person → an aloof etc. kind of person
It's a compact book[39] → It's a compact little book
a half hour → (a) half an hour
without doubt → without a doubt[40]
*pal mine → pal o' mine (but mother mine, lover mine, father dear)
Outside these I have no preference → Outside of these etc.[41]
Beware the Ides of March → Beware of Brutus (V3 534)

While they do not qualify as extant alternating constructions, we find cases parallel to these where a surviving form seems to owe its vitality to its suitability for accent. If *a little bread* was once *a little of bread*, as *Oxford* surmises, then *a little bread* and *a bit of bread* probably owe their contrast in form to the accentual clash in *a bit bread*. So with *a dozen eggs* but *a gross of eggs*. V3 523–526 instances the now obsolete *a morsel bread* vs. *a piece of bread*. The supplanting of *near* by *nearly* and *oft* by *often* may have accentual ties.

The *to* with the infinitive qualifies as an accentual insertion in a few rare cases. V1 86 ff shows, on the basis of about 300 quotations, that virtually all instances of *dare* without *to* are found in constructions where accents are already separated (often by an intervening *not* or personal pronoun), and that otherwise a *to* is inserted : *I dare not tell her, He dared adventure himself*, vs. *We dare to judge, The players dared to satirise*. So also formerly with *make*, as in Carlyle's *Amelia's love makes the burning sand grow green beneath him and the stunted shrubs to blossom* (V1 82).

The *to* with the dative also qualifies sometimes : *The lessons these things have táught us* vs. *The lessons these things have táught to áll of us* (cf. V3 536). Similarly the old *a-* prefix with *-ing*, as in *He's gone a-fishing*[42] ; what we do nowadays is partly to suppress the accent on *go*: *He's gone fishing*. The conjunction *and* serves a like purpose with *go* : *Why did you have to gó and téll her?* Again we may suppress the accent on *go* : *Why did you have to go téll her?* Relative *that* is a fairly regular insertion : *Who was it (that) told you?*

---

39. *Compact edition* gives no trouble. For some speakers, backshifting takes care of this : *a cómpact bóok*.

40. V1 54–55. Van Draat feels that the *a* has been inserted as a result of the fixation of the stress on the second syllable of *without*. He perhaps overlooks the matter of emphasis : *without a* ' without a single.'

41. The *of* in *out of, outside of, inside of*, etc., responds partly to accent, partly to other forces. In *outside the wall* there is no accentual problem and the position of *the* makes it clear that *outside* is a preposition. Similarly in *out the door* (vs. *out of bounds*). In *I prefer to live outside cities* there is an accentual problem and *outside* is too much like an adjective. Many speakers accordingly generalize the *of* to all situations.

42. Cf. V3 508–514. Compare *with lights aglow*, preferred to *with lights glowing* (cf. V3 515), and rhythmic preferences for *round* and *around* (V3 518).

with de-accented *it*, but not **Who was the man told you?*, with accented *man*. Accent and resistance to ambiguity combine in **I know the man came* for *I know the man that came*, vs. *I know the man they brought*. In the latter, where the relative is object of the subordinate verb, an unaccented element (most often a pronoun) normally intervenes.[43]

The inserted element may be merely transferred from another position. This is especially true of the indefinite article:

a quite long report	quite a long report (but a very long report, a terribly long report, etc.)[44]
**a só prétty girl	so prétty a gírl
só prétty a girl	súch a prétty gírl
**a that pretty girl	that pretty a girl
**a too remote place	too remote a place[45]

---

43. Cf. V3 505 for the type *He knows all there is to know.*

While it is easy to make a case for accent in the constructions where *that* can be omitted, it is difficult to make a convincing one about where what can happen will happen. I devised a test with sentences containing *that* flanked by accented and unaccented syllables and gave it to a class of 23 graduate students. The one item with unaccented subject— *Remember the time it happened?* vs. *Remember the time that it happened?*—showed a strong preference for omitting *that* (stronger than in *Remember the time Henry saw us?*), as would be predicted. But the accented subjects gave uncertain results. Listeners were as strongly opposed to omitting *that* in *He's the teacher (that) all respect* as in *He's the priest (that) all respect;* and they were as willing to omit it in *This is the brand (that) Dad insists on* as in *This is the label (that) Dad insists on.* Possibly the weaker influence of accent here is due to the potential pause at the end of the main clause. In *He simply isn't the friend George is, friend* can be given plenty of time for a turn of pitch. With a pronoun subject the pace is faster.

44. The overzealous writer does not transfer it: *a quite long book,* Van Wyck Brooks, *Helen Keller,* New York, 1956, p. 46.

45. J II 15.171,172 explains the word order here as based on the interrogative and relative, e.g. *How great a man.* This was undoubtedly the precipitating cause, but it does not explain why the resulting pattern was maintained against the more general tendency to put *a* first. As for *quite,* we may assume that the pattern *quite a man* ('completely a man', but now felt as an adjective, 'a real man') has influenced *quite a long report,* where *a quite long report* ('a completely long report') is possible. The significant thing is that the paroxytonic *very,* also an abverb, does not give **very a long report.*

For *too* we must allow an additional influence, that of the numeral *two.* While **a too small eye* is conceivable, **too small eyes* obviously has to be avoided. (I have heard *She has too small of eyes* as a solution to this, the *of* clearly articulated but undoubtedly a transformed indefinite article on the analogy of *too small a nose,* not, considering that the speech level was that of a thirteen-year-old, on the analogy of the formal *She is too small of eyes.*) Avoidance of the plural reflects on the singular. The addition of *of* in several such phrases is probably in part to get an extra margin of safety between accents: *If he's that much of a fool, If it's that new of a book* (overheard from a salesgirl

Being less popular and less frequent, synonyms of *too* do not displace the article: *an excessively remote place.*

The tendency to use the article as a buffer syllable may influence the choice between constructions. Normally I say *This is good water,* using *water* as a mass noun, not *This is a good water.* But in a comparison I have caught myself using it as a count noun: *It's as good a water as you'll find anywhere.*

Inversion is also resorted to with *enough*: *a góod enough réason,* vs. *a sufficiently góod réason.* The latter at least separates two of the accents, which would not happen in **an enóugh góod réason.* The medial position of *enough* not only separates adjective from noun but also results in a whole or partial suppression of its own accent: *a góod enough réason,* not *a góod enóugh réason.* Another solution is to put *enough* at the end, where it may be accented or deaccented at will: *a reason good enough.*

V2 § 4 mentions *good my lord* and *dear my liege* as having a rhythmic basis; so also—with inserted element in addition to inversion—phrases like *a day in June* vs. *September morn* (§ 33).

But the area where the relationship between inversion and accent can be most conclusively demonstrated is that of "binomials." As I have treated this elsewhere,[46] I shall merely summarize. Extant pre-adjunct binomials are almost all arranged so as to have the non-oxytonic member of the pair last, i. e., before the noun. This, coupled with the unaccented *and* between the members, causes the accents to be spaced out with at least one unaccented syllable between them: *free and easy manner, bright and shining eyes, gay and youthful laughter.* Tests with unstereotyped binomials prove that listeners react to this type of arrangement, not to the individual binomials as set phrases. When the binomial is in terminal position, i. e., with no noun following, there is less resistance to an oxytonic ending: *a hurried and curt note* is objected to more than is *a note that was hurried and curt.* Similarly when the following noun begins with an unstressed syllable: *a dreadful and dire warning* is less acceptable than *a dreadful and dire forewarning.*

The English comparative and superlative afford the best example of an alternate construction in which a pre-posed element competes with a suffix. The vitality of the *-er* and *-est* suffixes is almost certainly due to accent, in view of their near-restriction (especially for *-er*) to adjectives and adverbs which, on receiving the suffix, result in a non-oxytone of something less than three full syllables: *red, redder; simple, simpler; happy, happier; hollow, hollower.*[47]

---

in a bookstore), *kind of a, sort of a.*

Lapses are instructive: *You're góod a influence on me* for *You're a góod influence on me,* overheard from an adolescent speaker.

46. See pp. 129–138.

47. The two-syllable status of *happier* and *hollower* is of course arguable. From the standpoint of accent, however, it makes no difference; the stems *happy-* and *hollow-* end

Thus *a more extensive view* has no need for an interposed unaccentable syllable; *a broader view* is improved by it. The double comparatives *lesser* and *worser*, in the standard usage always pre-adjunct, are clear cases of lengthening for the sake of accent.

Accent affects the comparative in yet another way. If the adjective is placed after the noun, the form with *more* is preferred: *I've never known a girl more lovely*, *I've never known a lovelier girl*.[48]

The definite article with the superlative is probably selected partly on the basis of accent: *Hé sailed (the) fárthest* vs. *He sáiled the fárthest*. The decision whether to accent *he* or *sailed* of course depends on information values in the sentence.

Negatives *not* and *n't* are an interesting case of survival of competing forms in colloquial speech. The reduction of *not* to *n't* is accentual in the first place, since the suppression of the accent on *not* leaves the flanking syllables free to take an accent: *He isn't réady*. The contraction has been generalized and tends to be preferred even when a flanking weak syllable is no advantage,

---

in a syllable that is both weak and short, and adding the suffix makes a better buffer between accents. Jespersen (*Essentials of English grammar*, London, 1933, p. 222) also admits *-er* with polysyllabic oxytones, e.g. *politer*—a further argument in favor of accent; but I find most of these (**complexer, *corrupter, *diviner*) unacceptable. There are of course other restrictions: phonetic, as in **sourer*; related to frequency, as in **laxer* and in **winsomer* as against *handsomer*. The low-frequency restriction probably reflects homonymic conflict with agentive *-er*: *laxer* and *diviner* make me think of 'someone who laxes,' 'someone who divines.'

    48. Five listeners were tested with the following sentences:

I've never known a more gay man.

I've never known a man more gay.

I've never known a man gayer.

I've never known a gayer man.

They preferred the forms with separated accents.

But position is rarely a matter of accent alone—language is not that simple. We can be fairly sure that *I've never worked for a man more kind* and *I've never worked for a kinder man* select *more kind* and *kinder* primarily on the basis of accent. This is because of the governing expression *work for*, which implies no subordinate predication: *kinder* and *more kind* are both attributive. But in *I've never seen a man happier* (*prouder, madder*) we have the equivalent of *I've never seen a man be happier*, etc., which is similar to *I've never made a man happier*. These contrast with *I've never seen a man more happy* (*proud, mad*), which are almost, but not quite, unambiguously attributive. *I've never seen a man prouder* is active pride, e.g. that of a parent in the accomplishment of a child; *I've never seen a man more proud* is self-pride. By the same token I would avoid **I've never seen a view loftier* (*more lofty* is normal), since it both violates accent and implies the nonsensical 'I've never seen a view be (behave) loftier.' On the other hand, *I've never seen a view loftier than this* is normal, for both syntactic (juxtaposed ICs) and accentual (phrasal break after *view*) reasons.

but *not* maintains itself, under conditions that invite comparison with the notion of accent. To test this, I gave a group of subjects[49] a set of paired sentences in which each pair contained a *not* and an *n't*, and was matched (in all but one instance) with a following pair also containing a *not* and an *n't* but standing before something with a different accent pattern. They were told to express their preferences, which came out as follows in terms of " preference for *not* over *n't* " :[50]

> He's not (he isn't) afraid of anything. 45%
> He's not (he isn't) ready to go yet. 38%
> It's not (it isn't) advisable to delay. 48%
> It's not (it isn't) wise to delay. 35%
> It's not (it isn't) easy. 41%
> It's not (it isn't) so easy. 59%
> You're not (you aren't) to say a word about this, you understand? 80%

While *n't* was preferred in an absolute sense, in all cases there was a relatively greater preference for *not* when a flanking unaccentable *n't* would be useless than when the *n't* serves a purpose, and in the third set of pairs it exceeded the preference for *n't*. The last pair, with marked preference for *not* over *n't*, is a kind of emphatic stereotype.

III.   Adjectives and Verbs as a Class

For all the influence of rhythm as a symptom of the needs of pitch accent, it remains true that other forces are frequently more powerful, and that we are compelled to live with constructions that lack an advantageous spacing of accents. We must say *an acúte páin, a matúre mán*; there is no way to backshift the stress. The erosion of the past-participle ending has resulted in numerous oxytonic participial adjectives : *a declàred prìce, the desíred ánswer, a refórmed cónvict, an assúred víctory*. If it were not that pitch accent has a second line of defense (syllable-stretching ; see the next section), the apparent ease with which such forms come about might, in the long view, seem fatal to the argument. But as long as we are taking the long view, we are entitled to look for large-scale evidence of the residual effect of accent on the shape of words. Can we generalize about prenominal modifiers? A look at

---

49. A class of 23 graduate students. Thanks go to Edward L. Blansitt for permitting the use of his class at the University of Colorado, July 1961.

50. The instructions were to give the better-sounding sentence in each pair an A, and the other a B for ' almost as good ' or a C for ' obviously worse.' " Preference numbers " were reckoned as the number of B votes plus two times the number of A votes minus two times the number of C votes, and these were then converted to a percentage of preference for *not* over *n't*.

the stock of English adjectives suggests that they tend to congeal in non-oxytonic forms.

There is first the process of adjective derivation, which is mainly by atonic suffixes: *-ant, -ent, -ean, -ial, -al, -ate, -ary, -ory, -ous, -ive, -able, -ible, -ic, -ical, -ish, -ful.* The obvious contrast is with verbs, typically derived by atonic prefixes: *re-, un-, de-, dis-, mis-, pre-*: *pre-tést, misréad, untíe, defróst, re-téll.* An exception among the adjectives, such as *-ose*, is so quickly felt to be deviant that it is seized upon for some phonesthetic purpose (*verbose, grandiose, bellicose* are augmentative as well as adjectival); and many of these give in to backshifting: *béllicose áctions.* (For most American speakers *adipose* has permanently shifted because of the set phrase *ádipose tíssue.*)

A. L. Kroeber offers this bit of oblique evidence for an undercurrent among adjectives: "It is also possible that poetic form as well as choice of theme may influence frequency of the parts of speech. Testing what tendencies of this sort there might be, I came across a higher adjective rate in downbeat verse than in upbeat.... René Wellek suggests that most dissyllabic English and German adjectives and nouns are naturally trochaic in accent, whereas many verbs are not.... The tendency in both languages is for a higher proportion of adjectives in trochaic lyrics, irrespective of the characteristic frequency of individual poets."[51]

I cannot offer a complete census of adjectives, but I borrow a sample from the *Thorndike-Lorge teachers' word book of 30,000 words* (New York, 1944), pages 267-271, the first thousand words. I do not know of any count of English words separated according to parts of speech; here, I had to make my own rough estimates.[52] I separated monosyllables from polysyllables, because

---

51. "Parts of speech in periods of poerty," *Publications of the Modern Language Association of America* 73.309–314 (1958), p. 312. V1 97 says, "Most Adjectives, certainly most Germanic Adjectives, have the stress on the first syllable, or are monosyllabic."

52. The Thorndike-Lorge is a spelling list, with such words as *watch* being counted only once for *watch* as a verb and *watch* as a noun in the two senses 'vigil' and 'timepiece.' Whereas the semantic breakdown is to be found in the six-volume *Semantic count of English words*, Hektograph edition, Teacher's College, New York, 1938, this compilation too lacks an arrangement by parts of speech. I therefore had to guess. In deciding whether to count a word as an adjective or as a verb—the two categories to which I am directing attention here—I tried to estimate which part of speech comprised the majority usage. I assumed, for example, that *dress, favor, fear, issue, miss, name, note, place, price, ship, sort, sound, state, wind, charge, class, heat, order, pain, paint, shade, skin, smoke, store, train, picture, question, result,* had managed to get on the list by virture of noun usages mainly, and so did not count them as verbs. For the same reason I did not count *future* and *Indian* as adjectives. On the other hand, I counted *wonder, visit, surprise, produce,* and *command* among the verbs, and *direct, better,* and *present* among the adjectives. *Able* was not counted among the adjectives since *able man* is unquestionably insignificant beside *able to.* Among the verbs, only the form matching the infinitive

monosyllabic adjectives count as oxytones, and if large numbers of them are found and cannot be explained in some special way, the theory is weakened.

For monosyllables the figures are 106 adjectives, 164 verbs. Even in this category, where phonetic erosion has done its worst, verbs substantially outnumber adjectives. A thorough investigation would probably adjust these numbers by two other factors, even more favorable to the rhythmic interpretation. One is the number of normally unaccented adjectives which naturally bunch themselves in the first thousand words : *a, his, its, my, our, some, such* (except *such a,* but *such a* spaces the accents), *their, your,* etc. Among the verbs, only *be, can,* possibly *get,* and *have* would be similarly discounted. The other factor is the likelihood that the first thousand words includes a higher proportion of monosyllabic adjectives than of monosyllabic verbs—the commutability of nouns and verbs insures that the number of monosyllabic verbs will continue to run high.

Among the polysyllables we find 5 oxytonic and 49 non-oxytonic adjectives to 45 oxytonic and 27 non-oxytonic verbs. The adjectives are 91 % nonoxytonic, the verbs 63% oxytonic. In evaluating these numbers we should keep in mind that it is no DISadvantage, accentually, for a verb to be nonoxytonic, while it is distinctly advantageous for an adjective to be that way.

Are there factors in the sentence as a whole that will account for the different behavior of adjectives (and nouns) on the one hand, and verbs on the other ? Jespersen glimpsed that there might be when he said (I 5.73) that " the frequent position of the verb at the end of the sentence, thus followed by no word that might cause a rhythmic forestress, may have contributed to the distinction [of verb and noun or adjective by means af stress]." He lists (5.72, 73) 160 items thus distinguished, and in his list (5.59) of originally end-stressed French and Latin words that have retained the end stress we find that most of them are verbs.

But when Jespersen speaks of a rhythmic forestress, he thinks of smallscale combinations of the size of adjective plus noun, like the ones to which most of our attention has been devoted thus far. We need a larger perspective to see what are the forces that mold the smaller units when they enter into combination. In this wider view we see that the sentence itself tends to polarize its accents, to take its characteristic tonal shape from two main

---

was counted, e.g. *take* but not *taken.*

Mistakes in judgment are probably too few to affect the main proportions, which is all that such a comparison is good for anyway.

While it is not the kind of over-all count that one would desire for a comparison of this kind, the list of near-homonyms compiled, mainly from Daniel Jones's *Dictionary,* by A. J. Vanvik in his *On stress in present-day English,* Bergen and Oslo, 1961, pp. 42–58, esp. p. 55, confirms the impression of verbs having, as a class, a stress pattern differentiating them from nouns and adjectives. The list contains 248 entries, of which " 203 represent opposition between verb and some other part of speech."

pitch movements, one toward the beginning and the other toward the end. In fact, most of the examples offered in the earlier sections here have been citation forms tantamount to complete (though condensed) utterances with this typical shape.

There are semantic adjustments in connection with the two main accents —roughly they relate to the theme-rheme or topic-comment dichotomy; the last accent in particular attracts the contrastive, new-to-context item. But we are concerned here not with the semantic manifestations but with the fact that the sentence takes such a typical tonal shape even in the absence of normal syntactic interrelationships. In reciting *QED*, H_2SO_4, *do-re-mi*, consecutive numerals, and the like, we give the major pitch prominence to the initial and terminal items, despite the fact that they are not superordinate in any sense except that of position.[53]

The characteristic tendency toward major accents at the two extremes of the sentence exerts a push on the lexical items occupying the extremes, one that can be felt in the frequent shifting of the stresses, leftwise at the beginning, rightwise at the end. I offer some examples of rightwise shift. We find it in forms that are long and have the normal stress well toward the beginning. Typical are the adjectives ending in *-fiable*. I have repeatedly heard *jústifiable* rendered *justifíable* in terminal position, and have recorded

$$\text{Things} \quad \text{not} \quad _i\text{den}_{ti} \overset{\text{fi}}{} \text{able.}^{[54]}$$

Similarly adjectives in *-able* where the base verb has a stress at or near the beginning, as in this interchange:

Mason: Unrecog $\overset{\text{nizable?}}{}$

Tragg: $\text{Ye}^{s,}$ it was un $\overset{\text{rec}}{\text{ogniza}}$ ble.$^{[55]}$

We also find a good deal of right-shifting in emphatic speech. An accent at the end is climactic:

$$\text{Take} \quad \text{care} \quad \text{of} \quad \text{your}^{se}_{lf}$$

---

53. See Bolinger, " English stress: the interpenetration of strata," *Study of Sounds,* Tokyo, 1957, pp. 295–316, esp. p. 301.

54. Speaker, Dr. A. M. Liberman.

55. " Perry Mason " TV program, 5 Nov. 1960.

—a playfully sympathetic admonition overheard addressed to someone who was ill. The same speaker on another occasion, saying rather excitedly:

Why   trav   che
   didn't you get   eler's   ck$_s$?

—later, in a calmer tone, *tráveler's checks*, with checks de-accented in th~ normal way. Another speaker:

                                                          whe
What   the   pol   go   be   else
               icy   is   ing to   r$_e$.

This is fairly common with *elsewhere* in terminal position. The following example is from a long-repeated TV commercial:

                                     ca
Triumph   tooth
            over   de
                         y.

Normally, of course, *tóoth decay*, with *decay* de-accented. A person who has had three successive copies of the same book stolen may handle the normally unaccented pronoun *one* as follows:

                              on

                  third
It's   the
                       e !

Our preference for an end-stressed item in terminal position may be shown even when there is no shift of stress within a word. I gave eight persons the following to read aloud and indicate which seemed better:

    There was a mix-up at the baptism. We couldn't tell whether the
    infant was the wetter or the wettee.
    . . . was the wettee or the wetter.

Of the seven who stressed *wettee* on the last syllable, five unhesitatingly chose the first arrangement, thus getting the main accent on the last syllable in the utterance. The two others deliberated before choosing the second alternative (one observed that logically *wetter* is the more contrastive idea in this context).

Verbs are particularly subject to the end-shifting of stress. As with adjectives, the compounds are the most susceptible. Diachronically the "normal" stress has moved from the verb element to the adverb element in two-word verbs.[56] Synchronically compound verbs are like compound adjectives:

56. Cf. George J. Tamson, *Word-stress in English*, Halle, 1898.

end-stressed in end position, forestressed in pre-position: *He strúck out twíce, He struck óut* resembles *frésh-cut méat, The meat is fresh-cút.*

Unit verbs are also subject to shift, though less strikingly so in a rightwise direction than adjectives are in a leftwise one. I have recorded the following:

$$\text{The po}^{\text{si}}\text{tion} \quad \text{to be} \quad ^{\text{sub}}\text{sti}^{\text{tu}}_{\quad\text{ted}}{}^{57}$$

$$\text{It is} \quad ^{\text{beau}}_{\text{tifully}} \quad \text{do}^{\text{men}}_{\text{cu}\quad\text{ted.}}{}^{58}$$

And my own unpremeditated reading of a passage:

$$\text{The} \quad \text{e}^{\text{motion}} \quad \text{is} \quad \text{ma}^{\text{fest}}_{\text{ni}}_{\quad\text{ed.}}$$

Verbs with more than one recognized stress pattern are not uncommon, especially among those ending in -*ment*, e. g. *súpplement, supplemént.*[59] Presumably one who says *I couldn't locáte it*[60] would also say *I wonder why they couldn't lócate míne.*

We note another similarity between these rightwise shifts and the leftwise ones already studied: they apparently can occur only when the syllable to which the shift takes place is already long. Thus *locate* has two undegraded syllables regardless of which is stressed; so do the -*ment* verbs. I doubt that verbs like *whiten, picket, hurry, borrow, pillory, average,* and the like could right-shift the stress.[61] A speaker who says *to interest* [-əst] might conceivably shift the stress; one who says *to interest* [-əst] would not. This tendency probably cuts two ways: verbs retaining a long syllable may shift the stress, and the proclivity of verbs to a rightwise shift helps to retain the long syllable. Hence the numerous noun (or adjective) vs. verb pairs, the former with degraded syllable, the latter with long one, but spelled alike: *separate, estimate, intimate, compliment, ornament,* etc. (cf. J I 5.74.)

When the normally stressed syllable FOLLOWS another long syllable, we

---

57. Speaker, Dr. J. Donald Bowen, 2 July 1961.

58. Speaker, Professor Walter Starkie, 29 Jan. 1961.

59. I have heard the latter from Professors N. B. Adams and D. W. Reed. See p. 110 note 12. Vanvik p. 57 notes the tendency to which I call attention here in verbs ending in -*ment*.

60. So said by the character Will Gentry in "Michael Shayne" TV program, 9 Dec. 1960.

61. This gives us a structural reason for distinguishing the final syllables in *áverage* and *óutrage*. The latter may easily right-shift the stress: *He was simply outráged!*

readily get a shift to the left, as with adjectives and with the compound verbs already noted. So, *The énemy was outfóxed* but *our óutfoxed énemy* and *It's hard to óutfox Jóe there* (*Joe there*='that Joe,' with *there* de-accented).

I have given a number of examples of the accentual push to the end of the sentence, a result of the large-scale tendency toward having a marked prominence at the end of the utterance. We need some examples of the opposite of this, the marked prominence at the beginning. We find it in the major pitch jump normally occurring on the first long syllable, regardless of whether that syllable would receive an accent if the word occupied another position. In slow speech other prominences may be present, e. g. that of the "normal" accent on *constitution* in

tees
Con_{sti}^{tu}tion   guaran
The   it.

but the most sweeping changes of pitch are usually at the beginning and the end; other prominences seem to ride on the crest that has already been attained with the first and is held until the last. And in rapid speech, the medial prominences may all but disappear:

tees
Constitution   guaran
The   it.

In the following, we see how initial position shifts the stress:

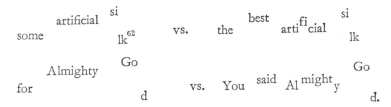

Other examples, contrasting initial position with final position:

He's an ámbidextrous ácrobat.	The acrobat is ambidéxtrous.
His repútation was rúined.	It ruined his reputátion.
Your próposition is no góod.	They rejected his propositíon.
A télegraphic stýle.	His style is telegráphic.[63]

62. Jassem p. 46.

63. This example is D. W. Reed's, in a talk at the Modern Language Association meetings, 28 December 1961.

In a word like *violin* I go much farther in my speech. I stress it on the last syllable in terminal position: *He plays the violín.* But I have caught myself saying

Two-word verbs behave like unit words:

> Then cást aside your féars.
> Just rún along to béd.

In terminal position, these are *cast asíde* and *run alóng*. Compare the similarity, within a potentially one-accent phrase, between the unit word *Constitution* and the two-word verb *clean up*:

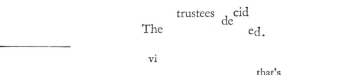

the   Consti^{tu}_{tion.}   Then   clean^{up}   a bit.

And in a two-accent sentence:

The Constitution ^{bids} for it. Then clean up ^{gra} your ft.

In the first pair, the syllables *Con-* and *clean* can be completely de-accented. In the second it is more difficult: for my speech a de-accented *Con-* (and an accented *-tu-*) would be unlikely, and a de-accented *clean* (and an accented *up*) quite impossible.

Our aversion to holding back on the initial prominence can be appreciated if we try to say

*The   trus^{tees} de^{cid} ed

reserving the prominence for the normally stressed syllable of *trustée* instead of giving it to the first long syllable. Instead, we say

The   trustees de^{cid} ed.

When the ^{vi}olins come _{in,} that's when . . .

with an appreciative emphasis on the word—not merely raising *vi-* beyond the level of *-olins* but completely smothering the latter. I am at a loss to account for this exceptional treatment; a similar appreciative emphasis on *Constitution*, e.g., would affect the syllable *-tu-*, not *Con-*. Perhaps we go to greater extremes with words where there is dialectal wavering, as I suspect there is with *violin*. I would probably do the same with *oatmeal*, *icecream*, and similar compounds.

For the same problem with a rightwise shift, consider the shiftability of *justifiable* and the unshiftability of *solitary*. I have recorded an instance of shift on *ordinary* (p. 115), but I doubt that any amount of emphasis could produce an utterance like *Sólitary confinement is so solitáry!* Stability of stress pattern seems to vary all along the scale.

To show that backshifting normally occurs only on long syllables, compare *retire* 'withdraw' vs. *re-tire* 'furnish with new tires.' In the following two contexts they are not necessarily distinguished accentually, as there is only one major accent: "These issues should not be left outstanding"—"*Then retire them*"; "These wheels are in pretty bad shape"—"*Then re-tire them*":

```
                          tire
              Then   re
                              them.
```

But with two major accents, as in "We're in a dangerous financial position" —"*Then retire the issues*," vs. "We're not going to get much farther in this condition"—"*Then re-tire the wheels*," the first comes out

```
                                    is
                    tire    the
        Then    re
                            sues.
```

and the second

```
                                   whee
                    re-tire    the
        Then                 ls.
```

One result of the initial prominence is that a distinction such as the one between *ránsacked* and *ran óff* is erased in initial position:

```
            ransacked        prem          They  ran  off  their     en
    They              the                                          emies.
                             ises.
```

Another is the creation of stereotypes where intermediate pitch prominences are lost: *Cónstitution Háll, Índependence Squáre.*

There remain many unexplored possibilities in the realm of shifts of accent from one lexically independent item to another. For example, whereas the phrase *not only* is normally accented on *on-*, it is not unusual to hear, at the beginning of a sentence,

```
                              sult
        Not
            only  did  he  in
                              me...[64]
```

My examples have been declarative. The shift of stress does not depend on this, however. The questions *Do you understand it?* vs. *Do you understand it now?* ('at this time'), one with a single accent, the other with two, normally come out

---

64. Cf. Jones's examples *He pút on his hát* (§ 973), *Ás I was sáying* (§ 999).

stand it?   understand it now?
Do you under   Do you

—with -*stand* getting the pitch contrast in the first, but *under-* in the second.[65]

Enough has been said, I think, to show that stress patterns are apt to congeal in the way position in the sentence may predispose them, which means that nouns and adjectives will tend to be forestressed,[66] verbs to be endstressed, and ultimately, in many cases, to carry this stress with them regardless of position. The influence of the major sentence accents in crystallizing the stress in the first place has been overlooked mainly because of our reliance on citation forms, which has fixed in our minds the conviction that we ought to be able to find " the " stress pattern of every lexeme. Since citation forms coincide, in their stresses, with what we find at the END of an utterance, the almost equally potent initial accent has not been given its due.

IV. " STRESS-TIMED RHYTHM " AND SYLLABIC LENGTH

Many commentators have reported a tendency, presumably affecting English more than some other languages, to equalize the time intervals between the accentual groups in an utterance. As Edgar H. Sturtevant puts it, " The intervals of time between accents are virtually the same throughout."[67] Kenneth Pike popularized the term " stress-timed rhythm," defined as follows : " rhythm units . . . tend to follow one another in such a way that the lapse of time between the beginning of their prominent syllables is somewhat uniform . . . . Since the rhythm units have different numbers of syllables, but a similar time value, the syllables of the longer ones are crushed together, and pronounced very rapidly, in order to get them pronounced at all, with-

---

65. We should not be fooled by something like

Do you under stand it now?

an utterance with one accent, *now* being only a trailer. This is an area of tonal ambiguity.

66. English seems to be more averse to postponing the first of the two major accents than to anticipating the second. While nouns and adjectives are certainly free to occur in terminal position, their somewhat greater frequency early in the sentence brings them under the influence of this more consistent pull to the left. The pull to the right at the end is weaker, except in emphatic utterance, but since verbs are less free to roam they are more subject to it.

67. *Linguistic change*, Chicago, 1961, p. 56.

in the time limitation."[68]   The contrary case, a deliberate pacing of syllables, Pike terms " syllable-timed rhythm," exemplified in English by a type of chant.

We need to determine two things : how accurate the notion of stress-timed rhythm is, and what significance it may have for pitch accent.

Pike's examples are the following : *The mán's hére* vs. *The mánager's hére* and *If Tóm will Í will* vs. *If Tóm'll do it Í will*, in which *man's* compares to *manager's* in length, and *Tom will* to *Tom'll do it*. Essentially this amounts to demonstrating that the monosyllabic *man's* stretches to the length of the polysyllabic *manager's*; similarly with *will* and *do it*, if we may equate, and cancel out, *Tom* and *Tom'll* (this is a poor example because of the pause after *will* and *do it*—terminal groups can be lengthened as one pleases, and so made equal).   I shall try to show later that monosyllables are a special case.   What we need now are some utterances in which a two-syllable group, say, is compared with a four- or five-syllable group ; and not between one utterance and another, but in a single stretch of speech.

It seems a bit implausible to expect equal intervals in a phrase like *the quite unnecéssary incomprehensibílity of his wórds*, where the two-syllable group *quite un-* is followed by the nine-syllable group *-necessary incomprehensi-*. While in this example we might stretch a point and more or less equalize the groups by creating an extra one out of *incomprehensi-*, in another example like *such íntricately devéloped strúctures* it is impossible at normal tempo to equalize the two groups confined by the accents.   Even in a more usual conversation piece like *I tóld him to téll his móther* we are not apt to equalize *told him to* and *tell his*, in spite of the fact that all we would need to do is to slow *tell his* down a bit.

To get some idea of actual measurements, I had six speakers record the following two sentences : *The experiment in adult education described in the article below is of general interest.   What has been done in Vancouver can be attempted elsewhere*.[69]   I then identified the accents, marked them on the tape (recorded at 15 ips), and measured the intervals in sixteenths of an inch. As not all six speakers distributed the accents in the same way, the recordings cannot be matched precisely, but within each separate recording the intervals can be compared without difficulty.

Certain precautions are called for.   First, if a pause intervenes, it is necessary to start over and declare a new standard after it—we cannot assume that the speaker will resume at the same pace (it is already a large enough assumption that he will not change the gait of his horse in midstream).   This means, too, that we have no right to compare intervals in the second sentence with intervals in the first—all comparisons should be within what Pike

68. *Intonation of American English*, Ann Arbor, 1945, p. 34.
69. Taken from *Atlas* 2 : 1.35, July 1961.

calls one of those "recurrent bursts of speed." Second, we have to measure from accent to accent, not including anything before the first accent or anything after the last one.

In the table I have arranged the intervals according to the maximum number that was used by any speaker. In the one case where one divided into two but others combined into one, I have entered the figures between the lines *What has* and *been* for those who made one group, *What has been*. Blanks mean either that an initial group contained no accent (this is how Speaker I read *What has been*) or that a pause broke the measure and invalidated what came after (for example, a pause after *below* meant a "new standard" but only one interval and hence nothing to compare with).

The intervals were measured from approximately the center of the accented syllable to the corresponding center of the next accented syllable, this point having been located by rolling the tape back and forth over the playback head. For convenience I list them as if each group contained all of its initial accented syllable and none of its terminal one; thus *-periment in ad-* really means the interval including half of the syllable *-per-* and half of the syllable *-ult*.

To make comparison easy I have given in addition to the intervals in sixteenths of an inch, the proportionate numerical value of each, setting the shortest one in each sentence at 100; these comparison numbers are italicized. Thus for Speaker IV the shortest group in the first sentence was *general*, set at 100, and the figure 194 for *-periment in ad-* indicates that this interval was almost twice as long.

Table

Number of syllables	Accent group	Speakers I	II	III	IV	V	VI
5	periment in ad		100 *129*	160 *154*	132 *194*	124 *141*	148 *115*
3	ult edu	108 *101*	*156 *200*	132 *127*	108 *159*	96 *109*	140 *109*
3	cation des	149 *140*	150 *192*	147 *141*	129 *190*	120 *136*	166 *130*
3	cribed in the	107 *100*	80 *103*	104 *100*	106 *156*	92 *105*	128 *100*
4	article be	120 *112*	131 *168*	135 *130*	128 *189*	88 *100*	152 *118*
3	low is of		108 *139*		112 *165*		
3	general		78 *100*		68 *100*		
2	What has		78 *115*	§90 *131*	64 *142*	96 *148*	122 *100*
1	been				45 *100*		
3	done in Van	125 *174*	144 *212*	157 *228*	136 *302*	117 *180*	190 *156*
5	couver can be at	171 *237*	180 *265*	176 *255*		146 *225*	
2	tempted	72 *100*	68 *100*	69 *100*		65 *100*	

* This speaker stressed *ádult*, and the group is therefore *adult edu-*.

§ This speaker accented *have* rather than *what*, and the interval is therefore *has been*.

The results give little support to the idea of isochronous rhythm. Of the 53 intervals, 13, or almost a fourth, have comparison numbers of 170 or higher—effectively double the length of the shortest interval. This figure would be higher if we relaxed the requirement that after a pause the standard must shift—if, for example, we took the measurement 72 for all of the first speaker's role instead of only for the second half. The shortest interval, that for the one-syllable group *been* as spoken by the fourth speaker, is, to be sure, considerably more than half as long as the groups *general* and *what has* (I repeat that we have something special with monosyllables), but one can make out a good case for number of syllables as the determinant by examining the last three intervals in Speakers I, II, III, and V—they maintain the same order, with the two-syllable *-tempted* shortest, the three-syllable *done in Van-* next, and the five-syllable *-couver can be at-* longest.

The lengths are not random, as can be seen by looking at the comparison numbers for Speakers II and IV in the first sentence. Except for the first two intervals (Speaker II said *adult*), which trade places, all intervals have the same rank order. By arbitrarily eliminating for the four other speakers the comparison numbers that correspond to the intervals that had to be cut out because of pauses, we get the following ranks for all seven intervals and all six speakers:

Interval	I	II	III	IV	V	VI
1		3	7	7	7	5
2	3	7	3	3	5	3
3	6	6	6	6	6	7
4	2	2	2	2	3	2
5	5	5	5	5	2	6
6		4		4		
7		1		1		

(This assumes that if all speakers had produced all intervals, the last two would have ranked 4 and 1. We can be pretty sure about the 1.) The repeated identical numbers in the horizontal rows suggest that there are forces at work to determine the length of intervals, probably involving syllable structure, nearness to initial or final position, syneresis, and relative semantic importance, besides the number of syllables. But as these factors have nothing to do with isochronism, we can dismiss them with the observation that they seem to have a good deal more influence than rhythm has in determining the length of accentual groups.

I conclude that if we are to talk about "stress-timed rhythm" in English, a more cautious statement is in order, like the one given by František Daneš for Czech: "The rhythm-units in Czech are both syllable-timed and stress-timed...." Regularity in rhythm manifests itself "in so far as it is compatible with the requirements of the other planes of linguistic structure . . . ."[70]

Stress-timed rhythm is not entirely illusory. Its dominant position in verse would alone be enough to provoke some reaction in prose, if indeed its roots were not in prose to begin with. But to find it extensively we must look beyond offhand discourse toward speech that is esthetically contrived or often repeated. A proverb or a prayer is apt to congeal in rhythmic form, and every writer or public speaker at some time indulges in poetic prose.

Now what of the peculiar status of monosyllables, at which I have twice hinted? Here I believe we have what more than any other one thing has promoted the feeling that accentual groups tend to be of equal length. If a one-syllable word tends to be as long or almost as long as a two-syllable word, and one- and two-syllable words make up a high enough running count of English words, it is not hard to see how an impression of isochronism might be created. This is especially true as the most radical difference in number of syllables—100%—is between one- and two-syllable words ; a three-syllable word might be half again as long as a two-syllable one, but this could not catch the ear so readily as the more radical difference between one and two.

To appreciate the length of accentable monosyllables, take an utterance like *Pa made John tell who fired those guns.* As we fit single unaccentable monosyllables into this frame, we see how instead of adding length to the whole, they subtract enough from the preceding long syllable to make room. In *Pa can make John tell who fired those guns,* *Pa* is shortened to make room for *can.* If *John* is replaced by *the man,* *the* steals from *made.* If *me* is added to *tell, tell* gives up some of its length. If *those* is replaced by *the,* most of the length of *those* is lost, and *the* takes from *fired.* The accentual rather than syntactic nature of this give and take is manifest in the subtraction that *the,* for example, makes from the preceding *fired,* rather than from its own

70. " Sentence intonation in present-day Standard Czech." p. 2, reprinted from *Intonace a věta ve spisovné češtině,* Prague, 1957.

Vanvik pp. 101-102 reports a set of measurements similar to mine, and a similar lack of isochronism ; he observes that the impression we have of equal time intervals is not borne out by the physical measurements. I. Fónagy and K. Magdics note (" Speed of utterance in phrases of different lengths," *Language and Speech* 3. 179-192 [1960]) that " only the sounds of phrases consisting of two or three syllables lengthen to a considerable extent " (p. 186) while " in the longer phrases . . . the relation between the number of syllables and speed is blurred " (p. 189)—in other words, in longer groups the total length responds to the number of syllables rather than to a tendency to isochronism, which agrees with my observations.

The most extensive recent study on isochronism in English is Yao Shen and Giles G. Peterson, *Isochronism in English* (*Studies in Linguistics, Occasional Paper No. 9*), Buffalo, New York. The conclusions are again the same : that " isochronism as postulated " (mainly by Pike) does not exist (pp. 4, 22, 34). Martin Joos, in a series of comments included in the same monograph (30-31) goes so far as to hypothesize that by allowing a certain average time for each segmental phoneme, each internal open juncture, and each terminal juncture, one can predict how long the interval will be—in other words, that length is chiefly a matter of phonetic bulk.

immediate constituent, *guns*.

The monosyllables which readily occur in accented position are those which, when strung together, tap out a regular, slow beat. The monosyllables which do not readily occur in accented position (articles, pronouns, prepositions, conjunctions, forms of *be*, etc.) are the ones that borrow length when they are distributed among the others. In *Did you take those things home?* the last four words are of approximately equal length ; in *Did you take your things in the house?* both *take* and *things* have ceded some of their length.[71]

The key to this I believe lies in the intimate relationship between syllabic length and accent, a relationship that has its beginning in the need to assist pitch accent in the absence of flanking unaccented syllables (and its end in the much misunderstood " plus juncture " of the phonological grammarians, of which more in a moment). A monosyllable that readily falls in accent position cannot execute a clear pitch turn unless it is stretched. But if it is followed by an unaccented syllable it does not need to be stretched, since the pitch turn can be divided between the two syllables ; the accented syllable can then afford to give up some of its extra length. From repeated use in accent position, this stretching feature is built into the syllable and is encountered whether or not the syllable is actually accented. Or it might be more accurate to say that accentableness has kept the syllable from being shortened. In either case, it is the demands of pitch accent that have helped to turn the trick.

Van Draat's example of the presence and absence of syllable-stretching (V1 14 ; see also V1 10–11) is *Money makes the mare go* contrasted with *Money makes the mare to go ;* in the former, " we pronounce *mare* in two syllables." Compare the following :

	nev		curred		lo	great		tha	
I've	er	in		a	ss		er	than	t.

	nev		cur		los	great		tha	
I've	er	in	red		ses		er	than	t.

	nev		curred,		loss	great		tha	
I've	er	in		a		as		as	t.

In the second, the dropping of the indefinite article forces the speaker to stretch -*curred* in order to negotiate the pitch movement. In the second and third the addition respectively of the plural -*es* and the first *as* enables us

---

71. In a checked syllable such as *take*, we achieve additional length to some extent by prolonging the following silence; " shortening " *take* then means that this silence is occupied by something else.

to give up the stretching of *loss,* which was needed for the pitch turn before the accented syllable of *greater.*

There is perhaps some connection between syllable-stretching and the stress-shifting of adjectives we have noted. I believe that one may almost as readily find the first of the following as the second, with a syllabie that lends itself so well to stretching as *-deal*:

	de	mar		i	mar
an i al		riage	an deal		riage

I have shown that isochronism of accentual groups is to be found in pairs like *tell* and *tell me.* We are now in a position to see how the built-in length that I have described can make for isochronism among accent groups having other unequal arrangements of syllables, say two versus three. In an utterance like *Did you pút those things in the clóset?* the syllable *those* is stretched because it is followed by normally accented *things.* *Things* gives up some of its length to the following unaccentables *in the,* but as there are two of them they just about balance the long *those,* equalizing *put those* and *things in the.* For the conscious stylist, manipulating stretched and unstretched syllables gives unlimited possibilities for rhythm. But we must remember that the essential thing is not rhythm but intelligibility: *Did you pút those things hére?* has *things* duly stretched, but is not rhythmic.

The rhythmic law with which I would replace stress-timed rhythm can be stated in the following three steps:

1. SYLLABLES THAT ARE READILY ACCENTED ARE LONG, THOSE NOT READILY ACCENTED ARE SHORT. The length is built into the syllable and, in the course of the evolution of a word, it is not lost immediately when the stress shifts to another syllable. This is one of those rare places where synchronic understanding needs diachronic insight. The number of loanwords in English, especially from French, has been so considerable that we can observe the process of assimilation in all its stages—the three-stage development from (1) borrowing a word (especially a noun) with stress on the last syllable, to (2) shifting the stress to an earlier syllable but retaining the originally accent-conditioned length on the last syllable, to (3) reducing the length of the last syllable and degrading the vowel concomitantly. In many such words the process is going on now, within idiolects. In my speech I waver in placing the stress of the following: *millionaire, parrakeet, perfume, recourse, recess, lemonade* (and other *-ade* words), *intrigue, ally, chaperon.* Others that commonly waver include *routine, alloy, romance, interne, Leon, soiree, caviar, pecan.* However stressed, these regularly retain the old length on the last syllable. In some others all three stages survive among different speakers: *address* [ədrés, ǽdrəs, ǽdrəs], *autopsy* [ɔtápsɪ, ɔ́tapsɪ, ɔ́təpsɪ], *astrakhan* [æstrəkǽn, ǽstrəkæn, ǽstrəkən]. Even a Frenchified pronunciation like

that of *prestige* [prɛstíž] adopted in competition with a fully assimilated [préstɪdž] will not resist the shift of stress—I have heard [préstiž]. There are so many words still at the middle stage that we may be witnessing the formation of a pattern that will in some cases resist further degradation; this has perhaps happened with words like *creole, turquoise, furor, typhoid,* and possibly *format* (the low back vowels are probably more stable).[72]

2. WHEN A SHORT SYLLABLE FOLLOWS A LONG ONE, IT BORROWS LENGTH FROM IT. This has been fully explained.

3. WHEN TWO LONG SYLLABLES STAND SIDE BY SIDE, THERE IS NO BORROWING AND EACH RETAINS ITS LENGTH. We have observed this happening in the shift of stress that results from the partial assimilation of loanwords, where a word like *recourse* moves its stress to the centralized *re-* and in the process restores the length and the full-grade vowel, without at the same time degrading the syllable that originally had the stress. We can observe it happening in the generation of new nouns (*blástoff, cómmute*) by shifting the stress of two-word or other verbs. And we can observe it in compounding where two long syllables are brought together: *bedpost, hambone*. The notion that in the latter there was some sort of phonological indication of 'compound' enjoyed considerable favor for a time, and such "plus junctures" were liberally marked. But what is involved is a prosodic and not a grammatical law: the compound *bedpost* answers to it as does the unit word *compost*, and *hambone* the same as *trombone*.

V. The Influence of Types of Pitch Accent

Skeptical of Van Draat's sweeping conclusions about prose rhythm, Jespersen points out (II 14.19) adjectives like *great, big, good, hard, blind,* etc., for which "there has never been any disinclination" to use them prenominally. We could put this down merely as an exception to the rule for which the proofs are already abundant enough to dispel any heavy doubts. We know that accent has to compete with contrary forces and does not always prevail against them; phonetic erosion cannot be resisted absolutely. We also know that accent has other resources and can circumvent an occasional collision of stressed syllables.

One such resource is the syllable-stretching discussed in the preceding section. For example, *Instead of a small dog it turned out to be a large cat* gives

	sma	do		la	ca
a	ll	g		a	rge	t.

---

72. The matter of stress shift has been fully treated by others; see esp. J I 5.5–5.8. But the matter of retained length has been overlooked.

Another resource, implied in many of the examples cited but not made explicit, is simply to sacrifice one accent for the sake of another. In the old form of the proverb *Money makes the mare to go*, the spacing of *mare* and *go* enables both to be clearly accented. With the passing of the *to* infinitive, instead of stretching the syllable *mare*,

ma   go..
   re   o

as would be entirely possible, speakers instead give up the accent on *go*:

                  mare
makes   the
              go

—the *go* now merely supplying the downmotion for accented *mare* ; cf. V1 49. This device is common in verse.[73] In prose, it seems to be feasible when the element sacrificed is somewhat less important semantically. In *He seldom ate at the hotel. Perhaps the only meals he had there were occasional lunches, which he had sent up to his suite,*[74] the last part gives

       had   . up   sui
he   sent   to his
                 te.

The need to accent *had* compels the de-accenting of *sent*, as may be seen by what happens when *had* is omitted:

        sent up   sui
he   to his
             te.

Maria Schubiger points out the sacrifice of the accent on *English* in *an Old English grammar*, in contrast with *an English grammar*.[75] Examples like *cóme on úp* (vs. *cóme ón*), *cóme back hóme* (vs. *cóme hóme*), and the like hark back to the " stress shifts " discussed in Section II. Actually an example like *a cléar-cut próblem* can more accurately be described as a sacrifice of the accent on *cut* than as a shift of the accent " from " that syllable " to " *clear*, since *clear* normally has an accent anyway (though one which in terminal position can itself be readily sacrificed:

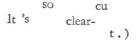

           so   cu
It 's   clear-
               t .)

73. V1 12 quotes Burns's " To Mary in Heaven," e.g. the line *Till too, too soon the glowing west*, in which the second *too* is lower in pitch than the first.

74. Charles Angoff, *H. L. Mencken, a portrait from memory*, New York, 1961, p. 54.

75. *English intonation, its form and function*, Tübingen, 1958, p. 102.

The process is reminiscent of the one by which a one-accent compound is created out of two elements each of which is stressed : *White House, crab-grass, soul mate, heartbeat.*

But possibly under some circumstances it is not necessary either to sacrifice an accent or to stretch a syllable. We may be able to find in the conformation of the pitch accent itself an occasion for indifference to the spacing of stresses. I have described elsewhere[76] three manners of pitch obtrusion, two of which, Acccents A and B, combine in different ways. In some of these ways a separation of stressed syllables is more necessary than in others.

Accent A is distinguished by a relatively wide downward movement of pitch. But in order to attain the height from which this movement can start, there usually needs to be a preceding upward movement. It follows that when two A accents stand side by side, a flanking unstressed syllable is the most convenient way of setting one off from the other, of making it possible for the first to have its characteristic drop in pitch and for the second in turn to recover the altitude for its drop. In

```
            had       few        man
    He         a          too
                                    y.
```

the syllable *a* is the drop for *had*, *too* is the drop for *few*, and *-y* is the drop for *man-*. Successions of A accents are frequent, since this accent is the one we resort to for separate bits of straight information. The contrast between

```
            saw       burn       hou
    We         a          ing        se.
```

and

```
            feels     burning    ha
    He         a                     tred.
```

is obvious if we try to remove the A accent from *burning* in the first one and make it

```
            saw       burning hou
    We         a
                                 se.
```

In *burning house* we have a separately informative *burning*. In *burning hatred* the participle is an enhancing modifier and part of a stereotype.

Accent B is distinguished by a relatively wide upward movement without a significant fall. In

---

76. See pp. 47-51.

Do they realize who was res pon s i b l e ?

there are two B accents, one on *re-* and one on *-pon-*. There are seldom more than two successive B accents, so that the problem of gaining altitude too fast and leaving insufficient room for succeeding rises does not often come up. But when it does, having flanking syllables is again convenient, since they can be slanted downward (not normally, as with A, skipped down to) :

Wasn't it Edward who brought the news o f the ac c i d e n t ?

—where *Ed-*, *news*, and *ac-* are B-accented syllables.

But when a B accent combines with an A, we have a different situation. The B has its characteristic upmotion, which automatically produces a height satisfactory for the A. No intervening unstressed syllable is necessary, and since the B is marked by the upward skip and the A by the downward one, the two can stand back-to-back with no loss to either. No intervening unstressed syllable is necessary. Such combinations are extremely frequent.[77] They include quantifying and degree modifiers :

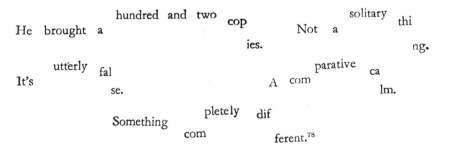

Enhancing modifiers :

---

77. See pp. 57–66.

78. For most of the examples I am sketching the more frequent of two shapes, in which the A accent does not take off from a higher point than the end of the B. But the contrary case is common enough, e.g.

something com pletely dif ferent

```
            beautiful da                          lousy de
What  a               y.           It's  a              al.


      really   needs                          clever  fel
He                                   He's  a
               you.                                    low.
```

Countless more or less stereotyped combinations which might be termed "intermediate compounds," which have not been fused to the point of entirely losing one of their accents:

```
      ternal  fe               Canada                quaking
the  e                              go          a           as
              male          a          ose                     pen


      master  ser           hoity  toi              lose his  shi
a                        so            ty    He'll
              geant                                            rt.


      never get a                            wasting your  ti
He'll            way                You're
                 with  it.                                 me.


      sailing  a                         flying  i
They're           lo              He  came
                ng.                                n.


      tumbled  apa                    throw it  awa
It            rt.            Then                y.
```

(As the last four examples suggest, the normal accent pattern of the two-word verb is this BA combination. We can show the contrast between BA and AA with an instance of this sort, the verb *pine away:*

```
                      pine  a
          She'll  just         wa
                              y.
```

as against a separately meaningful *pine* in *Keep the oak but throw the pine away:*

```
          throw      pine  wa
                 the       a
                            y.)
```

Any "coalesced" action, one in which there is a degree of expectedness between one element and another, the typical case being the noun object which more or less suggests the action of the verb:

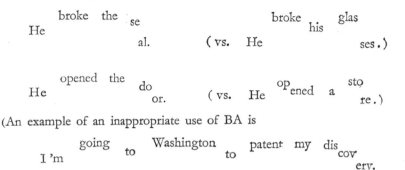

He broke the se al.   (vs.   He broke his glas ses .)

He opened the do or.   (vs.   He op ened a sto re .)

(An example of an inappropriate use of BA is

I 'm going to Washington to patent my dis cov ery.

which might be found in a context implying 'It's obvious, so there, and what are you going to do about it ?,' but is not suitable for a normal informative statement, which would have

I 'm go ing to Wash ington to' pat ent my dis cov ery.

—all the facts are new, and nothing is coalesced.)

The speaker is always free to replace the B accent with an A to imply a separation or a greater degree of assertiveness, e. g.

It 's real ly go od.

I have merely tried to illustrate certain prevalent associations of the patterns.

In the examples cited up to this point I have deliberately chosen BA combinations in which the two accents are spaced out. This was not necessary, but I did it to show that the flanking unaccented syllables remain relatively level—though present, they are wasted; no separation of accents is needed. Now it is time to ask whether any sizable proportion of the oxytones and especially the monosyllables— which give no difficulty with a BA combination[79] but are troublesome with successive A accents—are words which by

---

79. A monosyllable or oxytone can cause trouble not as between a B accent and an A, but as between a single A and its trailer, heard as a combination of B plus A. For example,

the e lite corps

is confusing—it can be heard as a B on -lite plus an A on corps, the latter being ex-nature would occur a large part of the time in phrases containing a B followed by an A. Examples :

```
      old  frie                    old  du                    far  cry . .
an          nd            an            mp            a            . .
                                                                      y

      close                   false  fro                   sure  thi
a          ca            a            nt            a            ng
           ll

      good  fel                dumb  id                   gone  gos
a           fel          that         id           a            lin
            low                       iot                        

      bad  ac                  that's  tha                no  pic
He's  a       tor.       And           t.           It's        nic.

      broke                   walked  o                 writes  nov
I          e             They          ff.         He           els.
           ven.

      ten  dol.                 plete  out               real  ni
for          lars.      a  com          fit         It's        ce.

      too  o                   all  o                        whole
I'm         ld.          It's        ver.         It's the         tru
                                                                      th.
```

tended somewhat to contain its own downmotion, or it can be heard as an A on -*lite* with no accent at all on *corps*, the latter serving as the downmotion for -*lite*. What causes the trouble is a combination of nuisances. In the first place, it is possible to have an A accent starting at a substantially lower pitch than the preceding B; all that is required is that it have the characteristic terminal downmotion of an A, but when the A starts very low, there is not much room for a further drop and this creates an ambiguity with the trailer—since a trailer also is generally downmoving, though non-distinctively so. If *corps* started at a higher pitch,

```
          lite    cor
      the   e
                  ps
```

Jespersen's example *bólt úpríght* (I 5.42), which he regards as an instance of rhythmic stress shift, for my speech must be marked *bólt úpright*, an instance of BA like the others cited here, with enhancing (or degree) modifier *bolt*, like the cliché modifiers in *stark naked, age old, brand new, sopping wet, bone dry*, etc.

It is clear that there is no dearth of examples in the categories I have named—quantitative and degree modifiers, enhancing modifiers, stereotypes, and other coalesced expressions. Since the first of these already embraces all the numerals, including ten monosyllables, as well as high-frequency quantifiers like *more, less, most, all, full, whole, complete, few, quite, entire*, and the second category includes equally high-frequency items like *good, bad, worse, fine, nice, cute, queer, odd, old, divine*, I think it is reasonable to suppose that we have found a breach in the requirement of spaced accents through which a good many monosyllables and a few other oxytones found it easier to make their way. But only a full census of adjectives and adverbs could tell us for sure.

VI. Contrary Tendencies

There is no more crowded world than the linguistic one. Forces jostle one another, a sign that points one way may be pressed into service to point

---

the ambiguity would be avoided. In the second place, *corps* is a monosyllable; a word such as *company*, where *-pany* could set off the higher pitch on *com-*, would make the ambiguity less likely to occur. In the third place, *-lite* is an exceedingly short syllable, one that is hard to stretch in order to cover a certain amount of downmotion and make an unambiguous A accent, as would be possible in

$$\text{the} \quad \text{w} \overset{\text{ne}}{} \quad \text{corps.}$$

The result is that we don't know quite what we are hearing. Other examples on this order are given on pp. 124–127.

It is possible that at least some forestressed compounds (in which the second element has become completely de-accented) have passed through this BA combination as an intermediate stage, the ambiguity facilitating the final step; e.g. *falseface*, starting as

$$\text{false} \overset{\text{fa}}{\underset{\text{ce}}{}}$$

with BA, but heard as

$$\text{false} \quad \overset{}{\underset{\text{face}}{}}$$

with A plus zero.

another, meaningless sub-units become significant in odd ways, hearers' and speakers' interests pull in opposite directions. The spacing of accents is too consistent not to be regarded as an established tendency in English, but it frequently fails because the phonological basis for it has been undermined or borrowed for some other purpose.

The undermining is chiefly due to phonetic erosion. A language with as strong a pull toward monosyllabicity as we find in English is obviously going to have trouble maintaining syllables just to have them to highlight other syllables. When pitch accent then tries to compensate for this by suppressing a remaining syllable so as to highlight one relatively more important, it may find that the lesser word is still too important to be held down. In *Come on in*, the speaker may decide not to sacrifice *on*, which means that he must resort to compressing the pitch turn on a single syllable.

Two additional contrary tendencies, one phonetic, the other semantic, are worth our attention.

The first is the tendency toward immobilizing patterns of stress. English words prefer stable phonemic shapes, and the stress pattern figures as part of this. Where for Shakespeare it was possible to vary the stress in many Romance words, particularly two-syllable adjectives and past participles used attributively, now that these words have been more fully assimilated it has become impossible to exploit most of them to the advantage of accent. Of the 23 two-syllable adjectives listed by Kökeritz (392-7) as having variable stress in Shakespeare (*austere, demure, extreme, profound*, etc.), only two, *impure* and *adverse*, vary in my speech (and one of these, *impure*, has a semantically separable prefix).

In a way related to this, accent sometimes defeats itself. I have pointed out the influence of prevailing position in the sentence, with accent a factor in fixing a forestress on adjectives and nouns and an end-stress on verbs. But once fixed, the word is no longer amenable to change in some other position. One even gets a kind of meaning of ' verbness ' attached to end-stressed forms, which makes for inflexibility since position is no longer the basis of it. I have this sensation of ' verbness ' in connection with end-stressed nouns : *reward, return, regard, receipt, concern, despair, regret, disgust, reply, consent, contempt, design, report, command*.

The other contrary force is the omnivorousness of meaning. One gets the impression that it hovers in the background ready to pounce on any contrast to fulfil any need. For many speakers *cóntrary* and *contráry* no longer mean the same ; the pairs *human-humane, antic-antique*, and *urban-urbane* have already undergone this bifurcation. We may retain the *-en* suffix as an adjectivized past participle in many forms because it gives us an extra syllable, but this does no good with *a swelled head*, which is not the same as *a swollen head*. In other cases the *-en* suffix has picked up a figurative meaning, as may be noted in the following when used attributively : *golden* vs. *gold, flaxen* vs.

flax, leaden vs. *lead, waxen* vs. *wax.* With *wool-woolly-woollen* there is a three-way contrast.[80]   The pair *near* vs. *near to* is no longer rhythmic, as Van Draat supposes (V3 529–532), but is tied to a literal-figurative distinction : *near Boston* but *near to my heart;* we still have a rhythmic recourse in *near* vs. *close to,* but *near to,* it seems, has been pulled into the orbit of *dear to.*

---

80. Cf. V2 § 29 for additional examples.

Part II

MORPHEMES

ON DEFINING THE MORPHEME

Word 4.18-23 (1948)

The title imitates W. F. Twaddell's *On defining the phoneme* (1935), but plagiarizes nothing else.

While " differential meaning " could be used as an all-or-none test for distinguishing phonemes, " referential meaning " was bound to lead, it seemed to me, into all kinds of traps, when used to distinguish morphemes; and as long as there was an appeal to meaning it had to be referential meaning, in spite of disclaimers. I therefore proposed a statistical measure for the morpheme— renaming the latter a *formative*—whose right to be classed as a morpheme was then to be gauged by its power to enter into new combinations.

This is the first place that I controverted the notion of the all-or-none, a theme that I took up again in *Generality, gradience, and the all-or-none,* 's-Gravenhage, 1961.

Implicit in Bloomfield's definition of the morpheme as ' a linguistic form which bears no partial phonetic-semantic resemblance to any other form ', and of the morpheme's semantic content (sememe) as ' a constant and definite unit of meaning, different from all other meanings, including all other sememes, in the language ',[1] is the assumption that a given phonetic concourse is either entirely with or entirely without meaning. The passage from the ' ultimate constituent' to the ' meaningless sub-unit' is abrupt : there is no meaning at all below the morpheme (if there is, we shall be suspected of not having analyzed far enough) ; and there is as much meaning, qualitatively, in morpheme plus zero as in morpheme plus morpheme plus morpheme....

I believe that this concept of the morpheme needs examination because (1) it is important to constituent analysis ; (2) it is a crossroads between diachronic and synchronic morphology ; and (3) it shows the necessity for a more rigorous treatment of meaning as it applies to synchronic analysis. I shall maintain : (1) That the transition from sub-unit to morpheme is, as regards meaning, not abrupt, altho there is a point below which we contemplate a world that is dead, or nearly so, but above which the degree of fluidity, the degree of animation, jumps upward at a rate far exceeding its increase elsewhere; this degree of animation, by which I mean the statistically

---

1. L. Bloomfield, *Language* 161–162 ; New York, 1933.

determinable readiness with which an element enters into new combinations, is the only sure linguistic evidence that the element has a meaning of its own. (2) That this increase continues as utterances are augmented in extent and still further as they are combined with other utterances, tho at an infinitely slower rate. In other words, instead of describing the access of meaning as a rectangle open at the growing end and closed squarely at the end that represents morpheme plus zero, I should diagram is as a parabola with the narrowest part of the curve standing for a least element capable of entering into new combinations (having meaning), and with the morpheme either at the same point or slightly to the right of it. The slow widening of the open end of the parabola is only a way of depicting the fact that $a+b$ will join more readily into new combinations than a or b alone, that $(a+b)+(c+d)$ will combine more freely in new arrangements than $a+b$ or $c+d$ alone, etc. —in other words, that the linguistic environment of a smaller unit tends to be more predictable than that of a larger unit. (3) That the morpheme, as defined, is a variable, and scarcely easier to pin down than a word. And (4) that the morpheme needs redefinition, as it represents at present a curious survival of the confusion of contemporary and historical analysis.

The application of the definition that I have quoted is illustrated by the statement that ' *unhesitating* is not a morpheme '.[2] Since *un-*, *-hesitat-*, and *-ing* are all encountered elsewhere with meanings similar to the ones that they reveal here, *unhesitating* is not an ultimate constituent, or morpheme.

The difficulty arises when we attempt to deal with words like *away* or *disease*. We know, of course, etymologically, that there are two components in *disease;* but this knowledge is diachronic, and cannot be invoked in a synchronic analysis. As far as the contemporary meanings of *dis-* and *-ease* are concerned, they are irrelevant to the contemporary meaning of *disease*— it would be impossible for a modern speaker of English to create *disease* out of *dis-* and *-ease* as we now use them, as he might, for example, create *de-hair* or *de-sugar*. Stimulated by our etymological information we may imagine to ourselves how the meaning of *disease* developed from the combined meanings of its etymological components; but this in no way represents any picture that the vast majority of the users of the language carry about with them. If we were limited to usage we could no more divide *disease* (as spoken, dizíiz) into *dis-* plus *-ease* than we can divide *curfew* into *cur-* and *-few*, or *copper* into *cop-* and *-er*. Etymology has undoubtedly motivated attempts at synchronic constituent analysis of many words, but needs to be carefully separated from it.

Now when we pass from words like *disease* in which the combination is different semantically from its elements (and the difference is not attributable to any tagmeme, such as order or modulation, but is a psychological trans-

2. R. S. Wells, " Immediate constituents," *Language* 23.81 (1947).

formation related to the frequency of the combination), to words in which the combination is clearly the sum of the parts, such as *unhesitating*, we traverse a zone in which there is every imaginable degree of relationship between the part and the whole. In some, the relationship is dim—one scarcely knows whether to affirm it, or to call the totality a morpheme-word; as indicated by the stressed -sal- versus the unstressed -si- of *motorcycle* and *bicycle*, we seem to have two cognate forms one of which is clearly separable and the other may or may not be. This wavering continues all the way up into fairly complex combinations, with of course fewer and fewer examples the farther we go. To most unsophisticated users of the language *a short circuit* has nothing to do with either *short* or *circuit* (except in so far as the phrase itself has been clipped to *a short*); and to not a few of these it has come to signify merely some kind of electrical mishap, completely removed from even that technical meaning which might, on reflection, be traced to *short* plus *circuit*. Ask one of these persons to account for the contrast *short circuit* versus *long circuit* and he will only look astonished.

If we abandon the etymological standard of analysis we resign ourselves to the fact that the *cept* of *receptive, concept*, and *except* is no more 'a morpheme', synchronically speaking, than is the *taf* of *taffeta, taffy*, and *distaff*, for neither meets the test of meaning. May we go a step farther? Suppose that a form which under many conditions does meet the test of meaning, such as the *re-* of *recall, reclaim, rebate, return, remand*, and a host of neologisms, under other conditions has its primary meaning swallowed up, as in *repertory, religion, recipe*, or again has it contrasting with itself as in *re-creation* versus *recreation*, or, finally, relates to a secondary meaning of the etymon as in *research*. Unless we resort to etymology there is no way to identify all these instances as a single morpheme. The *re-* of *research* ('diligent, intensive') of *recall* ('back'), of *rewrite* ('again'), and of *religion* (zero) are, synchronically, merely homonyms or near-homonyms. Besides identity and mere homonymy there may be partial synonymy, as in the *un-* of *undetermined* and the *un-* of *unwind*, which are related as negatives but distinguished by their peculiar connotations of 'yet to be' and 'in reverse'.

This raises the all-important question of WHOSE meaning, since meaning is the criterion. Clearly in the speech of the person who says *a three-wheeled bicycle* we cannot analyze *bicycle*. There are speakers of English who could never see a resemblance between the *com-* of *compare* and the *com-* of *compound* except the resemblance of sound, tho these same speakers would readily note the kinship of the *co-* in *co-worker* and *co-defendant*; there are others who might be taught to see the connexion in *compare* and *compound*, but would never think of it otherwise. For these people, who probably make up the bulk of the speakers of the language, can we rightly say that *com-* (*con-*) is a morpheme? It is doubtful whether for them any collocation of phonemes can be called a morpheme (as defined) unless it is still an active formative in the language, such as *un-*, *re-*, *anti-*, *de-*, in many or most of their combinations.

Obviously we cannot use meaning to determine an element in speech until we decide whose meaning, and what kind of meaning, we mean. As for whose, it can scarcely be other than that of the majority of speakers. As to what kind, it should be the kind that the majority would recognize as constituting a basis of similarity among complex forms that are otherwise dissimilar in meaning.

For the latter, we might speak of 'proper meaning', referring to the meaning that can be assigned to a segment taken separately. The *in-* of *infer* and *intense* would not have proper meaning because the majority of speakers would never take it separately; it would not, therefor, be a morpheme. It follows that proper meaning, as the determinant of a morpheme, is intimately connected with freedom. If it is a bound form, the element must—in order to be a morpheme—be active; for the moment that it becomes inert the new generation of speakers take it merely as a sound element, not a meaning element, of the larger signal. How proper meaning begins to dim the moment a combination becomes stereotyped is illustrated by a class in which the twelve students attempting to use the *he* (*him*)+*who* (*that*) construction to translate Spanish *al que* were divided equally between those who called it *he who* (as verb object!) and those who chose *him who;* fifty per cent made the wrong choice because *he who* had partially lost its active relation to the independent use of the pronoun.

Attempts to identify morphemes by formal means will probably bear little fruit, for juncture and stress are too erratic and bear no simple relationship to meaning. The open juncture in *an aim* and the close juncture in *a name* do not distinguish *an* as a morpheme and *a* as a non-morpheme, but rather distinguish *an aim* from *a name* as wholes. Tho *holiday* is not a phonemic phrase by the Bloch-Trager definition, the *-day* is a morpheme in the sense that most speakers would immediately use the word *day* in defining it, and would associate the similar sounds with similar meanings. Freedom rather than form is what marks the morpheme, tho the form is affected in loosely predictable ways. An utterance can perhaps be speeded up until all open junctures disappear, and yet it is understood, because its morphemes are identified thru memory. *Holiday* has often been encountered alone, and it is tied to a similar verbal habit or memory in *birthday* and *washday;* freedom in the sense of not being phrasally bound, and freedom in the sense of the manipulability of its parts, both REMEMBERED, enable us to identify it as a word and its ending as a morpheme.

We thus arrive at a definition of the morpheme which parallels that of the word. If a word is a least element that can be used by itself, a morpheme is a least element that can enter into new combinations. Potentiality for new combination has two distinct advantages, as criterion for the morpheme. In the first place, it enables us to replace the ill-defined *meaning* with a measurable fact, the recurring appearance in new environments. In the second place, we shall discover that it is necessary in our definition of the word; for if a 'minimum free form' is one which merely HAS appeared in varied contexts, it would actually be BOUND to those (extensive but finite) contexts; only its potentiality for new combination keeps it from being phrasally bound. The actual number of new combinations made out of any given morpheme may be extremely small, but the appearance of only one in the lifetime of a speaker is still sufficient proof that the element has proper meaning, that its user views it as something existing at least partly to itself. Admittedly such a definition will not be altogether easy to apply ; but it is an improvement on the definition that it replaces, which is just as difficult in application and is impossible in theory.

The definition, however, rules out meaningless residual forms as morphemes —such as the *cran-* of *cranberry*—as well as etymological components. There is no way by which they can be included without opening the door to forms that we should not wish to include. This is an inconvenience, as it flies in the face of usage of the term *morpheme*, and the change would involve correcting too many things already written. Since very little constituent analysis has been done, it will be easier to leave *morpheme* alone and to give a new name to the KIND of morpheme that I have described as pertinent to constituent analysis. I therefor propose *formative* in place of *morpheme* as I have defined it, and *component* for an etymological entity (as used by Bloomfield, *component* and *constituent* are precise synonyms, so that we can utilize the surplus term), whence a *morpheme* is 'a formative, residue, or component'. But we must remember, if this is done, that synchronic meaning is no longer the criterion for the morpheme; tho meaning of some sort there would be, whether diachronic or synchronic. Formatives would include morpheme words (whence *formative* might be defined also as 'a minimum active form'). (Tho there is wide duplication between residue and component and between formative and component, we still need to distinguish them, for there are residues which are not components such as certain portions of *discombooberate*, and there are even formatives which are not components, such as the *-aroo* as encountered in the originating word *buckaroo*).

Constituent analysis is more and more hemmed in as it moves from the open end of the parabola toward smaller and smaller units at the closed end. The smaller the unit, the more likely it is to be partially or wholly bound. I do not refer now to the kind of bondage which mechanically limits certain forms to one or a few environments, without altering materially the value of the parts, such as *brand*, adj., limited to *new* (or *span new*), or *hard of* limited to *hearing*; I mean the bondage which makes the whole radically different from the sum of its parts. *By all means* in present-day speech belongs to the focus class of *yes* or *certainly*, not to that of *in every way possible*; it is even less analyzable than *certainly*, where *-ly* affects *certain-* just as it affects *glad-* in *gladly*, whereas *by that method* is not semantically parallel to *by all means*. *How do you do?* belongs to the focus class of *Hello*, not to that of *How do you know?* *Like nobody's business* belongs to the focus class of *like sixty, like fun, like hell*, not to that of *like my brother*. *Why don't you be careful?* (admonition or reproach) versus *Why not be careful?* (suggestion or hypothesis)—unlike the semantically related *Why don't you try it?* and *Why not try it?* or *What do you say we—?* paralleling *Suppose we—?*, etc., are to be analyzed or not depending on how much the analyzer insists upon fidelity between meaning of the whole and meanings of the parts. The analyst will generally elect to analyze, and rightly so, for he cannot assume the impossible burden of identifying all the stereotypes in a language. Bondage—in the sense of uniqueness of meaning—is virtually complete by the time we reach down to the word, and quite complete when we reach the formative. It is true that there are hints of meaning with vague resemblances of form at inferior levels, such as the *n* of *un-, in-, non-, nude, numb, nix, no*, or the vowel of *goof, boob, google*, etc., the occupants of the sharpest part of the parabola that describes the access of meaning ; but constituent analysis should stop before it reaches this stage. Its problems are too specialized to be included.

CONCLUSIONS

1. Constituent analysis as undertaken up to the present works successfully—reflecting not perfectly but with a high degree of accuracy actual practice in the language—in larger groups, less successfully as groups are made smaller, until, at the point of the 'morpheme,' it breaks down a large part of the time. This necessitates a redefinition of the morpheme so as to separate morphemes that are valid for constituent analysis (formatives and residues) from those which are valid for diachronic morphology (components). The pluralizing component of *Cincinnati* and the genitive component of *Evans* are irrelevant to a constituent analysis of contemporary English.

2. The redefinition of the morpheme suggests a clarification of freedom and bondage. This is called for also because *bondage* is now used in two different senses : a sub-word formative is 'bound' by the very fact that it is not a word, that is by never appearing alone, tho the variety of its environments may be almost infinite; a word, on the other hand, is 'bound' when it is restricted as to its environments. Let us say, then, that : (1) Components are locked in 'inert bondage.' (2) Formatives and residues may be locked in 'active bondage.' (3) Words are locked in 'phrasal bondage' when the combination is mechanical and the meaning of the parts answers to the mean-

ing of the whole. The phrasally bound *gob* in *Shut your gob* has the same meaning as *mouth* in this context, and admits of the same ornamentation as in *Shut your silly gob* (or *mouth*). Phrasal bondage is in turn divided into (a) 'complete phrasal bondage' when the word is used only in enumerable combinations such as *full* adv. in *full well* and *full many* or *tapis* in *on the tapis*; (b) 'partial phrasal bondage' when the word is used only in certain types of context such as *budge* (largely in negative contexts); and (c) 'complex phrasal bondage' (itself either complete or partial) when a phrase is phrasally bound, such as the *no uncertain* of *in no uncertain terms* (*words, phrases*) or *suffice it* in *suffice it to say* (*point out*). (4) Words are locked in 'semantic bondage' when a set phrase, made up of words which may or may not be perfectly free under other circumstances, has a meaning which does not answer to the sum of the meanings of the parts. Semantic bondage comprises most of the so-called 'idioms' in the language. Since no expression is ever quite as free as the focus class to which it belongs, semantic bondage affects in greater or lesser degree every utterance in the language—this is to say that (even disregarding supra-segmental modifications) the whole is never quite the same as the sum of the parts. In practice, the difference can as a rule be safely ignored. Thru analogic creation, any form of bondage may be released into its corresponding form of freedom: the phrasally bound *hard of hearing* (not *hard of seeing, hard of smelling*) may become 'Is your car hard of starting?'[3] The inertly bound suffix in *delicious, luscious* may become actively bound in *galuptious, curvaceous, crematious*.

---

3. PDQ commercial announcement on Abbott and Costello program, 19 Nov. 1947.

2

WORD AFFINITIES

American Speech 15.62-73 (1940)

An early interest in synonyms led me to notice the similarity in form that synonyms are apt to assume, and this, in turn, to what came to represent for me a fundamental principle of the lexicon: the tendency of a form to gather about it an aura of meaning which clings to it in spite of the more strident demands of practical communication. It seems to me that verbal counters have both an x value and a picture value, and that the two are often in conflict. For the transactions of language, the x value dominates; for the allusions of language, the picture value dominates. The x value is potentially variable—it decrees that *home* "might as well" be *swurish* or *locyx*. The picture value is absolute—it decrees that *home*, once embedded in the language, forms semantic alliances that make it impossible to dislodge (except by a slow historical process), and once embedded in the mind of the speaker, becomes something more than a substitute for a thing—to a certain degree it *is* the thing, or part of it.

"Word affinities" was a first attempt to show the metastasis of forms linked with meanings, and reveals somewhat of the naivete of all first enthusiasms.

That certain words naturally go together, and being encountered drag each other along a train of thought like the barbed atoms of Democritus, anyone who has used any of the multitude of associative devices in English, from alliteration and rime to homonyms and puns, cannot fail to observe. Why, when I am writing this line, do certain words emerge as carriers of my idea, and not others? I do not, except on rare occasions, deliberately choose them; and even when I revise and correct the same mechanisms are at work, suggesting other expressions which I happily or unhappily seize upon, but have not myself 'consciously' brought forward. Connections of various sorts, most of them learned but a few of them accidental, do exist among words and become, by imposing a kind of prior framework on the expression of our ideas, in part the determinants of those ideas. The larger and more extensive a vocabulary becomes, the more of such interconnections there must be; English, with its enormously accumulated store of words, has more than its share of them. This inquiry has to do with one type of verbal affinity—the grouping of similar meanings about similar sounds.

How deeply rooted in English is this 'sound symbolism' the keen insight of Jespersen has already perceived and explained.* He taxes linguistic historians with an unwillingness to admit the obvious connections that exist between certain sounds and certain meanings, and proves that the adequacy of sound to sense has not only originated countless words but has also helped others to survive which were, to begin with, not provably imitative. He points out that others have not gone far enough in admitting this principle; yet, one feels that he may himself have stopped somewhat short of its fullest implications.

The shortcoming, if such it be—no one could call it a major one, considering the size of his contribution—consists, I think, in an overemphasis of the notion of adequacy. He has sought consistently to find some near or remote connection between a sonic element of the word and an element of nature —meaning by 'nature' everything except language itself. This ignores a phenomenon that recent psychology reveals: that relationships may be set up between things that have no outward similarity whatever, and that, once established, the relationship seems the most 'natural' thing in the world; find the relationship in configuration or in conditioned reflex, it makes no difference. Indeed, many 'naturally adequate' symbolisms are born in just this way, and the similarity which we think to find between word and thing is only fancied. Hardly a more artificial connection could be had than that between the bell and the food offered to Pavlov's dog; but no one whose salivary glands have been stimulated by the peals of a dinner bell would fail to agree that the sound and the food are admirably connected. The word *sour* is devoid of sound symbolism, but by this magic of identification has become as vivid a word as any in the language, to which the number of its figurative uses—a good measurement—bears witness.

It is not necessary, then, to look for resemblance between sound and sense when treating of 'sound symbolism' in the broadest meaning of the expression—'sound suggestiveness' might express it better. More often than not there is or has been at one time such resemblance, but it is never alone in binding together the word and the idea; for once the kinship is established it is as real as if it had been truly adequate to begin with, and the word becomes, in its own right, a bridge to still further associations. It may be the only basis of new connections, or it may supplement the idea in establishing them; the word *fresh* in the sense of 'bold,' 'forward' may have started by reason of its meaning, literally, 'nonchalant' (with the fairly obvious sound symbolism of chattering teeth in *freeze, frigid, fright,* etc.), but has ended by annexing itself to *rash* and *brash,* imitating *words* rather than any 'natural' *sound.* There is a cumulative tendency of symbolism within symbolism—a symbol may symbolize not a thing but another symbol; most often, however, it suggests both the thing and other symbols. A great deal

---

* Otto Jespersen, *Language,* New York, Holt, 1922.

of sound suggestiveness, as well as no small amount of philosophy, has resulted from symbols which stand at just such a second or third remove from things.

So while resemblances are active at the beginning, and doubtless play a part in the persistence of certain words rather than others, the appearance and sound of the word itself become in the end the more important factors. The business of symbolizing seems ultimately to be the creation of counters or tools which in essence are not suggestive but manipulable. As with currency there is to begin with an intrinsic value in the symbol—gold in those cultures where gold is valued, elsewhere pearls, hides, or tin cans—but in the end convenience gradually erodes the less useful attributes. We now prefer paper money (and again the analogy parallels words, in that we frequently value it for itself rather than for what it symbolizes) ; and other signs, from semaphores to Braille, are conditioned more by the exigencies of the method of signaling than by the idea signaled, and have become more and more abstract.[1]

Onomatopoeia in Reverse

The significance of words as words is illustrated by a number of expressions, particularly exclamations, where not only is the word assimilated to the sound, but the sound is also assimilated to the ' wordness ' of the word. From the long habit of using words as vocables of consonants-plus-vowels, we have taken the expressions *humph*, *ahem*, *pish*, and more recently *tsk* (the youngsters say *tusk*) and *umph* (or *oomph*), and have made them like ' real words ' by pronouncing them as spelled rather than articulating the sounds that they were intended to represent; we do this not only when reading them, but also sometimes when employing them spontaneously as interjections of our own.[2] The fact that they have gained currency, that they produce the desired response in our hearers, gives them a status from which the fact that they have sacrificed some of their imitativeness detracts not at all. Though not claiming to be an unusually deliberative person, I sometimes catch myself uttering a feeble and half-hearted *ouch* some seconds after I have received a trifling hurt; *ouch* is seen to be one might say the socially ' official ' thing to say under the circumstances, and its verbal capacity supersedes its value as an exclamation. In a similar way children soon accustom themselves to the ritual of kissing, and the symbolic kiss which may be

---

1. Cf. the rejoicing of Wm. McDevitt, *Book Collecting*, 9 : 1—' NEON LITE speling : Mechanical economy naturally produces betr speling. Much of th recent popularity of LITE NITE TRU BLU is DU to economizing LITE space and powr.'

2. Cf. the way in which many persons render the colloquial *th'* encountered in direct quotations in written stories : it frequently comes out as *thuh*—a ' real ' word. One serial cartoon goes so far as to print it *thuh*.

'tossed' becomes to their minds a real kiss; the symbol supplants the genuine article.

This kickback of the idea into the word, wherein without any imaginable sound symbolism the word is nevertheless vested with unusual suggestive power, is seen in verbalizations of things which are spectacular in themselves —names of jewels, meteorological phenomena, swift actions such as running, leaping (the mode of articulation here may contribute a true sound symbolism), dancing, etc. The poet appreciates these words, and the times that pearls, rubies, dawns, dusks, sands, shores, smitings, and slayings appear in his verses go beyond calculation. One of the most dazzling words in English, to my thinking, is *sapphire*, joining in one breath the sparkle of the jewel that it names and the gleam of the fire that it suggests. Yet there is no sound symbolism to speak of in these words, save what we impart (as we often do) when we say them.

Accretions Due to Sound

But once a partnership is fixed between a sound and an idea, nothing more is needed to cause that sound to give the cast of its idea to many words, alike in sound, that previously symbolized something different. If in addition there is some resemblance between the ideas themselves, eventually an entire family—by adoption—may knit itself together. I was lately much puzzled on reading a letter from a friend to learn that one of her family had 'exclaimed with much delight and embellishment.' It finally dawned that the sound element which had stuck in her ear and made that transformation possible was probably the *-ish* of *ravishment*, plus (I suspect) a dash of *embelesamiento*, from her having lived a year or two in Spain.

Such connections are inescapable. We are all potential creators of them, and not one but has at some time contrived some ridiculous or felicitous coupling of words. To my mind *ramifications* are followed out by *ramming* hither and yon. *Scrutinize* implies a screwing up of the face in response to mental effort, and *inscrutable* implies a similar screwing up due to perplexity. Freshman themes seldom omit the phrase 'literally covered with,' which obviously derives from the silly symbolism of *literal* and *litter*. A current magazine yields 'Fadiman is a carbolic ad libber,' wherein *carbolic*, besides suggesting 'acid' by its meaning, reechoes the *-olic* of *vitriolic*, *colic*, and perhaps also *alcoholic*.

It is not strange, then, that this phenomenon, in action every day of our lives, has made many permanent additions to the language in the form of constellations of words held together by similarity of sounds and a partly or wholly *induced* similarity of meaning.

Words with Imitative Elements. Jespersen's Points

Certainly it would be impossible to disentangle the purely imitative from the affinitive suggestiveness of words. The two overlap and reinforce each other; in fact, it is probably the affinitive element which, as the years take us farther and farther from the original echoism, has preserved to our day many of the kinships of sound-to-sense. What may have been the original sound significance of *gl* and related sounds for the eye and visual appearances would be difficult to single out—that there was sound symbolism seems to be indicated by the great number of words that show this uniformity; yet the disappearance of the sound symbolism has not affected the vigor of the constellation, which has gone on attracting other words into its system: besides *gleam, glance, glow, glare, glitter, gloat, glower, gloom, glaze, glass, glimmer, glimpse, glim*, there are *ogle, goggle, glory*, and most recently *glamor*, which colloquially is coming to refer to visual appeal; even *owl*, in the form *owlish*, refers oftener to a look than a sound, and there exists the variant *ogle*. But as Jespersen has dealt with the imitative side of the problem, we may make the division into imitative and affinitive as a matter of convenience, and examine some of his proofs, adding to them new examples.

Under 'Blendings'[3] Jespersen gives a number of examples of the creation of new words out of closely associated synonyms—*scroll* from *scrow* plus *roll*, *slender* from *slight* and *slim* plus *tender*, and so on. Short of the actual blend is the word-family of *sli-* and *sle-*, in which *slender, slight, slim, sleazy, sliver, slick, slip, slipper, slit*, etc., join with the general idea of 'neat' or 'trim'—an implication which was not developed. A knowledge of the constellations involved is fundamental to an understanding of blends, as they oftenest occur not between two isolated sounds but between two (or more) sounds either or both of which belong to a constellation. It is unlikely, for instance, that *scroll* would have developed (if it is a genuine blend and not a contraction of *scrow roll*) had there not already existed a large family of *scr-* words having to do with writing and an equally large family of *r-l* words (*roll, furl, curl, spiral*, etc.). How this happens may be seen experimentally. Take, for example, the *-ush* words, suggesting 'moist' and 'oozy': *lush, slush, mush, gush, crush* (attracted by the trade name *Orange Crush*), and the *-ash* words: *wash, slosh, hash, mash, plash*, merging with the idea of 'breaking' or 'fragments': *dash, crash, trash, slash, smash, bash, gash, ash, clash* (perhaps explaining why we hear mentally the clatter of small pieces when we use the word *cash*, and why *dishes* are so rattly and breakable). Now combine the foregoing sound with the swollen *bl-* group of *blubber, blimp*,[4] and *block*, and you get, 'The bladder became more and more bloated with blood until, suddenly, it *blashed*.' I submit that no other verb could as vividly depict the bursting of a membrane gorged with liquid. The word *vanquish* also

3. *Language*, New York, Holt, 1922, pp. 312 ff. and 396 ff.

4. Object of a recent word-play by Charlie McCarthy, 'She was a little *blimp*,' for *plump*.

provides a footnote, for it is stronger than *conquer* from its suggestion of *quash, smash,* etc. Again, combine the sounds of *droop, drip, drape* (cf. also *drop, drizzle, drivel, drool*) with *drupe,* and you get a very pictorial word for an earring—*droupe.* When Jespersen says[5] that he suspects that *swagger* comes from *swashbuckler* by the addition of a slang ending, it seems to me that he misses the application to the word *stagger* (or possibly *braggart,* or to the *-ag* family—*sag, wag, flag,* etc.) of the *sw-* constellation indicating 'flourish' or 'sweep'—*swoop, swell, swoon, swing,* etc.; *swashbuckler* certainly belongs with this constellation, but is, it appears to me, too narrow as an exclusive source. With these facts in mind, it is hardly necessary to point out that classical etymologists have restricted themselves beyond reason in their determined search for 'the' etymon of a word; the whole language can hardly be left out of account, and it appears that the old fallacy of the over-simplifiers, searching for 'the' cause where there usually is a complex of causes, has also bedeviled philology.

Of *plumbum* and related words Jespersen shrewdly observes, 'I see sound symbolism in *all* the words *plump.*'[6] He associates them with *-ump* as the sound of a heavy fall. As this sound is articulated by blowing out the cheeks, particularly when reinforced by initial *b, p,* or *m* (*bump, bomb, plump, mump, pompous*), there appears also to be an attempt to picture size; I find that these words, speaking more generally, signify heavy masses or the movement of heavy masses: *dump, rump, hump, crump, lump, stump, slump, gump* (a heavy-witted person), etc.

Vulgar Latin *magis* is cited by Jespersen as showing, in its derivatives Italian *ma,* Spanish *mas,* French *mais,* a vigorous survival in the sense of 'but,' because of the appropriateness of the initial *m.* One hesitant enough to use an adversative conjunction would be likely to fill in with *m-m-m* while making up his mind.[7] An example in English is the persistence of the illogical *a* in 'kind of a,' 'sort of a,' etc.[8] Something similar must have happened to bring about the well-nigh universal use of *n* in negatives, attracting into its meaning-system words not originally negative, from Spanish *nada* to English *nuts.*[9]

Of direct imitation there is no need to speak at length. The prickly, staccato sound of *st, t,* and *z* gives us *zest, zip, sting, tang, tingle, stick,* and the newest addition, *zing.* There is a flaccid sameness about *slop, flop, plop, lop,*

---

5. P. 300.

6. P. 314.

7. The supplanting of *mas* by *pero* in colloquial Spanish does not seem to invalidate the argument, as there is a dissimilation, not found in French or Italian, from *más* in the original sense of 'more.'

8. *Words* 4:2, Feb. 1938.

9. English *nod,* affirmative, is a curious contradiction.

and *lap*, an unmistakable garrulity about *babble, blab, gabble, bluster,* and their newest brother, *blat* (to say nothing of the kindred *pr-, br-* words, *prattle, prate, bray, brag, brawl,* etc.), a creepy sense to *lurk, skulk,* and *slink,* and a busy sound about *hustle, jostle, bustle,* and *rustle* ('to rustle up a meal'). We are sometimes conscious of sound symbolism even when it is hard to say exactly in what it consists—*butcher,* for example, is far more adequate to the sense than *killer.*

'Originator of the Sound' we may dismiss as not important to the argument, as such words as *parlez vous* for 'Frenchman,' *god-damn* for 'English soldier,' etc., would not be likely to serve as nuclei for word clusters, although they might themselves join with existing clusters—*bigot,* for example, with *big, bigwig, bogey,* etc.

'Movement,' in which the sound produced by the action is used to name the action, is a fertile source. The sound of motion through an inspissate medium, *sl-,* gives us words indicating slowness or inertia : *slow, sluggish, slothful, slack, slush, slosh, slubber, slog.* Liquid in motion runs the whole gamut of *seep, sip, sap, sup, sop, soap,* and *soup.* The gurgling of the throat gives *gullet, gorge, gargle, guttural.* The 'nasal' *n* predominates in words relating to the nose : *nuzzle, nozzle, nostril ;* and the sound of certain nasal functions is apparent in *sniff, sniffle, snuffle, snivel, snore, snort, snout, snoot, snot, snuff; snub* has been drawn into line probably by *snob* and *snooty,* all three implying arrogance ; and *schnozzle* testifies to the continued vigor of the constellation.

Under 'Things and Appearances' Jespersen analogizes between the 'natural association' of high tones and light, low tones and dark; and farther on[10] he extends this association to size, the high tones indicating smallness. Since dark gives the impression of bigness, by preventing us from seeing objects in detail, it may well be that the association was extended from size to light, instead of, or along with, the imagined kinship of high tones and light, low tones and dark. Size in this connection would seem to be verbalized by the fact that short *i* and long *e* make for brevity of utterance, and hence imply smallness and neatness. *Drip—pour, slip—slope, nick—gash, leak—gush,* are pairs that point to the distinction. I remember an entertainer's once ending a joke, depicting the extermination of a fly, with *squish*—the fly presumably being too small to *squash.* Jespersen remarks the re-formation of *pipe* into *peep* after the *i* ceased to be appropriate ; other examples are the childish word *teeny,* existing alongside of *tiny,* and *seep,* which has supplanted *sipe.*

Of 'States of Mind,' as leading to interjections which in turn give words, one of the deepest-rooted is admiration and the accompanying exclamation *m-m-m;* and since to our simple minds size more often excites admiration than anything else, *m* goes most naturally with bigness : *mammoth, megatherian,*

---

10. Pp. 402 and 407.

immense, magnus and its descendants, *mogul, muck-a-muck, mighty, mountainous* (*Man-Mountain* Dean), *Moloch,* the Octavus Roy Cohen favorite *magnolious,* and recently *monolithic.*[11]   The *growl* of the *grouchy* person gives us *grumpy, gripe, grouse, crusty, crabby, cross, cranky, crotchety ;* the proper name *Scrooge* also finds its place here (with the added suggestion of a wry face), and Jespersen adds *Mrs. Grundy*; 'don't be an old *granny*' is perfectly clear in its reference to the *cr-, gr-* words. *F-f-f* as an exclamation of disgust gives us *faugh, fol-de-rol, phooey, fiddlesticks, fiddle-faddle,* and has probably helped to weld together the synonyms of failure, which exhibit *f* plus *l* : *failure, fluke, fizzle, flop, fiasco* (*i* being here etymologically *l*). The lusty *whee* and *whoop* are heard in *whale* (of a good thing), *whopper* (of a lie), *gee-whiz,* and the interjection *what!* Jespersen mentions the Italian suffix *-accio* and *-uccio* (Spanish *-acho* and *-ucho*), used for ungainly things ; we may add the English suffix, still in the jelly stage and with no pejorative meaning to begin with, *-osity : pomposity, verbosity, religiosity, preciosity,* etc.; *-aster,* attempting to convey a pejorative meaning with a similar sound, has never caught on in English, the reason perhaps being that, like *-osity,* it seems rather to connote bigness : *medicaster, poetaster, criticaster,* etc., have remained in the realm of learned expressions.

Word Constellations

Proceeding now on the assumption made at the beginning, that the associative power is stronger than the merely imitative, I give some examples of word groups through which runs the thread of similarity in sound, many of which are truly imitative, some of which are not.

1. Affixes. The commonest uniformity in spelling and pronunciation is to be found among the elements used to compound words—prefixes and suffixes ; if a sonic constant is to pick up some special meaning, we should expect affixion to afford the best opportunity for it—and the new meaning like as not will be entirely different from the original one. *Delight, delectable, delicious, delicate* come to us from Latin, and have contributed a winsomeness to the group *del-.* Does it not come more naturally to say '*delirious* with joy' than to say *mad* or *insane* with joy? On the same stem was coined, in 1937, the word *delovely.*[12] There is no traceable symbolism in this sound. The *-cious* words, however, are suggestive of smacking the lips : *luscious, delicious, voluptuous, salacious, galuptious, scrumptious, voracious,* and a recent trade name, *Stillicious.* The *-sh* of *relish* and *ravish* (with *lavish* in the offing) puts them into a neighboring category, which obviously adverts to the moist and oozy *-ush* and *-ash* words given above. Another prefix, or rather a combination of prefixes, has a sound which, though devoid of symbolism to begin

---

11. *The Nation* 142 : 2, July 10, 1937, p. 32a.
12. Cf. movie ad., Kansas City *Star,* June 8, 1937.

with, is striking enough to have been made symbolic through use and ac-cretion—*irre-*, with its suggestion of 'utter': *irremediable, irreparable,* 'utterly beyond help'; *irresponsible,* 'utterly undependable'; *irresistible, irrefutable, irreverent, irresolute, irrespective*—all more utterly utter than if the initial *ir* were changed to *un.* Ring Lardner perceived this when he invented, or copied from popular speech, his *irregardless.* Three groups which parallel and strength-en each other in the suggestion of violence are *tor-* in *torture, torment, tor-tuous, torrent, torrid* (two distinct etymologies here), *tur-* in *turbulent, turmoil, turbid, turgid,* and *ter-* in *terrible, terrific,* etc. The popular *turrible* reveals the interplay here, and to my mind even *turbine* hints at intense power under control. The *ob-* words have picked up the sense of 'offensive': *objectionable, obnoxious, obtrusive, obsessive, obloquy.* I suspect that the unpopularity of *be-nignant* is at least partly due to the fact that the *-ignant* field has been usurped by *malignant* and *indignant,* its contraries in meaning. The accumulated mean-ing of a suffix may be quite consciously exploited, as with the *-ic* and *-ics* words, which have a legitimate cognate in *-ician: mathematics, mathematician; rhetoric, rhetorician; logic, logician; physics, physician; dietetics, dietician;* etc. Recently the guilds have laid hold of this professional-looking suffix and coined a *beautician* (with no corresponding *beautics*), a *mortician* (without a *mortics*), and a *radiotrician* (no *radiotrics*). The suffix *-orium* has undergone a similar treatment, as in *preventorium.* It only remains for some genius to call the keeper of a *sanatorium* an *idiotician.*

2. Visual similarity. Who doubts that *thorough* is more thorough than *thoro?* (Add the makeweight *going* and you have, in *thoroughgoing,* about the limit of expressiveness.) To a highly literate people spelling as well as sound can result in a kind of symbolism. Ernest Weekley says that for him the letter *h* 'makes a ghost all the more "ghostly" '[13]—and one quickly remarks the resemblance to *ghastly* and *ghoulish. Flabbergasted,* which Jespersen places among the mouth-filling words, I think belongs more properly here—'flabby and aghast with astonishment'; to have been perfect it should have been *flabberghasted.* Per contra, sometimes a difference in spelling can help dis-tinguish words that might otherwise appear to belong to a group to which their sense would not admit them. The *-aze* family suggests confusion: *daze, haze, craze, maze, amaze, faze* (in sense of 'disconcert'), *raze graze* (cattle grazing eat 'aimlessly' and 'in no order'); but *baize, pays, weighs,* etc., do not echo their cramboes in *-aze.*

3. Rime and alliteration. These two factors interlock with sound sym-bolism; but as they frequently serve to support a symbolism that is weak-ened or lost, they deserve to be separately entered. The *-ag* words, for example, which with a broad *a* doubtless symbolized the sagging of the jaw to picture that which is droopy and flabby, still carry that force with the assistance of

13. *Something about words,* New York, Dutton, 1936, p. 41.

rime, although *ăg* by itself suggests nothing in particular: *lag, flag* (v.), *fag* (v.), *hag, rag, sag, bag, nag* (n.), *tag* (-rag-and-bobtail), *wag* (v.), etc. *Hurry, scurry, worry, flurry, blurry* combine the notions of haste and confusion. For alliteration note the long list of *v-*, and especially *vi-*, words associated with intense ill-temper: *vituperative, vitriolic, vindictive, vengeful, vicious, vixenish, violent, vehement, virulent, vile* and its verbal cognates, *vesicant, venomous, villainous, vinegary*, and, following a prefix, *invective, evil, invidious, envy*. This group has such a spread that even the word *evict*, uttered with just the right curl of lip, is more powerful than *oust* or *exclude*. The virility of the constellation is partly due to a twofold symbolism—the hint of suppressed power in the sound, and the accompanying facial expression; but the alliteration provides the cement. For me, at least, as remote a word as *verdigris* is most potently uttered with a sour face; and we speak of a *volley* of (uncharitable, of course) questions. More generally, *v-* is indicative of power without unpleasantness; *vigor, vitality, verve, vim*. Who can fail to hear the powerful swoop of the verb *volplane*? Initial *f-*, related in sound, is also related in sense: 'He defended himself *vigorously, forcefully*' carries more weight than *strongly* (the *sturdy, stout, stanch* family being apparently weaker) or *energetically; emphatically*, combining the bigness of *m* and its mouth-filling length with the force of *f-*, outweighs its synonyms. Oddly enough *v*, with voiced *th*, suggests when terminal almost the opposite: *bathe, soothe, smooth, suave, lave, wave, curve, carve* (contrast the smoothness of *carving* with the sharp outlines of *chiseling*). Terminal *-f*, however, does not yield to gentleness: *rough, tough, bluff, cuff*. The *j-* initial words, building perhaps on the symbolism of the discordant sound, signify that which departs from the smooth or even, especially as regards motion: *jiggle, jounce, jump, jolt, jar, juggle, jagged, jangle, jut, jitters*,[14] *jog, jazz* (as, 'to jazz up a schedule'), and extends to marginal words such as *jam* (of traffic), *jungle* (disorder), *jeer, jab*, etc.

4. Other examples of consonance. The *oo* words suggest foolishness, with perhaps a symbolism in the staring expression with which they are uttered: *rube, boob, galoot, loon, moon* (v.), *nincompoop, stooge, coo-coo, goof, spoof*, etc. Perhaps *dunce* at one time belonged here, before joining with *stunt, runt, blunt*.

5. Pairing. Striking in their individuality are certain pairs of words which, though they may more or less dimly recall a sonic constellation, most noticeably suggest just each other. How often our writers have used the phrase 'to *banish* the mists'—because it suggests *vanish*! *Pendulous*, for all its Latin origin, is a more vivid word in some contexts than *dangle*, probably because it has been enriched by *tremulous*. *Roistering* brings *boisterous* to mind. *Damning* and *damaging* are exact synonyms in the phrase '*damning*' or '*damaging*

---

14. Peter Tamony (*News Letter* 83 : 9, March 3, 1939, p. 5) explains as a spoonerism on 'gin and bitters,' supplanting *heebie-jeebies*. The *j*-initial in both these words undoubtedly helped them to 'catch on.'

evidence'—certainly more because they sound alike than because they are cognates. ' He ate the soup with *gusto* ' means more than pleasure—it means *gusty* pleasure. *Ravage* is more devastating than *raze* or *despoil* because of the overtone *savage*. The use of *abysmal* to describe ignorance is a favorite with our literati, and comes not only from the meaning deep but also probably from the echo of *dismal*. There is apparently no etymological connection between *strain* and *strenuous*, yet the virtual disappearance of all meanings of *strenuous* except that of 'accompanied by strain' intimates that these words are related—the kinship being helped along, of course, by the *struggle*, *strive*, *stretch* constellation. *Lubberly* shifts the mental scene almost irresistibly to *rubbery*. In *Ariel*, according to the *Century Dictionary*, there is an allusion to *aerial*, *airy*; similarly the 'received' pronunciation of *aerial* as applied to radio has been effectively resisted by the general public, and *aeroplane* has long since gone down before *airplane*. How easy it is to make mistakes in this direction has already been pointed out; Mencken uses the expression ' to *waive* aside,' clearly a confusion with *wave*; *careen* of recent years has come to mean ' to rush headlong,' or ' hurtle,' doubtless because of its resemblance to *career* —but this is rather an example of displacement than of pairing, for one rarely hears or reads the word *career* nowadays. An example of pairing that may eventuate in displacement is *mumbo-jumbo* for *mummery* (helped along by *flummery*, *mumble*, etc.). The adjective *trivial* has re-attracted its cognate *trivium*, which is now being used, in the plural *trivia*, with the meaning ' trivial things.'

The phenomenon is not restricted to pairs of words, of course, but may spring from any limited number. *Flabbergast* was seen to reflect two other words. *Sarcastic* is a cutting word in more than its etymology; part of its tartness comes from the insinuation of *sour* and *caustic*.

CONCLUSION

After assembling a number of instances of verbal affinities, one can hardly escape the self-accusation of having indulged in special pleading. It is tempting to imagine that all the words we use are in some way contaminated with a suggestiveness that points beyond their literal meaning, as more of them than we are wont to realize do, in fact, so point, but the argument can be overemphasized. If the tendency to commerge meanings were left unrestricted, language would run together like melted butter, and soon we should be unable to distinguish anything. Where necessity imposes itself, our ears can be totally deaf to echoism—the Latin learning English is embarrassed when he attempts to say *sheet* or *piece*, yet we never notice the barely distinguished sounds unless our attention is expressly directed to them. *Dank*, *rank*, *tank*, *sank*, *drank* give us the hint of dampness, but *flank*, *crank*, *lank*, *hank*, and *blank* do not even remotely summon the idea. Here and there forces are at work to curb the association of words and sound symbolism. 'Refined' people object, for instance, to the interplay of vulgarity and vividness—*gut*, *victuals* (hinged to *vitals?*), *sweat* (too powerfully suggestive of *wet*), etc., have been ostracized. Literary associations may countervail imitative ones, as when we prefer the neutral *neighing* of the horses to *nickering* or *whinnying*. But word affinities are vastly pervasive, and many a proudly 'logical' phrase can be made to look primitive by singling them out.

There is no denying that the question is largely—too largely—speculative; all one can hope to do is partially to delimit a field for more exact investigation. Discovery of affinities is not devoid of a certain utility. We have already seen that advertisers have made unconscious use of them (perhaps a mixed good, the furtherance of which might be calamitous). Then, we live in a changing world, demanding a constantly wider application of our verbal store, expanding old words as well as adding new ones. Can we predict to some extent what words will be expanded? Might we not have known that 'reckless driving' rather than 'careless driving' would come to be the accepted phrase, given the suggestion of *wreck*, *rack*, and *ruin?* Knowing the affinities may help to guide us here.

In another sense the tracing of constellations is of special interest in English. The language is almost totally lacking in an orderly system of derivatives. Words like *comparable* and *impious* are turned so as to show no connection with their cognates. *Enthuse* as a back-formation from *enthusiasm* does not imply *refuse* as a back-formation from *refusiasm*—examples of this sort have been multiplied time out of mind. If the language is settling into a species of interrelationship, it is probably high time.

3

RIME, ASSONANCE, AND MORPHEME ANALYSIS[1]

Word 6.117-136 (1950)

After writing " On defining the morpheme," I felt more and more that while descriptivists had declared their independence of etymology in the analysis of morphemes, they were still behaving as if the only morphemes worth recording were the ones to be found in paradigms (like the common element in *him* and *them*) and cognates. It seemed to me that by merely generalizing the descriptive standards being used to discover etymological " morphemes " like *-cept*, a host of other morphemes could be discovered with no etymological kinships at all, and that by exposing some of the absurdities to which such an excursion would lead, I might supply a worthwhile corrective. This article has been referred to at least twice as " negative." Part of it is, frankly, a reductio ad absurdum. But there was a positive side, which was to reveal a gradience among forms—degrees of similarity between wholes rather than the absolute identity of parts.

The question has lately been revived by Norman U. Markel and Eric P. Hamp, in " Connotative meanings of certain phoneme sequences," *Studies in Linguistics* 15.47-61 (1961). They propose the term *psychomorph* to replace phonestheme, and Markel thinks that the meaning of psychomorphs " is a function of the connotative meanings of the words in which they appear " (footnote 8). This is undoubtedly correct. But Markel and Hamp still seem to feel that the typical psychomorph is an unbroken sequence of phonemes that can be isolated in about the same way as the traditional morpheme. By selecting the data one can make a strong case for this, but it remains true that psychomorphs can be found in all shades from most concrete, like *gl-*, to most diffuse, like the *-isten* of *glisten* whose /s/, in its association with the /s/ of *gloss, moisten, mist*, differs only in degree from *gl-* in the latter's association with *glitter, glow, glare*, etc. I offer one more test of the countless vague associations that hardly yield to segmentation : the verb *bolster*. Its regular meaning is ' to support.' It is based on a noun meaning ' pillow,' and the kind of support originally meant is the kind one gives by underpadding something. But most of us when we think of supports do not visualize pillows but some-

---

1. For their valuable suggestions I am indebted to Allen Walker Read and to Fred W. Householder, Jr. The latter's help has been extensive, so much so that not all of it can be explicitly acknowledged in these footnotes.

thing solid, and *bolster* vaguely echoes *bolt, brace, buttress*, all with the initial /b/ but otherwise related to *bolster* heterogeneously : the first through /ol/, the second through /s/, and the third through /t/ and /s/ in reverse order. The initial /b/ is hardly substantial enough to isolate as a psychomorph common to these four words, and the remaining ties are inconsistent. Nevertheless, the soft *bolster* has been solidified phonesthetically one way or another. I asked a group of seventeen college undergraduates to indicate which of the two following seemed more appropriate as a definition : ' to give a stiff and rigid support to something ' or ' to give a softer or more yielding support to something, as with a cushion.' They preferred the first, 13 to 4.

1. Analysts, returning from their impressive conquest of phonology, bring with them the weapon that stood them in good stead : the principle of oppositions, of absolute identity versus absolute difference. It is only natural that a weapon which proved itself in one field should be favored by those who used it there when they pass to another field, much as sea power may be favored in an air age because it won earlier wars for its advocates. In the little that has been done with morpheme analysis up to now, linguists have displayed their bias for identity-difference.[2] But new wars demand new weapons, and a different kind of work demands different tools. I shall try to show that in describing the morphemes of English, the principle of identity-difference will have to be modified to make room for mere similarity-dissimilarity.

2. IDENTITY-DIFFERENCE VERSUS SIMILARITY-DISSIMILARITY. The phonologist regards any two phonemes *qua* phonemes as absolutely distinct, with whatever similarities may subsist between them being relegated to another level of investigation. This procedure of absolute oppositions (whether reified, as by some linguists, or frankly regarded as expedient, as by some others) has worked very well with phonemes, which may number a dozen, or forty, or a hundred. It even works with morphemes when one addresses only a few morphemes, as analysts have done thus far in English within the narrow zone of tense, number, case, and one or two other safe-and-sane inflexions. But the exploring analyst must face the multiple and pluralistic stock of English with its twenty or thirty thousand discrete—or not so discrete?—forms popularly used.[3] Are absolute identity and opposi-

---

2. Voegelin looks to ' equivalence in meaning ' to determine morpheme alternants (*Language* 24.132, 134) ; Bloch separates into two or more morphemes verbs that have even a slight difference in their meaning and that have identical bases, if the conjugation type differs in the barest degree (*Language* 23.405).

3. Twenty thousand probably lies somewhere between the extremes of active vocabulary on the one hand, and recognition vocabulary on the other, of a highly literate person. An approximate figure is the best we can do, though if a comparison with

tion any longer practical, and is the area not too crowded for such compartmentalization? Whatever formulations we may eventually set up on the basis of lines sharply drawn, it is first incumbent on us to find our landmarks, and to do so, to treat facts which are themselves, at the level of exploration, loose facts, we need to trace associations rather than identities.[4]

3. INFERENCES FROM PRESENT PROCEDURES. Though not much has been attempted in English morphemics aside from the most easily systematizable phenomena of paradigms, a few hints have been dropped as to what might be done should these safe moorings be cut. Bloch writes: 'the base of the verb *sing* has the alternants / siŋ /, /sæŋ/, and / sʌŋ / before the inflexional morphemes, but the alternant / sohŋ / before a zero derivational suffix in the noun *song*.'[5] He adds, in a significant footnote, 'It goes without saying that historical considerations play no part in structural description. The actual historical relation between *sing* and *song* is irrelevant here; all that is relevant is their morphological relation in the structure of present-day English.'[6] Hockett lets fall a more conservative hint : 'Even if *men* were an isolated

---

phonemes is valid, our reliance upon it is not misplaced : alphabetic writing was also an approximation, which roughed out the phonemes before phonemic theory was hit upon. Now in what proportion did phonemic theory reduce these crude original phonemes? By fifty per cent? Let us suppose a reduction of seventy-five per cent in the number of our morphemes, once all duplications have been weeded out—the resulting figure of five thousand is still far larger than any complement of phonemes. On the other hand, it is unlikely that any such reduction, using the methods proposed by Bloch, could be effected: his system calls for such an apparatus of homonyms and other subdivisions (*n't* a separate morpheme for *not*, *bite*, *get*, *have*, etc. divided into two words) that the total might be increased rather than reduced.

4. This is not to say that a given instance of similarity may not be reduced, at the level of psychology, to a something held in common which is identical, against two somethings, or sums of things, which are different. Identity at this level would be, perhaps, the stimulation of a single nerve by two stimuli separately presented—the identity resting upon the oneness of the nerve stimulated. When we attribute the sameness to the stimuli, however, we are extrapolating. I would go along with the assumption that similarity and identity are quantitatively distinguished, and that similarity can be reduced to identity plus some difference. But I do not believe that we are equipped to discover enough identities in morphemics to justify the extrapolation and make the concentrated search for identities in English worth while.

5. To Nida (*Morphology*, Ann Arbor 1949, p. 72), *song* would not be an 'alternant' but would contain a 'replacive morpheme.' The latter may consist of nothing more than stress (cf. ibid. 74), or, what is still more nebulous, an epiphany of stress (*Language* 24.441). This is more realistic, but since there is utterly no way, in English, of predicting where such replacives will fall, what function they will perform (in verbs like *heave-heaved-hove* they are transitive-intransitive markers as well as tense markers), or even what form they will take, it is hardly rewarding to do more than list them.

6. *Language* 23.407 (1947).

case in English, this resemblance would be worthy of mention. But it is, of course, far from isolated; we have also *mouse: mice, foot: feet, woman: women* (IF *woman* IS A SINGLE MORPHEME[7]), *slide: slid, sing: sang,* and many others.[8] Says Nida: 'The forms *him, them,* and *whom* bear a partial phonetic-semantic resemblance to each other, and we are thus obliged to regard *-m* as a morpheme (even though its distribution is very limited).'[9] In most dialects *whom* would have to be dropped, leaving only *him* and *them;* Nida also lists[10] the forms / wəz / and / wər / as containing ' a recurrent partial, namely /wə-/.'

We infer : (1) that etymology is irrelevant ; (2) that given phonemic similarity and semantic similarity of two forms, we have enough to justify analysis into separate morphemes one or more of which have constant meaning and are held in common, the difference being due to other morphemes not held in common and having meanings (including zero meaning) of their own ; (3) that syntactic classes may be crossed (*sing* is a verb, *song* is a noun) ; (4) that a distribution as narrow as two forms is sufficient to establish a morpheme ; (5) that differences in phonemic shape may be rationalized (*song* is an alternant of *sing*). Since (5) is a concession to necessity, if we can avoid it in establishing a given morpheme, our case will be all the stronger.

4. IMPLICATIONS OF THESE INFERENCES. Making bolder than has been attempted thus far, let us see what happens when we apply the reasoning of the preceding paragraph.

Syntactically *often* and *off and on* are the same : *He does it often, He does it off and on.* In view of the kinship in meaning (degrees of frequency) and of the formal similarity, the two contain the same morpheme /ɔfn̩/, without suffix, or with zero suffix, in *often,* and with the added suffix /ɔn/ in *off and on.*

If *shine* n. and *shine, shone* v. contain the same morpheme, then *sheen* (etymologically ' beautiful ' but now a type of ' shine ') contains it too.

If *handle* (the act) and *hand* (the organ performing the act) contain the same morpheme, then *hear* (act) and *ear* (organ) likewise contain the same morpheme, despite probably dissimilar origins.

If *sing* (the act) and *song* (that upon which the act is performed)[11] con-

---

7. The emphasis is mine.

8. *Language* 23.339 (1947). But can etymology be so easily dismissed? Undoubtedly it ought to be, and synchronic analysts would like to be regarded as uninfluenced by the etymology of the forms that they analyze. That they do not have the courage of their convictions is shown, however, by the almost complete lack of examples, in their works, of any analysis that cannot be justified on etymological grounds. When etymology and non-etymology are in the balance, the former is likely to weigh more heavily, as in Nida's implied analysis of *solemnize* (*Morphology* p. 30) (English has no formulable *-nize* for *-ize*).

9. *Language* 24.423 (1948).

10. Ibid. 429.

11. Here using *song* as an entity apart from the act of singing : *A composed a song, B sang it,* or *What he sang was not so much a song as a chant.*

tain the same morpheme, then the same is true of *see* and *scene*.

Probably no native speaker can escape the impression th⁀t gangrene is attended by a greenish color of the necrosed flesh. Hence *gan/grene*.

If the etymologically related *sue-suit, live-life, trail-train, crumb-crumble, sear-sere, shove-shovel, drip-drop*, and *shake-shock*, and the doubtfully-etymologically related *harass-harry, tackle-attack, ruffian-rough*, and *knock-knuck* are to be analyzed as pairs showing the same morpheme, the same must be done with the etymologically unrelated *cover-hover-over, crape-drape, sway-suasion, bloat-blow, strut-straight, face-phiz, bride-breed* (or *bride-brood*), *bride-broad* (the latter a name for ' woman'), *futility-utility, discomfit-discomfort* (discounting the common affixes), *coffin-sarcophagus, mold-mildew, slim-lean, tie-tight, dope-dip, wile* v.*-while* v., *sponge* v. t.*-expunge* v. t.

We need not limit ourselves to pairs, but may look for larger patterns. One tempting example is the cross-patterning of / gl / ' phenomena of light' and / fl / ' phenomena of movement' with (1) / ɪtr / ' intermittent,' (2) / ow / ' steady,' and (3) / ɛr / ' intense':

glitter . . . . . . flitter

glow . . . . flow

glare . . . . flare

I leave the question of / gl / and / fl / to the later consideration of the large cluster of forms attached to each one. As for the terminal ' morphemes' in the above words, we find (1) evidenced also in *titter, jitter, litter, iterate*; (2) in *slow, grow*, and *tow*; and (3) in *blare, stare*, and *tear*. But a number of things mar the neatness of the pattern: we might add *gleam-flame*, but *flame*, along with *flare*, and also *flicker* and *flambeau*, has to do with fire and hence ' light' as much as ' movement'; *glide* refers to movement, not light, and *fleer* is a glance, not a movement. Still, these difficulties can be explained away as homonyms if there is any value in doing so.

A pattern which shows numerous intersections but little or no cross-patterning is that of / kr / ' bent' : *crawl* (' slow'—encountered also in *drawl*), *cringe* (' evincing pain'—also in *twinge*), *creep* (' secretive'—also in *peep*), *crouch* (' slovenly ' or ' low '—in *slouch* and *couch*), *crumple* (' wrinkle'—also in *rumple*[12]), and probably others.

Patterns as well as pairs may show the complete irrelevance of etymology, despite close formal and semantic kinship. One such is the *-amble* family, all of whose members except *bramble*[13] have at least one homonym referring to locomotion and differing in origin from the others : *amble, ramble, scramble,*

---

12. Householder assigns *crumple* and *rumple* to a group that also includes *wrinkle, dimple, crinkle, crumble, bundle*, and, *mangle*, all with hormorganic nasal plus stop plus /əl/.

13. But ask what someone's feelings are as to the difference between *bramble* and *brier,* and the reply is likely to be that brambles are *rambling* thorny bushes.

gambol, and *shamble* (*scamble* may relate to *shamble* or *scramble*). Etymological morphemes may be recombined into new 'morphemes': the *-ust* of *must*, *rust*, *crust*, *fust*, and *dust* evinces perhaps the synonymy of 'surface formation'[14]; but with the increment of the suffix *-y* the resulting *-usty* in *musty rusty*, *crusty*, *fusty*, and *dusty* gives several clear-cut synonyms for 'old.' (Compare *bat* dissimilar to *fat* but *batten* v. i. almost precisely synonymous with *fatten* in some dialects.) *Irre-*, combining *in-* and *re-*, means 'utterly.'[15] *-Lessness* has become so suggestive of 'indifference' (*lawlessness*, *carelessness*, *worthlessness*, *shiftlessness*) that I unconsciously used the term *librarylessness* in the sense of 'indifferent use of a library.'

5. THE TRAP OF MEANING. Meaning has, with good reason, been shunned in the handling of phonemes, except the minimal 'any difference in meaning at all' necessary to establish contrasts like *log-lag*. Some would like to continue doing this with morphemes.[16] But meaning is the criterion of the morpheme, and unless we are willing to develop a theory of meaning and apply it consistently, morpheme analysis will have heavy going. I list some of the facts that must be accounted for in such a theory, and try to show how each one affects the analysis of one or more morphemes:

Meanings occur in clusters. There are few words in English that have but one clear-cut meaning. In analyzing *dusty*, for example, are we to prefer the primary meaning 'covered with dust' and analyze *dust/y*, ignoring the derived meaning which analyzes *d/usty*? And in what sense is a meaning 'primary'? It may be primary historically, but etymology is banned; it may be primary statistically, but there is no time to make repeated counts whenever the wind blows from a different direction. This could be obviated by recognizing each sense as a separate form and analyzing accordingly, but the result would be an unmanageable number of derivatives. A refractory case is that of *pact*. We have the words *pack*, *packet*, *package*, and *cómpact* (pack of cosmetics) which seem to contain the same morpheme. Since *pack* v. is defined as 'to put together compactly,' and also because of the formal similarity with *cómpact*, we should have to include the adjective *compáct*. Now *cómpact* also includes 'pact' in its cluster of meanings, but this meaning is comparatively remote from that of *pack*. Do we then analyze *compact* twice, once for the adjective *compáct*, the verb *compáct* in one of its senses, and the noun *cómpact* in one of its senses, and a second time for the other senses of the verb and noun? The noun *flight* has a neat cluster of meanings that do not make for splitting it into two homonyms; yet it belongs to both *flee* and

---

14. Suggested by Householder.

15. See pp. 198–199.

16. Bloch notes the morphological identity of *sew* and *sow*, and says wistfully '*Sew* and *sow* differ only in meaning (and spelling), but perhaps not more widely than different senses of certain verbs listed only once.' *Language* 23.413 (1947).

fly.[17]   Or take *ideal*. It includes in its cluster the principal meanings 'something worshiped' and 'something perfect.' The first of these verges upon *idol*, the second upon the chief modern sense of *idyl* ('a perfect state of happiness'). We can hardly identify *ideal* with either unless we identify it with the other, and it is hardly possible to identify it with both unless *idol* and *idyl* are themselves identified. But this kind of ad hoc solution is so cavalier with the obvious main differences in meaning between *idol* and *idyl* (against the twofold unity of *ideal*) that were we to attempt it there would be no good reason for excluding *idle* (since idyllically people should not have to work), whence we would want to take in *dole* (that upon which *idle* people live), and from there *doleful* (the way people on the dole feel), and so on.

Continuity of meaning is rare among sub-word morphemes, if they are traced through all of their occurrences, for the free form is almost invariably more or less than the sum of its parts. Stanley S. Newman expresses it as follows: 'In spite of rationalizations from etymology regarding the semantic force of the component elements in *dispúte*, the word is a close-knit semantic unity.'[18] He distinguishes two types of affixes, 'fused' and 'unfused,' which only partly solves the problem because *all* affixes are affected in some degree. In Von Planta's title *Wörtwörterbuch* the 'same' morpheme appears twice, once fused and once unfused. The base is also likely to be affected: derivatives of *facere* defy attempts to base a potentially infinite series upon them, even when the items are selected so as to preserve the greatest formal similarity. *Defect*, *affect*, *perfect*, *infect* are vaguely related in meaning ('having or keeping a state or condition'—a meaning chosen ad hoc, for it is not primary in any of them). *Confect* and *effect* (verbs) are mutually related, but bear little resemblance in meaning to the others. *Perfect* is entirely out of the orbit, and further derivation only confuses the picture, for in their primary meanings *affection* and *affect*, *defection* and *defect*, and *confection* and *confect* have separated completely, while *factitious* and *fictitious*, and *fact* and *fiction* (popularly associated), have brought together the results of disparate origins. Where a form is infinitely productive, as with the pluralizing morpheme, we do not go astray; but with narrowly limited distribution 'potentially infinite' founders on 'actually finite.' When there is sufficient phonemic bulk, as in *Greco-*, *pseudo-*, *-ology*, *-ism*, and *-itis* we have enough to identify the morpheme, or react to it, when it is alone (proved by the fact that the three suffixes named here are now and then used as words). But in the diminutive /ɪ/, without much consistency in either sense of the word, there is little anchorage for meaning: it is obvious in *doggie*, dubious in *honey* and *pretty* (endearments),

---

17. If this problem is solved by positing two morphemes, then *modest* is also two morphemes, one (with a moral sense) which can combine with the prefix *in-* and one (non-moral) which cannot: we can have a modest house but not an immodest one.

18. *Word* 2.182 (1946).

capable of creation in *falsie*, dead in *bully*, and nonexistent in **earie*. In many of its occurrences it is hardly more than a sub-morpheme differential, as, to reduce it to an absurdity, one might find in /h/ versus /d/ in *hog* and *dog*, where /h/ = 'porcine,' /d/ = 'canine,' and /ag/ = 'animal.' The problem of 'morphemes' with low phonemic content will appear in bolder relief as we treat more extensive constellations of related words.

Meanings fluctuate with speech level. To a person of some sophistication, *breakfast* may contain two morphemes, clearly identifiable as to meaning and with the compound the clear resultant of the combination. To others *break-fast* is not analyzable at all.

Meanings vary in specificity.[19] A working principle would be that THE LOWER THE SPECIFICITY OF MEANING, THE LARGER IS THE NUMBER OF FORMS THAT MAY BE SUBSUMED UNDER ONE MORPHEME. Theoretically it would be possible to find a few lowest common denominators for all the words in English, thereby, with extensive rationalization, deriving them all from those few 'morphemes.'

Low specificity may be illustrated by a few absurd examples. Take, for instance, the concept of 'energy.' Now the manifestations of energy comprise virtually every verb in the language, and a large proportion of nouns, adjectives, and adverbs as well. But 'energy' is deceitfully clear-cut and unified, and if we are unaware of the level of specificity at which we are operating we may seize upon the word *erg* 'unit of energy,' set up *irk* 'energetically annoy' as an alternant with zero suffix, and go merrily on to:

1. *w/ork* 'apply energy' (prefix also in *w/ill*)
2. *sh/irk* 'fail to apply energy' (prefix also in *sh/all, sh/ucks, psh/aw*)
3. *p/erk* 'enliven, apply energy to' (prefix also in *p/ep*)
4. *l/urk* 'hang about actively' (prefix in *l/oll, l/allygag, l/oiter, l/inger, l/oaf*)
5. *m/urk* 'active, fluid opaqueness' (prefix in *m/ud, m/oil*)
6. *j/erk* 'snatch energetically' (prefix in *j/olt, j/iggle*, etc.)
7. *B/urke* 'kill energetically' (prefix in *b/atter, b/low*, etc.)
8. *d/irk* 'wicked, energetic little knife' (prefix in *d/agger*)
9. *k/irk* 'place where clergyman works' (prefix in *c/lergy, c/urate*)
10. *qu/irk* 'a lightning notion or energetic turn of character' (prefix in *qu/eer*)
11. *cl/erk* 'hard-working person'

Or by taking the low-specificity 'having to do with the earth' we are able to relate *t/amp, tr/amp, st/amp* (all 'earth-striking'), *d/amp* (a typical earth condition), *cl/amp* ('fasten down'), and *r/amp* ('slope of earth').

Low specificity has been seriously resorted to in order to demarcate certain English affixes. Nida refers[20] to the 'suffix' /-ər / in *hammer, ladder, spider,*

---

19. The semanticists' 'level of abstraction.'
20. *Language* 24.430 (1948). What of *ly/re* (cp. *li/ar*), *fire*, etc.?

otter, *badger*, and *water* as having some sort of 'grammatical meaning,' which he refrains from defining.[21] The suffix *-age* demands recognition because the majority of its bases exist as independent morpheme words (*breakage*, *mileage*, *stoppage*, *wreckage*, *steerage*, *package*, *leakage*, *truckage*, *drayage*, *cartage*, *trackage*, *baggage*, *luggage*), and because it is still active (*voltage*, *amperage*, and *wattage* are comparatively recent, and *gruntage* is a humorous coinage[22]). We cannot say that its meaning is 'nounness,' since it is added to bases that are already nouns; and it is impossible to assign it a logical meaning broad enough to include all that needs to be included without including too much—without taking in, for example, *nonage*, whose ostensible analysis is *non* plus *age* 'majority.' Yet by not taking it in we spoil the high-specificity comparison of *nonage* and *dotage*, unrelated etymologically.[23]

From the standpoint of the analyst, the *irk* and *amp* connexions seem preposterous. But such low-specificity kinships are by no means irrelevant to the description of English—description as distinguished from formulation.[24] Take the low-specificity 'sinister' and apply it to words in /awl/: *owl* (symbol of the sinister in birds), *prowl* (sinister lurking), *foul*, *scowl*, *growl*, *howl*, *rowel*, *bowel*, *jowl*. To test the power of this echoic family the terms *wimple*, *toque*, and *cowl* were written in view of a class of twenty persons, who were told that all three signified a type of head-dress, and requested to write on a slip of paper the one of the three which suggested to their minds something sinister or bad (no mention was made of rime). It was assumed that the majority of those present would not know the precise signification of any of the terms, but in order to make certain of this, the subjects were given a few seconds, after making their choice, to write a definition, if they knew one, of the word they chose. Only four did this (all had elected *cowl*), and of the four three gave the (possibly monkish and hence vaguely sinister) equivalent 'hood'; the fourth gave 'hood' but in the neutral automotive sense. The choice was *cowl* 15, *toque* 4, and *wimple* 1. The influence is plainly associative. *Wimple* could not be favored because of the innocent rime with *dimple*, *pimple*, *simple*.

Meanings differ in intension. When I refer to the *shoemaker* around the corner, I use a term that, as applied to him, is analyzable, for he is a *maker* (a connotative word which not only identifies him but fits him into a class) and he works in *shoes*. When I address my friend *Shoemaker*, however, I use a term that is completely denotative and hence unanalyzable. This is the problem of all proper names. They have little or no meaning in the con-

---

21. Nida also recognizes differences in meaning which are sub-morphemic. Ibid. 433.

22. George Woodbury, *John Goffe's Mill*, New York, Norton, 1948.

23. Householder suggests that formulation may be possible if several homophonous suffixes are set up, an arbitrary procedure.

24. And have actually been used in formulation. See *Word* 5.32 (1949).

notative or intensive sense, but merely point; and they point as wholes—their parts, whatever they may be and whatever their origins may have been, do not of themselves point (i. e., are not separately denotative) or classify (i.e., are not separately connotative). *Johnn/y* may be analyzable to the extent that its suffix classifies the object as small, although it is doubtful that *-y* is more than a differential here. *Joan, Jane, Jean, Jan, Janet, Jeanette, Jenny,* and *Juanita* cannot be analyzed as containing the same morpheme, for aside from etymology they have nothing in common except the fact that all are female names —a level of specificity so low that if it is resorted to there is no reason not to include *June, Ginny,* and *Regina.*

In an ideally constituted lexicon, the elements of the word would relate it to more inclusive genera precisely and scientifically (connotation), and the word itself would refer to a species, or to a less inclusive genus, something at a higher level of specificity (denotation). This the botanist achieves, not fully but in part, with that portion of his terminology which names a species by combining the generic name with modifiers, e. g. *Brassica campestris, B. rapa, B. oleracea,* etc. Morphemic analysis of such forms is significant—they have been synthesized for the express purpose of showing interrelationships. The essential denotativeness of English nouns, however, is shown in their contempt of nice interrelationships, their resistance to meaning more than one definite thing at a time. The *Brassica* family itself has, or had, a base form *cole* whose meaning comprehended all the members of the genus. Yet despite its importance to nutrition and the resulting familiarity of the words, the popular names instead of drawing closer to *cole* have dispersed from it, and the uncompounded base word has not only disappeared from everyday speech but its derivatives have become more and more disguised. *Cabbage* loses *cole* entirely, *brussels sprouts* does not acquire it, the accidentally similar *broccoli* evolves no further, *colza* competes with *coleseed* and *kale* with *borecole,* while *colewort* is corrupted to *collard* and *collet* and *coleslaw* to *cold-slaw.* THE NEED TO DIFFERENTIATE OUTWEIGHS AND SUBMERGES THE NEED TO INTERRELATE in our concrete vocabulary; where a relationship causes confusion it is dropped, as witness the old pair *starboard-larboard* now *starboard-port. Kale, kohlrabi,* and *cauliflower* are denotative words whose ties with *cole* have been weakened to the point where they may SUGGEST, but no longer SPECIFY, an interrelationship. Their vague suggestiveness probably contributes a sense of fitness when one reflects upon the family relationship; but this is not enough to sustain a 'morpheme' /k-l/ when a realistic description shows that the language itself has moved away from it. To this extent historical linguistics is relevant to structural analysis.

Finally, meanings vary in their degree of attachment to a given form. 'Sinister' is more closely attached to *howl* than 'energy' is to *quirk.* The attachment must be close in order to enable us to single out ONE element of the word as 'having' that particular meaning and therefore as responsible for the presence of that meaning in the whole word. It is easier to say that /awl/ 'means' sinister (making gr/owl a 'sinister gr/unt') than to say that /ərk/ 'means' energy (making qu/irk an 'energetic qu/eerness'). But, withal, attachment is only a question of degree.

Problems of meaning do not occur singly, but interlace in a bewildering way. Take the -oil family. As a first step, it may be divided into an orderly set of pairs;

toil-moil 'to work'	roil-soil 'to dirty'
boil-broil 'to cook'	foil-spoil 'to frustrate'

Moil, however, includes in its cluster the meaning 'to dirty'; in this sense, then, we have

roil-soil-moil 'to dirty'

By taking a lower-specificity meaning, 'to mar,' we add spoil, and get

roil-soil-moil-spoil 'to mar'

But in roil and boil we can factor out a reference to liquid; since this also affects oil, we get

roil-boil-oil 'liquid'

Etymology, however, associates roil and rile, and since both have in common 'to stir up,' we may, instead of -oil, take r-l as our constant and get

roil-rile 'to stir up.'

This same process is equally valid, though not etymylogical, in

coil-curl 'round,'

and resorting to the roundness of the movement of stirring, and the very low-specificity association of roundness and smoothness, we have

coil-oil-boil (cp. 'rolling boil')-curl.

6. 'DISCOVERING' MORPHEMES. Says C. F. Voegelin, 'To investigate the entire linguistic structure of any language requires two discoveries. First, . . . we must find the phonemes; secondly, we must find the morphemes.'[25] 'Discovery' is not the same in these two areas. No speaker of any language is more than dimly conscious of the phonemes of his language until they have been set up by elaborate and more or less indirect processes and then taught to him. Every speaker must know something of the morphemes of his language before he can speak it (though the non-speaker may be ignorant of both). Or are there morphemes of which the speaker is not at all aware, and which must be 'discovered' by indirect processes, even when the analyst is himself a speaker, similar to those used in phonology? The answer depends partly upon our definition of 'awareness.' If we mean the

---

25. *Language* 24.133 (1948).

ability to talk about a thing with little or no reflexion, then we can probably say that despite (and because of) its automaticity, the average speaker of English is aware of the pluralizing morpheme, since he could make a quick and sensible answer to the foreigner's question 'I know how to say *an egg*, but how can I speak of more than one?' This awareness would vary from speaker to speaker where certain other recurring phenomena are concerned, but if we entirely rule out such naive reactions we open the door to fantastic 'discoveries' some of which have already been detailed, for we have lost the key to the CONSISTENT part of consistent recurrence. All speakers are forced to correct, to paraphrase, and to explain constantly in their verbal intercourse, thereby developing knowledge of their medium as well as skill in its use. We depend upon them even at the lowest level of 'mere difference in meaning,' for things are not abstractly different but different in some respect, which respect must be known to be judged.[26]

What are we to do with such 'discovered' morphemes when the speakers of the language show that they do not believe in them? One could argue plausibly for a common morpheme in *make* and *break*, in view of popular associations like *This experience will either make him or break him*, or *a make-and-break circuit*. But while the etymologist can point out, and the morphemicist discover, that the same morpheme exists in *aurochs* as in *ox*, assuming both to be found in the same dialect, this does not square with a full description of the language, in which we find the alternant *auroch*—proof that if morphemes depend on meaning, the two words do not contain the same morpheme for many, probably for most, speakers. Formulation of a common morpheme is opposed by a full description of English.

7. CONVERGENCE AND DIVERGENCE. Let us suppose that it should become the custom in our society, all the time or a good part of the time, to prepare *bacon* by *baking* it. The two words would have converged sufficiently to create a common morpheme /beyk/.[27] Such actually happened with *whetstone* and *wet*, and with *belfry* and *bell*. When the noun *rocket* was converted into a verb, 'to dash headlong,' it became synonymous with the verb *bucket;* convergence made it possible to discover a common morpheme. When the verb *kid* 'to hoax, humbug' came to be used in the sense 'twit, tease', it drew close enough to the older verb *cod* to share a common morpheme. It seems obvious that morphemes dependent upon such haphazard events, or at best upon a mutual attraction that cannot be predicted, would be too unstable to be worth recording; yet until better principles of analysis are

---

26. Cf. Nida, 'the answer to the difficulty of identifying morphemes must be found at least partially in the native speaker's response to the meaningful units in his speech.' *Language* 24.435 (1948).

27. In fact, their both being handled in the same kitchen is sufficient for this. Householder reports that *baking powder* was *bacon powder* to him as a child.

laid down there is nothing to debar them, and they have undoubtedly operated in cases where etymologists would recognize a common morpheme—*scrawl* and *scribble*, for example, drawn to *scribe* and *script*. It is more plausible to find a common morpheme in *kid* and *cod* than in *sing* and the *song* of *He sold it for a song.*

Sans etymology, a problem of convergence may be refractory indeed. Take the nouns *chute* and *shoot*. These have converged to the point that the *Century Dictionary* says ' *Chute* coincides in pronunciation and sense with *shoot*, *n.<shoot, v.*; but the two words are independent of each other.' Independent, of course, etymologically ; to the synchronic analyst they are one and the same. But, in their convergence, have they also attracted the cognate verbs ? The popular phrase to *shoot the chutes* indicates something of the kind, yet *chute* v. is not the same as *shoot* v., in view of the preterits *chuted* and *shot* (but again, the nonce word *parashot* partially erased this distinction). The convergence has caused complications in another quarter. It causes a minimum of trouble with *parachute* and *bumbershoot* ' umbrella,' if one is willing to accept a generous dose of metaphor ; but *parasol* and *parachute* are popularly identified by the OTHER half of the related words, and the fact that it is *para* which here stands for the object in question is proved by the coining of *paratroops*, in which only *para* is left. Can a situation of this kind be efficiently dealt with by oppositions? It would seem that there is simply the fact that *parachute* AS A WHOLE resembles *bumbershoot* and AS A WHOLE resembles *parasol*, while *bumbershoot* AS A WHOLE resembles *parachute* on the one hand and *umbrella* on the other.

The opposite problem may be phrased as ' how far must two forms having the same morpheme diverge before they cease to contain the same morpheme?' A special case is that of forms deliberately altered in order to escape a taboo : e. g. minced oaths like *gosh* and *gad* for *God*, *darn* for *damn*, *shoot* for *shit*, *jeepers, gee-whiz, gee-whillikers* for *Jesus*, etc.[28] Do these have the ' same ' morphemes as their originals—for speakers who recognize the connexion?— for speakers unaware of any connexion? Most divergence is gradual. Does *deed* still contain the same morpheme as *did*, *steed* that of *stud*, *serve* that of *serf?*[29] *Snivel, sniffle, snuffle, sniff*, and *snuff* have diverged, but not far. A form may sire other forms which resemble it but differ from each other. *Caliber* gives us *caliper*, the two relating as to ' measurement,' and also *caliver*, related to as ' gun '; but *caliper* and *caliver* are not akin in meaning. Are there, then, two *calibers*, two different morphemes, to be assumed to account for the divergence-cum-similarity? Two forms may remain in the same low-specificity area but diverge in a high-specificity area : *stroke* v. derives from *strike* v. and both still signify ' a touching motion,' but the one refers to a

---

28. See Mencken, *American language*, Supplement I, New York, Knopf, 664–5 (1945).

29. Nida combines *serve* and *serf*, *Morphology* 72.

'caress' and the other to a 'violent blow,' in the commonest of their senses. *Sever* has now diverged, except in the very lowest-specificity sense, from *several*, and has drawn closer to *severe* in the somewhat higher-specificity sense of 'cutting'—is it then to be reanalyzed? The identification of the now diverged *plaintiff* and *plaintive* evokes surprise in anyone but an etymologist; yet their connexion in meaning is obvious once it is pointed out, and by existing rules they contain the same morphemes.

Homonyms are a special problem. *Shorts* 'middlings' and *shorts* 'underdrawers' have diverged in meaning but not in form. Purely formal analysis must identify them unless 'form' is taken to embrace a series of contexts that cannot be stated in grammatical terms. Accurate description demands separation in forms such as *mettle-metal*, where the visual morpheme of the first, the same as in *fettle*, bears witness to the duality.

8. Dialectal and Individual Differences. Meaning is personal, and varies throughout the lifetime of the individual. As a child I related *first-rate* with *straight*—both, to me, 'contained' *straight*. The linguist naturally rejects such idiosyncrasies, but with dialectal differences he faces a more delicate problem. For English at large, *scary* and *leery* would not, in all likelihood, be regarded as having the base morpheme in common. Where *scary* becomes *skeery*, however, the division into *sk/eer/y* and *l/eer/y* is more insistent.

9. Attraction. When two forms are encountered in the same area of greater or lesser specificity of meaning, and are also closely similar in form, they are likely to exercise a kind of magnetic attraction one upon the other. *Disburse* is more forceful than *spend* because it suggests intensive *dis-* plus *burst*. The word *pick* has veered from one of its meanings ('select') to another in the phrase *Why pick on me?* because of the formal identity of *pick* v. with *pick* v., similarity with *peck*, *poke*, *pike*, and a predisposing context. When one of the attracting elements is a whole system to itself, the gravitation becomes more pronounced. There exists in English a family of words with the fairly low-specificity meaning of 'sharp movement plus dull (or dull ringing) sound': *plunk* (*He plunked down the money*), *clank, clunk* (*They clunked him over the head*), *spank, dunk, honk;* and there is a related pair containing the vowel / ɔ / in which the ringing is not dull—*bong, gong*. The formal similarity of *conch* with these two groups is apparent, and an expression like *He hit him on the conch*, meaning 'on the ear,' could date back a long way. Somewhere the shift was made from 'ear' to 'nose,' and then, because of the real or imagined resonance of a blow on the head, *conch*, or *conk*, became 'head' (now unknown to some speakers except as a verb, 'to strike on the head').[30] The orbit of *conch* was thus contracted toward *clunk* and gave us *to conk one on the head*—but not contracted all the way, since one may be clunked on the posteriors but conked only on the head.

---

30. Further extended onomatopoetically in *The engine conked out.*

The attraction may be extremely remote. *Renounce* is felt to be more vigorous than *abjure* because of the echo of *bounce, pounce, flounce, jounce*; but it would be too much by any standard to say that it contains the same morpheme.

Most speakers of English, when they hear *ambush*, are likely to think of someone hiding in the bushes. Likewise with *hierarchy* one tends to hear the element *higher*.[31]

Now the linguist is bound, by habit and training, to abhor the kind of vague resemblance that I point to here and that I stress as unavoidable in the accurate description of the English lexicon. It is possible, however, to demonstrate their validity statistically. Elaborate tests are not necessary, for the evidence is abundant. I offer a brief study of *literally* made on a group of twenty-five students, to determine the extent to which *litter* has influenced it (evidenced in *He reads current topics and litterly* [*sic*] *buries himself in trade magazines*[32]). The following sentences were presented, to be graded A for good, B for fair, and C for not very good, along with instructions to assume that some were better than others and to grade them relatively. The sentences and the votes were:

		A	B	C
1.	He was literally overwhelmed with questions	8	9	8
2.	The floor was literally covered with paper	13	9	3
3.	The ground was literally carpeted with leaves	8	7	10
4.	We were literally soaked with the wetting we got	6	9	10
5.	Her face was literally smeared with mud	6	9	10
6.	The garden was literally overgrown with weeds	5	8	12
7.	The air was literally black with smoke	10	11	4
8.	The dog was literally mad with excitement	4	4	17
9.	We were literally awed by the sight	4	5	16
10.	His head was literally crushed by the blow	4	9	12

The 'C' votes on 8, 9, and 10 are significant, for there we find that the notion of 'covered' or 'filled' is absent—senses primary to *litter*.

As with intensive *literally*, so with intensive *scrupulously*, which, by virtue of the 'cleanliness' of *scrub, scrape, scour, score, scarify*, is practically monopolized by the 'cleanly' phrases *scrupulously clean* and *scrupulously honest*. *Limb* is more graceful than *leg* because of *slim* and *trim*. The French word *flair*, dropped unceremoniously into English, was magnetized by the *fl-* words (*fling, flaunt*, etc.), and also probably by *air*, since a flair is had with an air; in any case, accommodating itself to the dynamics of English it has all but

---

31. A. W. Read has collected a quantity of such 'submerged' words. See his article "English words with constituent elements having independent semantic value," in *Philologica: the Malone anniversary studies* (Baltimore, Johns Hopkins Press, 1949).

32. *Topeka Daily Capital*, 11 March, 1940.

lost any suggestion of 'sense of smell.' When a group of cognate synonyms show definable divergences in meaning, those divergences often betray the gravitational pull of the rimes and assonances to which each word bears the greatest resemblance. The synonyms (1) *distrait*, (2) *distraught*, and (3) *distracted* relate as follows: (1) 'absent-minded,' referring to a mind that has *strayed* (cf. also *away*, *pay* out a line, *ray*, *spray*, and other words suggesting centrifugal movement); (2) 'in troubled confusion,' with the unmistakable suggestion of '*wrought* up' and '*fraught* with trouble'; (3) 'in frantic confusion,' with no close kinships but with more numerous attachments than its two congeners, to words suggesting vigorous action: *attract*, *react*, *contract*, *act*, *racked*—mostly clustering about the vowel /æ/.

Where we start with a close formal similarity, chances are good that two attracted forms will merge entirely or in part. Thus *burden* 'something borne' and *burden* 'refrain' have, in *the burden of proof* and *the burden of his speech*, become practically identical. But a given form may also echo a number of other forms not very closely related among themselves, and be attracted to them sufficiently to take on a cast of their meaning. To test this I offered the coined word *desticate* (suggesting *decimate*, *castigate*, *devastate*, *desolate*, *desolation*, *degradation*, and other vaguely unfavorable words[33]) to a group of twenty-eight college freshman students, giving them the choice of two contexts, *We were hungry because our provisions had been completely desticated* and *We liked the picture because the colors were so nicely desticated*, and asking them to choose the one that seemed more appropriate. The vote was twenty-two for the first, six for the second.

10. Two Classes of Sub-words. Up to this point I have lumped together two classes of forms which pose much the same problem to formulation but which have to be distinguished for further description. They might be termed 'neutral morphemes' and 'affective morphemes' or 'phonesthemes.'[34] In view of their elastic boundaries, the latter should perhaps not be called morphemes at all, though since they fit the definitions of the morpheme I continue to treat them as such. In this way the problems that they pose will better reveal the need for some change in our technique.

Also it would be impossible to say where the neutral ends and the affective begins. I prefer to believe that once a phonation and a meaning are attached, the two thenceforth are felt to be appropriate to each other and become potential centers of phonesthetic radiation. Be this as it may, a large segment of English exhibits the traits that go to make up phonesthemes, as I shall now show.

11. Phonestheme Patterning. It is generally recognized that English

---

33. Compare the rough *reprobate* with the mild congener *reprove*.

34. I adopt the term *phonestheme* from Householder, who in turn has it from J. R. Firth.

contains a pool of forms interrelated through rime and assonance.[35] What is not appreciated is the vastness of the pool. A true description of this part of English shows not here and there a few pristine forms adhering together and forming neat little bundles of morphemes, but rather shows form A merging with form B, B with C (and farther away from A), C with D (and still farther away from A), and so on, until all resemblance of A with remoter steps is lost. Over-simplifying, we get a series of steps like:

ride (a horse)
stride (a horse) —*straddle*
spraddle—*spray*
splay—*splatter*
spite   *spatter*—*patter*
spat—*pout*   *batter*—*bludgeon*
pet—*peeve*   *truncheon*—*trounce*
miff—*huff*   *pounce*
gruff—*grumpy*
dumps

or a metastasized cancer like:

wriggle
wiggle——*wag*   *snicker*—*nicker*
squiggle   *snigger*
higgledy-piggledy—*jiggle*——*juggle*——*jigger*
snuggle
struggle—*strive*
strain—*might and main.*

We discover what looks like a tidy little set of synonyms for *utter*, all containing the same morpheme as *utter: mutter, stutter, sputter,* and *splutter*; but we must then deal with the fact that not only in these words, all of which may be used with the meaning 'say,' but also in *shutter, flutter,* and *putter* the meaning of 'discontinuity' is present, and we get a picture like the following, which, to be adequately drawn, needs more than two dimensions:

---

35. Cf. Sturtevant, *Introduction to linguistic science*, New Haven, 1947, 111-112.

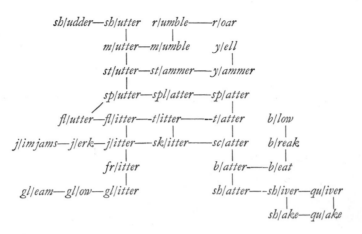

The couplings noted here are not artificial; among other evidence for their association we have phrases like *shiver and shake, quiver and quake*.

12. MORPHEMES AND SUB-MORPHEME DIFFERENTIALS. No sharp line could be drawn between those collocations of phonemes which, through relative uniqueness of one sort or another (unique context, unique content, unique position, etc., or combinations), show comparatively little deviation in meaning, and those which are shared by so many occurrences under such varied conditions that we must either admit extensive homonymy or not consider them as morphemes at all, in the sense that a morpheme depends on constancy of meaning. I have remarked the contrast between the diminutive /ɪ/ and the pluralizing morpheme in point of productiveness, and its contrast with affixes like *Greco-* and *pseudo-* in point of substance. *The Century Dictionary* calls many words containing it 'intractable to classification,' as we discover for ourselves when we try to class *movie, lovey-dovey, comfy, taxi,* and *buggy*. I have referred to it in these occurrences as a sub-morpheme differential.

Where, within or between morphemes and mere differentials, would our rimes and assonances fall? If we can show enough regularity in use, a rime or an assonance should be, or come very near to being, a morpheme. Let us take the form /gl/, already noted as referring to 'visual phenomena,' and assay its possibilities as a morpheme. Discarding technical, learned, and dialectal words, we may list, in seven columns showing graduated fidelity to the meaning 'visual phenomena,' all the base words, excluding obvious derivatives, that begin with /gl/:

Visual				Non-visual
glacé				
	glacial			
	glacier			
				glacis
		glad		
				glade
				gladiator
				gladiolus
	glamor			
glance				
				gland
				glanders
glare				
	glaze	*glass*		
gleam				
				glean
			glee	
				glen
				glib
				glide
glim				
glimmer				
glimpse				
glint				
glisten				
glister				
glitter				
gloaming				
	gloat			
				globe
				globule
gloom				
	gloriole			
	glory			
gloss				
				glove
glow				
glower				
	gloze			
				glue
				gluten
				glutton
				glycerin

(Admitting dialectal words would favor the visual side slightly because of the—mostly Scottish—words *gley, glime, glisk,* and *glunch.*) If this necessarily subjective distribution is accepted, roughly half of the popular words in English that begin with /gl/ either have or are very close to the implication 'visual' (and running frequencies doubtless would compare equally well). As percentages go this is better than some of the paradigmatic suffixes, though of course /gl/ is never more than sporadically productive.

Although of a somewhat lower level of specificity, the monosyllabic rimes in *-ash* make an even better showing. The meaning is 'headlong,' 'hit,' and result of hitting, 'fragments.' There are twenty-one common or fairly common forms that fit: *ash, bash, dash, fash, gash, hash* (attracting *goulash*), *lash, plash, splash, clash, flash, slash, mash, smash, gnash, pash, rash, crash, brash, trash, thrash.* (Neighboring *quash, squash, cosh,* and *slosh,* and probably also the rejective exclamations *bosh* and *tosh,* suggest related meanings.) One dialectal word conforms: *blash.* Three existent forms do not fit: *cash* (which is nevertheless strongly suggestive of money in fragments), *tash,* and *sash* (with its obsolete congener *shash*). Twenty-four phonemically possible forms do not exist, though some of these, such as *gwash,* embody low-frequency combinations. To test the potency of this rime, I offered to a group of twenty-eight students of freshman English the dialectal word *blash,* telling them that it was an invented word, suggesting no meaning for it and making no reference to rime or assonance, but asking each person to use it in a sentence that would show clearly what the word meant to him. Three had no opinion, four others used contexts too ambiguous to classify, and the remaining twenty-one employed the word in ways that clearly showed a relationship to words in *-ash* (17) or to *bl-* words (3) or to one or the other (1).

What has gone before is not an argument for saying that all rimes and assonances are related. To assume this would be as absurd an extreme as the opposite one of paying no heed to the connexions that do exist. I recognize no kinship in *spindle-bindle, lever-clever,* or *pray-ray.*

Where such unrelated rimes and assonances occur, and intersect others that are related and meaningful, we have sub-morpheme differentials. Take, for example, the group connoting 'twisting motion' and characterized by initial /tw/: *twist, twirl, tweak, twill, tweed, tweezer, twiddle, twine, twinge.* The differential in *twirl* also occurs in *whirl* and is therefore not sub-morphemic.[36] That in *twist,* however, does not seem to match anything else, and accordingly,

---

36. Which will be considered the base and which the differential is probably best determined by the number of examples in either direction. Since there are about as many /r̩l/ words relating to 'round'—*twirl, curl, furl, burl, knurl, whirl, hurl, swirl, purl* —as there are /tw/ words, it does not matter whether /tw/ be considered the base and /r̩l/ the differential, or vice versa, or both be given equal rank in some special procedure for such cases.

besides creating *twist* as a unique word, serves only to distinguish it phonetically from other—especially other /tw/—words. It is a meaningless residue, like the *cran-* of *cranberry* or the *cray-* of *crayfish*.

Yet we can never say that these forms are entirely 'without meaning.' The alternant *crawfish* is used as a verb in the sense 'crawl backwards,' showing perhaps the 'same morpheme' as *crawl*. In the noun *fatso*, the *-so* is unique as a suffix,[37] but it reflects the sportive *-o* of *jocko, bucko, bozo*; similarly in *sockdolager*, in which the suffix *-dolager* plays upon any number of associations, including that of mere verbal bigness. We see, therefore, that the outlines of meaningless and meaningful rimes and assonances are infinitely scumbled, and that the analyst faces a hopeless task if he attempts to formulate them by oppositions.

It is even possible, so pervasive are meanings, to discover a sub-phoneme differential. Take the groups

dumb	*numb, numbskull*
dimwit	*nitwit*
dolt	*(nut)*
dunce	*(nonsense)*
dense	

If we accept *dumb, numb, slum,* and *bum* as containing the same morpheme /ʌm/, we then have differentials /d/, /n/, /sl/, and /b/. But we find that in this group *dumb* and *numb* are more alike than are any of the others, and we note from the vertical list above that both /d/ and /n/ appear in synonyms for 'stupid.' Therefore we are tempted to the conclusion that *numb* and *dumb* show their greater resemblance by virtue of the resemblance between /d/ and /n/. But if /d/ and /n/ are also the differentials, then we have two words which are both differentiated and assimilated by the same elements. This is untenable, so that the real differentials of *numb* and *dumb* are reduced not to /d/ and /n/ but to nasalization versus non-nasalization plus whatever other phonetic differences separate /d/ from /n/. The same is true of *guile* and *wile*, where the closer similarity of /g/ and /w/ is matched by a closer resemblance in meaning than, say, between either word and *rile*.

The smaller the phonemic content, the greater the likelihood of extensive overlappings. How much overlapping would be needed in order to drop a form from the category of a morpheme to that of sub-morpheme differential is a matter of definition, for the language will not furnish us with a clear-cut line. Initial /st/ has a variety of uses, but one clusters about the meaning 'arrest': *stop, stay, still, steady, stanch, stall, stump, stick (at)*; it is almost equally common, however, in words having the opposite sense: *stimulate, sting, stir, start, startle*. To suit his taste, the analyst might find morphemes

---

37. Disregarding obsolete *catso*. Or should the analysis be *fats/o*? (Householder).

here, or just sub-morpheme differentials.

Finally, there are certain interlockings which put us in a quandary as to whether to regard an element as a sub-morpheme differential or as part of a base. Thus if we compare *loot* and *boot* (both 'plunder') we find the sub-morpheme differentials to be /l/ and /b/; if we compare *boot* and *booty* (both 'plunder,' and of different origins) we find the differential /ɪ/; if we compare *booty* and *boodle* the differentials again change. We cannot declare the morpheme to be /uw/, because to do so would sacrifice obvious resemblances. The only recourse, for the formularian, would have to be a complicated and artificial rationalization.

13. INFIXED DIFFERENTIALS. *Refrain* is the intransitive aspect of *restrain*; *infect* is used when the parasite is a microorganism, *infest* when it is a macroorganism. Pairs such as these give us discontinuous morphemes, with infixed differentials (the latter called 'morpheme components' by Z. S. Harris[38]). Striking are the groups that show internal vowel alteration as in *sing* and *song*. The set /s-p/ practically runs the gamut of the vowels: *seep, sip, sap, sop, sup, soup, sipe,* and possibly *soap*.[39] The set /sp-t/ refers to 'rush of liquid': *spit, spate, spurt, spout*; the set /str-p/ to 'line having breadth': *strip, strap, strop, stripe*. The set /st-nt/ 'a piece of performance' (*stint, stent, stunt*) shows a regular semantic gradation as well.[40]

14. CREATIVITY. A great many, perhaps most, of the resemblances of rime and assonance look to the casual observer like phenomena that once were active but have since become dead. Doubtless numerous initial consonant combinations may be traced to a common origin; but this is far from exhausting the sources of resemblance, others of which we have seen in more or less accidental convergence; and it is even farther from exhausting the resources of resemblance, which are constantly building upon each interrelated family, whether that family got its start with a single etymon, as an instance of onomatopoeia, as a verbalized gesture, as an accidental convergence, or simply as a single word whose tremendous frequency or close analogy impressed itself upon other words surrounding it. Consider the potent family of /sk/ initial and final, referring to 'swift movement': *brisk, frisk, whisk, scour, scamper, scatter, scurry, scuttle, skedaddle, skip, scoot, scramble, scat, skiddoo, skid, skim, scull,* with marginal *to scale* (a mountain or wall), *skittish, escape, skiff, scuffle, scrap, scrounge, scrabble, scare,* and *sketch*. The interjections *sic!* to a dog and *sk!* (for *scat*) to a cat must be included. *Scram* and *skiddoo* are fairly recent inventions. When C. E. Seashore, referring to 'making scattered trials so as to locate where to make intensive trials' says 'We first *skirmish* about to find

---

38. I owe this reference to Householder. See also footnote 5.
39. Householder adds *syrup* and *slurp*.
40. *Word Study*, October 1949, p. 6.

for what difference the observer is likely to get about 75 per cent right,'[41] the influence of the /sk/ constellation is obvious. Likewise when I once caught myself saying *Let's skin out of here*. The well-known family of *-ump* ' awkward, heavy, lumpish ' (*dump, rump, crump, hump, mump, bump, slump, stump, grump, gump, thump*, etc.) has recently been enriched by the addition of *schlump*, defined as ' a guy who waits outside a revolving door until some vigorous person comes along to push it—so that he can walk through with his hands still in his pocket.'[42] The initial ' morpheme ' in this neologism is familiar from three other recent epithets : *schnook, schmo*, and *schlamiel*—besides nonce words heard frequently in the interval 1946–1950 (this heretofore foreign-to-English initial /ʃ/ plus consonant other than /r/ is unique in being shared by practically no other popular words). Creativity is as active in these ' morphemes '—and active in the same way—as in the conventional affixes, as, for example, *-ese* in *journalese* or *-ster* in *lamister*.

15. CONCLUSION. If announced principles of morpheme analysis are carried to their logical conclusion in English, not with the selection of a small body of affirmative data but with a firm resolve to face up to the whole lexical spread, three facts emerge : (1) within a comparatively narrow zone, formulation is both possible and valuable ; (2) in a wider zone it is possible but valueless ; (3) in the remaining zone it is impossible. Point (1) is not demonstrated here ; it is assumed from the writings on morphemics which have dealt with identity-opposition analysis of paradigms.

Point (2) may be phrased ' a formulation that takes care of an insignificant number of forms is fruitless.' We have a comparatively easy test for worth : that the statement of the law shall be more economical than the mere enumeration of the phenomena for which it is supposed to account. (By this measure, nothing is gained by prodding a morpheme /-m/ out of *him* and *them*.) Says A. Martinet, ' Morphematic analysis has only one justification, that of helping us understand cetain features of linguistic reality.'[43] It should stop before it reaches the point of creating more problems than it solves.

Point (3) is borne out by the array of forms—especially phonesthemes— which are too fluid to be penned within limits or which, when one attempts to limit them, lend themselves to contradictory formulations. I give one more example : *covert* can be matched with *covered* as a redundant past participle, like *burnt* with *burned*; but so to analyze it contradicts the almost invariable pairing, in some idiolects, of *covert* with *overt*. With the principles in vogue, unarbitrary formulation is impossible, for the two equally valid analyses are mutually exclusive. The sensible answer is to recognize that there are units

---

41. *Psychology of musical talent*, New York, Silver Burdett, 1919, p. 49.
42. *Life Magazine*, 15 March 1948, p. 23.
43. *Word* 5.31 (1949).

which show two-way (or three-way or multifarious) resemblances, to describe the latter fully, but to accept the units as organic entities.[44]

---

44. From long practise in matching and cultivating morphemes for associative effects, the poet, who knows almost instinctively that *rasp* is a rougher word than *file*, can give no little to the linguist where phonesthemes are concerned. See remarks of Jeremy Ingalls on ' chromaticism' and ' tone color' in *Word Study*, Oct. 1949, pp. 1-3. The vowel phonesthemes, in the shape of ' tone color' relating to size (/i/ for smallness, etc.) have been investigated by several linguists and psychologists since A. H. Tolman called attention to them in 1887 (*Andover Review* 7.326–337). They continue to be the basis of popular coinage: ' *Poopsquawk*—that's an elderly *pipsqueak* ' (Fibber McGee and Molly radio program, 9 Nov. 1948) ; ' A *myth* is a female *moth* ' (It Pays to be Ignorant radio program, 24 April 1949).

4

SHIVAREE AND THE PHONESTHEME
American Speech 25.134-135 (1950)

Shivaree is a favorite of dialect geographers because of its competition with the synonyms *serenade, tin-panning, bull-banding, skimmilton, belling, horning,* and *callathump.* Why has it raced ahead in popularity? One reason is probably its phonesthetic ties with other firmly-rooted words in English.

To the list of *-ee* words given here, add *razee,* 'a drunken spree' (listed by Wentworth, *American dialect dictionary,* 1944, and in " A Word-List from South Carolina," *Publications of the American Dialect Society* 14.56 [1950]).

Shivaree illustrates how the sound of a word often helps it to make its way in the world. It might be instructive to add an example of a word whose phonesthetic ties have weakened it. Someone recently called my attention to the aversion that many speakers seem to feel toward the past participle *swum,* to the point that they will avoid using the perfect tenses: *I have swum* etc. I sense this awkwardness in my own speech. It is probably due to the almost consistent association of [ʌm] with unfavorable meanings and overtones: *bum, dumb, scum, slum, numb, rum, crumb, glum, chum* ('fellow'), *drum (drum out of the corps), plumb (plumb dead:* this synonym of *quite* clusters with unfavorable modifiers—*plumb tuckered out* is more likely than *plumb delighted), vum, hum (ho-hum* for boredom), *clumb* (viewed as substandard for 'climbed'). Even *to strum* is a careless kind of playing. Not only perfect rimes are involved; other words have a bearing, such as *grumble, humble, stumble, fumble, jumble, crumble, lummox, flummox, lump* (and the other *-ump* words, likewise on the gauche side: *rump, frump, dump, slump), clumsy, grumpy,* etc. Strong past participles live precariously, in an exposed position. The majority of verbs get along without them, and it is harder for them to defend themselves against a hostile influence.

To the Editor, *American Speech:*
In their interesting article on *shivaree,*[1] Messrs. Davis and McDavid look to competition among *shivaree's* synonyms in the secondary settlement areas to explain the triumph of *shivaree.* The borrowing of the French word, they feel, was partly a compromise.

But this explanation disregards the fact that at the moment of its adoption into English, *shivaree* was itself in competition with the other terms, and was in a weaker position than they, for it was forced to make its way among

---

1. *American Speech,* XXIV (December, 1949), 247-55.

synonyms that were already more or less established. The speaker who discards his own word in favor of someone else's does not go to a neutral person, so to speak, to find a new term with which his old one does not compete; he imitates another speaker, and, circumstances being equal, is no more likely to imitate B.'s *shivaree* than C.'s *callathump*. He gives up as much one way as the other.

To one who accepts the reality of phonesthemes, the explanation of *shivaree's* greater viability is obvious; it is such a shining example, in fact, that it practically proves the case for phonesthemes by itself. Our authors give as the last of their several reasons for *shivaree's* interest to dialect geography the word's accent pattern, 'atypical for nouns in American folk speech, which predominantly have the primary stress on other than the final syllable.' The key to *shivaree's* success lies in this very stress on a final [iː], which accommodates it to a family of similar words with similar meanings. In fact, 'atypical' is misleading, for while the stress pattern is unusual for the folk lexicon in general, it is precisely what marks the constellation of words in question, which includes *jamboree, corroboree, jubilee, husking* (etc.) *bee, spree, whoopee, whee, gee, free, yippee, glee*, and probably *massacree*, with a possible reflex in *smithereens* (1841) and *shivereens* (1855).

How much *shivaree* owes to these words, and how much they owe to *shivaree*, could be ascertained only if we knew the earliest dates of oral occurrence for each. Since the *OED* and the *DAE* do not record the highly frequent interjections *gee* (except for a horse, or in combination) and *whee*, we cannot pin much faith upon a correlation between the dates of first written occurrence of the other words, and the dates of oral occurrence. But the evidence does imply that the loud- or medial-stressed final [iː] with the meaning 'absence of restraint,' particularly in reference to unrestrained celebration, was active at the time when *shivaree* made its bid for supremacy, which appears also to be the time when *shivaree* took on its new pronunciation. *Glee* and *free* are an ancient heritage (and their stress pattern, in phrases, accords with that of the polysyllables—note stress and intonation highlights in *Yippee! I'm free!*). *Jubilee* dates from 1526 in the general sense, and there is a *jubilee masquerade* in 1749. *Husking* (etc.) *bee* appears in 1769; *massacree*, also in the eighteenth century; *spree*, in 1804; and then in quick succession *corroboree* with modern spelling in 1835, *shivaree* with modern spelling in 1843, and *jamboree* in 1864. The strength of the constellation is attested by nonce formations like *whoop-jamboree* (1873) and *shooterie*.[2] Its pre-existence has undoubtedly contributed to the success of the suffix *-eroo*,[3] which manifests the same 'atypical' stress pattern and wears the same festive countenance.

---

2. *Ibid.*, XVI (December, 1941), 306.
3. *Ibid.*, XVII (February, 1942), 10–15.

Jakobson has pointed out[4] that the potency of what I here call phonesthemes is in inverse ratio to their frequency in the over-all phonological
system. The very uniqueness of the stress pattern of these words has, therefore, helped to maintain them as a family. They exert their pressure still, as
can be demonstrated by a simple test: I offered to two groups the invented
words [mæskə'rɔː] and [mæskə'riː], in this order, telling them to indicate
which seemed better to fit the definition 'a noisy, riotous masquerade party.'
Both groups favored the word with [iː], the first by 7 to 2 and the second
by 22 to 3. One person's later remark was typical—she preferred [iː] because 'it seemed so much gayer.'

---

4. Reported to me by Fred W. Householder, Jr.

5

THE SIGN IS NOT ARBITRARY

Boletín del Instituto Caro y Cuervo 5.52-62 (1949)

Ask two children to draw a picture of a clock, and the results will be pretty much the same: a circular face with numbers on the circumference and two hands extending from the center. The agreement will be at least as close as between two pictures of a dog.

But the clock is arbitrary—is a product of our culture—and the dog is not. A clock is something to measure time, and could as well be built like most radio "dials," with a calibrated strip and a needle that goes to 12:59 and then shifts back to one. In this respect most words are like clocks. They might as well be something different.

A child or a naive speaker realizes the "might as well" hazily if at all. He accepts clocks on a par with dogs, since he has grown up with both; he accepts *bee* on a par with *buzz*, and will take alarm as quickly on hearing the word *bee* as on hearing the buzz.

This article is an attempt to show what I was leading up to in "Word affinities": that an "arbitrary" form, once integrated into the system, assumes all the affective and associative privileges enjoyed by the most obvious onomatopoeia.

One of the cardinal assumptions of linguistics is that the signs of language are, by and large, not appropriate to the meanings that they convey. I do not mean that linguists have assumed that signs are inappropriate, but only that there is no bond between the sign and its meaning which could not as well be dissolved in favor of some other sign with the same meaning: *perro* is a historical accident that has perpetuated itself, but has no more intrinsic right to symbolize 'perro' than has, say, *becerro* or *alma*.

The assumption of the arbitrariness of the sign has had its causes and its effects. To a great extent I suspect that it was born, or at least confirmed, at the hands of the comparativists, who observed the series *perro-dog-can-chien-hund* etc. and concluded that since forms differing as radically as any set of forms can differ in their phonetic content are yet able to convey a meaning with equal aptitude, the question of aptitude is irrelevant and resemblances for the most part are to be studied as indications of related origin or contact, not as suggesting any kind of psychological or semantic necessity.

Among its effects the most far-reaching has been the divorce between linguistics and semantics. If the sign is arbitrary, forms can be studied apart from meanings—indeed, to attempt to involve meanings in the study of forms is to invite confusion. This has bred a generation of linguists who display acute symptoms of fright and its accompanying compensations when m e a n-i n g is mentioned, who have elaborated subtle techniques for circumventing it in their analyses, and who have left the investigation of meaning adrift and at the mercy of a few competent semanticists among a legion of charlatans. It has, to be sure, restricted their field and relieved them of a burden that a young science would have found it hard to bear; but linguistics has now gone far enough no longer to be excused from assuming that burden. To convince our linguists, it is necessary to attack their fundamental assumption of the arbitrariness of the sign.

If the sign is not arbitrary, there must be an intimate connexion between form and meaning—sufficiently close at times for form to influence meaning, and for meaning to influence form. This influence can take two directions: transformation and inclusion or exclusion. In the first, 1. a meaning alters a phonemic shape or 2. a phonemic shape alters a meaning; in the second, 3. a meaning may spell the difference between the existence and non-existence of a given phonemic shape within the language, or 4. a shape may do the same for the existence of a meaning.

To put the question in its proper perspective, let us take a position from which we can get a concrete view of language. In a physical sense language is a series of movements, articulatory or auditory, that take place within the physiology of individual human beings. To the comparative linguist it has a sort of existence of its own, independent of the individual, wherein utterances may be matched across space and time. To the physical positivist it has no existence apart from its realization by separate speakers and hearers, and no comparisons are productive unless effected within the speaker's daily activity. Language from this point of view is systemic[1], and is controlled by a dynamics that is the same as for any other physiological activity involving goals, be it dancing, table etiquette, courtship, musical composition, or wood-carving. The activity and its goal are largely learned from others, but they become p a r t of the individual the moment that he acquires them; his role is paramount, for it is only within him that forms and meanings jostle one another.

It follows that no new movement, and no new goal, can be ingested without adjusting itself to the apparatus already on hand, and that a process of continuing adjustment goes on forever among all the parts of that apparatus. So long as we use the same arms and legs for playing golf as for riding a

---

1. The systemic nature of language is maintained by J. R. Firth, e. g. in "The semantics of linguistic science", *Lingua* 1: 393–404, 1948.

bicycle, neither skill can be acquired without drawing upon the other that has already been learned, be it ever so little. So we must say that in a systemic view of language, cross-influences will be as pervasive as in the currents of a river.

Against this generalized background we see that the " substitutive " or vicarious function of words is substitutive only at first. We are accustomed to regarding the reaction of mouth-watering at sight (visual image) of a lemon as " natural ", and the same reaction on hearing (auditory image) the word *lemon* as " arbitrary ". But once the activity of the word has been integrated into the individual's system the reactions based upon it are as " natural " as any other. The sound *lemon* becomes a part of the sensory complex ' lemon ' just as the sound of a bell, heard frequently (but not always) when other bell-stimuli are presented, becomes part of the sensory complex ' bell '. The " form " *lemon* is now a part of the " meaning " ' lemon ', and may be abstracted from it to represent it, on the basis of the part standing for the whole, just as a pictorial image or a smell or a taste may be abstracted from the whole and used to represent it[2]. To the language-learner already familiar with the sound of galloping, the word *galloping* may have seemed appropriate at the very first; but, once learned, *run*, with little or no onomatopoeia, is just as vivid. Whatever its origin, be it as pictorial as an imitative word or as abstract as the numeral *ten*, once part of the individual's equipment it can no longer be arbitrary, and cannot " just as well " be something else. " Arbitrary " things are learned in the same way, and with exactly the same systemic results, as " natural " ones. The synapses of the brain are no respecters of any such dichotomy[3].

---

2. I am here using *meaning* to signify a psychological Gestalt, so related that the whole may be set in motion by the movement of one part. The parts usually abstracted are those most convenient to handle and carry about—in particular, language and graphic representation; but they are not s u i g e n e r i s by that fact. It might be better to consider *meaning* to signify the r e l a t i o n s h i p between the abstracted part and the whole; but for the purposes of this study it makes no difference, since we can consider a given form to be affected either by other forms (" other forms " being *meaning* by my definition) or by its connexion with other forms—in either case meaning cannot be divorced from form. I avoid the simplistic conception of meaning as a tie between a symbol and a thing, since it is too dependent on concrete nouns for its cogency and since it implies a theory of reality which is psychologically untenable unless *thing* is specially defined.

3. For an event to become linguistic, however, a great many brains must play in unison. It is possible for one person to produce an utterance like *The grain terminals were gluttered*, in which the forms and meanings of *glutted* and *cluttered* are blended. While this is exactly the same thing, as far as the individual is concerned, that occurs when sight of snow produces a remark about snow (an old linguistic event is reproduced) or when for the first time the English word *goof* is used for ' fool ' (a new event

When we speak of sound-suggestiveness, then, we speak of the e n t i r e
l a n g u a g e, not just of a few imitative or self-sufficient forms. And we
speak of units of that language smaller (and from the etymological point of
view more disorganized) than anything which linguistic formalists have con-
ceded to suggest or have meaning, as I shall now try to prove.

It has never been contended that complex utterances are arbitrary in the
same sense in which *arbitrary* has been applied to morphemes. When I say
The fire consumed the house I " might as well " say *mabu*, an arbitrary sign to
symbolize the entire occurrence. The fact is, however, that in my language
experience p a r t s of the utterance correspond to p a r t s of the event—and
the whole utterance is to that extent not arbitrary, for it is articulated in
some such way (remote as you please to call it) as the event itself. Here
meaning and form affect each other. Now there is no reason why this habit
of non-arbitrariness, of point-to-point correspondence, should stop at the level
of complex utterances. It continues to the level of morphemes and beyond.
And herein, at the floor of language where phonologists and morphemicists
have made their stand and where signs have been pictured as unimpeachably
arbitrary, we are challenged to find proof that language is still systemic.

1. *A meaning alters a phonemic shape.*—This includes the traditional " popular etymology ", which comparative linguists have been wont to class among
the museum pieces of their craft. Examples are common and a few will
suffice. The alternating Spanish forms *tajamanil* and *tejamanil* ' shingle ',
which Santamaría derives from Aztec *tla* ' thing ' and *xamanilli* ' broken,
split ', show each an assimilation to another word : *tajamanil* to *tajar* ' cut '
and *tejamanil* to *teja* ' roofing tile '. A colleague writes *peatón* ' pedestrian ' as
pietón (pie ' foot '). A relative pronounces *hybrid* identically with *high-bred*, an
obvious inference from modern genetics. To me, as a child, *Jew's harp* was
juice harp, for saliva played its negative part in the instrument's performance.
The name of a variety of watermelon, *Kleckley Sweet*, which crackles when
cut, has been heard as *Crackly Sweet*. In all such instances the form is made
analytically meaningful as well as meaningful in its entirety. The articulatory
movements in *Kleckley Sweet* and *Crackly Sweet* are sufficiently similar to
create interference and confusion— the movements in *crackly* are so intimately tied to their meaning that similar movements suggest the same meaning
if other circumstances are favorable, whence the initial phonemic shape becomes itself a cause of its alteration. The favorableness of the circumstances
need not be nearly so striking as in *Kleckley Sweet;* the oilworker's device
called a *Schlumberger* (with a correct French pronunciation) became *Slumber*

---

occurs and is made linguistic through repetition induced by the linguistic frequency of
[u] for ' foolish '), it is not linguistic, for it is not perpetuated.

Jay[4], with only the vaguest significance in either element of the new form. The phonetic elements of a language are like the keys of a piano. They have been played so often and in so many combinations that even a random cord, struck by an object accidentally falling on them, will have some vague semblance of meaning.

But popular etymology is only one manifestation of the phenomenon, an easy one to single out because whole words, and comparatively few of them, are involved. It is revealed in another of its aspects in the identification of parts of words which are partially synonymous, where it is difficult if not impossible to regard the parts as separate morphemes. English *smash* is converted from *mash* under the influence of *smear*, *slash*, etc. *Regardless*>*irregardless* comes through attraction to *irrespective* and other words with initial *irre-*. A broader aspect is that of larger units, whose shape may be determined by the suggested meaning of one of their parts. English *rapt*, for example, is homonymous with *wrapped*, and phrases like *rapt attention*, *rapt expression*, where the observer is 'wrapped up' in what he observes, enjoy a higher frequency in spoken English than others attributable to the lexical meaning of *rapt*.

The ideal conditions under which to test the influence of meaning over phonemic shape are those obtaining when new expressions at the level of morphemes are deliberately created. Such conditions are infrequent, but are found occasionally in the work of poets and often in the work of advertising men. Examples of the latter are the trade names that have been applied to soaps and soapless detergents in American English. The first and best-known of the latter is *Dreft*, an obvious echo of *drift* (and of other monosyllables with final *-ft* which suggest pleasant or poetic meaning: *soft*, *oft*, *lift*, *sift*, *tuft*, *deft*). Not to be outdone in this hint of drifting suds, another manufacturer has come forward with *Tide* and a third with *Surf*. In such terms, of course, the primary meaning is the product; a secondary meaning, which the seller wishes to suggest, influences the form.

2. *A phonemic shape alters a meaning.*—Ideal conditions here are also those of invention. If we coin a nonsense word, and get substantial agreement from a number of hearers as to what it "seems to mean", we have evidence of the pressure that shape can exert on meaning. To make such a test I coined the presumably non-existent English word *smuck* and submitted it to a group of sixteen persons asking them to state in writing, first, whether it seemed "nice" or "not nice", second, what the word seemed to mean. Responses were as follows:

---

4. Lalia P. Boone, "The language of the oil field", *American Speech*, 24:33, 1949.

Nice 2
Not nice 13
(No reply .... 1)

Definitions:

1. Dirt, mud 5
2. Something slimy or sticky 1
3. Worthless (low-bred, socially unacceptable) person 4
4. Stupid act 1
5. Stupid person 1
6. Opprobrious name for a foreigner 1
7. Slap 1

Meanings 1 and 2 echo *muck, mud, mire, marsh, moor, morass,* etc. Meanings 3–6 reflect the unfavorable implication of the former and add an echo of the recent epithet *schmo.* Similar tests that I have run, and which there is no space to report here, have shown equally striking agreement. Perhaps even more significant than the figures is the cooperativeness with which speakers enter into a suggestion of this sort: it seems natural to them that sound should affect meaning.

In the foregoing, however, we have started with an assumed zero meaning. What of a form that is already established in the language? Probably, for form to affect it radically, its prior meaning must be attenuated. Instances of this sort are numerous among the mistakes that speakers make in attempting to use words that they have heard but imperfectly understood, inferring a meaning from an insufficient number of contexts. A critic's reference to a novel as having a *somewhat portentous title,* echoing *ponderous* and *pretentious,* is probably an individual lapse; but *mitigate* is frequently heard in the sense of *militate* (both followed by *against*). The English *shambles* 'slaughter house' was extended to 'carnage' which is close enough to 'destruction' so that the echo of *shoddy, shamble* (gait), *shanty, shack, shiftless,* and other *sh-* words could carry it through and beyond to 'mess' of any kind, which is its current meaning.

The prior meaning may be one that is thoroughly known, however, but with conditions so favorable that two forms converging phonetically also converge semantically. This has happened with the English nouns *shoot* and *chute,* and probably for many speakers with the Spanish verbs *acechar* and *asechar.*

Subtler examples, though less convincing to the skeptic, are more numerous and more typical. The primary meaning of *jacket,* for instance, is 'short coat', which, being fabric, is perfectly flexible. Yet *jacket* echoes *jagged* and *rigid* besides the hardness so characteristic of [æ] in English; this fact has undoubtedly supported its extension to 'rigid covering', as in *strait jacket* and *steel-jacketed.*

Where subtle examples become undeniable, however, is in constellations of words having similar meanings tied to similar sounds. How such constellations originate is immaterial : it may be that a given sound, as has been maintained by many writers for [i] in the sense of 'smallness, tenseness', has a pre-linguistic meaning ; it may be that some one word is used so often that phonetically similar words are affected, as has apparently happened with English *bulge* reflected in *divulge* and *indulgent*, suggesting 'expansiveness'; or it may be that two or more forms coincidentally resemble one another in both form and meaning, thereby drawing closer together and pulling other forms into their orbit, as seems to have happened with *chary, wary,* and *scary* (*skeery*) in their effect upon *leery*. The result is the same : the cluster maintains itself and attracts outside matter to it. Examples in Spanish are *tajar rajar, ajar, bajar, fajar, majar, sajar,* and *desgajar,* analogizing closely with English *bash, mash, smash, crash, dash, lash, hash, rash, brash, clash, trash, plash, splash,* and *flash.* The whole e s d r ú j u l a family in Spanish is peculiarly dramatic, and Carlos García Prada writes mockingly, " Dice *férvido me mande* porque ese adjetivo es más enérgico que el acostumbrado *fervoroso,* y que *ferviente* ". The coined forms mentioned above were suggested by constellations and the persons tested clearly felt the attraction exerted by the constellation. In Spanish there exists the cluster *derrabar, derramar, derrenegar, derrengar, derretir, derribar, derrisión, derrocar, derrochar, derrotar, derrubiar, derruir, derrumbar,* and *derriscar,* all hovering about the related meanings 'destroy, bring down, mistreat'. When I coined the word *derrufe* and asked three speakers to imagine meanings for it, the replies were 'vagabundo', 'payaso', and 'derrumbe' (the first two possibly combining the alliterative *rufián* with 'hombre caído')[5].

---

5. The literature on morphosemantic constellations in English includes : Albert H. Tolman, " The laws of tone color in the English language ", *Andover Review,* 7 : 326–337, 1887 ; " Expressive power of English sounds ", *Atlantic,* 73 : 478, 1894 ; " Symbolic value of English sounds ", in his *Views about Hamlet,* 141–72, Houghton Mifflin, 1904 (Tolman adopts the term *sound symbolism*). Otto Jespersen, *Language,* 312 ff and 396ff, New York, Holt, 1922. Edward Sapir, " A study in phonetic symbolism ", *Journal of Experimental Psychology,* 12 : 225–239, 1929 (Sapir contends that phonetic symbolism is pre-linguistic and not primarily caused by word associations; this is probably true within the limits of his study, but not in general). Charles E. A. Moore, " A preliminary study of the emotional effects of letter-sounds ", *Quarterly Journal of Speech,* 24 : 134–149, 1938. E. H. Sturtevant, *An introduction to linguistic science,* 111–112, New Haven, 1947. J. Gonda, " The comparative method as applied to Indonesian languages ", *Lingua,* 1 : 86–101, 1948 (a major part of the Indonesian vocabulary shows morphological effects of semantics). There are also unpublished studies by Fred W. Householder, Jr., of Indiana University.

Another test in Spanish : The feminine names *Teresa* and *Alicia* were offered to two groups, one of nine persons working at the Caro y Cuervo Institute in Bogotá and the

But, our critic may ask, do events occur thus in a natural situation, or only under the artificial conditions of intentional coinage and interrogation of speakers? An answer is supplied by the word *magnolia*, from *Pierre Magnol* and hence etymologically without bearing upon the phonetically similar *magnificent*, *magniloquent*, *magnify*. Yet the suggestion of 'magnificent flower' is so obvious that speakers of English have brought them together, creating *magnolious*, a humorous synonym of 'magnificent'. When *miniatures* ($<$ *minium* 'red lead') were introduced, their customary smallness offered no resistance to the attraction of the numerous *min-* words for 'small' (*minimum*, *minion*, *minnow*, *minute*, *minutia*), and it has now come to signify 'small' itself. *Minikin* is another non-etymological accretion to this family.

3. *A meaning keeps or destroys a phonemic shape.*—A form which is tied to one tabooed meaning among a number of respectable meanings, may be destroyed in all of its senses by that one meaning. This is a familiar phenomenon; it has occurred with *huevo* in Mexican Spanish (replaced by *blanquillo*) and with *coger* in Argentine Spanish (replaced by synonyms of the approved meaning). To be sure, the "destruction" here is not complete with all speakers, since tabooed forms maintain a clandestine existence for a time or indefinitely; but the forms are not openly heard, and consequently disappear from the vocabulary of the more innocent.

Taboo that is not connected with metaphor begins with the prohibition of larger units and ends with the prohibition of a recurrent partial. Thus *belly* as an anatomical term is inoffensive, but *belly* is also appropriate to all the situations in which the part of the body that it names might figure (*He groveled on his belly*—besides many unprintable contexts—where *abdomen* will hardly do). Some of these situations are forbidden, and *belly*, now impregnated with them, is replaced with *abdomen* or *stomach*. The partial is usually a word, but now and then is something less: English *spissed* was probably helped to oblivion by its rime.

4. *A phonemic shape keeps or destroys a meaning.*—The conspicuous examples are those of "conflict of homonyms". Contexts employing Spanish *veneficio* 'maleficio' clashed with those using the identical antonym *beneficio*, and the first gave way. Similarly with English *let* 'hinder' and *let* 'allow'. We

---

other of twenty-five students in upper-level secondary school in the same city. They were asked to write the name that seemed to them more 'deleitoso'. In the first group, *Alicia* was favored by six to three, and in the second *Alicia* was also favored, twenty-one to four. This probably shows the influence of *delicia*, perhaps supported by *primicias* and *albricias*. Compare, in English, the creation of *delovely* about ten years ago from the word-family *delicious*, *delightful*, *delectable*, *delirious* (*with joy*). A similar test with nonsense-words *sabo* and *saba*, to show an assumed relationship between gender and size, failed of effect, possibly because the "feminine augmentative" is no longer productive in Spanish, or possibly because the sonic element is too small—much smaller than any others tested.

cannot explain the disappearance of one meaning simply as an intellectual choice made to avoid confusion, for languages do not evolve intellectually. The reason is again the bond between a meaning and a form, resolved in favor of the stronger bond when two are in conflict.

Less conspicuous are examples where a prior meaning is lost by attraction of the form to similar forms with different meanings. English *callow* means 'beardless', and, by extension, 'immature'. As used by fledgling writers, however, it has so fallen under the influence of *sallow* (reinforced perhaps by *pallor* and *hollow*) that it is made to refer to the complexion.

CONCLUSIONS

Maurice Bloomfield wrote in 1895, " The question as to how much plasticity may have been imparted to the lexical value of words by the cloud of formally assonant words, with meanings not too far removed, that hover about them, would form one of the most fruitful and profound investigations in linguistic history "[6]. My brief study makes no pretense of being profound, but it does attempt to dignify such an inquiry by proving its absolute relevance to anything that linguists may attempt to do with meaning—as they increasingly must as they go beyond phonemic analysis.

While I have attempted to prove the vast importance of cross-influences, I have not aimed at demonstrating their omnipotence. We can be singularly deaf at times to an assonance that seems as if it ought to clamor for attention. The existence of a constellation in *blob, gob, cob, knob, daub, bob, fob, hob,* and *job* implying 'compactness' reflects little upon *snob*. *Toilet water* remains a delicacy despite the unfavorable implications of *toilet*. This is not fatal to my thesis, which was that a given form is physiologically tied to a given meaning. Any discriminable form, however similar (and discrimination here includes non-linguistic context), may be tied to a totally different meaning. It is sufficient evidence if we find that a large part of the time similar forms will tend in the direction of similar meanings. We are in the position of a doctor who proves the existence of a disease by pointing to an infallible symptom, but does not disprove the disease by the symptom's absence. Language, like health and like disease, is systemic.

---

6. *American Journal of Philology*, 16 : 413, 1895. I owe this citation to Professor Allen Walker Read of Columbia University.

6

THE LIFE AND DEATH OF WORDS
American Scholar 22.323-335 (1953)

In the Summer 1951 issue of the *American Scholar*, the historian Jacques Barzun and the linguist D. J. Lloyd bared their differences on whether *disinterested* should be allowed to mean 'uninterested' and whether English in general should be allowed to go to the dogs. Barzun is a cultivator of clear expression (the unbelievable happened when he became Dean of the Graduate School at Columbia University—the next edition of the graduate catalog was *readable*); he has no patience with writers or speakers whose ideas fall into place accidentally. Lloyd recoils from anything with the scent of purism. The result was a controversy with no middle ground.

As in most arguments, both litigants were right, or wrong. The descriptive linguist was off limits in censuring, rather than describing, an attempt to regulate language. The defender of pure English was wasting his ammunition trying to rescue a word that was already fatally wounded.

In "The Life and Death of Words" I try to show two things: the associative forces within a language that make some changes inevitable, and that the purist should recognize; and the conservative forces that nip many incipient changes in the bud, which the linguist should be willing to recognize—and to describe, as just another linguistic phenomenon.

"A major revolution now looms" is a journalistic phrase, and I am afraid that much of this carries a journalistic tone; but the organic view of evolution I believe is correct.

A major revolution now looms in the science of words, not known in all its significance even to some linguistic scientists. Its prime movers and pacesetters, working independently but convergingly, are Professor Yakov Malkiel of the University of California and the school of linguists in Germany known as the Neo-Humboldtians, after the great nineteenth-century naturalist philologist Baron von Humboldt.

Malkiel is the meticulous, profound researcher. His work is in Spanish and related languages, but his method is valid for all languages and will be applied to them sooner or later. The Neo-Humboldtians are the avant-garde theorizers, shorter on demonstration but bolder in drawing conclusions. No one who ventures to pronounce on how words and meanings evolve will in the future dare to overlook their work, for it gives at last a ground for the fusion of the time-honored study of how languages change in form and the newer science of semantics.

Briefly, the implication that concerns us is that words evolve in masses of forms and meanings with infinite cross- and counter-influences, like soft bodies that crowd together and modify one another's shape and function. Linguists have always known that words behave in some such fashion, but they have not had the courage to depart from their straight-line etymologies, mainly because they lacked the vast information that Malkiel has amassed to prove that no form or meaning in a language ever changes in isolation. As Jost Trier of the Neo-Humboldtian school says, " Nothing in language exists independently."

Straight-line etymologizing, the hunting down of " the " source of a word, cannot be displaced so long as there are words whose prime source is unknown. It gives us the ontogeny of words—their individual parentage— against what the new approach offers, an understanding of their phylogeny, their group survival, the history of the entire species. A recent example of the straight-line quest, brilliant as a display of tenacious searching, was the discovery by Professor Allen Walker Read of Columbia University—wading through the Greek *óla kalá*, the Choctaw *okeh*, the Andrew Jackson *Oll Korrect*, and other origins proposed by the indefatigable guessworkers who plague the borders of etymology—that O. K. comes from the Martin Van Buren O. K. Club of 1840. But what the new school wants to know is why *O.K.* caught on, and why it has grown in popularity every year until within the last decade or two it has partially displaced *all right*. Not all of the answer lies in the language necessarily, any more than all that explains the popularity of a style in women's clothing is to be found in the history of styles—some of it may be the appeal of sheer newness or nonconformity, or persistent plugging by an advertiser. But as much as the life or death of a term or meaning is due to its relationships among its own kind, linguistics provides an answer; and that is a lot.

An example of Professor Malkiel's methods is the Spanish *pech-*, a root that developed from several Latin sources: *pactu*, 'agreement' (including terms of agreement, fines, taxes) ; *pectus*, 'breast, chest'; *pessulu*, 'bolt or bar of a door'; and the group represented by *despectus*, 'contempt,' and *suspectus*, 'suspicion.' Not all of these left descendants in all parts of Spain, but as speakers migrated from one section to another, the forms tied themselves into what Malkiel terms a " lexical tangle," with each wielding some influence to support or weaken each of the others. For instance, the *despechar* from *pactu* meaning 'to levy excessive taxes on,' hence 'to ruin,' merged with the *despechar* from *despectus* meaning 'to offend,' which had already been infused with *pecho* from *pectus*, 'breast,' as the seat of the feelings, so that *despechar* covered the range of ruin, anger and despondency.

A less complicated tangle in English is that of *shoot* and *chute*. The words of a language form a gravitational system, with some forms being pulled into the orbit of others and some rotating at a safe distance in a sort of mutual tolerance and stability.

This is all in a manner of speaking, of course. Words are not things, but activities. Language is a system of movements like figure dancing—but the most complicated system under human control. If two similar steps in a dance can condition each other so that both are confused or so that the dancer must exercise special care to keep them apart, imagine what happens when the steps are increased from the possible hundred or two in the dance to the eight or ten thousand that constitute the stock of verbal movements at a speaker's command. Imbed these ten thousand movements in a layer of ten thousand meanings, and it becomes obvious that something is going to be done to align meaning with form, purely for economy of effort.

Here is the most important inference to be drawn from our knowledge of word-families: that the life and death of words in large part depends on our need to economize, to make what words really mean agree with what they seem to mean. There is a connectedness in our experience of reality—dogs are dogs, but they also have four legs and so relate to cats; they eat almost anything, and so belong with other carnivores. Unflaggingly, but not always successfully, we seek the same connectedness in the imaging of reality, our language.

To picture the word within the system of which it forms a part, imagine an orb like the sun with gaseous satellites revolving about it. The central body is the core of the word's meaning, what it is taken to signify under normal conditions by those who hear and use it. The gasiform satellites are the aura of all its apparent meanings. When the core is relatively hard, the aura continues to haunt the fringes but does not move in upon the central meaning. When the core is diffuse, the aura may blend with it and alter it completely. The aura is like an accumulation of cosmic dust given off by all the other orbs in the galaxy of the language with which the one in question is associated in meaning or use. As our word drifts its way about the verbal universe in the daily converse and intercourse of speech, it accumulates this billowy sort of envelope that presses in upon it hard or softly, depending on circumstances.

Our astrological picture is necessary to get the facts in focus. The essential fact is that every word or combination of words lays the stamp of its form on the meaning that it conveys. Once we say *onion* and associate it with a certain adjunct to culinary art, *onion* is available to come to mind whenever anything that sounds like *onion*, in either form or meaning, is mentioned. In form, it may be a rhyming word like *bunion*; in meaning, it may be a kindred term like *soup*. (Meaning is ultimately form, for it comes by way of the actual use together of *onion* and *soup*.) Until the connection is unusually close, no threat is posed to the stability of the word. Once the bond is firmly set, a reaction begins to take place.

Disinterested will serve as an example. This word is a kind of binary star, one-half being the prefix *dis-* and the other half the base *interested*. Its stuff is pretty thin, like that of which astronomers tell us a roomful would weigh only a fraction of a gram, for it names not a precise thing but an attitude—in a nutshell, you cannot diagram or picture *disinterested*. So the aura begins to mingle with it. Its first half, *dis-*, takes on the coloration of almost all the *dis-* words in spoken English, which is that of an "unfavorable" meaning (*disgust, distrust, dislike, disturb, distress, dissatisfy*), while its second half pulls in upon itself the only popular meaning of *interested* nowadays, which is not 'having a stake in something' but 'being emotionally attracted by something.' There you have it—*disinterested* not in the sense of 'impartial,' but as an unfavorable term signifying 'indifferent': the disinterested judge, to quote Jacques Barzun, becomes the judge who goes to sleep on the bench. What *disinterested* "really" means has moved toward what it seems to mean.

All the evidence of the power of what we might call the "organon" of the language—its vocabulary in action, with form engraved on meaning—has been at hand, but not until now has it received more than piecemeal recognition. Some of the pieces wear traditional labels in linguistics.

There is, first, folk etymology. One may occasionally hear a plant or animal referred to as *high bred*, in place of *hybrid*—an obvious, though false, inference based on the achievements of modern genetics. Folk etymology is the interpretation of something strange in familiar terms—the odd word is taken really to mean what it seems to mean. The American political expression *doughface* originally meant a face covered with a mask of dough; then, when the practice of wearing such masks disappeared and the original meaning was lost, people began to apply the term with 'easily molded person' in mind. Probably everyone remembers childhood guesses that later had to be revised—one of mine was *juice harp* for *jew's harp*.

Then there is "verbal taboo." Here the speaker knows what his term signifies, but the aura includes an apparent meaning that is indecorous, and so he refrains from using it. In Perry County, Tennessee, the word *peanut*, writes Kelsie Harder, "contains a double-barrelled taboo, and red-faced farm boys, or even their parents, seldom used the term among mixed company." The word *goober* replaced it, but trouble cropped up again because "*goober* had formerly been identified with the anatomically distinctive organ of young boys." The not entirely satisfactory *peas* was the compromise. The linguistic geographer Raven McDavid tells of the taboo on *Helena*, Montana, with accent on the first syllable, aggravated perhaps by little boys who disguised their profanity in *Go to Helena*. (In my set it was the supremely fumigated *Go to Halifax*.)

" Conflict of homonyms " is the collision between two words which sound alike and, owing to use in similar situations, cause such confusion (or, if one is tabooed, embarrassment) that one eventually disappears or changes its meaning. Professor Edna Williams of Smith College has documented the rivalry between *queen* and *quean*, ' harlot,' where *quean* was finally exiled from standard English; that of *strait* and *straight*, where *strait* has disappeared in all but a few phrases, such as *the strait and narrow path*.

" Blends " are compromises, usually accidental, between two forms, both of which fit a situation—the meaning wears a dual stamp. When Erle Stanley Gardner writes, " Many the night we have paced the floor," he combines *many a night* with *many's the night*. The student who claims to be " listening intentively " has joined *attentively* and *intently*. Others are " imitray " for *imitate* and *portray* (Red Skelton), " tremorous " for *tremulous* and *timorous* (Hart Crane), " sophomoronic " (Francis Hayes), " bugabear " for *bugaboo* and *bugbear*. Usually a blend is a nova in the verbal heavens that flashes and then fades. But now and then one continues to glow. The common *every now and then* is probably a blend of *now and then* with *ever and anon*. Many speakers contradict themselves when they use " He isn't far from wrong," blending " He isn't far wrong " and " He's far from wrong." Blends require not only meanings that will match but forms that mate easily ; *most places+almost everywhere=most everywhere*.

Given a long enough stretch of history, even the few blends that survive can accumulate a respectable total. And here we reach the most spectacular proof of the workings of the organon of words, entire families built by slow accretion through the centuries in a process more subtle than blending but closely similar to it. The thirteen-year-old boy who said, " Jones is *plumpier* than Smith " remolded *plump* along the lines of *chunky, chubby, roly-poly, tubby, pursy, paunchy, pudgy, portly* and *fleshy*, re-creating a form as old as Shakespeare. Here the aura is one of form: about *plump* hover all its synonyms, and they have borne in upon it and changed its shape to agree with them. Instead of a change of meaning to make the word really mean what it seems to mean, there is a change of form to make the word seem to mean what it really means—two sides of a single process, the mutual fitness of form and meaning.

Thus constellations of words have been born. The Danish linguist Otto Jespersen noted the grouping of *rump, clump, dump, stump, hump, bump, lump* and other *-ump* words about the notion of heaviness and clumsiness. The family of *slap, clap, rap, tap, flap,* and *lap* denotes actions that strike and then glide off, while that of *dab, grab, stab, tab, nab* and *daub* covers striking that does not glide off but stops in or on something. A lighter or sharper blow or its result is suggested by the group *nip, clip, tip, sip, dip, grip, pip, quip, yip* (contrast *yap*), *flip* (contrast *flop*) and *drip* (contrast *droop* and *drop*). But another constellation crosses this one at the point of *drip*, that of *drip, drop, drizzle, drench, drool, dribble, drink, drain*, relating to liquids.

After *shivaree* first appeared in English about 1800, it had to make its way against several other expressions with the same meaning: *horning, belling, skimmilton, bull-band*. It triumphed because arrayed behind it was the family of accented -*ee* words: *jubilee, husking bee, spree, whee, gee, free, yippee, glee, jamboree, corroboree*. It is easy to prove the linguistic reality of such families. A group of thirty-four persons, asked whether *m. skeró* or *maskerée* better expressed the idea of 'a noisy, riotous masquerade party,' voted six to one in favor of *maskerée* because, said one, " it seemed so much gayer." The British linguist J. R. Firth calls these sound-sense groupings " phonesthemes."

Some families were undoubtedly imitative in origin. *Bang, clang, clatter, batter, spatter* imitate sounds. Other families have no trace of imitativeness. Roughly half of the popular words in English that begin with *gl-* (*glimpse, glow, glare, glitter, glance*), for example, have to do with something visual. Whatever their origin, they now serve as gravitational centers, growing as they overpower other centers or fading as they are overpowered by them.

Members of a constellation may be few or many, from mere pairs like *banish-vanish* (with looser ties with *finish, anguish*), *abysmal-dismal* (ignorance), *damning-damaging* (evidence) to multitudes that cluster in all degrees of affinity and branch out in a score of directions. All point to the one inevitable drift—the accommodation of form to meaning and meaning to form.

What is the effect of the organon of lauguage, of the aura of meanings that cling to a form and of forms that cling to a meaning? Words are born—how, we can never predict: they may be deliberately coined, like *aspirin* or *gas*, or adapted, like *gatling* or *bowie*; they may be borrowed from another language, like *buckaroo* or *flair*, or from another dialect, like *ornery* based on *ordinary* or *heist* based on *hoist*; they may come from having an extra word lying around somewhere that is not really needed, which gradually becomes infused with a special meaning—" Whip him *good* " no longer means the same as " Whip him *well*." By fusions of misunderstanding or borrowing, a single word may propagate several—*gentle, gentile, genteel, genty* and *jaunty* are all ultimately the same. Easy as it seems to do, words are seldom invented—they usually just happen. If they fulfill a need, they are seized upon and made secure in the language. If not, they are lost. What is important in the life of a word is that once launched it has to run the gantlet of all the existing forms and meanings in the organon.

The result may be fortune or disaster, a straightforward course or distortion or oblivion. Of the immediate failures no record is left, but we may be sure that mortality far exceeds survival, as witness the accidental blends already mentioned which died aborning. Our interest lies with the successes, with how they have managed to endure the ordeal of a hostile environment.

Like people, these words achieve success by adaptation. Of all the terms of electrical measurement named after men famous in electronics—*ohm*, *joule*, *ampere*, *coulomb*, *volt*—only *volt* has taken hold outside the lingo of specialists and become a part of everyone's speaking vocabulary; *volt* could readily adapt itself because *bolt* and *jolt*, also used in popular reference to electricity, were there to help. *Catty*, as in "a catty remark," at the outset had no more promise of success than *waspish*, *shrewish* or *vixenish*, also named for animals, and besides had to brave their competition; but it is now better known than any of the others to the speaker on the street, thanks to *cutting*, *curt* and *sarcastic*. *Magnolia*, named for Pierre Magnol, was so suggestive of glorifying words like *magnificent*, *magnanimous* that it not only caught on but gave rise to *magnolious*. Such as these are the rousing successes.

The course of others has been more tortuous. *Flibbertigibbet* originally meant a fiend, but the pull of the family of *flippant*, *flighty*, *flimsy*, *flirt*, *flit*, *fly-by-night* and other words signifying something light, harebrained or inconsequential has been too powerful, and now it means a flighty person.

Still others have been struck a fatal blow, some early in their career and some late, by an enemy elsewhere in the organon. An enlightened society will no longer tolerate *niggardly*, though it has nothing to do with *nigger*. As soon as the ending *-ific* became associated, through *terrific*, *horrific* and *prolific*, with the idea of drive and power, *pacific*, 'peaceful,' was doomed in the spoken language. Association turns purely relative elements like *-ific* and *dis-* into absolute ones and destroys or changes words where they do not appear in the dominant sense.

One way of avoiding this fate is a change of form—usually just enough of a change of pronunciation to disguise the unwanted kinship. *Fatima* is still listed by the dictionaries with accent on *fat-*, but few speakers will tolerate so unfeminine a pronunciation. *Communal* is traditionally accented on the first syllable, but political sensitivity (plus the growing use of the word *community*) has pushed the accent to the second syllable for many speakers. The pronunciation of *nascent* with the *a* of *pass* was too reminiscent of *nasty*, with the result that the *a* of *nay* is now recorded.

The chooser or inventor of a word must grope his way in the organon of language exactly as a composer in search of an apt musical phrase gropes his way in the organon of music. There are no clearly formulated rules; success is determined by fitness.

Fishing in the subconscious, when we are coining or choosing, brings to light the wayward associations that attach themselves like lily pads and old shoes to the hook, along with an occasional catch. The interacting bonds of form and meaning can summon any related form for a related meaning and any related meaning for a related form, as well as summon form by form and meaning by meaning.[1] One comes to understand von Humboldt when he says, as Professor Harold Basilius of Wayne University expounds him, " Words result from the totality of speech." There is no more real invention in *temptatious*, combining *temptation* and related forms with *delicious, luscious, scrumptious* and other *-cious* words, than in saying " Quigley fiddles," though neither may ever have been said before.

To give all possible examples of these and other manifestations of the organon would be to quote the dictionary, for all show potentially an infusion by the aura of form and meaning. The tendency of forms to mold themselves on other forms with like meanings, and meanings to mold themselves on other meanings conveyed by like forms, is universal.

But here arises a dilemma. Why has this not completely regularized the English language, so that now the conformity of the two is perfect? Partly, there has not been time. Partly, the accidental origin of new words precludes their being regular to begin with, which is a corollary of the same thing. Most importantly of all, we resist it.

What speakers avoid doing is as important as what they do. Self-correction of speech and writing, and the correction of others in conversation (" I can't understand what you say "), in classrooms and over editorial desks is an unending business, one that determines the outlines of our speech just as acceptances determine its mass. Correction, the border beyond which we say " no " to an expression, is to language what a seacoast is to a map. Up to now, linguistic scientists have ignored it because they could see in it nothing more than the hankerings of pedants after a standard that is arbitrary, prejudiced and personal. But it goes deeper. Its motive is intelligibility, and in spite of the occasional aberrations that have distracted investigators from the central facts, it is systematic enough to be scientifically described.

Correction is largely the process of throwing an expression into sharper relief. It works automatically in some instances of pronunciation. We can say, " Industry is working for de*fense* " and put the accent on one syllable, but in " A good offense is the best *defense* " we shift it to the other, for the sake of contrast.

Another example is our exasperation when we start a sentence and then find that somewhere along its course we have used two identical or closely similar sounds in different senses: " I'll take the doors outdoors to paint them "; " He charged me too much for charging the battery "; " It is good to be in a position to be in possession of the facts "; " It's an oasis in the wastes of Africa "; " The second weakness is one that he does not to my

---

1. See the examples in the next article, on " Verbal evocation."

knowledge acknowledge." A colleague at a committee meeting said, "Yes, merit increases—I think the idea has merit," then paused, laughed and corrected herself. "Before you leave, be sure to brush your hair" is all right, and so is "Before you leave, be sure to brush your teeth," but "Before you leave, be sure to brush your hair and teeth" would be rejected in favor of "brush your hair and clean your teeth"; for the implied repetition would use the same word in different senses.

What one linguist belittles as "the school admonition to use synonyms instead of repeating a word" is the basic need to achieve clarity through contrast carried to an extreme. Purists have made a fetish of not permitting repetition even in the same sense. But this is unimportant. What matters is that in order to be understood, meanings that we want to distinguish we must represent by clearly distinguishable sounds. The purists are right, but for the wrong reason: we do not avoid repeating because it sounds bad, but it sounds bad because we avoid it—the prime reason for the avoidance is the prompting of contrast.

So, except in the most unreflecting speech, we are likely to shun, "He had an idea, and jumped up and wrote it down," where, even though there is no repetition of sound, *up* and *down* are incongruously matched.

The reason we fail to realize the contrastive impulse in language is that we are seldom aware of its functioning except when it breaks down. The crude examples that I have given illustrate a few of the commoner disorders.

The drive for contrast goes counter to the drift toward similarity. Here is the explanation of why a language will tolerate a multiplicity of words for the same thing—why masses of synonyms have grown up and works like Roget's *Thesaurus* are possible. If the aura had its way, all synonyms would sound alike; but we know that they do not. The reason is that meaning is nebulous and has to be condensed by the context in which a word is used. The way we resolve that condensation responds to the need for contrast. Two expressions otherwise synonymous may be resolved in different ways. Let us say that I express an idea as "I was running for the train because my watch was not running and I was late." Here, within a narrow context, *running* has been condensed in two ways; the result is nonsensical or funny (funniness is a social reaction to nonsense). So I reach for an expression completely different in form, but synonymous ("my watch was out of order," "needed fixing," "wasn't working"), which condenses the meaning contrastively. If all synonyms sounded alike, either clarity or brevity would have to be sacrificed.

If our language had a large enough inventory of sounds, we might retain both similarity and contrast to the full—have a set of synonyms of similar form, and a stand-by set to be called in when needed. But the stock of distinctive sounds ("phonemes") is too small, and when sharp contrast is needed, we have to use them up more than one at a time. *Tiny* and *tidy* are not bothersome in referring to a small woman's figure, but if *a tidy sum* is likely to be misunderstood as *a tiny sum*, just the contrast of *d* and *n* is not enough—the speaker must clutch at something entirely different, such as *respectable, large* or *sizable*. Competition keeps similarity and contrast moving in upon each other all the time.

The fight between the purist and his linguist foe is not part of our immediate business, but the theme of drift and contrast holds a moral that it would be inopportune not to point out.

A language might be likened to a machine with two economies: the economy of social effort, which is that of maintaining existing contrasts and keeping the machine in repair; and the economy of individual effort, which is that of letting it float into a homogeneous state of bliss that will tax the speaker least when he tries to remember what he wants to say. As speakers, regularity is what makes us happiest, and our children are working hard at it every day with their self-created as well as propagated *I doed it, you was, a orange.*

But speakers are also hearers, which makes the division a false one. From the hearer's standpoint—which is the same as saying from the social standpoint—the trouble is that there are many children and many points of departure for regularization which may therefore run at cross-purposes. Language is a sensitive and infinitely layered and segmented machine, and its owners cannot afford to let new parts be inserted or old ones moved from one place to another unless they represent a minimum of disagreement. There are vested interests even in the absurdities.

The purist and the anti-purist maintain this false division, the one championing society as the stockholder in stability and the other the individual as the focus of change.

The purist takes a short view of history, refusing to see that languages are always on the move. His mistake is his unhappy penchant for defending positions that the majority have long since willingly abandoned. He will fight for a senseless *whom* as fiercely as for a sensible distinction between *mitigate* and *militate* or *foreboding* and *forbidding*. Like the prohibitionist, he makes a moral issue of a certain kind of abstinence.

The anti-purist sees the massive changes that language has undergone through the ages, and watches with contempt the handful of pipsqueaks in his own generation who would try to arrest an irresistible process. To him, Speakers are the great flowing stream, which he emotionally identifies with Nature, and purists are a small hive of busybodies outside Nature trying vainly to divert it. In his Olympian view he overlooks our immediate concerns and fails to see the purist as but one part of the assertion of things-as-they-are reflected in language, revealed in other ways in the hour-by-hour hesitations and self-corrections on the part of speakers—their "I mean this, not that," the "What was that you said?" on the part of hearers, their insistence on some alternative mode of expression, the frowning-down of rude intonations and laughing-out of oddities, the life-or-death substitution of *flammable* for *inflammable*, the constant and inescapable decisions that one must make on how to put a thought more clearly or pronounce, for the benefit of a stupid or noisy audience, a word more intelligibly. Interference with language is inescapable. The individual interferes, automatically, when he forgets or fumbles or is careless or lazy; society bent on self-preservation interferes whenever he strays, and drives him back into line—almost—the extra amount beyond the almost being the quantum of change.

Society hugs its practices to itself, and the purist hugs them too close; but anti-purists are as powerless to prevent the embrace as purists are to make themselves immortal. Both the long and short views are true in their proper setting. To side with drift against contrast is to side with the nether against the upper millstone.

VERBAL EVOCATION
Lingua 10.113-127 (1961)

About 1928 I began collecting English synonyms for my own use, to make up for the lack of close equivalents in the average thesaurus or book of synonyms. For instance, if I had forgotton a term that I knew meant 'inbreeding,' there was no way for me to lay my hands on *endogamy*. If I wanted *taskmaster, slave-driver,* or *Legree* as synonyms of *disciplinarian*, Roget was of no use. One byproduct of the memory-cudgeling that this led to was an awareness of the subconscious links that enable one eventually to drag a fugitive word into the light. I began to jot them down. The following is a compilation, which I hope has some significance for the relationship of form and meaning.

Linguists have typically left problems of association and memory to psychologists, just as psychologists have typically left questions of linguistic form to linguists. Their common ground is the relation of form to meaning, and association and memory, to the extent that they bear on this, assume an importance for scientists in both fields.

In a recent article[1] Roman Jakobson reopened the question of a *signatum* with zero *signans*, treated by Kurt Goldstein. Crudely stated, this has to do with a sign whose meaning is known but whose verbal form has been forgotten. Its symptom is the recognition of an absence. The speaker (or writer, or thinker) is aware that there is a vehicle for his idea, may even recall something about it such as that is is long and starts with *d*, and that this vehicle is better than any other within reach, but he is unable to lay his hands on it.

In pathology, the obliterated *signans* may never be recaptured, or may be recaptured only after psychiatric treatment. But psychopathology is not the only area in which the obliterated *signans* is to be found: it is of everyday occurrence in normal speech, where it reveals itself in the temporary loss of some verbalization and a slight delay in recovering it. It may be that there is always a time lapse between the issuance of a summons for a particular expression and its delivery; if this is true, as a rule the lapse is no greater than the time the speaker would need in any case for phonation, and no in-

---

1. *Journal of Individual Psychology,* Vol. 15, 62–65, May 1959.

terruption results. But occasionally, especially with the careful writer or speaker who will not be satisfied with less than a precise word, delivery takes an appreciable time. By observing during that period of waiting and searching, we are able to learn something about the associative mechanisms that give speech its continuity and enable us to summon up from among countless stored words, phrases, and complex verbal responses to earlier stimuli, the desired one to fit a new stimulus. For the linguist or psychologist who likes to see in language something analogous to a mechanical translator, this is worth looking into for the light that it may shed on lexical storage and lexical searching.

For anyone but a linguist or a psychologist, the moment of search is linguistic chaff. The important thing about the hunt is the catch, and when the catch is in the bag, the hunt is forgotten. Also, this form of hunting is such an unremitting fact of our lives that there is no room for remembering, and the memory span at best is short—recapturing an associative link is like recalling a dream: unless one puts the dream into words while it is still warm, there is no recovering it later. Willis R. Whitney, Director Emeritus of the General Electric Research Laboratory, played a game with himself when he found that he was staring at an emptiness where there should have been a signans. He wrote his experience down, as in this example: " The other day I tried to recall a certain senator. *Blutgut* popped into my mind. *That's nothing like it*, I thought disgustedly. Nevertheless, I made a note of it. Pretty soon my subconscious gave me another nudge: *Carney*. I put that down too. Later I thought *Gormley*. Then, in a flash, I had it: *Kilgore*. Reading back on the notes, it was obvious that the associated ideas of blood and gore assumed a German disguise in Blutgut, became Latinized in Carney, were Anglicized as Gormley, and crystallized as Kilgore. But if I hadn't written the words down, I'd never have known how I got the answer."[2]

What Whitney describes was of course noted many years ago by E. W. Scripture and called by him the " mediate association of ideas ".[3] Scripture's experiments, coupled with those of Aschaffenburg, " found these intermediate ideas in all degrees of consciousness, from full consciousness, in which the succession appears as a series of three ideas, down to complete unconsciousness, where the idea is completely forgotten, or is not even recognized when shown."[4] There is no magic in the number three—Whitney insists on a succession of four. Actually the mediation can be of any degree of length and complexity, though the more steps there are, the harder they are to retrace and the more likely it is that the whole series will escape attention.

In the discussion to follow I shall use the term " field " for multiple things

---

2. *Saturday Evening Post*, Oct. 13, 1945, p. 6.

3. *The new psychology.* New York: Scribners, 1898, pp. 199–207.

4. *Op. cit.*, p. 206.

tied together in any kind or degree of relatedness that is not based purely on linguistic form (under which I include syntax). Thus three things whose names start with the phoneme /m/ and belong to the same form class, e. g. nouns, but are not as far as can be discerned related in any other way, such as *moan*, *mule*, and *mitt*, are not in field relationship. But *mule* and *mink* are both 'names of animals', and to this extent are in field relationship. The concept is necessarily vague; one may conceive of a field relationship between *mule* and *mitt* on the basis of 'names of material objects'. Since the focus can be as broad as one cares to make it, there are hardly any two things, however disparate, that might not be brought into some field or other. But the broader the field, the less operative, I should think, would be the association within it, and anything as comprehensive as 'material objects' could be disregarded. Despite its vagueness, the concept is useful, for otherwise we have no term that will distinguish between a series like (A) hermit → (B) acolyte → (C) anchorite and one like (A) hermit → (B) anchor → (C) anchorite, the first having its intermediate step in field relationship with the starting point ('terms of religion'), the second not.

If at the broader end we exclude from "field" something as inclusive as 'names of material objects', at the narrower end we should also exclude synonymy. In the series (A) name of the man I met last night → (B) Jim Blade, or (A) happy → (B) joyful, the focus is too narrow to take in what can properly be called a field, and the association may well be immediate.[5]

Why exclude linguistic form from "field"? It might seem just as reasonable to include 'all things with names starting with the consonant cluster /str/' as to include 'all things green'—the irrelevance of one to any more meaningful association is about as great as the irrelevance of the other. There are two reasons. First, it is worth while to set up what may turn out to be a null hypothesis, namely, that linguistic form is in any way different from other things that may occur as associative links; if it is difficult to show such a difference, then we have evidence that lexical storage in the brain depends no more on linguistic similarities than on similarities of any other kind. Second, linguistic form is in a rather special category anyway in that the final link in the chain is itself a verbalization—not the mental image of a lemon nor the selection of one thing remembered out of a physical set of alternatives, like one culprit from a police lineup, but a form like *George List* or *irrecusable*, something drawn wholly from storage and capable of being pinpointed by a speaker's performance. While the playing of a forgotten piece of music

---

5. I qualify this statement in order not to have to prove a negative. Until we can trace the mechanisms that tie *happy* to *joyful*, we cannot say that there is no third term between them. Meanwhile we must assume that it is at least possible that there is no third term at all.

or the dancing of a forgotten step would do as well, the verbalization has obvious advantages—its familiarity and physical brevity.

In the examples that follow I accordingly keep the linguistic and the non-linguistic associative links separate from each other, and different kinds of each separate in turn, as far as I am able to distinguish them. They are drawn mostly from personal experiences, recorded over many years, but I shall refer to myself impersonally as O. I divide them into two major classes, the first being cases of " successive delivery ", where the links precede the end result and do not interfere with its articulation, the second cases of " simultaneous delivery ", where the end result and one or more links are uttered at the same time, resulting in a *lapsus linguae*.

I. SUCCESSIVE DELIVERY

(1) Association via linguistic form : shared phonemes and shared morphs.

Case 1. O tried to remember the name of Al Capp's heroine. All he could grasp was *Lulu Belle,* a reflection of the fact that the desired name also consisted of two words (plus the—here ineffectual—field relationship of ' rustic names '). Two days later, while cycling home at night when the air was balmy, O mused to himself how pleasant it was to ride in the long *days in May.* Immediately the order of two days earlier was filled : *Daisy Mae.*

Case 2. For a pair of pictures illustrating a grammatical problem in Spanish, it was suggested that one show an Indian woman with a child on her back, and the other the same Indian woman carrying a large jar. As the word for *jar,* O proposed *cacharro,* a word that he had never used before, in place of the more familiar *jarro.* Retracing, he found that the intermediate step had been *cachorro* ' cub ', suggested by the name of the other burden, *niño* ' child '.

Case 3. O was on the track of a word more or less synonymous with *arbitrary.* The phrase *to alienate affections* came first to mind, then the desired word, *inalienable.*

Case 4. O tried to remember the term for *ingestive or egestive action of the alimentary canal.* The word *Gestalt* came to mind, with the conviction that the desired word was akin to it. Presently the latter emerged : *peristalsis.*

Case 5 illustrates a purely formal association that turned out to be a blind alley. Trying to recall a word similar to *carotid,* O succeeded in grasping it as *caryatid.* But on the way he unaccountably thought of some kind of bug, and later realized that he had been sidetracked by *katydid.* (Or did the *y* of the spelling help out?)

Case 6 illustrates an exceptionally remote association. A friend called and left a message with O to be delivered to O's wife. O forgot the message until a few hours later when he started to discuss with his wife a Christmas card just received from an acquaintance in a distant city. The forgotten message was immediately remembered. The distant friend had had a child named *Lynn*, seen only briefly five years earlier and whose name O would probably not have been able to recall had he been asked it; and the friend of O's wife, the lady who had left the message, was also named *Lynn*.

It seems to make no difference in the power of the association whether the shared elements are merely phonemes or are recognizable morphs. In *cary-atid-katydid* the shared elements are phonemes and nothing more. In *alienate* and *inalienable* there is a shared morph. In *days in May* and *Daisy Mae* there are two shared morphs, but the first, [dej], is only an etymological fossil in *Daisy*, and the second, [mej], represents nothing more than a pair of homophones.

Although the formal links in Cases 1–6 outweigh all others, one cannot absolutely exclude the possibility of a field relationship unless the end result is completely irrelevant to what mediates it. This seems to be true of *Daisy Mae*, but in *Gestalt-peristalsis* there is a vague field of 'behavioral terms', and in *Lynn* a vague field of 'names of female acquaintances'.

Case 7 is another with a dim possibility of some kind of field. Trying to recall *a certain kind of covered wagon*, O first picked up *Saratoga*, and then the sought-for term, *Conestoga wagon*. Possible field, 'names of places'.

(2)   Association via linguistic form: shared frame.

Case 8.   O tried to remember the names of two persons to whom he owed reprints. One of them came promptly. *Mrs. Perry*, but the other held back. O then got the distinct feeling that the two names were connected in some way other than the present context. Finally the second name emerged: *Daniel Gregory Mason*. The frame shared by both was of course Erle Stanley Gardner's lawyer, *Perry Mason*

Case 9.   Listening to a radio program on which one personage got himself into trouble by admitting to his real name, O thought, "Under those circumstances I'd give an assumed name—I'd call myself *Terhune*". Then, wondering what would be the right first name for this, O hit upon *Bayson*. Some time later the realization came that the suggestion of *Bayson* had come from *Albert Payson Terhune*.

In 8 and 9 the shared frame is a linear sequence in which the immediate and mediate items both occur, but which is otherwise irrelevant to both.

(3)   Association via meaning: rival signans, or synonymy.

I have already rejected relevant synonymy on the ground that we cannot be sure the association is not immediate. This is particularly true as synonyms are frequently linked as sets at some stage of learning. Trying to capture the word *incarnadine* from a starting point of *red* may lead across a memorized quasi-paradigmatic frame *red-scarlet-ruddy-crimson-incarnadine* rather than over a semantic bridge. Besides, a relevant synonym often discharges the energy of the search in a wrong direction: delivery of an undesired one is apt to block the delivery of a desired one. Irrelevant synonymy, on the other hand, is better proof of a semantic link.

Case 10. *O* was on the point of saying *radio depot* but rejected it in favor of *radio station* in time to avoid an overt lapse. While the formal resemblance of *radio* and *railway* undoubtedly helped to evoke the latter as a middle step, and the association of both *depot* and *station* with *railway* in turn helped to evoke *station*, there is more than a formal association here: *railway station* and *railway* (or more likely *railroad*) *depot* have virtually identical ranges of occurrence, and the irrelevant synonymy must have played a part.

Case 11. *O* was unable to recall the name of a small town in Costa Rica. The name of a town in California emerged, *La Jolla*, and after it the desired word, *Alajuela*. *Alhaja* and *joya* are both Spanish words meaning 'jewel'. There is of course also a field relationship here: 'names of towns'.

(4) Association via meaning: rival signatum.

Case 12. *O* was trying to recall a word referring to *polite usage*. The notion *a word referring to formal attire in Spanish* emerged, and following it the word itself, *etiqueta*. The word desired was the English cognate *etiquette*.

(5) Association by a series of linguistic forms.

Case 13. Running across the word *polymathia*, *O* was unable to recall a certain synonym. The first thing that came to mind was *polygraph*. This led to a mental picture of a drawing device in the shape of a movable parallelogram, and after a while to the latter's name, *pantograph*. This in turn brought home the desired word, *pansophist*. The series was AB via *poly-*, BC via *-graph*, and CD via *pan-*.

(6) Field associations.

I group here the numerous evocations in which more than local form or local meaning is involved. There seems to be a kind of reserved space for collective stocks—a storage for names-of-people, names-of-places, terms-of-religion, terms-of-politics, etc., as if anything that reduced the semantic distance between a mediating and a mediated item would somehow establish itself. In a general sense, the field is always the prime evocative agent: one seeks a word fitting a given context referring to sailing craft and the word is delivered without any mediation of which one is aware. But a general field is too broad to map, and we must merely recognize its existence while tracing the local steps along an associative pathway. The remaining examples involve more or less intricate interlacings of form and meaning in an associative field.

Case 14, field plus shared morph plus shared phonemes. Searching for the name of an *occupational disease of miners*, *O* first encountered *psittacosis*, then the desired term, *silicosis*. Field, 'names of diseases'. Shared morph,

-osis. Shared phonemes, /si/.

Case 15, two fields plus shared phonemes. *O* was trying to recall the name for *a system of agriculture midway between sedentary agriculture and nomadism.* For a time the term that obtruded itself was *nopal*, the prickly pear—here the field was 'things-in-view' (*O* was motoring through Western desert country at the time). This led to the desired word, *milpa*. Second field, 'Spanish-words-of-Aztec-origin'. Shared phonemes, /p/, /l/, /a/, plus nasal.

Case 16, field plus near synonymy plus shared initial phoneme (alliteration). *O* referred to a *Mr. Peacock* as *Mr. Partridge*. Field, 'names-of-persons.' Synonymy, 'bird-with-fantail'. Phonemic similarity, initial /p/.

Case 17, two fields plus shared phonemes. *O* tried to recall the word for *a certain kind of choice*, vaguely thinking of it in terms of philosophy. The first emergence was a nonce-form, *Hobbesian choice*, followed by the right one, *Hobson's choice*. First field, 'philosophy' (the philosopher Hobbes and questions of choice). Second field, 'names-of-persons'. Shared phonemes, /h/, /a/, /b/, /n/, plus sibilants.

Case 18, three fields plus riming shared phonemes. *O* tried to recall the term for a small size of can, which seemed vaguely reminiscent of a sporting term. Two intermediate words appeared, *portmanteau* and *coney*, and finally the wanted one, *pony*. First field, 'sports': *pony* and *coney*. Second field, 'small things': *coney* and *pony* in the relevant sense. Third field, 'objects-for-carrying-things': 'can' and *portmanteau*. Shared phonemes, all but the initial of *coney*, and the initial of *portmanteau*.

Case 19, two overlapping fields plus shared phonemes plus shared morph. *O* tried to recall the name of a certain well-known actor. The sequence was (A) *Jascha Heifetz* → (B) *Mischa Elman* → (C) *Mischa Auer*. Overlapping fields: 'names-of-entertainers', 'names-of-musicians'. Shared phonemes in *Jascha* and *Mischa*, /š/, /ə/, plus same syllabic and prosodic structure. Shared morph, *Mischa*.

Case 20, shared phonemes plus shared morphs plus synonymy plus rival signatum. *O* was trying to remember a word applied to *a prematurely intelligent child*. At first the only thing that obtruded itself was *procacious*, with a tinge of *prodigious* or *prodigy*. Then it occurred to *O* that there was some connection with the meaning 'to cook beforehand', and Spanish *cocer* gave the clue to *precocious*. Shared phonemes, everything in *procacious* and *precocious* except /e/ vs. /i/. Shared morphs, suffix *-ious* in *procacious, precocious*, and *prodigious*, intensified in the neologistic suffix [šəš]; and the shared stem in *prodigy* and *prodigious*. Synonymy, *prodigy* and *precocious*. Rival signata, 'prematurely intelligent' and 'cooked beforehand'.

II. SIMULTANEOUS DELIVERY: BLENDS AND LAPSES

If in recalling an item D, a series ABCD can be retraced, is it certain that B and C were effective links in the successful delivery of D? Where some stimulus is involved that is obviously external, like *days in May*, the link must be regarded as effective. The contrary case, where a mediate step is negatively effective, is illustrated by Jakobson's example of the woman with a violent aversion to worms who was unable to produce the Russian verb *kishet* 'to swarm', which is frequently used in describing worms. But in other cases of successful delivery, we cannot be sure whether the mediate steps are indispensable turns in the main road or are merely bypaths branching out from it: in other words, whether the first or the second of the following diagrams applies:

Fig. 1   Fig. 2

In the first case, D would not have been arrived at without B and C. In the second, it would have been arrived at anyway.

If what we are interested in is what might be termed "proximity in storage", it does not matter that the process moves in one direction at a time or more than one. In either case we have evidence that two points are linked, and hence are in some way probably "close to" each other.

The same holds for simultaneous delivery. If B and C are delivered at the same time, we cannot be sure whether B is a link to C (or vice versa), or whether both are directly linked to A. Simultaneity seems to argue for the direct link; but since phonation takes a finite amount of time, it is possible that B precedes and is partially uttered but then rejected in favor of the more satisfactory C which it has suggested, the whole thing taking place so fast that elements of both B and C appear in the final result. In either case the obvious conclusion is that the bond between B and C is extremely close. It is probably no accident that B and C are usually at least partially synonymous besides being as a rule similar in form.

(1)   Accidental blends involving elements that are not closely synonymous and have relatively low formal resemblance:

imitate + portray → imitray[6]
Norwegian + Swedish → Norwedish
courteous + cordial → cordious ([kɔrdʒəs])[7]
exactly + actually → exactually

---

6.   Red Skelton, Dec. 30, 1951.
7.   Hazel Messimore, Sep. 7, 1949.

leeway + freedom → freeway (*to have more freeway*)

(In addition to the formal resemblance between A and B, there is generally a resemblance between C and some existing normal English morph or morphs—here C becomes identical with such a morph, *freeway*. And the blend is more likely in proportion as the meaning of the existent morph thus arrived at is consonant with the utterance as a whole, evidence of the field relationship. When I said *The so-called medial strength is length*, I (1) blended *stress* and *length*, (2) produced an existing morph, and (3) gave something roughly synonymous with the intended word, *stress*.)

under the guise of + on the pretext of → on the guise of[8]
to waive + to lay away → to waylay (*waylay a requirement*)

(2)   Accidental blends involving close synonymy but relatively low formal resemblance :

gorged + bulging → gorging (*cupboards gorging with clothes*)
trepidation + disquietude → trepitude
at her wit's end + at the end of her rope → at her rope's end
many a night + many's the night → many the night
high spirits + fine fettle → high fettle
agape + with bated breath → with gaping breath.

(3)   Accidental blends involving less synonymy and more formal resemblance :

canteen + container → cantainer
pressed + fresh → preshed (*a beautifully preshed collar*)
portentous + pretentious → potentious (*a potentious house*)
glut + clutter → glutter (*grain gluttered the terminals*)[9]
Knott's Berry Farm + Watts-Hardy Dairy → Watt's Dairy Farm.

(4)   Accidental blends involving close synonymy and close formal resemblance :

protuberant + protrude → protruberant
attentively + intently → intentively (*I listen intentively*)
glare + leer → gleer
prating + ranting → pranting
glum + grim → grum, glim (*What's the matter, son, looking so grum—glim?*)
abandon + disband → disbandon (*Book club being disbandoned*)
from $ 6.50 up + $ 6.50 and up → from $ 6.50 and up (price marker)

As with the earlier examples of successive delivery, blends may also involve more than two terms.   A triple blend occurred in the following : a speaker wishing to refer to the *Flatirons*, a landmark near Boulder, Colorado, called

---

8.   Drew Pearson, Jan. 12, 1953.
9.   New York, *Star* July 11, 1948.

them the *Flagstones*, blending *Flatirons* with *Flagstaff* (the name of a nearby park) and with *stones*, which is what the Flatirons are. Note the formal resemblance between *flat* and *flag*, between *flatiron* and *flagstone* as compounds; and note that the end result is again an existing form. Following is an example of a four-way blend: "And the passage goes *as this—as thus—as so—as follows*".[10] The speaker blended *as follows* successively with *this way*, *thus*, and *so*.

The natural interconnectedness of accidental blends[11] is revealed in the readiness with which many of them are unconsciously adopted, especially those containing looser elements of syntax. In the following, many speakers are not aware that they are using what was originally a blend; in fact, some of them have become standard:

twenty-some + twenty-odd → twenty-some-odd (*twenty-some* was perhaps already a blend of *some twenty* and *twenty-odd*)

most places + almost everywhere → most everywhere (influence of the blend is seen in the fact that *most* for *almost* is limited to situations like this; few would say *most ten*)

hardly had...when + no sooner had...than → hardly had...than (*He had hardly eaten his supper than he had to leave*)

I won't stand that! ('tolerate') + I won't stand for that ('uphold, support') → I won't stand for that! (the blend is between the intonation of the first and the lexical elements of the second, plus the pattern of verbs with *for*: *hope for*, *look for*, *wait for*, etc.)

He has the most of all + He has more than any → He has the most of any (*has the most notes of any of the other woodwinds*[12])

It's been nine hours since I ate anything + It's been nine hours that I've not eaten anything → It's been nine hours since I've eaten anything

He didn't stay any longer that ('so far as') he could help + He didn't stay any longer than he had to → He didn't stay any longer than he could help

(5) Other lapses:

An accidental blend is by definition a lapse. Other lapses on inspection appear to involve the same processes, and it may be that there is no useful distinction between one kind and another. When a speaker says *I broached a few people* ('*approached* them on a subject newly *broached*'), we can probably

10. President of the University of Nevada, speech, Oct. 14, 1960.

11. I have left out of account the intentional blends coined for some literary purpose: words such as *anecdotage*, *sophomoronic*, *tremorous* (Hart Crane, "Legend"). The spontaneous blend is rarely quite as incongruous as most of the inventions, though the process is probably the same.

12. Golden Record Library No. 2, issued 1960.

still set up the equation *approached + broached → broached,* since such a substantial phonemic part of *approached* is retained. The false start in *a chain—train of thought,* in which *chain* is corrected to *train,* similarly allows of *train + chain → chain.* When a doctor writes *The reaction to mosquito bites is not always alike* we can set up the equation *reaction is the same + reactions are alike → reaction is alike* or *reactions are the same + reactions are alike → reaction is the same + reaction is alike.* This is a blend of *same* and *alike* in the sense that while *alike* has not assumed any phonemic resemblance to *same,* it has assumed the latter word's distribution. The now widespread confusion of *substitute* and *replace* evidences a similar blending of distributions.

When a lapse is imitated, the fault is no longer one of delivery but of storage: e. g., the use of *flaunt* for *flout* in imitation of other speakers. Or the storage may reflect an initial act of confusion, especially with words that are relatively long and comparatively rare: the first speaker who said *to mitigate in one's favor* may well have had the word *militate* so imperfectly learned that *mitigate* displaced it. Similarly with *hypothecate* for *hypothesize.* But imperfect acquisition or acquisition from doubtful models has little to reveal about the nature of lexical storage.

As with lexical searching and blends, now and then a lapse will involve strung-out associations. The speaker who said *Like in New York, when our friends would fall—drop in* was looking for a certain synonym of *to visit,* which apparently evoked first *to call,* then, by formal resemblance of *call* and *fall* and irrelevant synonymy of *fall* and *drop,* bridged the gap to the desired expression, *drop in.*

Blends and lapses tell us not only about what items are close to what, but also somethnig about the KINDS of items across which links are forged, the relation that they bear to the language of the speaker. They appear to be in the shape of dominant word- and syllable-types which are typical of the language ("canonical forms") though they may not correspond to the morphs of segmental analysis. The speaker who referred to a person as *plumpier* than someone else brought over not only the comparative suffix *-er* but also the double suffix found in words that are based on nouns: *chubbier, tubbier, chunkier. Cordious* involves a "suffix" that is present in *outrageous, gorgeous, rampageous. Exactually* reflects not only *actually* but also *factually. Grum* and *glim* reproduce highly frequent clusters and correspond to canonical types quite central to the lexicon: *slum, drum, prim, slim, brim,* etc. *Gleer* adds one more to a list of *gl-* and *g-* words meaning 'look': *glance, glare, glower, goggle, gape.* Similar linkages occur in spoonerisms, with the difference that whereas in lexical searching they are entirely out of sight and in blends they are only partially in view, in spoonerisms they are fully exposed: *audio radiance* for *radio audience* results in existing words; *set asiding* for *setting aside* and *assign assailum* for *insane asylum* are a reassembling of already stored morphs.

CONCLUSION

Until a way is found to get more direct evidence, observations like those here are useful to tell us something about what our linguistic stock in trade consists of and how it is stored. Three characteristics stand out:

(1) The stored units are in themselves of every imaginable degree of complexity, from single phonemes (even from mere distinctive features, as in the nasal of Case 15 or the sibilants of 17) on up through various kinds of phonemic clusters (*gleer*), syllabic structures (*Jascha-Mischa*), rimes and alliterations (*Knott's Berry Farm, Watt's Dairy Farm*), prosodic types (*flagstaff-flatiron*), individual morphemes, intonations (*I won't stand for it!*), and high-level syntactic stereotypes (*to alienate affections*), some helped along the way by a transformational relationship with another term in the equation (*at the end of her rope—at her rope's end*). What impresses one with this assemblage is its heterogeneity. It is not even confined to one sensory field: spellings, which are of course visual, undoutedly play a part.

(2) The " resemblances " (associative pathways, proximities in storage, or whatever analogy is appropriate)—by which we prove the existence of the units—may be of any order of form or meaning. Two items may be similar, and one may serve to snag the other, on the basis of any feature whatever: internal form, such as shared phonemes or shared morphs, external form such as a shared frame (*Perry Mason*), or meaning, in the broader " field " sense or in the narrower sense of relevant or irrelevant synonymy. This last is perhaps only a very generalized kind of external form—since synonyms have identical or near-identical ranges of occurrence, there is a formal connection between, say, *to buy* and *to purchase* in the shared frame *He—the goods with his own money.*

(3) While the elements are linguistic, the processes do not take place in an orderly linguistic manner. A first step may be in terms of phonemes, a second in terms of irrelevant synonymy, a third in terms of a syntactic relationship, a fourth in terms of some fixed memorized frame, and a fifth in terms of any of these steps applied to a second language of which the speaker has a command. It is as if the relationships and mobility were such that all the resources for search could be made available at once.

What remains unresolved is whether cases of instantaneous delivery—uninterrupted utterance—are different in kind or only in speed and accuracy from those described here. Though unable to settle this question, we can pose it in a way that will make answers easier to seek. One side of the question is whether a given instantaneous utterance is an innovation or is merely a unit drawn bodily from storage. If it is possible for the sight of a dog to elicit the automatic response *dog*, it should be possible for a more complex situation that has been met (or the like of which has been met) before to elicit the same more complex verbalization that was previously used—it is highly probable that a large percentage of linguistic responses are repetitions either of what we have ourselves said before or have heard said, and their syntactic complexity is at a different level, like the complexity of a sound wave in relation to a phoneme, and is therefore irrelevant. If so, it is not surprising that such responses are given trippingly on the tongue, for they are recovered as wholes. A second side of the question is the degree to which search and organization take place before phonation starts; that is, whether we think out our sentences during normal breaks in the rhythm, and then give them all of a piece. A third side is the speed with which it may be possible for us to capture an item during the very act of uttering the sentence of which it then becomes a component. If it turns out that delays can be infinitesimal, then all recoveries from storage may be like the ones I have described or even like some deliberate search for a pun or a metaphor, the difference being that the latter are just a slowing down, a sort of magnification, of the re-assembling, creative process that always takes place in speech. This would in turn imply that associative links come into view only exceptionally, and when they do they tend to be discounted because of their apparent irrelevance.

One final observation. As the stored items are more or less discrete, a search that goes through them must take place in jumps. This appears to answer to the facts—there is not a smooth transition from clue to discovery, but a series of hops and skips from one clue to the next.

8

VISUAL MORPHEMES
Language 22.333-340 (1946)

Intended originally as a follow-up of William F. Edgerton's article "Ideograms in English writing," *Language* 17.148–150 (1941), this article was redone along lines suggested by Bernard Bloch. The title also reflects Bloch's principal criticism, which was to view spelling forms as parallel to audible ones, or morphemes.

Edgerton had confirmed my feeling that it was not quite accurate to relegate writing to the status of a merely derived system. It may have been only this in a genetic sense; but it had something in common with all systems: once set going, it acquired a propulsive power of its own.

I. WHY THEY MUST EXIST

The fact that most writing is the graphic representation of vocal-auditory processes tends to obscure the fact that writing can exist as a series of morphemes at its own level, independent of or interacting with the more fundamental (or at least more primitive) vocal-auditory morphemes. Recognition of visual morphemes is also hampered by the controversy, not yet subsided, over the primacy of the spoken versus the written; the victory of those who sensibly insist upon language as fundamentally a vocal-auditory process has been so hard won that any concession to writing savors of retreat. Yet, so long as a point-to-point correspondence is maintained, it is theoretically possible to transform any series of morphemes from any sensory field into any other sensory field, and keep them comprehensible; the only condition is that contact with the nervous system be maintained at some point. More than theoretically: it is actually done for the congenitally deaf-and-dumb reader of Braille, who 'reads' and 'comprehends' with his finger-tips. Just as here is a system of tactile morphemes existing with no connexion (other than historical) with the vocal-auditory field, so there is nothing unscientific in the assumption that a similarly independent visual series may be found.

In part, the subordination of writing, and with it the visual side of language, has been due to the interpretation that many linguists have put upon the behavioristic explanation of language. The emphasis upon laryngeal processes was so heavy that other processes tended to be slighted. So it is relevant to point out that there is nothing in behaviorism which excludes eye movements, detectible and implicit, from the language organization. All that behaviorism requires is that language be viewed as having an anatomical basis. Watson is explicit on this point: 'Throughout the text we have spoken of laryngeal processes as though they were responsible for all language organization. This manner of speaking was chosen for brevity's sake. We hasten to add now that the anatomical basis of language habits involves, of course, the whole body but specifically the neuro-muscular system in the head, neck, and chest segments.' Also—and note especially the author's own italics: 'From our standpoint it is not necessary to assume that all thought is laryngeal even if we use "laryngeal" to include the whole mechanism described [in the preceding quotation]. We have learned to write words, sentences, and paragraphs, to draw objects and to *trace them with the eyes*, hands, and fingers. We have done this so often that the process has become systematized and substitutive.'[1]

Finally, it is not only good behaviorism, but the better part of positivism as well, to give visual movements their due. We present a subject with the sign DANGER and observe him as he avoids the object designated as dangerous, avoids it exactly as he might avoid it if the visual stimulus had been a threatening gesture rather than a written word. The sign and the response are the only parts of the process that can be demonstrated, which gives little basis for supposing that the sound or sub-vocalization cannot have been short-circuited completely. With reading, eye movements are the only overtly demonstrable movements in the process; whatever concomitant vocal movements there may be can be progressively reduced and perhaps eliminated entirely, but no material reduction of eye movements can be effected. They provide an always fully operative physiological correlate for reading, with all that reading implies for comprehension and thinking.

Lest the discussion be detoured by too narrow a definition of language, let me say that I use the term in the sense in which it is used by Watson: communicative behavior. Any written sign capable of effecting like responses in different members of a community is by this definition a part of language.

II. Evidence that They Do Exist

Having seen that there MAY be visual morphemes (reconcilable even with the point of view thought to be hostile to giving importance to mere writing), let us see what proof we may find that there ARE such morphemes.

Once more the teaching of defectives provides the most direct proof: the congenital deaf-mute who reads ordinary writing and print is obviously handling a system of morphemes that for him is basically visual. But it is

---

1. *Psychology from the standpoint of a behaviorist* 310 and 324 (Philadelphia, 1919).

more interesting to inquire the extent to which normal persons come in our culture to depend upon visual morphemes.

For convenience we may distinguish three types of visible arbitrary signs, according to their connexion, or want of it, with speech:

1. Signs existing independently of vocal-auditory morphemes, or having only a fortuitous relationship with them. Such are the red color of gasoline containers, the death's-head on bottles of poison, lines (curved, straight, bent, etc.) to mark the direction of highways, etc.

2. Signs which supplement audible morphemes, interacting with them just as two parts of the vocal-auditory system (pitch plus tongue movement, for example) interact to form a meaningful integration, or just as one may join hearing with close watching of lip movement and gesture in order to grasp a meaning (i.e. to respond appropriately).

3. Signs which, under certain conditions (such as silent reading), to a greater or less extent supplant the audible morphemes, just as READING a dot-dash progression may entirely supplant HEARING a dot-dash progression in receiving a code message.

The most important class is obviously the third, for it embraces the whole of writing. If we grant it, we grant that *lose* and *beat* are different visual morphemes just as /lúwz/ and /bíjt/ are different vocal-auditory morphemes. Plausible as this seems, it may yet be denied by those who assume a necessary laryngeal basis for all language behavior; and while such a basis cannot be proved, neither can it be disproved. In order to convince those who make this assumption, we must look to another class.

The first class exists independently of or is prior to speech by definition; but on this account many will object that it has nothing to do with 'language'. If we can demonstrate, turning to the second class, that even granting the absolute necessity of the laryngeal concomitant, a response still depends in part upon some visible factor, then eye movements and visual morphemes have to be admitted as part of the language organization.

Such interdependencies are abundant in modern English, largely as a result of our chaotic spelling. In the examples which follow, I assume a visual factor only where the laryngeal one fails absolutely to account for the full response.

1. HOMONYMS. These are exemplified by the schoolman's remark, '*Sea* is an ocean and *si* is a tone, as you can readily *see*.' Through eye movements, the referents are identified without need of context. Even more marked is the effect when the whole context of sounds, implicit or explicit, is identical, and the distinction of meaning more or less indifferent, as in *The big clock tolled* (*told*) *the hour* or *The danger is safely passed* (*past*).[2] The identification of

---

2. Edna Rees Williams, *The conflict of homonyms in English* 15 (New Haven, 1944),

distinctive spelling with distinctive meaning in English is so close that we are shocked when the connexion is broken. At a naturalization hearing recently in Los Angeles, the petitioner's testimony was recorded by the stenographer as follows:

Q. Do you believe in the Fascist or Communist ideologies?

A. I don't know.

What the candidate alleged that he had intended was *I don't. No.*[3]

The visual separation of homonyms may be demonstrated in another way: by showing the degree to which the eye-movement complex of one member of the pair blocks recall of the other member. I offered, as a test of this kind, a set of matching homonyms to a class of twenty-four college students. Two sample pairs were first presented—*bard-barred* and *sighs-size*—and then the following list was distributed to the class: *plane, to, vain, gourd, phrase, rein, grate, prey, peak, board, wee,* and *led.* The students were directed to fill in any word with identical sound, or a definition of such a word if they did not know how to spell it. The number of those who did this successfully was, for each word in the order given, 23, 24, 24, 12, 4, 24, 21, 24, 21, 18, 17, and 24. The significant result is, of course, that of *phrase.* Here, despite the existence of TWO homonyms (of identical spelling), *frays* 'conflicts' and *frays* 'makes or grows ragged', at least one of which everyone knew, almost ninety per cent were distracted by the total dissimilarity in spelling. If *phrase* had induced none but laryngeal movements, there is no more reason for its homonym to have been missed than for that of *board* to have been missed, assuming a like degree of familiarity of both terms.

A second test, conducted in the same way but involving a contextual phrase (*I bear no sword here for thee, O Great One*) and offered to thirty-four students, resulted in successful identification of homonyms as follows, for the words in the order given: 31, 32, 31, 11, 34, 33, 30, 34, 32, 28. As predicted, the significant figure is for *soared.*[4] These tests prove that, other things being equal, the more unlike the spellings are, the less likely it is that the identification will be made. For all the fallibility of self-observation, it is well to remember that one can FEEL a difference of eye movements in passing from *beaut* to *butte,* from *key* to *quay,* and from *rapt* to *wrapped.*

---

recognizes the principle as possibly operative even in speech, in preserving otherwise conflicting homonyms, and quotes Henry Bradley in support of it. Such a spelling reflex in speech goes a step farther than the main thesis of this paper.

3. A complete phonetic record would probably, though not necessarily, have shown the difference. The intonations could be identical, with a high upskip followed by a downglide on the second and also on the third syllable.

4. The *I-eye* pair would seem to offer the most radical difference; but what undoubtedly raises the number of identifications here is, more than the familiarity of the terms, the fact that this pair is an oft-noted example of homonyms.

2. SEMANTIC EVOLUTION OF SPELLINGS. This is of at least two kinds: spelling bifurcation and spelling constellations.

BIFURCATION. The clustering of repetitions of a given distinctive spelling about a given meaning (*passed* versus *past*) can result just as surely in establishing a fixed written sign for that meaning as can a similar clustering of sounds result in establishing a fixed morphophonemic sign (*let us* vs. *let's; good and* vs. *good'n*, as in *good and hot*, the Spanish *bien caliente*). Raymond Macdonald Alden twits this tendency: 'To think, as some do, that " gray " and " grey " are quite different colors, and that a ghost which through the triumph of spelling reform had lost its " h " would also have lost its terrors.'[5] That *gray* and *grey* have separated, at least for some readers, is evidenced by the answer that I usually get from my advanced students when I ask them which of these two spellings they would prefer in a good sense (*She has lovely— eyes*) and which in a bad sense (*It was a—, gloomy day*). *Grey* is preferred for the good, *gray* for the bad.

Other pairs: *check-cheque; controller-comptroller; compliment-complement.*[6]

CONSTELLATIONS. The accident of association of certain spellings with certain uses comes to invest the spelling with a meaning related to those uses. This is evidenced in the *-or* of *expeditor* (adopted after much discussion by the members of this occupation), which has appeared also in *advisor*,[7] *publicitor, realtor,* and *weldor.* The existence of some examples (as *sailor*) semantically outside the constellation does not necessarily weaken it. The *-or* suffix is a visual morpheme of prestige.

The association of the spelling *ea* with words which suggest awkwardness, inconvenience, abnormality, and other over-the-left connotations, make this spelling suitable for humorous use, as in *They sank the Swiss fleat*; *It's all Greak to me*; *In all things, seak to know*. The *gh* links *ghost, ghastly, ghoulish,* and *aghast,* so that a nonce spelling such as *He ghulped and ghasped* can be most expressive.[8] Edward Lear uses the mysterious *gh* and the exotic grave accent to good effect in the name of his imaginary figure, the *Yonghy-Bonghy-Bò.*

An instance of a constellation which is also a bifurcation of which one half has withered as an active formative is that of *-y* and *-ie*, the latter being the form that is now generally used as a diminutive in new words.

3. DIALECTAL SPELLINGS. These John S. Kenyon calls ' pseudo-dialectal '

---

5. *Nation*, 9 Nov. 1911, p. 443/2.

6. For some speakers, the differences here are phonemic. I have heard ['kamptrolər] spoken by university instructors. For the *Century Dictionary* and for *Webster*, *compliment* and *complement* are distinct; for the *Standard*, they are not.

7. See Raven I. McDavid Jr., " *Adviser* and *Advisor*: Orthography and semantic differentiation," *Studies in Linguistics* 1.7 (1942).

8. The *h* may be, in some ridiculous way, phonemic, standing for a lingering on the initial sound, or for heavy breathing.

and Harold Wentworth 'eye dialect'. Wentworth defines as follows: 'Eye Dialect is phonetic respelling of words, not in order to show a mispronunciation (e.g. Eye-talian), but merely to burlesque the words or their speaker. Since /'wɪ-mɪn/ is a standard pronunciation of *women*, the corresponding spelling *wimmin* is eye dialect.'[9] The spelling here is a visual morpheme which implies, 'The person quoted is one who would use a vulgar pronunciation if there were one.' Examples: *licker, vittles, sassiety, whut*. Misspelling is made to substitute for mispronunciation: i.e. it is suggested that the speaker is at the level of ignorance where one misspells in this fashion, hence mispronounces as well.

4. VISUAL PARONOMASIA. This is of two kinds, puns and intentional misspellings.

VISUAL PUNS. These depend on the ludicrous juxtaposition of some reference of the written sign, and the suggested other meanings of the same morphophonemic sign: *Belleigh Acres; Bedside Manor*; letter addressed to The Tax Collector, *City Haul*. All puns of this type have to be written in order to be fully appreciated, and some, such as the last, are meaningless unless written. The more extended the puns become, the more difficult they are to grasp from hearing, while visual comprehensibility remains unimpaired. This is illustrated by the childish jingle, *How much wood would a woodchuck chuck if a woodchuck would chuck wood?*

INTENTIONAL MISSPELLINGS. The form *sinema*, which *Time* defines[10] as 'a naughty movie', is a visual blend. Humor or ridicule is the intent in the title of an article, *The Compleat Military Expert*,[11] where the archaic *compleat* suggests *The Compleat Angler*, and, by implication, something out of date.

Misspellings may be used for swank. This is especially true of girls' names, such as *Steffiny* for *Stephanie*,[12] *Alyce, Bettye, Edythe*; sometimes also of surnames, especially the common ones, giving *Smythe, Murfee*, etc. A similar amelioration is noted in the following quotation, where misspelling softens the oath: *To which he replied, " Why, goddamit, I waited around ... for somebody to come along and buy my breakfast."*[13]

Trade names make widespread use of misspellings, being visual for the product and morphophonemic for something else: *Duz, Odorono, Neet, Krumbles*, etc. Misspelling may be used simply to mystify; the puzzle of *Mairzy Doats*, for example, is acknowledged by the authors of that song to have been responsible for its enormous sale.

---

9. *American Dialect Dictionary* s.v. *eye dialect* (New York, 1944).

10. 13 March 1939, p. 33/2.

11. *New Republic*, 12 Jan. 1942, p. 50.

12. *Stephens* [*College*] *Standard*, Dec. 1941, p. 31/1.

13. W. G. Clugston, *Facts you should know about Kansas* 22 (Girard, Kan., 1945).

Besides spellings, there remain many other signs used in writing which are probably not phonemic. The punctuation of the phonemically identical phrases *the dog's masters* and *the dogs' masters* locates the proper referents through eye movements. So with *the longest undiscovered vein* and *the longest-undiscovered vein*.[14] Combinations avoided in speech are possible: *the too-happy people*. Quotation marks are largely non-phonemic; this fact has forced the adoption, in speech, of the terms *quote* and *unquote*, so as to make a quotation stand out as such. In the essay, non-phonemic quotation marks imply 'I use this term critically'; see 'reads' and 'comprehends' in the first paragraph of this article.[15] Capital letters are signs, usually non-phonemic, of importance.[16] Writing employs various schemes of decoration and other effects that are non-phonemic. Such is the Sears catalog advertisement for S-T-R-E-T-C-H-A-B-L-E-S.

Examples such as I have quoted are less important in themselves than as symptoms. If our writing were perfectly phonemic, and could remain so for a reasonable length of time, we might go on without suspecting the integration of eye movements as part of the terminal or implicit response to a written stimulus. When something goes wrong with our graphic representation, however, as has happened with English, the necessary functioning of our visual apparatus in the terminal response is forced upon us. A little reflection then shows that the integration is so close that eye movements may be present even when the stimulus is spoken. Every teacher of a foreign language using our own alphabetic system has encountered students who will, for instance, upon being told that a word is spelled *manto*, pronounce it ['mæn-to] even though there is no written sign of it anywhere about—and this in spite of the fact that [a] is by no means foreign to English. The mispronouncer has 'seen' the word implicitly. Such implicit 'seeing' is often cultivated, as, for example, when giving dictation. There is possibly a visual

---

14. Equivokes of this kind are the basis of much written humor: for instance, the advertisement of the British couple who announced that they 'had cast off clothing of all kinds' (Frank Colby column, *Kansas City Journal*, 7 Feb. 1942, p. 16/4).

15. So closely have quotation marks come to be identified with 'something cut off from its environment' that in direct discourse they are sometimes omitted by contemporary writers in order to give the effect—especially if the speaker is talking to himself—of blending the quotation with the setting.

16. The scholastics, writes Erasmus (*The Praise of Folly*, Hudson translation 85 [Princeton, 1941]), 'say it is a sacrilege ever to write MAGISTER NOSTER except in capital letters.' Capitals are often used to burlesque the importance of something, as in *They visited all the Interesting Places and got to know all the Best People*. They are sometimes phonemic, as the following example shows: 'One of the gayest and pleasantest expressions in any language is a Texas exclamatory expression of joy at seeing a friend: "Come in this house!" "Why, if it's not Johnny and Marylee—Come In This House!"' (*American Speech* 20.83 [1945]).

basis to some of the lightning calculations made by mathematical prodigies. Finally, anyone who has observed himself carefully in a moment of close concentration (as when 'thinking hard' to remember something), has been conscious of roving movements of the eyes, in an effort to focus on the desired object. It is unthinkable that a race which looks at the calendar in order to decide when to light the fire, reads a thermometer in order to decide when to call a doctor, and in other ways strives to get visual correlates for almost everything—our eyes being our most precise exteroceptors—should not have integrated eye movements into the language system.

III. THE VISUAL AT THE EXPENSE OF THE ORAL

There are two present-day incentives toward increasing the importance of visual morphemes:

1. MODERN TECHNIQUES OF TEACHING CHILDREN TO READ. Eye movements are encouraged at the expense of vocal movements. The contrast between the two is seen in the fact that the top speed of reading with full vocalization lies approximately between three hundred and three hundred and fifty words per minute, while the top speed of silent reading is almost three times as high. Speeding up the rate gradually reduces the time that can be allowed for subvocalization, and comprehension is attained through eye-jumps that take in whole syntax-groups at one time.

2. VOCABULARY-BUILDING BY WAY OF THE PRESS. Says Reese D. James, 'The eye plays the major role in adding to the number of words at our disposal.'[17] Says Erik Wahlgren, 'Government proclamations, newspaper jargon, advertising clichés, military and technological idiom, all these modern man takes in through the eye rather than through the ear. What is true of one's mother tongue follows for the other *Kultursprachen*, however the situation may be with Choctaw or Burmese.'[18] People in our cities nowadays probably read as many words as they speak, not only because more reading matter is forced upon them, but also because the old active relaxations of conversation and recitation have given way to passive relaxations such as the radio and the movies, in addition to reading. Not only neologisms are affected, but to an increasing extent old forms as well, as the schools absorb more and more persons of limited verbal background and bring them into contact with a written literature far more extensive than anything they have ever heard. Writers use, and readers recognize, forms that are not spoken or heard; many of these forms are then reflected in the spoken language by countless spelling pronunciations, and even, occasionally, by the creation of a new morpheme (*awry* mispronounced, its meaning misinterpreted, and recommitted

---

17. *Quarterly Journal of Speech* 31.83/1 (1945).
18. *Modern Language Forum* 29.75 (1944).

to paper as *orrie*; *tsk* creating the interjection *tusk*, etc.).

IV. An Analysis of Visual Morphemes?

Segmentation in the visual field has not been touched upon in this paper, as being beyond the scope of the arguments offered here. A brief comparison may not be amiss, however, if for no other reason than to guard against the easy assumption that one may extrapolate vocal-auditory methods into this area.

The most radical difference lies in the fact that in vocal-auditory communication there are two processes which have to be synchronized: the process of producing the sound and the process of intercepting it (that the latter is not mere passive absorption is evident in the varying degrees of 'attention' of listeners). Linguists have concerned themselves almost exclusively with the first of these processes. In visual communication, however, the output-process is largely relegated to machines, so that the one that involves the majority of us most of the time is the intake-process, or reading.

A second difference is that an audible message has to be taken as it comes. A visible message may be read, reread, speeded up, or slowed down at will.

One could list other dissimilarities that might or might not be significant for analysis. It may be that the procedures will turn out to differ only in degree; but, pending exploration, nothing of the kind should be taken for granted.

V. Conclusions

1. Visual morphemes exist at their own level, independently of vocal-auditory morphemes. Even a perfect phonemic transcription would, if used for communication, immediately become a system of visual morphemes. In modern English, education has made the visual system part of the public domain, so that it exhibits some evolutionary tendencies unsecured to vocal-auditory morphemes.

2. In the implicit reactions of literate people, eye movements combine with other implicit movements. There is as good reason to posit eye movements as the physiological correlate of 'thinking' and 'understanding' as there is to posit laryngeal movements as such a correlate.

3. In view of the close integration of the 'language organization', it is probably necessary to revise the dictum that 'language must always be studied without reference to writing'. This in no way detracts from the value of that dictum as applied to all languages at some stage of their development and to largely illiterate speech communities today; it is merely a recognition of a shift that has taken place in the communicative behavior of some

highly literate societies.

4. If it is true that the residue of language after the vocal-auditory is subtracted has provided a redoubt from which attacks could be made on linguistic science, then an appreciation of visual morphemes by both parties to the controversy may prove a step in the direction of reconciliation.

Part III

ORDER

I

LINEAR MODIFICATION

Publications of the Modern Language Association

67.1117-1144 (1952)

When I wrote this article I was not aware of the earlier work of V. Mathesius and the recent work of Jan Firbas on what Firbas calls " functional sentence perspective," a broad concept covering all the means by which an utterance enables the hearer to establish a hierarchy of parts of the utterance—specifically, to distinguish " thematic, transitional, and rhematic" elements (see Firbas, " Some thoughts on the function of word order in old English and modern English," *Sborník Prací Filosofické Fakulty Brněnské University* A5.72–94 [1957]). Word order is the most usual of the means, and much of what I say appears to harmonize with Firbas's views. Both approaches are concerned with the interferences between grammaticized word order (e.g., position as indicator of modifier and modified in *glass window, window glass*) and " natural " word order, but differ in that I look to a " broad-to-narrow " sequence and Firbas to a " theme-to-rheme " sequence, i.e., the progression from topic to comment, from known and shared to unknown and questioned.

My first glimmering of the principle of linear modification came in the course of trying to find a foothold in English for the contrasting positions of the descriptive adjective in Spanish. The closest analogy turned out to be the position of the adverb : *She sweetly kissed him* compared with *Le dio un dulce beso* ' She gave him a sweet kiss '; *She kissed him sweetly* with *Le dio un beso dulce* ' She gave him a kiss [that was] sweet.'

[Elements as they are added one by one to form a sentence progressively limit the semantic range of all that has preceded. This causes beginning elements to have a wider semantic range than elements toward the end. The concept of linear modification thus developed knits together a number of otherwise heterogeneous manifestations of sentence order in English, and provides a plausible theory of adjective position.]

The linear geometry of the sentence imposes certain relationships upon the elements that compose it. These relationships are conveniently expressed as dichotomies. Two dichotomies are, figuratively, spatial : they are CONTIGUOUS versus SEPARATE (*A* is next to *B* or is distant from *B*) and WITHIN versus WITHOUT (*A* is contained within *B* or is outside *B*). Two dichotomies are temporal : FIRST versus LAST and BEFORE versus AFTER.

While it does not follow that any of these pairs necessarily has linguistic importance, given their location at the very foundation of sentence structure it would be strange if they had not been seized upon for some use in communication. I think it can be shown that all of them have, probably in all languages, though I am concerned here only with the last two, the temporal dichotomies, and even with these, only in two languages.[1]

Though I assume that the temporal dichotomies probably have some importance in all languages, the particular importance that I should like to attribute to them is hypothetical. For English and Spanish, I believe that the hypothesis has enough footing to be called a theory or even a principle. My reason for not daring to bite off more than English and Spanish at this stage is the extremely subtle nature of the over-all manifestation, something that costs a good deal of effort to see just in one's own language, and which it would be hopeless to attempt to trace in any language where one must assume the extra burden of teaching an informant to look beneath the tumble of hills and valleys that make up the surface of his language, for a patch of common ground beneath. Languages are jerrybuilt structures, and the relationships of before and after are boards that lie handy and are likely to be nailed on anywhere. It is an arduous task to determine from the size and shape of the board where it is likely to be nailed and where not. No one could possibly have foreseen, for example, that *He told the squad off* 'bawled out' and *He told off the squad* 'assigned' would be in different semantic ranges, while *Let's take the money out* and *Let's take out the money* would be in the same. Side-effects are unpredictable. In many of them sentence order as such has channeled in a certain way the meaning of the stereotype, but usually we cannot determine whether it has or not, since the external features are so gross that our attention is distracted from any possible underlying influence. IF we are to find what it is that order contributes of its own, we must seek it in expressions that have the least possible difference in meaning, where stereotyped side-effects are least in evidence. In approaching an informant we must say something like " I am not asking you for clear and important distinctions, but for hazy and unimportant ones." So I beseech your willingness to listen for tones that are often elusive, though I expect to offer some that are unmistakable.[2]

---

1. As an example of WITHIN vs. WITHOUT, take the remark of H. Poutsma, *A grammar of late modern English* (Groningen : P. Noordhoff, 1928), Part I, First Half, p. 390, that the arrangement *We went to school together* " could hardly be altered." We note that *to go to school* is a stereotype with the sense ' to attend school '; but, contrary to Poutsma, we can transfer *together* into the phrase, breaking it up, and destroying the stereotype. *We went together to school* is less likely in the sense ' attended school ' and more likely in the sense ' journeyed to school.'

2. We are caught in the same circumstantial web as when we try to determine the

LINEAR MODIFICATION

I. The Principle

Let us consider what happens when elements—call them words, for convenience—are laid end-to-end to form a phrase. Before the speaker begins, the possibilities of what he will communicate are practically infinite, or, if his utterance is bound within a discourse, they are at least enormously large. When the first word appears, the possibilities are vastly reduced, but that first word has, in communicative value for the hearer, its fullest possible semantic range. The second word follows, narrowing the range, the third comes to narrow it still further, and finally the end is reached at which point the sentence presumably focuses on an event—usually aided by a gesture, a physical context in which only one of several possibilities can be elected, or what-not. This crude picture deliberately oversimplifies the fluid and automatic readjustment that presumably takes place when we ingest an utterance from its beginning to its end. Actually the interaction of situation and spoken symbol is in play from the first; furthermore, in a continuous stream of speech words are not, of course, heard as sharply defined units, either semantically or phonologically. But to the extent that the speaker creates a phrase (that is, to the extent to which the hearer cannot predict a following part of an utterance from what he has already heard) the hearer is taxed to re-shape continuously, and the degree of discreteness or fluidity of the process does not materially affect the argument.

Though circumstances would distort it more or less, we can, therefore, say that the sentence as a complex semanteme has a pointed structure with hyperbolic-flaring sides:

The open end of the horn represents the moment of pre-speaking, followed by the first word and each additional word in course. The narrow end, which focuses on the event, never quite comes to a point, since language is necessarily ambiguous and to sharpen it we must carry it beyond into a non-linguistic setting. But for practical purposes we may represent it as a point.[3]

---

meaning of an intonation contour—the intonation is there, and we know that it means something, but to separate it from the particular locution with which it is used imposes a heavy burden of patience and abstraction.

3. Though my hypothesis has not so far as I know been explicitly announced in the literature of linguistics, there are a few hints of it. One is provided by Sapir, *Language* (New York: Harcourt Brace, 1921): " It seems to me that there is a rather important psychological distinction between a language that settles the formal status of a radical

It follows that words toward the broad end of the horn will be broader in meaning, those toward the narrow end will be narrower, than the same words would be if their positions were reversed. Breadth and narrowness will undergo many transformations depending on the class of words that we are dealing with and on the degree of relevant or irrelevant stereotyping that may have taken place; but with care it is possible to filter out the primary colors from the welter of shades.

An example is the sentence *John eats*. At the moment of pre-speaking, anything is possible; when the word *John* appears this possibility is modified, though John, until we are told otherwise, could be doing anything; the term *eats* then appears and restricts this activity to one kind of act. *Eats* is not a modifier in the terms of Latin grammar, but it just as surely modifies *John* as would the adjective *young* in *Young John*.

The example is inserviceable, however, because it could be argued that *John* also modifies *eats*, as, in a sense, it does,[4] and there is no way of testing the linearity of modification because the order subject-plus-predicate has been stereotyped in this kind of sentence.

It is not, however, stereotyped in Spanish. The Kahanes found[5] that the type *Juan canta* is used in Mexican Spanish more often than not to signify what John does for a living, whereas *Canta Juan* more often than not means that he is singing now. Actually these particular meanings are secondary, but they derive logically from the fact that in *Canta Juan* it is primarily *Juan* that narrows *canta*—starting off with *canta* the speaker suggests an action that anyone might be doing, hence some such situation as a concert where several persons have been singing and it now comes John's turn. The *canta* is general and the *Juan* is restrictive. On the other hand *Juan canta* suggests pos-

---

element before announcing it . . . and one which begins with the concrete nucleus of a word and defines the status of this nucleus by successive limitations, each curtailing in some degree the generality of all that precedes. The spirit of the former has something diagrammatic or architectural about it, the latter is a method of pruning afterthoughts. In the more highly wrought prefixing languages the word is apt to affect us as a crystallization of floating elements, the words of the typical suffixing languages . . . are 'determinative' formations, each added element determining the form of the whole anew" (p. 135 n.). He calls such distinctions "elusive, yet important." Sapir is speaking of the architecture of bound forms, not of the architecture of sentences, but the analogy is apparent, and one of my points (*overrun* vs. *run over*, II, §8) would also be an example of his argument. See n. 9 for another hint, from Samuel Gili Gaya.

4. Modification in the most general sense can work backward as well as forward, just as two objects exert a mutual gravitational pull. I do not argue that backward modification is non-existent, but that forward modification is of a peculiar kind by being forward.

5. *Language*, XXVI (1950), 238.

sible activities for John[6]—he sings for a living rather than writes or weaves. The one answers the question *¿Quién canta?* The other answers *¿Qué hace Juan?* Note particularly that the differentiator, the contrasting element, comes last.[7]

Now for an equally striking example in English. It is obvious that there is a clear-cut difference between *Why did you abruptly back away?* and *Why did you back away abruptly?*, though not one so radical as to put them in different semantic ranges. The first asks essentially 'Why did you back away at all?' while the second asks 'Why, having decided to back away, did you do it abruptly?' The first can be contrastive, but only as a whole; we might say *Why did you abruptly back away? Why didn't you courteously accept as I wanted you to?* The second is contrastive on either part, depending on the accent: *Why did you back awáy abruptly when I told you to dart fórward abruptly?* and *Why did you back away abrúptly when I said to do it grádually?* When *abruptly* precedes the verb, it is difficult for contrastive accent to set it off against *back away*. We should seldom if ever say *Why did you abruptly back away when I told you to slowly back away?*[8]

Precisely this same change of meaning cannot be effected by changing the position of the average English adjective, where again we are blocked by a stereotype. *The red house burned down* cannot be worded *The house red burned down*. As might be expected, then, the adjective modifier, unlike the preposed adverb modifier, can readily be differentiated by means of contrastive accent: compare the ease of *Why did you choose the réd house?* with the difficulty of *Why did you slówly back away?*

The Spanish descriptive adjective, however, exhibits almost identically the same traits as the English descriptive adverb. In *un hermoso edificio* the speaker has in mind only one building—the phrase is a semantic unit, just like *abruptly back away*; in *un edificio hermoso*, however, the building is contrasted with others that are not beautiful, just as *back away abruptly* contrasts one kind of backing away with another kind. What W. E. Bull calls the " holotomic " or whole-splitting function of post-posed adjunct adjectives in Spanish

---

6. Progression is partly crowded out by competition from the *está cantando* construction, which causes *Juan canta* to favor the durative present.

7. In *Language*, XXVI (1950), 240, the Kahanes reported that in *Los tecolotes llegaron* " the *tecolotes* are expected," whereas in *Llegaron los tecolotes* they are not. This is too narrow an interpretation, for it depends on keeping the same accentual pattern, but it nevertheless illustrates our point. The authors probably intend a like accent on *tecolotes* in both sentences, so that any extra " contrastiveness " that the word may possess will come about by its position, not by any other form of highlighting. Despite the accent on *tecolotes* in BOTH sentences, it is more pointed, more contrastive, when it follows the verb.

8. It is just as nearly impossible to say in Spanish *¿Bien se portó o mal se portó?*

is also true of post-posed adverbs in English. When the qualifier precedes, it overshadows the whole of the following noun or verb, as we might expect from their relative positions in the horn of the sentence; when it follows, it splits the noun or verb. Diagramming, we get:[9]

9. Samuel Gili Gaya, *Curso superior de sintaxis española* §164 (Mexico: Minerva, 1943), discussing the *hermoso* example cited above, gives the nearest approximation to my hypothesis that I have encountered, and then, curiously enough, rejects it as central though accepts it as ancillary. "From the logical standpoint," he says, "the element that follows determines the scope of the one that precedes. In *un hermoso edificio* the substantive restricts the quality set forth in the adjective by applying it to a particular object. On the other hand, in *un edificio hermoso* the adjective excludes from the general image of 'building' all buildings that are not beautiful." This reasoning, he says, underlies Bello's view that following adjectives are "specifying." His motive for considering it secondary is his belief that the "determining" function, which Bello had attributed to the position of the adjective, is largely subsumed by the articles and other determinative adjectives that the grammarians allowed to creep into their examples. He then gives sentences without such determinatives, for instance *Valiosos cuadros adornaban el salón* versus *Cuadros valiosos adornaban el salón*, with presumably only a "stylistic" difference, to prove that what is paramount is a "synthetic style" for pre-position and an "analytical style" for post-position. This so-called stylistic difference can be reduced, even in his examples without determinatives, however, to the same pattern of adjective-embracing-whole or adjective-splitting-whole: querying a Spanish colleague as to which phrase— *valiosos cuadros* or *cuadros valiosos*—would be used of a poorly-appointed, run-down art-gallery, I received the unhesitating reply *cuadros valiosos*. My colleague agreed that in *valiosos cuadros* the *valiosos* overflows the *cuadros* and extends to the rest of the gallery. Gili Gaya's impressionistic terms "synthetic" and "analytical" are excellent if we concentrate our attention only on the effect that adjective position has on the noun; we saw in the instance with the English adverb that *abruptly back away* is synthetic as far as the verb is concerned. These are special cases of linear modification.

Despite the example of the Spanish descriptive adjective to suggest it, no Spanish grammarian to my knowledge has hit upon the fact that the Spanish descriptive adverb exhibits the same traits as the English descriptive adverb. Gili Gaya seems to be alone in extending the analogy of the adjective a little way, in the direction of the *gerundio* (see below, n. 20). It is curious that the phenomenon has been so completely overlooked by grammarians of English, or perhaps not so curious if we reflect that the most comprehensive grammars of English have been written by non-natives, and the distinction is not a highly obvious one. Non-natives are handicapped by having to work with affirmative data only; but a pattern cannot be fixed unless in addition to what CAN be said we

I have said that the stereotyped position of most English adjectives makes selective contrast impossible except by means of contrastive accent. This is true if we allow no modification of the wording, and in the main I think that avoiding modification should be a principle in seeking examples of our phenomenon. Taking a few liberties at this one point, however, will show us that fundamentally the same forces are at work even with the English adjective. Take the example of a man house-hunting in a certain neighborhood. He is asked *Are you looking for something?* and replies *I'm looking for a vacant house.* Or, if he assumes that house-hunting is obvious under the circumstances, he may confirm it selectively by replaying *I'm looking for a house that's vácant.* Unable to say *a house vacant,* he does the next best thing and expresses the selective contrast by means of an adjective clause. Now why did he not say *I'm looking for a vácant house?* Because contrastive accent on pre-position would rarely be used in such a situation unless *house* had already figured, verbally, in the conversation. Asked *Are you looking for a house?* or *What kind of house are you looking for?* he might readily reply *I'm looking for a vácant house,*[10] but this reply would come, so to speak, at second hand—the sentence would not be of what I term the "first instance," that is, a sentence that can begin a discourse.

If we take participial adjectives into the fold, we can illustrate the point without resorting to any verbal alteration at all. Thus if we reword *The advancing soldiers hálted* as *The soldiers advancing halted* (moderately prominent

---

determine what CANNOT be said. Poutsma's principle, to which he keeps recurring in the body of his chapter on word order, is (387) : "The best way of throwing any element of the sentence into particular relief is to give it end-position. . . The first words of the sentence, like the cautionary words of a command, put the listener on the alert. As the discourse proceeds, he is kept in suspense, so that his mind is prepared to receive that part of the communication on which his attention should chiefly be centered." Poutsma also recognizes front-position for emphasis, but does not reason it further. "Emphasis," "suspense," and "relief" are vague terms ; we need to know more, for instance, about the nature of the relief that is provided by end-position.

Curme, in *Syntax* §16, 2 (New York : Heath, 1931), says that "an adverb can freely stand in almost any position except between a verb and its direct object. . . . This usage rests upon the principle that an adverbial element is usually more important than a direct object and, like important elements in general, gravitates toward the end." He cites, among other examples, *Yesterday I met your father* and *I met your father yesterday.* In what sense *yesterday* is more "important" in one example than in the other is hard to see—in one it is more important by being more inclusive, in the other it is more important by being more selective. "Importance," "stylistic difference," and the like are traps. The adverb *again* may be both more "important" and more "emphatic" in *Again he told me* than in *He told me again,* but it precedes, nevertheless, for a reason that neither importance nor emphasis can explain.

10. Two different intonations to answer the two different questions.

accent on either *advancing* or *halted*), we achieve a selective contrast that does not depend on any previous sentence in the chain of discourse. But if we said *The adváncing soldiers halted*, we should almost certainly be in the " second instance," setting someone right who had mistakenly asserted that it was the retreating soldiers.[11] So we may say that selective contrast of the first instance is most typically (if not always) achieved by position rather than by contrastive accent. And since the other type of sentence is imitative, it is of secondary importance; its order is not its own, but is that of the real or supposed sentence that it imitates.

I have dwelt upon selective contrast because it is the most striking manifestation of linear modification. It is not the only one, however, as we shall see as we examine other examples of " free position " in English.

II. ENGLISH EXAMPLES IN DETAIL

1. Simple adverbs. I include here the majority of adverbs except subordinating adverbial conjunctions; I shall not attempt a definition—to do so would require an article in itself.[12]

My example of *abruptly back away* used a descriptive adverb. It was, however, limited to a certain type of question. We shall now see, first, whether other descriptive adverbs in other contexts behave similarly, and second, whether shifting the adverb through a progression of steps creates a semantic gradation.

The selective contrast that we observed in *back away abruptly* is evident in the following example from Poutsma (p. 464), *A man she respected too highly to deliberately tease*, if we end-shift the *deliberately*: *A man she respected too highly to tease deliberately;* the latter arrangement would have given the unwanted implication that she might tease him *unconsciously*, hence the split infinitive. In the original order, *deliberately* modifies all of *tease*.

The same is true of James Bryant Conant's remark: " I am afraid there has been traditionally in the United States a tendency to equate good education

---

11. Or, with prominent accent on *halted* as well as on *advancing*, be intending to go on ourselves to add something like *And the retreating soldiers were thrown into a róut*—in any case, contrastive accent on a pre-posed adjective seems to refer to some other VERBALLY EXPRESSED element.

12. The adverbs that I have included mainly give a mental picture of an action. Though I leave out subordinating adverbial conjunctions of the *when-where-as-because* type, since they are fixed in a single position, I include non-subordinating conjunctive adverbs of the *afterward-then-therefore* type. The latter behave much like descriptive adverbs—which is just as well, since drawing a sharp line between them is practically impossible.

with long education. With any such equating, I want *to violently disagree.*"[13]

Poutsma points out (p. 439, n.) that certain adverbs of time are "decidedly the rule" in end-position when the verb is imperative. But he could have included practically all adverbs, since in commands like *Do it carefully, Carry them slowly, Take it easy,* the adverb is the contrastive point of the command.[14]

If a following adverb so often suggests the possibility of two or more types of the action in question, it follows that a preceding adverb will often suggest only one type of the action. If—and such situations are typical—we already know from the context something about the action in question, the preceding adverb may then be almost expletive, adding nothing to our information. Some examples are: *He was badly shaken* (*cut, bruised, wronged, surprised*)—such things may be naturally bad. *You are cordially invited, He politely held the door open for me, They courteously stepped aside, He rudely insulted me, I selfishly thought only of myself*—innumerable expressions like these involving the amenities show actions which in our society are normally regarded as right or wrong. By the same token, adverbs of praise and dispraise are highly frequent in pre-position—precisely the same is true of both the adverb and the adjective of praise and dispraise in Spanish.[15] *The thing doesn't automatically stop now* refers to a machine which normally does not stop in any way except automatically; in reference to machinery, expressions like *After the third phase it automatically stops* are common. *The commanders in the field may not nicely weigh the claims of individuals or groups to special treatment*[16] refers to an action which under the circumstances could be nothing but "nice." If *They courteously stepped aside* implies 'It was courteous of them to step aside,' *I was curiously alarmed* virtually means 'It was curious that I was alarmed.'

Coming to our second point, whether progression in position creates progression in meaning, we are handicapped more than ever by a variety of side-effects. This is only natural, since given several positions of a word one might expect that some of them would be captured for specific stereotypes or

---

13. *Time,* 23 Jan. 1950, p. 46. The writer not perfectly versed in English betrays himself in the following from J. Gonda, *Lingua,* VIII (1950), 316: "Notwithstanding his shortcomings the disinterested and idealistic Swiss scholar *has essentially contributed* to the advancement of Indonesian studies." As it stands, this is probably a feebler compliment than the author intended.

14. Commands are typically short. We are not likely to combine two orders in one. Thus in *Do it carefully,* the *do it* part is almost certainly resumptive, *carefully* being the only new datum. If the *do it* is also a new datum, the dual command will probably take some such shape as *Do it, and be careful about it.*

15. *Cortésmente me abrió la puerta* implies '*cortés* to be expected.' *Furiosamente se abalanzó sobre mí* produces the same effect as *furioso león.*

16. *Bull. Amer. Assn. of Univ. Professors,* XXXVI (1950), 684.

distinct grammatical functions. Take for example the progression *Generally he made himself agreeable, He generally made himself agreeable, He made himself generally agreeable,* and *He made himself agreeable generally.* We can compare the first with the second and the third with the fourth, but not either of the first two with either of the second two (unless there is radical alteration of pause and intonation); this is because the two front positions have been captured by the meaning 'as a rule,' and by the function of sentence adverb, leaving the meaning 'in all ways,' and the function of modifying a single word, to the two back positions.[17] The adverbial *rotten* in *rotten spoiled* (*PADS*, xiv, 57) is not comparable with the predicative *rotten* in *spoiled rotten.*

So we must seek an adverb that is not made captive in this fashion. Again we may use our example with *back away: Slowly he backed away, He slowly backed away, He backed slowly away,* and *He backed away slowly.* Selective contrast is unlikely until we come to the third position, and is frequent only in the fourth position. On the other hand, the type of intonation typical of pre-posed adverbs (*Slo-o-owly he backed away*) shades off slightly from first to third position and becomes least likely in fourth position. The third position therefore shares both possibilities—drawling and selective contrast; and there is no mistaking the difference between the first position and the last. We may conclude that gradation of position creates gradation of meaning when there are no interfering factors.[18]

The effect of pre-position is that the adverb colors everything that follows. In *Slowly he backed away* the whole picture, not just some part of it, is in slow motion. I believe that this is significant for what is commonly called the " sentence adverb "; and I think it suggests that adverbs cannot be sharply divided into sentence-modifiers and word-modifiers, since, depending on its position, and with no side-effects to interfere, an adverb can modify all of an utterance or a unit consisting of almost any major or minor portion.

The adverbs commonly recognized as sentence adverbs would then be those which frequently gravitate toward the front. We have already seen how *generally* not only gravitated toward the front but was made captive there. It does not follow, of course, that adverbs which modify larger units than single words must stand at the beginning: in *Recently he has not been around, to be around* is a unit, and accordingly we may say *He has not been around re-*

---

17. There is a further side-effect in the fact that *agreeable generally* admits of two types of selective contrast: 'agreeable in all ways instead of just some ways' and 'agreeable in an over-all sense but maybe specifically disagreeable.'

18. An example where the adverb has been half captured is *Well he knows that it is not true, He well knows that it is not true, He knows (perfectly) well that it is not true, He knows that it is not true (perfectly) well.* Here there is partial interference from intonation. Many adverbs of time may be captured by one or the other of two or more verbs: *Often I hope he will suffer, I often hope he will suffer, I hope he will suffer often.*

cently and still have *recently* modify a phrase. In spite of this, *recently* is more inclusive when it stands at the beginning.

Similar to sentence adverbs are conjunctive adverbs, which have as an additional reason for standing at the beginning the fact that they throw a line to a preceding locution and therefore tend to be as close as possible to it. As with sentence adverbs, an ordinary adverb may be made captive in pre-position in some conjunctive sense. Thus if we reword *I believe it absolutely,* as *Absolutely I believe it,* we get *absolutely* in the sense of 'indeed' and confirming some previous statement. *Yet* is even more striking. In *We yet have nothing to show for it* (I conceive this as possible though infrequent), *We have yet nothing to show for it, We have nothing yet to show for it,* and *We have nothing to show for it yet,* there is the gradation that we noted earlier; but in *Yet we have nothing to show for it, yet* has been made captive, and to get anything like the former sense we must replace it with *as yet.*

There need not be any such side-effects, however, and the conjunctive adverb may remain one in any position, with the same gradation that we have noted. Thus *He called me; accordingly I went—I accordingly went—I went accordingly.*[19]

2. Adverbial clauses. These larger blocks evidence linear modification just as clearly as words do. Compare *If you come I'll help you* with *I'll help you if you come;* the first envisages more affirmatively the possibility of the person's coming—has, that is to say, a meaning that goes a little beyond mere condition and may amount almost to an invitation; the second lends itself more readily to the implication 'I'll help you ONLY if you come'—selective contrast. When the *if* clause is placed first, it serves as a frame for all that follows; Professor Hatcher suggests the example *If you drop in this afternoon we'll have tea and play a few hands of bridge,* which proves the point in that it is irreversible: *We'll have tea and play a few hands of bridge if you drop in this afternoon* is an improbable sentence. Compare also *When you come I'll help you* with *I'll help you when you come;* the second lends itself to the implication 'but not before'—selective contrast. In *When her husband died she died* there is a suggestion of 'because' as well as 'at the same time as,' while *She died when her husband died* is more likely in the sense of time alone. The *before* clause in *Before the note came due he had made all arrangements* is broader in meaning than that in *He had made all arrangements before the note came due.*

3. Participial phrases. When adverbial or quasi-adverbial, these behave very much as adverbial clauses. In *Going that way you'll get lost* the phrase covers the meanings of hypothetical *if, when,* and *by* clauses as well as, potentially, the literal implication that the person is actually going or about to go

---

19. The term " conjunctive abverb " does not satisfy me, but as it is not material to the thesis I copy it from Poutsma (e.g., p. 444).

that way. In *You'll get lost going that way* the hypothetical senses more or less fade—the person is probably actually in the process of going that way. Compare also *Cursing his luck he walked out* with *He walked out cursing his luck;* in the first, we tell what else he did while he was cursing his luck; in the second, we tell what else he was doing when he walked out. Samuel Gili Gaya observes this identical effect in Spanish, comparing it to the effect of transposing the attributive adjective in the type *hermoso edificio* and *edificio hermoso* which we have already studied.[20]

The *-ing* form as a gerund shows a similar peculiarity: in post-position it tends to be limited to the REALITY or IMMEDIACY of the action designated, while in pre-position it is broadened to include the potential as well as the real. Consider *Playing golf is fun,* an utterance which is appropriate when merely imagining the game as well as when actually engaging in it. The alternate form *It's fun playing golf,* however, is less likely to be used unless one is really playing.[21] Later we shall see that much the same is true of adjunct present participles: *a working man* emphasizes the potential, *a man working* the real.

4. "Prepositional" adverbs. Though it is difficult at times to discern a difference in the types *They left out both pages* and *They left both pages out,* when differences can be discerned they accord with the theory.

First, there seems to be a tendency for the terminal adverbs to be more literal, that is, narrower in their semantic range, while the pre-posed adverbs take on a looser sense which sometimes is so completely transferred that the adverb becomes a captive there in the given sense. *She is going to take her mother out tonight* is made ludicrous in my dialect when worded *She is going to take out her mother tonight*—the latter means 'remove.' But even when not made captive, the adverb still exhibits a broadening when it is moved forward: the *down* in *They broke the door down* is narrower than in *They broke down the door.*[22]

Second, post-position is the one that lends itself to selective contrast.

20. He says (§146) the *gerundio* "is generally placed after the verb; but it can go before, and in this case the adverbial modification takes on...a relief similar to that of the adjective put before its noun."

21. There may be a partial side-effect here. My feeling is that when we say *It's fun playing golf* the *it* has to some extent retained the status of a true subject, and is not merely a vicarious subject. We might, for example, ask, *Is it fun?* (*it* a true subject = 'what you are doing'), and receive the reply, *Yes, it's fun playing golf.* In this way it is possible for the effect that we observed in the participle-as-adverb to carry over to the participle-as-noun.

22. It might be argued that contiguity with the verb rather than the relationship of before-after is responsible for this. If so, the examples lose their value, though the theory is not contradicted.

Poutsma says (pp. 419–420, n.) it is not "difficult to account for the arrangement of the following examples, in which the notion expressed by the adverb is contrasted with that indicated by another adverb; thus that of *back* in *Try to force this bolt back* ..., *off* in *He pulled his dog off.*"[23]

5. Factitive and causative phrases. These, involving as they do a more or less stereotyped verbal phrase, are much the same as the prepositional adverbs. *I pushed the door open* is appropriate for selective contrast, *I pushed open the door* is not; *This thanklessness will make any further effort on our part useless* is more appropriate for selective contrast than *This thanklessness will make useless any further effort on our part.* Note the resemblance of the latter example to the corresponding adverbs in *Why protest uselessly?* and *Why uselessly protest?* As with the prepositional adverbs, these modifiers may also be made captive in front position: *He let fall that silly hint* means that he made it; *He let that silly hint fall* would probably mean that he let it flop.

6. *Only.* One or two adverbs deserve individual treatment. In *I only want ten*, *I want only ten*, and *I want ten only* there is the same progression that we observed with *slowly*. In the first is a suggestion of 'It is only that I want ten,' which is mixed in the second and entirely lacking in the third; yet all three signify fundamentally 'only ten'—the difference is that the preposed *only* takes on a broader meaning. The same may be noted in Palmer's example (Poutsma, p. 447) *I only saw my friend yesterday*, which he uses to show that *only* owes its proper understanding to intonation. This is mainly correct, for intonation does single out the chief element for modification; but the role of sentence order is not abated, for—keeping the intonation of *friend* the same—*I only saw my friénd yesterday* is not identical with *I saw only my friénd yesterday*: the first gives a hint of 'All I did yesterday (of importance to our discussion) was see my friend,' which the second lacks.[24]

7. *So.* *So* may have alternating positions either as a pro-word (pronoun,

---

23. The contrary effect may be noted in the manner in which a terminal adverb weakens a contrast on some other element even when that element bears contrastive accent. Thus *Put your hát on* is less effective as regards singling out *hat* than is *Put on your hát.*

24. *Only* can be made captive in a variety of ways. In *Only, I saw my friend yesterday* it is 'except for the fact that.' In *Only Í saw my friend yesterday* it is 'I alone.' In *I only saw my friend yesterday* there are various major implications according to accent, plus a minor one due to position. In *I saw only my friend yesterday* there are two major implications according to accent (*mý* or *friénd*) plus a minor one due to position, and the latter implication competes with *I saw my friend ónly* [optional pause] *yesterday.* In *I saw my only friend yesterday*, *only* is captured as an adjective. In *I saw my friend only yésterday* we get either 'no other time but yesterday,' competing in its order implications with some of the foregoing, or the stereotyped 'no longer ago than yesterday.' In *I saw my friend yesterday only* we get 'no other time but,' with competing order implications.

pro-adjective, pro-adverb) or as an adverbial conjunction.

In "*John is a good dancer*"—"*So he is*" we have *so* resuming something from the previous utterance. Since resumptives set the stage for what is to follow, cast their shadow so to speak over the whole of the coming utterance, we find them often in pre-position. In "*John isn't a good dancer*"—"*He is so!*" we find selective contrast. The greater definiteness of *so* in post-position is also evident in "*They came early*"—"*So you told me*" against "*How do you know?*"—"*They told me so*," and even, though it has to contend with lack of accent, in *It was useless—at least, so they said* against *It was useless—at least, they said so.*

As an adverbial conjunction, take the example *She got into the habit of insisting so, that ...* where the result is more or less incidental, and compare it with *She got into the habit of so insisting, that ...* , where the result is colored by something like purpose or inevitability—in any case the *so* is broader than in post-position.[25]

8. Terminal prepositions. Jespersen[26] quotes Fowler as saying that a preposition at the end of a relative clause is admissible "only when used in the literal or most obvious sense," as in *It was a cab* [but not *high indignation*] *that he rode away in.* It is in accord with our theory that a word placed toward the front should take on a broader meaning; Fowler says in effect that when a preposition includes figurative as well as literal meanings, it must go forward.[27]

With interrogatives we get phrases liké *Where from?* versus *From where?* and *What for?* versus *For what?* Take a question-and-answer set like "*He'll get the money*"—"*Where from?*" as against "*He'll get the money*"—"*From where?*" In *where from* the *where* is more inclusive: *Where from?* may be skeptical about there being any such place at all, while *From where?* stresses the difficulty of finding the place. The same contrast is evident in *What for?*, where *what* is so inclusive that the phrase as a whole is practically interchangeable with *Why?*, against *For what?*, in which the referent of *what* is pointed to starkly.

With verbs, comparison is more difficult because of the stereotyping of forms

---

25. The first is an announcement of mere result; we might expand to *She got into the habit of insisting so, that as usually happens in such cases she got her way.* The second is more: an interpolation pointing to mere result is less suitable.

26. Part III Syntax 2nd vol. 10.3₅.

27. Another relevant effect is noted by Poutsma (p. 472): that end-position of the preposition is sometimes avoided "when the verb or nominal is felt to be of particular weight." Thus in "On some of the most important issues of modern life there is no free discussion within the groups *on* whose decisions everything *depends*." It is desired to focus on *depends* at the narrow end of the sentence, and a following *on* would dilute this, even though *depends* is still accented.

like *overlook, overrun*.   Nevertheless, if comparison be allowed, we note the usual contrast between an expression like *They ran over the field* and one like *They overran the field:* the pre-posed *over* becomes broader.

9. Simple adjunct adjectives.[28]   English has a few adjectives which, through French tradition or some other influence, may stand either before or after the noun—for example, *royal battle* and *battle royal, positive proof* and *proof positive, payable accounts* and *accounts payable*.   Most of them, however, have been captured by some side-effect.   Thus *God Almighty* has been spoiled for comparison with *Almighty God* by the fact that it is seldom used except as an oath.   *The members present voted* is hard to compare with *The present members voted* because the one means 'not absent' and the other means 'having that status now' (but this may be a derivative side-effect, since the more literal meaning, 'not absent,' is the one that follows).

We find an occasional adjective that does, however, compare closely with the descriptive adverb in admitting two positions in the same semantic range. In *He belonged now to the world everlásting* we find a selective contrast, *everlasting* being opposed to *temporal*, and taking the same position that our adverbs did for selective contrast.   In *the everlásting wórld,* as with the adverbs, only one world would be under consideration.[29]

Similarly in *If we'll all work and get together the money necessary . . . , necessary* gives selective contrast (heightened by the fact that in this order it usually calls for further qualification, like *necessary for our aims*), whereas in *the necessary money* it overshadows and hence binds together the whole.[30]   Poutsma likes to point out the resemblance of the first type, *the money necessary,* to undeveloped clauses like *the money that was necessary*.   We have already noted

---

28. The entire paper, and this section of it particularly, has benefited from the detailed and painstaking criticism of Professor Anna Granville Hatcher of Johns Hopkins University.

29. See n. 11, above, and accompanying text for the effect of contrastive accent on pre-posed *advancing*, analogous to the effect of contrastive accent on pre-posed *everlasting* here.   The two examples just given correspond respectively to a theologian's and an astronomer's view of the world.   The latter speaks of a world whose existence is the very measure of time—whence *everlasting* is expletive.

30. One must guard against distracting elements such as occur in Poutsma's example *If the nation will rise to the occasion and make the united effort necessary, it can overcome this German machination*.   We "feel" that the position gives the same effect here as in the example in the body of the text (*the money necessary*), but discover that selective contrast seems to be ruled out by the fact that in both *the united effort necessary* and *the necessary united effort* only one particular effort is under consideration.   The reason is the presence of the added modifier *united*, which of itself particularizes the noun and which must, by the mechanics of the English sentence, go in pre-position.   In order not to be misled we must then either strip away the surplus adjective, or bear in mind that BOTH *united* and *necessary* particularize, but that *united* is fixed in position.

the relationship in the case of *a vacant house.*

There is also marked selective contrast in the example (Poutsma, p. 489) *It is the man who makes music because he loves it who is the true musician. He is the musician pure.* But this example is revealing in that it shows one device by which English gets around the disability of not being able, ordinarily, to put an adjective after a noun in order to get selective contrast. We note that in the example, *true musician* gives practically the same effect as *musician pure,* and is, in fact, repeated by the latter. The reason is that in *the true musician* (or *the pure musician*) we have re-defined the noun *musician* to exclude all would-be musicians. This gives selective contrast between *musician* and *would-be musician,* which is the same as that between *musician pure* and *musician impure.*[31]

Parallel constructions enable us to get selective contrast by means of postposition with a great many adjectives. So in the examples *In the body national as in the body natural*[32] and *[The dictograph] has figured … in the undoing of dynamiters, legislative bribe-takers, grafters high and crooks low* (Poutsma 489).

Grouped adjectives have more freedom of movement than single adjectives. Thus in Spencer's dictum (Poutsma 503) *A three-year-old urchin playing with an open razor, cannot be allowed to learn by this discipline of consequences* shows *three-year-old urchin* with its literal significance plus that of 'young urchin in general'; worded *urchin three years old,* the meaning would be pared down to its most restrictive. In *three-year-old urchin* the point is 'urchin.' Similarly in *the three-mile-long passage* the point is 'passage,' while in *the passage three miles long* the point is the differential.[33] Sometimes the accrued meaning re-

---

31. At the risk of laboring the point, I again insert the caution that *He is the pure musician,* with contrastive accent on pre-posed *pure* and with *musician* de-accented, is iterative.

32. Jespersen, *Syntax,* 1st vol. 15.54 (Heidelberg, 1914).

33. A troublesome case of grouped adjectives is provided by comparisons of inequality. In *We use a fairly bright light in indoor photography, like this one, because a dimmer light than this would slow the photograph too much,* I feel that *dimmer* in pre-position is slightly inappropriate because of the faint suggestion that the alternative light would be actually dim, whereas the context says that it probably would not be. A better contrast seems to be got by saying *a light dimmer than this, dim* in post-position being more contrastive. Similarly in *For this job we need an older man than John,* which suggests 'really old,' as against *For this job we need a man older than John,* which leans more to the purely contrastive, relative sense of *old.* It is hard to manipulate comparisons like these for three reasons. First, all comparatives imply a contrast regardless of their position. Second, ungrouped comparatives are required to precede most nouns (*a dimmer light,* not *a light dimmer*), and grouped ones assimilate to them. Third, there is a side-effect from the use of such expressions to pay compliments. In *There is no prettier girl here than Mary, pretty* overspreads and makes Mary a pretty girl; but *There is no girl here prettier than Mary* can be either the matter-of-fact 'and she is not necessarily pretty' or the hyperbolic 'none CONCEIVABLY prettier than she.' An identical effect is observable in the

sulting from grouped pre-position is emotional or poetic, as may be seen in the rather lyrical *A broad, level, and verdant plain* as against the matter-of-fact *A plain broad, level, and verdant*, or in the insulting *He is an evil-tempered and malicious man* as against the more matter-of-fact *He is a man evil-tempered and malicious*.[34] Precisely the same is true of Spanish.[35]

The examples of simple adjunct adjectives that I have cited up to this point seem to have been rounded up from the scraps and left-overs of the English language, and to present no traceable pattern of any consequence. Is there, then, no broad patterning of adjectives that follow their nouns for some effect or purpose that accords with linear modification? If our general principle can aid us in discovering a specific formula, we shall have a test of its usefulness as well as its validity. I believe that there is a pattern, and that examples like *Such countries friendly would be a great asset to us, Mary beautiful is something hard to imagine, There is nothing more delicious than grapefruit fresh, A man unhappy is a social risk, Lions are always fearsome beasts but a lion hungry is the terror of the jungle, The people sick had to stay in bed*, etc., represent a type than can be defined. To arrive at it, let us enter by the back door, so to speak, along a corridor where post-position cannot be employed.

Spanish *deliciosas comidas*, which makes *delicious* non-differentiating and so implies a compliment, against *comidas deliciosas* which may be either an insult or a hyperbolic compliment.

34. The latter paraphrases Poutsma 498.

35. The expression *Es un infame hombre* does not appear in the textbooks, but is good colloquial Spanish, such as might be used by a woman complaining to a judge about the treatment she received from her husband—is more emotional, less matter-of-fact than *Es un hombre infame*, where *infame* has less spread. The same would be true of the grouped *Es un perverso e infame hombre*. In *Es un estudiante pervertido* we get the figure

estudiante | | pervertido

'a student who happens to be perverted'; *Es un pervertido estudiante* gives

pervertido | | estudiante

'a perverted one who happens to be a student'—perverted in all senses, not merely *qua* student. It might be argued that since Spanish can convert almost any descriptive adjective to a noun, in the second construction we have the eqivalent of *Es un pervertido*, with another noun in apposition, which is therefore not comparable with *Es un estudiante pervertido*, where *pervertido* has to be an adjective. The argument can be countered in part, however, by casting about for an adjective that would be unusual as a noun; thus *Es un inicuo*, though possible, is distinctly unusual, while even the person unfamiliar with the meaning of the word would accept *Es un inicuo hombre*. This seems to suggest that in *Es un pervertido hombre* the *pervertido* is an adjective and so is comparable with *hombre pervertido*. In any case our main thesis is unaffected, for even with noun-noun combinations the effect of linear modification may be noted: *mi viuda madre* refers to only one mother, a widow, while *mi madre viuda* would give a ludicrous selective contrast (Gili Gaya §164).

One of the most important questions about position has to do with the "standardizing" effect that is produced by placing a qualifier before its noun. Obviously the phrase *underseas craft* names a standard type of craft in our culture, whereas *craft underseas* does not. Linear modification enables us to relate this phenomenon to the more ordinary one just mentioned, *an unhappy man* versus *a man unhappy*, where the notion of "standard type" is not so evident. The relationship is a real one in English, though my development of it may seem circuitous.

We begin by inferring, from the comparative rarity of the post-position of ordinary adjectives in English, that if a pattern can be found where post-position is regular, that pattern will show a trait of "restrictiveness" that is more exaggerated than would be found where post-position is common. Now in the type *a man unhappy, the people sick, the guests absent, the tools ready, a person busy*, etc., adjectives may regularly follow their nouns. Applying our reasoning to *a man unhappy* we get

in which *unhappy* does not cut off the whole of *man*. Do the parts that it does not cut off represent other men? Let us try a sentence in which there might be a contrast between *a man unhappy* and some other man who is happy: *A man unhappy fell down and broke his leg.* Such a sentence is clearly un-English, whereas *A man unhappy is seldom in control of his emotions* is acceptable English. The parts of *man* that *unhappy* fails to cut off in our diagram therefore do not primarily refer to other men, but to the same man: the contrast is between the man unhappy and the SAME man happy. It is not thing-to-thing, or selective, contrast, but self-contrast. This situation has been reduced to a stereotype with the adjective *proper:* compare *the proper test* (thing-to-thing) and *the test proper* (self-contrast); Spanish *mismo* behaves identically. We thus find the conditions of our inference satisfied—not only is there restriction, but the restriction is of a particularly narrow kind; and as we look at other expressions within the same pattern, we find that it is mostly limited to adjectives which can describe varying states of the same individual person or thing—most of the adjectives in the pattern show a striking similarity to participles and adverbs: *unhappy* suggests *dashed* or *disappointed*, *sick* suggests *diseased* or *stricken*, *absent* suggests *away*, etc. So germane is this to English that the language has preserved a small group of adjectives which are stereotyped in post-position and which reveal their kinship to adverbs by having been at one time prepositional phrases: *afloat, agog, alive, apart,* etc.; their reference is to some transitory state. *Overweight* is similar, though occasionally met in pre-position. The same is true of *money galore*—we note the ludicrous suggestion of " standardization " or " characterization " if we try to say *galore money.*[36]

I chose the example *a man unhappy* because it is an extreme case, pointing up the unsuitability of post-position to imply much more than temporary state. The example proved that the adjective had to apply to the same man as would its opposite, *happy,* not to other men, and therefore that it could not CHARACTERIZE the man, but could only picture him in a more or less momentary condition. Actually the only essential of the pattern is that the adjective suggests DETACHABILITY FROM THE NOUN—usually the notion of ' that happens to be '; it may at times be used to set thing against thing as well as thing against some other state of the same thing. We can say, for instance, *People unconscious are unable to hear,* where there is self-contrast, or *The only man unconscious was John,* where there is person-to-person contrast; but in both cases the meaning is ' that happen(ed) to be unconscious.' In *Roast beef rare is a dish fit for a king* the detachability is evident. The same is true of adjectives with the *-able* suffix which retain their verbal sense; they freely admit post-position in certain inclusive-exclusive constructions with *all, only, the few,* and the like: *the person desirable* (' to be desired '), *the tools usable* (' that may be used '), *the money spendable, the houses acceptable, the argument defensible,* etc.; e.g., *The few stars visible were plotted.* All these express ideas that are detachable from the noun, i.e., that do not characterize. But where the *-able* adjective has taken on a non-verbal sense, so as to be able to characterize, post-position is far more restricted: compare *All the people desirable were invited* with *All the people likable were invited,* or *the only argument defensible* with *the only argument plausible.*[37] A number of *-able* words have fairly well-defined dual functions depending on position. If we say *The only navigable river is to the north* we normally mean ' regularly navigable '—the river is so CHARACTERIZED; if we say *The only river navigable is to the north* we mean ' navigable at present '—out of several navigable rivers there may be only one river navigable. In *They collected on every taxable dollar* we have a predetermined class of dollars; in *They collected on every dollar taxable* all such dollars are included, whether classified or not. The characterization inherent in pre-position sometimes makes for partial or complete transfer of meaning. We can characterize a person as agreeable; hence *The only agreeable person was John;* but if we say *The only person agreeable was John* we use the word in the narrower sense ' willing to agree ' to some proposal. Similarly with *the only*

---

36. Compare *money ready,* a momentary state, and *ready money,* a prearranged class.

37. To put it subjectively, the " characterizing " *-able* words give a mental picture of the thing; the others do not.

passable (either literal or in the transferred sense of 'fair') *road* against *the only road passable* (literal only); or *the responsible man* ('trustworthy') against *the man responsible* ('to blame, bearing responsibility'); or *the only creditable* ('worthy') *amount* against *the only amount creditable* (to a given account). We can even use adjectives of a more "permanent" sort if the combination is something hypothetical, new, or surprising—i.e., if the connexion between the adjective and the noun is still loose and uncertain in the speaker's mind. The type *Such countries friendly would be a great asset to us* is more likely than the type *Such countries friendly are a great asset to us*—the hypothetical *would be* stresses the "non-belongingness" of the adjective and its noun. In a situation where persons of doubtful loyalty are being tested for their allegiance we might find *All persons loyal will be given jobs*, i.e., all persons 'found to be loyal' as a result of the test—the connectedness of adjective and noun is still new.[38] Similarly with *The officers explained their position and all members antagonistic were asked to withdraw; Any part defective will be replaced if returned within thirty days*. The implication of newness or unexpectedness is present where adjectives are post-posed after quantifiers like *few, only: The few men disloyal were discharged, The only house vacant is that one, No report unsatisfactory will be filed*. The non-connectedness of *Mary beautiful is something hard to imagine* is obvious.[39]

If the theory of pre-position for characterization is correct, it should be possible to find nouns whose semantic content admits of characterization by a given adjective, whence that adjective precedes, while other nouns of different semantic content will not, though the circumstances be similar or identical, admit of the same preceding adjective. Take the noun *party*, in the sense of 'one involved in litigation or controversy.' In this legal sense, parties can be CLASSIFIED, in our culture, as responsible and non-responsible, i.e., characterized as such. Therefore we may say *The responsible party will be prosecuted* where we should be far less likely to say *The responsible man will be prosecuted*—the latter, as we have already seen, becomes *the man responsible*, since something as transitory as responsibility for a given act does not normally characterize men as men. Or take the adjective *unconscious* and the noun *victims*. *Unconscious* is a normal classification of victims, who may be, standardly, injured, unconscious, or dead. *Unconscious* is not, however, a normal classification of *men*. So *The unconscious victims were given emergency treatment* comes more readily than *The unconscious men (persons, people) were given emergency treatment*.

---

38. If *Citizens* replaces *All persons*, the result is somewhat un-English. See the next section for the reason, *person* being a more inclusive noun.

39. Non-connectedness is made explicit by certain interpolations: *Mary being beautiful, Having such countries friendly, All persons found loyal*. It is commonest of all in the quasi-predicatives *I saw John unhappy, We found the report unsuitable*, etc. The pattern probably evolved from these types.

This leads us back to our initial question, why qualifiers that represent a "standard type" in the culture must precede. Since the qualifier that follows shows a detachable, especially a transitory, state, in order to represent something as fixed, i.e., to CHARACTERIZE (or, better, to STANDARDIZE or NORMALIZE, since characterizations like *all persons loyal*, where the application is in doubt, have been shown to take post-position), we must put the qualifier before the noun. This has led to the creation of odd compounds like *after-the-fact requisition, heavier-than-air craft, better-than-average person, under-the-counter sale*. Note the latter: an under-the-counter sale is one that is marked by certain stigmata; a merchant in totting up the day's receipts might conceivably have such sales in a separate column, which is the same as saying that they are a CLASS apart. *A sale under the counter* does not imply a class, but an incident.

Some terms are needed with which to label the two positions of adjunct adjectives. If we take "attributive adjective" in the sense of 'one that assigns an attribute,' then *attributive* should be limited to adjectives in pre-position. For post-posed adjectives such as have been described, Professor Hatcher suggests *appositional adjective*. We might simply continue to identify them by their position, but it is necessary at least to point out the danger of using the conventional term *attributive* of any but pre-posed adjuncts.

Our pattern provides one clue for the post-position of grouped adjectives. When a speaker combines a series of adjectives he gives the impression of improvising, and improvisation is the opposite of standardization.[40]

Further evidence for the pattern is provided by adjectives accompanying proper names. In *John unhappy is impossible to live with* we have but one person, John, who has his characteristics that remain unaltered by his being at the moment unhappy; he remains the same John. But to characterize him as an unhappy person we say *Poor, unhappy John!* The *unhappy* overspreads him completely; it is viewed as a trait of his character.[41]

---

40. We have noted the comparatives as one set of grouped adjectives. In the contrast between *A lovelier face I have never seen* and *A face more lovely I have never seen* the general principle is clear, as is also the suggestion of 'striking unexpectedness' (when coupled with the *never* phrase) offered by the post-position. In ordinary constructions, such as *You need a more intelligent manager*, the comparative is more likely to precede, though, in the nature of the case, comparatives are more detachable than non-comparatives and more readily follow. Note that the *-er* comparatives, except in the type discussed in n. 33, regularly precede; they are the most-used adjectives, those representing qualities most likely to be embalmed in standard types.

41. Spanish post-position is not limited to "detachability," the latter being relegated to a totally different pattern (*ser-estar*), whence "standard type" is not excluded from post-position. The chief use of pre-position is a special kind of "norm": that of known or assumed-to-be-known characteristic (cf. n. 15 and corresponding text). Just

10. The indefinites. Adjectives with pronouns such as *those, the ones, anyone, no one, somebody, something, somewhere,* etc., do not meet the condition of having more than one possible position; we can only say *anyone wealthy,* not *wealthy anyone* (*a wealthy nobody,* of course, transfers *nobody* out of the indefinites). Nevertheless, they seem to provide either a derivative or a contributing side-effect. Indefinites, by the statement of our problem, ought to precede, and we find that they do; further, there is a bearing on the position of indefinite nouns, where two positions are possible. The chief example is the noun *things,* though other semantically sweeping nouns such as *events, times, fortunes, matters,* etc., occasionally exhibit the same trait: *things incredible, events American, times medieval,* " people concerned with *matters Chinese,*"[42] and so on are phrases which, though somewhat rhetorical, are recognizable English and illustrate our principle of the pre-position of indefinites. Indeed, we might combine this as one and the same manifestation as that set forth in the preceding section. There, it was a highly precise, transitory adjective combined with an ordinary noun which admitted of post-position; here, it is an ordinary adjective combined with a highly inclusive noun. We could say that in either case it is the DIFFERENCE in semantic breadth between the noun and the adjective that determines post-position. The difference in pressure between these two potentials is what counts, and gives us the same feel of ' that happens to be ' in *things incredible* as in *man unhappy.*

11. Adjunct participles. These, both present and past, have greater freedom of movement than ordinary adjunct adjectives. The example *advancing soldiers* versus *soldiers advancing* has already been found to square with the theory.[43]

---

as English post-position is an extreme, so Spanish pre-position is an extreme: that of " standard " which given a setting is so standard that just mentioning the noun is supposed to suggest the adjective (as in *world everlasting* versus *everlasting world*). Chopping up the spectrum so as to fit the two languages, we get the following:

Pre-position in Spanish	Post-position in Spanish	
Known standard	Unknown standard	(Unknown) non-standard
Pre-position in English		Post-position in English

English groups " standard," Spanish groups " known." The important fact is that while the two languages divide the spectrum at different points, the polarity is the same. Thus all constructions admitting pre-position in Spanish would, on transposing them to the predicative pattern, demand *ser,* though not all constructions in the *ser* pattern when transposed to adjunct pattern would call for pre-position.

42. Charles Hockett in *Language,* XXVII (1951), 441.

43. Poutsma (506) attributes the pre-position in *At last one of the advancing bulls*

The present participles show better than do ordinary adjectives the "stand-ard" versus "non-standard" dichotomy that we have just considered. This is to be expected in the nature of participles: they show a process or its re-sult, and a process is impermanent, whence post-position is in the order of things. It is, then, rather pre-position which has special uses, than post-posi-tion. The fluid "characterization" in *advancing soldiers* as against *soldiers ad-vancing* is like that of *sick people* versus *people sick;* but in *traveling salesman* versus *salesman traveling* we have a characterization that has been frozen into a stereotype. It accords with the general theory, for in *traveling salesman* we have 'actually traveling' broadened to 'potentially traveling.'

Such compounds with present participles are numerous, but no different from others with adjectives, adverbs, or nouns plus nouns. It is a charac-teristic of the type that the qualifying word is transferred from its literal meaning and specialized in some figurative or restricted sense. So the parti-ciple partially loses its identity, and functions in the same way in *traveling salesman* as does the adverb *underseas* in *underseas craft*, the adverb *next-door* in *next-door neighbor*, the noun *light* in *light house*, or the gerund *reading* in *reading lamp*. As before, if two positions are possible, the shift will square with the theory—thus though *light house* cannot be compared with *house light*, it is possible despite the shift in semantic range to compare *underseas craft* with *craft underseas* and *next-door neighbor* with *neighbor next door*—in both, the sec-ond member of the pair has the more literal meaning.[44]

---

stood still to there being "no time association" in the participle when it precedes the noun. In many instances the time association of the post-posed participle is obvious, as in *working man* and *man working*; but the *advancing bulls* example is a poor one because post-position of the participle has as its primary effect a selective contrast; there is potential time association in both arrangements. This is best shown by a ludicrous rearrangement of another of Poutsma's examples, *She was now quite alone with the dying Henry*, where unless there are two Henrys no other arrangement is possible— time association is secondary.

44. However one may define "compound," the compounds that admit of simple change of position without a change of meaning too radical to apply the theory, are few indeed. *Heavier-than-air craft* is 'craft heavier than air,' reversible because grouped modifiers take both positions more freely—it is 'craft characteristically heavier than air' just as *under-the-counter-sale* is 'a sale characteristically under the counter.' But the stress-defined compound *drummer boy*, though it refers to a boy who is a drummer, is not the same as *boy drummer*, nor may other similarly stress-defined noun-noun compounds like *beggarwoman, teacher lady, washerwoman, soldier boy*, etc., be matched with their reversals. The meaning-defined *black death, horned owl, heavy water*, etc., cannot be reversed. Such varied extra-linguistic considerations seem to influence the order of the "dual capacity" meaning-defined compounds described by Hatcher (*Modern English word-formation and Neo-Latin*, Baltimore, 1951) that it is difficult if not impossible to draw any conclusions: the *sander-polisher, harvester-thresher* type gives the natural sequence of the two combined

A non-stereotype is *on the day following* and *on the following day*, between which Poutsma (519) confesses to seeing no difference. Though in a practical situation the two might be interchangeable, they are not identical. *On the day following* implies that time is being measured or fixed according to day periods—*following* contrasts with *preceding* or *same; on the following day* offers *day* as a new datum. There is potential selective contrast on the end-word in both examples.

Past participles exhibit best of all the self-contrast that we discovered in *a person unhappy. From the standpoint of combat efficiency, a soldier wounded may be worse than the same soldier dead* compares states of the same soldier; *a wounded soldier* would compare soldier *A* with soldier *B*.[45] Other examples of self-contrast: *A pound of coffee hoarded is just that much food likely to go to waste through spoilage; A joke misunderstood can cause plenty of trouble.*[46] In these, as in other examples with past participles, post-position keeps the participle more nearly a verb—that is, more literal, narrower, as we expect from our theory.[47] The same is true of grouped participles: *left-over food* versus *food left over, a broken-down car* versus *a car broken down.*

---

operations, and so cannot be reversed; the *theater-auditorium* type cannot be reversed without suggesting a proper name; *lend-lease* and *lease-lend* were interchangeable, though the latter was less frequent.

As might be expected, since the type *underseas craft* is stereotyped as to position, in order to get a non-iterative accent on *underseas* we must re-word just as with *vacant house*. If a person ignorant of the fact that a submarine is a vessel asks what a submarine is, he will not be told *It is an underséas craft*, for that would presuppose *craft*, but will be told *It is a ship that runs under the water*—the function of non-iterative selective contrast is taken over by a clause.

In all likelihood the participle that enters into the formation of a compound is contaminated with the sense of gerund plus noun, if, indeed, we can tell which is which in many cases. Thus *sewing machine* is not only 'a machine that sews,' but also 'a machine for sewing,' just as *reading lamp* is unambiguously 'a lamp for reading.' Though *the missing link* is clearly a participle, and a *losing battle* probably is one, it would be hard to say how to class *a working arrangement*.

45. Although combined with other modifiers there may be a selective contrast, e.g., *The jewels stolen were the ones she prized most of her whole collection*, where *the* gives *stolen* the power to distinguish jewels from jewels, there must always be an implied self-contrast as well. The same "jewel from jewel" distinction is present in *The stolen jewels were the ones she prized most of her whole collection*, but the example changes because of the missing "previous state versus present state" contrast.

46. Professor Hatcher notes that these have an element in common: they are gnomic predications with generic subject.

47. Pre-position assimilates participles to ordinary adjectives; post-position assimilates ordinary adjectives to participles. Note the "adjective" sense of *C and H is the best refined sugar* against *C and H is the best sugar refined* (*fallen woman—woman fallen; a given number—a number given; a studied remark—a remark studied*). In *He is an easily-satisfied*

As with self-contrast, so with thing-to-thing contrast. Since "detachability" inheres in their nature, the array of past participles following nouns is unlimited, and provides a repertory of selective contrast as full as that of adverbs. When an act is performed on a thing, the stigmata of the act serve to mark it off from other things. Cases such as *the countries discovered, the names called, the man invited,* etc., are too commonplace to dwell upon. A more difficult one is *appointed;* but even in *I attended the inquest at the appointed time* we think of but one time,[48] while *at the time appointed* suggests the possibility of some other time.[49] The same is true of *oft-repeated advice* and *advice often repeated.*[50]

In the past participle *born* we find a side-effect that accords with the theory. In *He was a gentleman born* the *born* adheres to the literal sense 'by birth,' while in *He was a born gentleman* it is broadened to mean 'genuine.'[51]

Similar to past participles and often using past participles are all phrases employing *with* and referring to a position or state—this, of course, is a special case of "non-characteristic." *He stood with head erect (head high, hands in pockets, arms folded,* etc.) denotes a contrast that is absent in parallel phrases like *erect head*—the latter might be used to describe an animal whose head is characteristically erect, not differentially erect at the moment.[52] The postpositions in this type usually come seriatim.

---

person the participle is not only adjectivized but broadened to suggest 'easy-going,' 'friendly,' 'comfortable,' etc. *He is a person easily satisfied* is verbal and restricted.

48. In the absence of iterative accent on *appointed.*

49. Poutsma (508–509) is unsure of any distinction here.

50. Poutsma's remark (523) that "Late Modern English hardly tolerates an attributive participle after a noun that is modified by a possessive pronoun or genitive" is pertinent as an incidental result of post-position for selective contrast (bear in mind that "attributive" here means 'adjunct'). His example is *He heard his dear and doted-on Mary Ann say,* where *doted-on* cannot follow the noun. Since a possessive usually pins a thing down so as to make it unique (and moreover in this instance the proper noun clinches it), to split it by means of post-position is not common. Rather than make this a mechanical rule applying to possessives, however, we must realize that it is due to the nature of linear modification. In *Our two articles accepted were both on natural science* we have post-position despite the presence of a possessive, because thing-to-thing contrast is possible.

51. Poutsma denies this (519), citing *He was a liar born* to disprove it; he reasons that one cannot be born a liar, hence the literal-figurative dichotomy won't work. But he forgets that it is always possible to employ a literal form rather than a figurative one for the purpose of a special figure: hyperbole. If I can say *He was literally a liar from the day he was born* I can also use the equivalent and equally manifest exaggeration *He was a liar born.*

52. The potential difference is not always actualized; thus *with arms folded* and *with folded arms* do not show the striking difference of *head erect* and *erect head.* Its absence

12. **Special adjectives.** *Each* in pre-position is more inclusive, in post-position more contrastive. *We each received five dollars* might mean 'each' (i.e. togetherness) loosely in respect of sharing an experience, which could be at any time or place. *We received five dollars each* almost necessarily refers to but a single transaction—the 'each,' or togetherness, is sharpened to a single occasion. Note that *What a coincidence! We each received five dollars on the same day!* is acceptable, but *We received five dollars each on the same day* is less so because redundant.

More, extra, and *additional* function alike. In *He gave me a dollar extra* the point is *extra*—we are talking about an enlarged AMOUNT. In *He gave me an extra dollar* the point is precisely *dollars*.

13. **Intensive pronouns.** *I myself seldom do it that way* is diffuse, including practically everything that may be subsumed under 'as far as I am concerned in the act.'[53] In *I seldom do it that way myself*, however, we focus a selective contrast on *myself*, conceding the right of others to act differently. The type *It was signed by John himself* is contrastive even though no other position is possible.

14. **Nouns plus nouns.** During the Second World War combinations of the type *Operation Pacific, Operation Claire,* etc., gained currency. The greater particularization of *Operation Pacific* over *Pacific Operation* is obvious. The invention gives us an opportunity of observing a "title" in the making; for if it continues, *operation* in this construction may take the same status as *king* in *King James* or *number* in *Number Ten*. A recent book on civil liberties is advertised as *Operation Gag*.

15. **Predicate complements.** Complements of *be* are striking. In *Here is the money that you requested*, *here* is broadened to include proffering as well as location; in *The money that you requested is here* one detects only literal location. In *Gone are the times when...*, *gone* overspreads mere *times* to suggest

---

is an accident. On the one hand, there is no creature characterized by folded arms as there are animals characterized by erect heads, so that a radical difference in meaning is impossible. On the other hand, there IS a standard pose "folded arms," which therefore admits the "standard" position of the adjective.

53. There is a side-effect with *myself* taken as a word-modifier of *I* alone: 'even I seldom do it that way.' This depends on intonation. To highlight the difference, change the locution to *I myself don't feel that I have the right to do it that way*. With an A accent on *-self*, approached from either a higher or a lower pitch but followed by a low level pitch, the implication is 'even I.' With the same conditions but with a rising (or fairly high level) terminal pitch on *-self*, the implication is as in the text. 'Even I' is again implied when *myself* is terminal with A accent and low fall. In both cases there is contrast with some other "self," which is sharpened by end-position; in one case the meaning is 'why should anyone else feel that he has the right to do it that way?' and in the other it is 'I concede another's right to do it that way.'

all that is bygone, while *The times when ... are gone* is strictly limited to particular gone-times.

On came the storm throws the whole picture into forward motion, an impression that is lacking in *The storm came on.* This is the same effect that we observed with descriptive adverbs like *abruptly* and *slowly.*

In " *Why do you want it in money rather than goods?*"—" *Money I can hide, goods I can't*" we have a resumptive, which, in common with other resumptives, overshadows what follows when placed in this position. It is as if we said ' As for money, I can hide it.'

16. Subject and verb. In certain contexts where direct discourse is reported, there is virtually " free variation " between the types *he says* and *says he.* To find what happens when the position changes, look at the second sentence in footnote 9, and change *he says* to *says he.* The effect is immediately one of sarcasm or disbelief: *says* becomes broader, taking in what others might say about the subject, and *he* is contrastive—it is his opinion against that of others.

III. INTERPLAY OF FORCES

At various points we have seen positions interlocking with accent and intonation to produce a certain effect. Lest we fall into the temptation of expecting to find one set of variables conditioned by the other, let us compare certain aspects of accent with what we have discovered about linearity.

Both Curme and Poutsma thought to see a conditioned relationship between movable position and accent. Curme notes (§ *16*, 2, n.) that the sentence adverb usually precedes the verb, verbal phrase, or predicate noun or adjective, and either is less prominent than when it follows the verb, or, if strongly accented, is joined to a verb that is also strongly accented. He gives the example *I útterly scórn your proposition.* But accent here is as in the example *I ónly want tén*, where it has a definite purpose: to connect two elements whose relationship is especially close, as well as to underscore their importance. That there is no arbitrary connexion between order and accent can be shown by examples like *Agáin I told him, Cértainly they did it*, where no other accent matches that of the adverb.

Poutsma says: " When an adverbial adjunct is placed between the verb and its object, this is mostly done owing to its being subservient to the other elements of the sentence, especially the object itself ... Compare *He heard again the noise on the stairs* with *He heard the noise on the stairs again*, and *He again heard the noise on the stairs*, and *Again he heard the noise on the stairs;* and observe the relatively weak stress [=accent] of *again* in the first example" (pp. 416–417, n.). But *again* is " weak " in this position only if made weak; I find it easier to weaken a terminal *again* than one standing anywhere toward the front. If accent has any automatic tie-in here it is more likely with the word *again* than with any feature of position; replace *again* with *sometimes* and the word can be weak in all positions.

We have seen how linearity establishes selective contrast, and how accent operates now with it, now across it, for its own special types of selective contrast. Thus in *Like strains of lóng-forgótten músic* we may reword to *Like strains of músic lóng-forgótten* in order to get selective contrast on the adjective and at the same time keep *music* a new datum; whereas if we retain the original order and de-accent the noun, we get a selective contrast that is iterative: *Like strains of lóng-forgótten music.*[54] Consider now an instance of selective contrast in which accent assumes the entire burden, the modifier going not at the end nor anywhere near the end of the sentence, but at the beginning—and going there because it has to by the principle of linearity:

In answer to the question *Do you see her Tuesdays?* one may reply *No, Tuesdays I stay home*[55] or *No, I see her Mondays.* The first order comes by reason of *Tuesdays* being resumptive, the second by reason of *Mondays* being contrastive and going where such contrastive elements go, at the end. We would not ordinarily find a combination like " *Do you see her Tuesdays?*"—" *No, Mondays I see her.*"[56] But observe now that a combination like " *Do you see her Tuesdays?*"—" *No, Tuesdays I stay at home; Mondays I see her* " is as normal as the same discourse with the last sentence changed to *I see her Mondays.* There is a selective contrast with the variable at the beginning of the sentence.

This is because in the order *Tuesdays I stay at home, Mondays I see her* we have an ENUMERATIVE CONTRAST, and it develops that any noun or " substantive adverb " (an adverb that names a place or a time) may be so employed. So combinations like the following are common: " *Tell me about your plans* "—" *Well, tomorrow I intend to work, and day after I'll go fishing* "; " *What's your work schedule like?*"—" *At home I put in three hours, at the office six* "; " *Tell me about your purchases* "—" *This couch we bought at auction, those chairs at a store.*" In each instance the pre-posed element is a logical subject which does not primarily limit what follows, but is limited by what follows, and hence stands first; but which stands in contrast with some other logical subject (not necessarily resumptive) and so receives contrastive accent. The key-word, the overshadowing word, in each such instance stands first, just as in the succession *First we write, second we read, then we play.*

I have not attempted to give more than a sample of the effects of mingl-

---

54. The same effect may be observed in Spanish with *Juan canta,* putting contrastive accent on *Juan* so that *canta* is resumptive. In *Canta Juan* both elements are new data, unless *canta* is given contrastive accent, in which case *Juan* is resumptive.

55. Or, as with sentence adverbs in general, put *Tuesdays* at the end following a pause.

56. No more than we would find " *How did you do it?*"—" *Carefully I did it.*"

ing accent and linearity. It would be just as difficult to do more than this as to attempt to describe all the possible shades that can be got by mixing two primary colors—even if we had identified the colors, which, with accent, we have not.[57]

---

57. I suspect, though the two do not automatically condition each other, that linear modification is one reason for a primary feature of the English sentence, viz., the tendency toward main accent at the end. If the " point " of the sentence is there, so will the accent be, more often than not. The same is true of Spanish.

2

MANEUVERING FOR ACCENT AND POSITION

College Composition and Communication 8.234-238 (1957)

Originally titled " Maneuvering for stress and intonation"

The collection ends on a practical note : one lesson on how to be a good writer.

Lack of markings for pitch often leads to misunderstanding. (We know that pitch is responsible because when the illogicality of a passage perplexes us, oftentimes we re-read, readjust the intonation that we had silently read in, and see through our mistake.) I recently asked eighteen persons to read aloud the Eugene O'Neill title *Mourning Becomes Electra.* All but two said

<pre>
                                     lec
           Mourning
                     Becomes E
                                tra
</pre>

with the main accent on -*lec*- and therefore the (I think) nonsensical meaning ' Mourning turns into Electra' (or the equally nonsensical meaning ' Of those we have discussed whom mourning suits, it is really Electra '). The most logical reading is

<pre>
                           comes
           Mourning Be
                           Electra
</pre>

but it is not cued by the writing. The readers followed a habit that we acquire in reading, which is to shift the major accent as far as possible to the right—a materialization of the tendency discussed in " Linear Modification," to put the most contrastive item last.

A way of partially avoiding such trouble has become an unwritten law of good writing. The good writer helps his reader by lining up three things : accent, position, and rising or falling pitch. I try to show how he does it.

The first lesson that every apprentice writer must learn is what he can and what he cannot utilize out of the store of spoken devices that he has been accumulating since he learned to talk. Everyone knows that language comes out the narrow end of the funnel when it passes from speech to writing. Something is gained, no doubt, in pictographic tricks and in the precision that is made possible by our freedom to revise what we have said before anyone sets eye or ear upon it. But more is lost. All the expressiveness that we associate with a living speaker is wrung out : gesture, the look on a face, a quality of voice, the warmth of physical presence.

Still, we can accept the fact that writing is language in a kind of cold storage, and thaw it out by an act of imagination. The writer can describe a smile or a quality of voice. He is apt to overlook a more serious defect of writing: the loss, not of the *circumstances* under which something was uttered aloud, but of certain grammatical ingredients of the sentence itself. The loss affects most of all the writing that we term expository: the essay, the historical account, the scientific treatise, where the personality of the speaker counts for least and the logical message is everything. In drama and novel the reader is challenged to guess at circumstances and emphases; he knows he will have to fill in. Expository writing lulls his wariness; safely ignoring the writer's *tone* of voice, he feels privileged to ignore the writer's voice altogether. To lead him around the traps he thus lays for himself, the writer must look to those lost grammatical ingredients.

The two that count for most, and to which we never got around to assigning written symbols except in hit-or-miss fashion, are accent and intonation. It is commonly felt that since they are left unmarked, they are therefore left out, and that it is up to the reader to restore the missing sense. To a degree, this is true. The reader sub-vocalizes as he goes along, or adds the accent and intonation overtly when he reads aloud, and no two readers performing the same passage will give identical interpretations. Yet it is not quite true to say that they are entirely unmarked. Over the centuries writers have unconsciously devised a scheme by which the reader is pretty reliably cued as regards the most important peaks of accent and turns of intonation. The scheme has congealed into an implicit convention of expository prose, as if writers had met and affirmed an agreement: " We recognize that we cannot play every tune of speech on the rigid scale to which we are confined. We therefore engage to play a single tune, and orchestrate the other variables to fit it." The variable most affected is sentence order, and this, along with the tune to which it is set, is the theme of what follows.

With minor variations, the tune consists of two beats, one toward the beginning and one toward the end; let us call them respectively " secondary " and " primary." Each is signaled by a rise in pitch. After the primary beat, or accent, the pitch drops rapidly and fades into silence. This is our normal reaction to two punctuation marks, the period and the semicolon. The pattern is one that we most often use in explanatory speech, and its adaptation to expository writing, whose primary aim is to explain and convince, is simply a matter of providing our reader with the most obvious clue. In questions, of course, the tune will change in some details, but the beats remain the same.

There is a difficulty. The beats are not always *at* the beginning and *at* the end. Their location is flexible, and the writer must enlist his skill to put them where the reader will expect them to be. To do this, he needs to know two of the main functions of accent, and how to reconcile them for the reader, who is pulled between one and the other.

The first function is a sentence-binder. It is mechanical, and easily demonstrated when we read aloud a series of signs that are barren of internal grammatical relationships. In the following examples, interpret the accent sign (`) as " secondary " and the sign (´) as " primary "; òne, twó, thrèe, fóur; T̀ R A Ṕ; Àpril tén; the tènth of Àpril; Hènry Jónes; Jònes, Hénry. In such utterances the major beats actually fall at the very beginning and end, betraying our tendency to put them there as a matter of course.

The counter tendency emerges in utterances that have true grammatical correspondences. It consists in putting the primary accent on the semantic " point " of the utterance, the element that carries the greatest freight of information, that answers the question uppermost in our minds. We have no clue to this other than our understanding of an entire passage, unless, as we shall see, the writer condescends to give us a hint. When James Stewart says, in a recent moving picture, He'll be back—his things are still here, he accents the word things: ' He'll be back because of his things ',—the things, possessions, will be responsible for the action expected. If in answer to Why didn't you stay longer at camp? we say The weather was too bad, we accent weather. The informativeness of the accented word is shown in that we frequently omit everything else: Why didn't you stay longer at camp?—The weather. How come you didn't get there sooner?—Our cár broke down, or just Our car, or Our car—it broke down, with two primary accents, splitting the utterance so as to make both items informative. We often have a choice. We might answer the last question by A tree blocked the road, accenting either road (' It was the road's fault ') or tree (' It was a tree's fault '). The grammatical construction of the accented element makes no difference. It may be noun, adjective, adverb, verb, or anything else that carries the burden of information. In The little girl didn't finish reading the story because there was a scáry place in it, we accent the adjective, which is the key to the explanation.

The recipe for reconciling the two functions is simple: the writer should make them coincide as nearly as he can by maneuvering the semantic primary into the position of the mechanical primary; that is, toward the end. A good practice is first to read the sentence aloud and note the position of the primary; then, if it is not already as close to the end as possible, rearrange the sentence. Since only one of the two accents can survive, the position of the mechanical accent serves as a signal for the semantic accent; if the latter goes too far from the end, it is liable to be lost, and the reader interprets something else as the bearer of the semantic accent.

Sometimes the maneuver can be effected by interchanging two positions. The author who wrote The " f " turned to " h " which became silent in its turn meant to say The " f " turned to " h " which in its turn became silent, accenting not *turn* but *silent* (not a mere question of "misplaced modifiers," for *became silent* and *in its turn* have equal claims on *which*). A simple inversion such as this one is possible only where English sentence order is free to do what sentence order in Spanish or Czech can do as a regular thing: start with the known or given and move to the unknown or problematical, which accords with the scheme of accents since the unknown or problematical is where most information lies, and our accent can go where we want it, at the end. Unfortunately, sentence order in English must also serve other purposes, those of grammatical relationships. There is nothing we can do with *The men ate the fish*, for the order of the words signals what is subject and what is object; or with *Cover shed* and *Shed cover*, where, as commands, it tells us what is the verb. Some arrangements are ruled out by our demand for symmetry in grammatical relationships even though the meaning is clear, as in *Looked at me the squirrel*.

To circumvent the arbitrariness of grammar, the writer may now choose between parallel structures differing only in sentence order. He picks the one that allows him to get his accent at the end. If he defines Canada as *the place where Canadian bacon was invented*, he miscues his reader, for he wants the accent on *bacon* (and can easily put it there if he says it aloud), but his order suggests that it falls on *invented*. A parallel structure, *the place where they invented Canadian bacon*, avoids the trap. (Spanish can simply invert: *the place where was invented Canadian bacon*). Observe how the reader is misled by the following from a popular magazine: "Why don't all the children come to the classes? For one thing, ... many ... kids go off to camps. ... *I also found that children both stay away and come according to what friends happen to choose*." Unforewarned that the primary accent belongs on *friends*, the reader takes *what* as a modifier and puts the accent on *choose*. It would have been better to write *according to what is chosen by friends* or *what happens to be the choice of their friends*. A part, perhaps the major part, of the survival of alternating structures like those of active and passive voice, which seem like syntactic luxuries since *The man shot the dog* and *The dog was shot by the man* "mean the same," is that by relieving sentence order of the responsibility of showing grammatical relationships they free it to carry our meaning.

In the examples thus far, the entire clause within which the primary accent falls may be said to "answer the question." *This is the country where Canadian bacon was invented* or *This is the country where they invented Canadian bacon* both answer the question *How may one identify this country?* The problem is merely one of getting the accent in the place where it is normally expected to fall.

But not only the accent may be thrown out of joint. The intonation may be as well. The reader looks for the primary accent at the end. He also expects to find at the end, in common expository statements, an intonational fall. Sentences like *I told him I would,* with a rise in pitch to the accent on *told,* a slide down on *him* and *I,* and an up-down-up pitch movement on *would* with its accent, are common in everyday speech, but reading *I told him I would* aloud one almost automatically puts a straight fall to silence in the last word, thereby perhaps falsifying the writer's intent. Again it is up to the writer to arrange matters so that this nearly automatic tendency does not conflict with the meaning of the passage.

To do so now calls for a different kind of shift, not one in which the internal arrangement of clauses or phrases is altered, but one in which whole clauses or phrases are interchanged. This is made necessary by the contrasting functions of what we may call " conclusive intonation," which falls more or less precipitously at the end and fades into silence, and " inconclusive intonation," which rises or maintains a comparatively high pitch. The usual function of inconclusive intonation in statements is to imply 'What immediately precedes is a circumstance or condition hedging the main idea.' If Smith says *Nobody likes it* and Jones replies *Brown likes it,* the chances are that Jones will use an inconclusive intonation,

$$B r^{o^{w^n}} \text{likes } it$$

—implying ' Your statement may be true, but not in this particular.' (A conclusive intonation would imply straightforward contradiction.) In this case, the main idea and the qualifier are divided between speakers; combined, they would give *Nobody likes it, except for Brown,* in the form

$$except \text{ for } Bro_{w}n$$

and this, rather than the division between speakers, is the usual thing in expository writing. In *We next consider how to divide the amounts: unfortunately it will come out uneven if we do it thus-and-so—*

$$come \ out \ un^{e}ven \ if \ we \ do \ it$$
$$t^{hu^s} \ and \ so^{o^o}$$

—the *if*-clause hedges *it will come out uneven,* and would generally fail to drop completely on the last word, *so.* But the main idea, *it will come out uneven,* is capable of receiving the conclusive fall. The good writer then obliges us by arranging his sentence as follows: *if we do it thus-and-so, it will come out uneven;* or, *Except for Brown, nobody likes it.* When the writer is aware of what he is doing, the procedure is clearly defined for him: put accented qualifiers at the beginning, and the answer proper at the end.

Again we may have to override grammatical structure in order to carry out the maneuver. In *Conditions were bad, but the government was hardly to blame. It was the world situation,* the question and answer, reduced to their least dimensions, are: Q. *Why were conditions bad?* A. *The world situation.* The blamelessness of the government is a qualifier, but we are not aware of this until we are past the period following *blame*—too late to avoid confusion over whether the blamelessness is conclusive. A possible solution is to write *but it was less the fault of the government than of the world situation;* or simply to combine in a single sentence without the apparently conclusive period: *but the government was hardly to blame—rather the world situation.*

Where the qualifier is a more intimate part of the answer proper, the operation becomes more delicate. The statement *John likes Mary* answers the question *Whom does John like?,* but also implies an answer to the question *Who likes Mary?* If someone wanted to dispute the statement *John likes Mary,* he might do so in terms of either the main question or the implied question or both: *John likes Jane. Jake likes Mary.* The latter, if spoken, would have an inconclusive intonation—

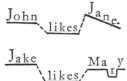

—for the answer to *Who likes Mary?* is *Jake,* and *Jake* is out of position— it precedes instead of following its qualifier ('It's Jake as far as Mary is concerned'). Changed to read *John likes Jane; Mary's boy friend is Jake,* the utterance acquires suitably conclusive endings all around.

I do not mean to suggest that inconclusive intonations and all that goes with them are undesirable everywhere. In speech they are often helpful. Someone asks *What about* **women**? *What do* **they** *want? And what about* **men**? We may reply, orally, *Equality is what women want. Men want superiority.* We signal our meaning with perfect clarity by means of an inconclusive intonation on *women want,* and we gain the advantage of exposed position, right at the front, for one of our two main answers, *equality.* But if we do this in writing, we invite misunderstanding, for the period after *want* seems to call for an intonational fall. A semicolon is a partially helpful compromise, but still ambiguous.

The inconclusive intonation may be desirable for itself in the spoken language, for it is our way of showing that the qualifier is contrastive. It is not perfectly clear that *women* is contrastively accented in *Women want equality,* unless the speaker puts a rise-fall-rise on it with a pause immediately afterward; but this is awkward, as it slows the pace too much. Inverted to *Equality is what women want,* the accent is clearly specified for this context: either *women* is markedly accented and there is an inconclusive ending ('As for what women want, it is equality')—

qual i ty
E̲   is what, wo men wa n t

—or there is no accent at all on *what women want* but rather a low pitch and a fall to silence:

qual
E̲   ity is what women want.

(We do this when *what women want* is felt to be repeated or merely incidental). But writing does not conduce to either interpretation: the former because the period militates against inconclusiveness, the latter because de-accenting the ending violates our rule about primary accent at the end.

At times there is no way out. Marilyn Monroe says *Sex is a part of nature, and I go along with nature.* The second half contains an answer about nature: 'What I go along with.' *Nature*, now, is a qualifier: 'As for nature, I go along.' But the qualifier is at the end, and the answer is at the beginning. The quip depends on the phrase *go along with*, and cannot be tampered with. Our only recourse is to treat the two clauses as independent of each other and give both an intonational fall.

I summarize with a precept: Arrange the order, or select the structure, to:

1. Wheel the heavy guns fore and aft. The points of most information, what the sentence is designed to answer, belong in the normal position of secondary and primary accent.

2. Make periods really say what they seem to say, 'This is the end.' Put accented qualifiers at the beginning of the sentence, to avoid an intonation that hangs in the air.

If the apprentice writer will listen, both things can be done by ear. An accent can be heard, and juggled into position; and anyone who can tell high from low can detect an inconclusive intonation. Even the novice can see that *I'm going to throw the others away, but I'd like to keep this one* violates both parts of the precept. Both *keep* and *this* are accented, but both stand at the end instead of being separated; and *this one*, with the meaning 'as for this one,' is an accented qualifier, and accordingly receives an inconclusive intonation. Write instead *but this one I'd like to keep.*

PUBLICATIONS

PUBLICATIONS
of
DWIGHT L. BOLINGER

BOOKS :

1. *Intensive Spanish*, Philadelphia, Russell Press, 1948.
2. *Spanish Review Grammar*, New York, Holt, 1956.
3. *Modern Spanish* (with J. D. Bowen, A. M. Brady, E. F. Haden, L. Poston, Jr., and N. P. Sacks), New York, Harcourt, Brace, and World, Inc., 1960.

MONOGRAPHS :

4. *The Symbolism of Music*, Yellow Springs, Ohio, Antioch Press, 1941.
5. *What Is Freedom?*, Norman, Oklahoma, Cooperative Books, 1941.
6. *Interrogative Structures of American English*, University, Alabama, American Dialect Society, 1957.
7. *Generality, Gradience, and the All-or-None*, 's-Gravenhage, Mouton, 1961.

ARTICLES, LANGUAGE :

8. " In Defense of the Purists," *Correct English*, Sep. 1939.
9. " Toward a New Conception of Grammar," *Modern Language Journal* 27. 170–174 (1943).
10. " Visual Morphemes," *Language* 22. 333–340 (1946).
11. " On Defining the Morpheme," *Word* 4. 18–23 (1948).
12. " The Sign Is Not Arbitrary," *Boletín del Instituto Caro y Cuervo* 5. 52–62 (1949).
13. " Intonation and Analysis," *Word* 5. 248–254 (1949).
14. " The ' What ' and the ' Way,' " *Language Learning* 2. 86–88 (1949).
15. " Complementation Should Complement," *Studies in Linguistics* 8. 29–39 (1950).
16. " Rime, Assonance, and Morpheme Analysis," *Word* 6. 117–136 (1950).
17. " Intonation : Levels versus Configurations," *Word* 7. 199–210 (1951).
18. " Linear Modification," *Publications of the Modern Language Association of America* 67. 1117–1144 (1952).
19. " The Life and Death of Words," *American Scholar* 22. 323–335 (1953).
20. " Identity, Similarity, and Difference," *Litera* 1. 5–16 (1954).
21. " The Melody of Language," *Modern Language Forum* 40. 19–30 (1955).
22. " Locus versus Class," in *Miscelánea Homenaje a André Martinet*, Canarias, 1957.
23. " Intonation and Grammar," *Language Learning* 8 : 1, 2. 31–38 (1957–58).
24. " Linguistic Science and Linguistic Engineering," *Word* 16. 374–391 (1960).
25. " Verbal Evocation," *Lingua* 10. 113–127 (1961).
26. " Syntactic Blends and Other Matters," *Language* 37. 366–381 (1961).

ARTICLES, ENGLISH :

27. " The Living Language " [monthly department on neology], *Words*, September 1937 to October 1940.
28. " Verbal Rarities," *Words* 3. 58–59, 163 (1937) ; 5. 77 (1939).

29. "Victory for *Gadget*," *Words* 3. 179 (1937).

30. "Whence the *A* in *Kind of A*," *Words* 4. 32 (1938).

31. "Our Migratory Adverbs," *Words* 4. 62–63 (1938).

32. "Distinguish Between *Infer* and *Imply*," *Words* 4. 118 (1938).

33. "Profanity and Social Sanction," *American Speech* 13. 152–154 (1938).

34. "A Reconsideration of *As* and *So*," *English Journal* 28. 56–58 (1939).

35. "*Different*—Comparative Degree?," *English Journal* 28. 480–481 (1939).

36. "Must We Use Fewer Words?," *Better English*, October 1939, pp. 39–41.

37. "A Leaf from Your Thesaurus," *Writer's Forum*, December 1939, p. 15.

38. "*Bozo*," *American Speech* 14. 97 (1939).

39. "How Do You Use *Data?*," *Better English*, April 1940, p. 167.

40. "The Unspoken Language," *Writer's Forum*, May 1940, pp. 14–15.

41. "Word Affinities," *American Speech* 15. 62–73 (1940).

42. "Ambrose Bierce and *All of*," *College English* 2. 69–70 (1940).

43. "*Trivia*," *American Speech* 15. 332–333 (1940).

44. "*Churchianity, Churchanity; Trojan Horse*," *American Speech* 15. 452, 453–454 (1940).

45. "Apposite and Opposite," *Writer's Forum*, January 1941, pp. 18–19.

46. "Among the New Words" [a continuing department], *American Speech*, April 1941 to February 1944.

47. "Neologisms," *American Speech* 16. 64–67 (1941).

48. "Plurals and Collectives," *Words* 7. 15–16 (1941).

49. "Whoming," *Words* 7. 70 (1941).

50. "Battle of the Matics," *Word Study*, November 1941, p. 7.

51. "*Need*, Auxiliary," *College English* 4. 62–65 (1942).

52. "*Fifth Column* Marches On," *American Speech* 19. 47–49 (1944).

53. "Split Infinitive," *Word Study*, February 1944, pp. 4–5.

54. "New Words and Meanings," in *Britannica Yearbook*, 1944.

55. "Note on the Volitional Future," *Notes and Queries* 188. 121–123 (1945).

56. "Inhibited and Uninhibited Stress," *Quarterly Journal of Speech* 31. 202–207 (1945).

57. "The Minimizing Downskip," *American Speech* 20. 40–44 (1945).

58. "The Intonation of Quoted Questions," *Quarterly Journal of Speech* 32. 197–202 (1946).

59. "Thoughts on *Yep* and *Nope*," *American Speech* 21. 90–95 (1946).

60. "Analogical Correlatives of *Than*," *American Speech* 21. 199–202 (1946).

61. "Transformación Inglesa de Dos Palabras Españolas," *América Comercial* 1:1. 16 (1947).

62. "Dictionaries Hate to Give Offense," *Correct English*, November 1947, pp. 39–40.

63. "More on the Present Tense in English," *Language* 23. 434–436 (1947).

64. "The Intonation of Accosting Questions," *English Studies* 29. 109–114 (1948).

65. "*Shivaree* and the Phonestheme," *American Speech* 25. 134–135 (1950).

66. "*Next* and *Last*," *American Speech* 28. 232–233 (1953).

67. "Intersections of Stress and Intonation," *Word* 11. 195–203 (1955).

68. "Intonation as Stress-Carrier," *Litera* 2. 35–40 (1955).

69. "English Stress: the Interpenetration of Strata," in *Study of Sounds*, Tokyo, 1957, pp. 295–315.

70. "On Certain Functions of Accents A and B," *Litera* 4. 80–89 (1957).

71. "Disjuncture as a Cue to Constructs" (with L. J. Gerstman), *Word* 13. 246-255 (1957).
72. "Maneuvering for Stress and Intonation," *College Composition and Communication* 8. 234-238 (1957).
73. "Stress and Information," *American Speech* 33. 5-20 (1958).
74. "On Intensity as a Qualitative Improvement of Pitch Accent," *Lingua* 7. 175-182 (1958).
75. "A Theory of Pitch Accent in English," *Word* 14. 109-140 (1958).
76. "Contrastive Accent and Contrastive Stress," *Language* 37. 83-96 (1961).
77. "Ambiguities in Pitch Accent," *Word* 17. 309-317 (1962).
78. "Binomials and Pitch Accent," *Lingua* 11. 34-44 (1962).

ARTICLES, SPANISH :

79. "Spanish on the Air in Wisconsin," *Modern Language Journal* 18. 217-221 (1934).
80. "Heroes and Hamlets: the Protagonists of Baroja's Novels," *Hispania* 24. 91-94 (1941).
81. "About Those Exchanges," *Journal of Higher Education* 13. 438-440 (1942).
82. "The Position of the Adverb in English: a Convenient Analogy to the Position of the Adjective in Spanish," *Hispania* 26. 191-192 (1943).
83. "Son of Something," *Hispania* 26. 184 (1943).
84. "Purpose with *Por* and *Para*," *Modern Language Journal* 18. 15-21 (1944).
85. "More on *Ser* and *Estar*," *Modern Language Journal* 18. 233-238 (1944).
86. "The Case of the Disappearing Grammar," *Hispania* 27. 372-381 (1944).
87. "Neuter *Todo*, Substantive," *Hispania* 28. 78-80 (1945).
88. "*Qué Tanto, Qué Tan*," *Hispanic Review* 14. 167-169 (1946).
89. "The Future and Conditional of Probability," *Hispania* 29. 363-376 (1946).
90. "Spanish *Parece Que* Again," *Language* 22. 359-360 (1946).
91. "Still More on *Ser* and *Estar*," *Hispania* 30. 361-367 (1947).
92. "1464 Identical Cognates in English and Spanish," *Hispania* 31. 271-279 (1948).
93. "Discontinuity of the Spanish Conjunctive Pronoun," *Language* 25. 253-260 (1949).
94. "The Comparison of Inequality in Spanish," *Language* 26. 28-62 (1950).
95. "Retained Objects in Spanish," *Hispania* 33. 237-239 (1950).
96. "*En Efecto* Does Not Mean 'In Fact,'" *Hispania* 33. 349-350 (1950).
97. "Evidence on *X*," *Hispania* 35. 49-63 (1952).
98. "The Pronunciation of *X* and Puristic Anti-Purism," *Hispania* 35. 442-444 (1952).
99. "*Ser Bien*," *Hispania* 35. 474-475 (1952).
100. "Addenda to the Comparison of Inequality in Spanish," *Language* 29. 62-66 (1953).
101. "—And Should Thereby Be Judged," *Books Abroad* 27. 129-132 (1953).
102. "Verbs of Being," *Hispania* 36. 343-345 (1953).
103. "Verbs of Emotion," *Hispania* 36. 459-461 (1953).
104. "Articles in Old Familiar Places," *Hispania* 37. 79-82 (1954).
105. "English Prosodic Stress and Spanish Sentence Order," *Hispania* 37. 152-156 (1954).
106. "Education Trend: a Spanish Boom," Los Angeles *Times*, editorial page, 30 May 1954.
107. "Meaningful Word Order in Spanish," *Boletín de Filología* (Universidad de Chile) 8. 45-56 (1954-55).
108. "Prescriptive Statements and Mallo's Anglicisms," *Hispania* 38. 76-78 (1955).

109. "The Relative Importance of Grammatical Items," *Hispania* 38. 261–264 (1955).
110. "More on Prescribers and Describers," *Hispania* 38. 309–311 (1955).
111. "Stress on Normally Unstressed Elements" and "*Contestar* versus *Contestar A*," *Hispania* 39. 105–106 (1956).
112. "Subjunctive *-ra* and *-se:* Free Variation?" *Hispania* 39. 345–349 (1956).
113. "Prepositions in English and Spanish," *Hispania* 40. 212–214 (1957).
114. "Indicative versus Subjunctive in Exclamations," *Hispania* 42. 372–373 (1959).
115. "The President's Corner," *Hispania* 43. 85–86, 245–246, 425–426, 579 (1960).
116. "Algo Más Que Entrenamiento," *Hispania* 44. 16–20 (1961).
117. "Three Analogies," *Hispania* 44. 134–137 (1961).
118. "Acento Melódico, Acento de Intensidad" (with Marion Hodapp), *Boletín de Filología* (Universidad de Chile) 13. 33–48 (1961).
119. "'Secondary Stress' in Spanish," *Romance Philology* 15. 273–279 (1962).

ARTICLES, MISCELLANEOUS:

120. "Victorian Styles in Fertilizer," *Commonwealth*, August 1938, pp. 19–20 (abridged in *Magazine Digest*, January 1939).
121. "Profits in Flesh and Blood," *Commonwealth*, December 1939, pp. 19–21.
122. "The Great American Lottery," *Writer's Forum*, March 1940, pp. 27–29.
123. "Press and Profundity," *Writer's Forum*, September 1940, pp. 14–15.
124. "Corina Rodríguez: Impressions of Isthmian Politics," *New Mexico Quarterly Review* 14. 389–402 (1944).
125. "Universal Military Training," *Bulletin of the American Association of University Professors* 31. 97–102 (1945).
126. "Famous Coincidences of Science," *American Journal of Pharmacy* 117. 431–435 (1945).
127. "There's Gold in Them There Sewers," *Progressive*, August 1949, p. 27.
128. "The Indivisibility of Tolerance," *Bulletin of the American Association of University Professors* 35. 661–664 (1949).
129. "Who Is Intellectually Free?" *Journal of Higher Education* 25. 464–468 (1954) (reprinted in *Bulletin of the American Association of University Professors* 41. 13–18 [1955]; abridged in *Education Digest*, November 1955, pp. 9–11).
130. "Ambassador Without Portfolio," *Hispania* 44. 692–693 (1961).
131. "Unwelcome Allies," *German Quarterly* 35. 98 (1962).

ARTICLES, PEDAGOGY:

132. "Are We Playing Fair with Our Students Linguistically?" *Hispania* 34. 131–136 (1951).
133. "Retooling Retrospect," *Modern Language Journal* 38. 113–117 (1954).
134. "More on Pitfalls in Modern Language Teaching," *School and Society* 89. 279–280 (1961).

FICTION:

135. "Glass," *Fortnightly*, December 1938, pp. 702–712.

VERSE:

136. "Streamliner," San Francisco *News Letter and Wasp*, 31 March 1939, p. 11.

137. " Cool Fountain," *La Voz*, November 1960, p. 3 (translation).
138. " To the Father of the Bomb," *Fellowship*, 1 November 1960, p. 9.

REVIEWS :

139. " Spanish Intonation " (on Tomás Navarro, *Manual de Entonación Española*), *American Speech* 20. 128–130 (1945).
140. " R. A. Hall, 'Spanish Inflection,' " *Hispania* 28. 582–583 (1945).
141. " American English Intonation " (on K. L. Pike, *Intonation of American English*), *American Speech* 22. 134–136 (1947).
142. " Comments on Pike's *Intonation of American English*," *Studies in Linguistics* 5. 69 –78 (1947).
143. " Ricardo J. Alfaro, *Diccionario de Anglicismos*," *Hispania* 33. 284–286 (1950).
144. " Anna Granville Hatcher, *Modern English Word Formation and Neo-Latin*," *Word* 9. 83-85 (1953).
145. " Salvador Fernández Ramírez, *Gramática Española*," *Romance Philology* 7. 209–215 (1954).
146. " James E. Iannucci, *Lexical Number in Spanish Nouns*," *Romance Philology* 8. 111 –117 (1954).
147. " Mary Reifer, *Dictionary of New Words*," *Modern Language Forum* 41. 53–55 (1956).
148. " Daniel M. Crabb, *A Comparative Study of Word Order in Old Spanish and Old French Prose Works*," *Word* 12. 148–151 (1956).
149. " M. M. Ramsey and Robert K. Spaulding, *A Textbook of Modern Spanish*," *Romance Philology* 11. 59–64 (1957).
150. " Kenneth Croft, *A Practise Book on English Stress and Intonation*," *Language Learning* 11 : 3, 4. 189–195 (1961).
151. " J. E. Jurgens Buning and C. H. van Schooneveld, *The Sentence Intonation of Contemporary Standard Russian as a Linguistic Structure*," *Language* 38. 79–84 (1962).

INDEX

GENERAL INDEX

The abbreviation N stands for Note.

Index of Authors

The abbreviation N stands for Note.